The Poets Laureate of the Long Eighteenth Century, 1668–1813

The Poets Laureate of the Long Eighteenth Century, 1668–1813

Courting the Public

Leo Shipp

LONDON
ROYAL HISTORICAL SOCIETY
INSTITUTE OF HISTORICAL RESEARCH
UNIVERSITY OF LONDON PRESS

Published by
UNIVERSITY OF LONDON PRESS
SCHOOL OF ADVANCED STUDY
INSTITUTE OF HISTORICAL RESEARCH
Senate House, Malet Street, London WC1E 7HY

Available to download free or to purchase the hard copy edition at https://www.sas.ac.uk/publications.

ISBNs
978-1-914477-30-0 (paperback edition)
978-1-914477-29-4 (hardback edition)
978-1-914477-33-1 (.epub edition)
978-1-914477-32-4 (.pdf edition)

DOI 10.14296/sner2422

New Historical
PERSPECTIVES

Cover image: A Writer Cutting His Pen, Jan Ekels (II), 1784. Object number: SK-A-690. Jonkheer J.S.H. van de Poll Bequest, Amsterdam, Rijksmuseum. Public domain.

Contents

Acknowledgements

I first started work on the poets laureate as a BA student, when I wrote my dissertation on Robert Southey's appointment to the post. Back then, I considered Southey a laughably obscure poet; my original idea had been to write something on Wordsworth's 1807 *Poems, in Two Volumes*, due to how much I had enjoyed studying *Lyrical Ballads* in A-Level English. I must therefore thank the teachers and schoolmates at Ravenscroft who steered me towards history and literature in the first place. In particular, my English teacher Ms Button was the one who introduced me to classic novels, poetry and the Romantics; and it was one of my oldest friends, Meqdad Jawid, whose homework on Alfred the Great made me realize that I ought to be taking an A-Level in History, rather than the Advanced GNVQs in Applied Science and Business Studies that I had signed up for. If I had not been enticed by the warm crackle of burning buns over that of Bunsen burners, things would have panned out very differently.

Over the course of my university career, many people have supported my work on the poets laureate. Jonathan Conlin agreed to supervise my BA dissertation at Southampton, accommodated my hopes of writing something interdisciplinary, and made the suggestion that I find a more neglected subject than Wordsworth. His supervision and subsequent advice over the years have been immeasurably helpful; without them, that dissertation's mutation into a journal article would never have been possible, and that focus on the laureateship would never have developed into a PhD thesis and monograph. Alex Barber then supervised my MA dissertation on the later Stuart poets laureate at Durham, and his generous references helped me into a funded PhD place at Exeter. I am also thankful to my upgrade examiners, Hester Schadee and Richard Ward, and my PhD examiners, Tony Claydon and Henry Power, for their constructive feedback. Tony encouraged me to develop my own definitions of the court and the public rather than following other scholars' definitions, and I hope he will not be too disappointed in the results.

Particularly effusive thanks must go to my doctoral supervisors. Martha Vandrei, my History supervisor, was my initial contact at Exeter, and her help was essential in securing me a funded PhD place; she was a friendly and fiercely ambitious supervisor thereafter. Since the completion of my PhD, she has provided the support, advice and encouragement essential for navigating postdoctoral academic life. It was Martha who recommended that I submit my work for publication in the New Historical Perspectives series, and read my application draft. Without her, this book would not exist and I probably would not have been able to find any postdoctoral job at all.

I was equally fortunate in my English Literature supervisors. Nick Groom was a source of endless information, suggestions and insights, and first brought my attention to many of the works referenced in the following pages. Stephen Bygrave's suggestions regarding my work's overall structure and concepts have been highly important, both to the doctoral thesis and to the monograph that followed on from it. Nick and Stephen each read my thesis at various stages of its composition and gave far-reaching feedback, constantly guiding and challenging my work, and have continued to support my work since the completion of my PhD. The fact that my time at Exeter was possible, and that such an excellent team of supervisors (spanning disciplines and universities) was assembled, was due to the South, West and Wales Doctoral Training Partnership and the Arts and Humanities Research Council, for whose funding and help I am hugely grateful.

While working on the poets laureate, I have been lucky to make a number of academic friends whose companionship has made difficult times bearable and good times good. If I started naming friends from Exeter, the list would either be overly long or unfairly selective, so I will have to confine myself to thanking anyone who ever shared a walk, board game session, football match, pub night or trip to the beach with me. Beyond Exeter, it has always been a great pleasure to meet up with the 'Merry Gang' of Clara, Hannah and David at conferences and elsewhere. Edward Taylor has been particularly liberal with his help and advice. With his expertise on politics, periodicals and Neo-Latin in seventeenth- and eighteenth-century Britain, and his Georgian geniality, his friendship has always fulfilled the ancient dictum of mixing the *utile* and the *dulci*.

I am likewise lucky to have been given such a warm reception by everyone at the Royal Historical Society and University of London Press, and especially by Philip Carter, Elizabeth Hurren, Jane Winters, Emma Gallon, Jamie Bowman and Lauren De'ath. They have made the publication process easy, and have aided me in making the book as good as it can be. So too has Stephen Conway, who read and discussed the first draft, providing me with both specific and general points that have been very helpful. And the diligence of Robert Davies and Karen Francis ensured that the copyediting stage was smooth and productive.

Lastly, I would like to thank my family. Mum, Dad, Grandma and Owen have all, in their different ways, provided a constant bedrock of support and motivation, without which none of this would have been possible. If they take any pride or pleasure in seeing this project come to fruition, then it will have been worthwhile.

Leo Shipp
Exeter
November 2021

Quotations, dates and abbreviations

In quotations, the original spelling and punctuation is retained, and the term '*sic*' is not used. Dates given before the introduction of the Gregorian calendar in 1752 are given in the old style, but the beginning of the year is dated to 1 January throughout.

For all publications dating to the period of study, the place of publication is London, unless otherwise stated. The names of the biannual odes produced by the laureates for New Year's Day and for the reigning monarch's birthday are abbreviated in the footnotes to the year of performance and 'NY' (for New Year's Day) or 'BD' (for royal birthday). Further details as to where each ode might be found are given in the Bibliography. For periodicals, naming and differentiation conventions follow those of the Burney Collection online database, except for those periodicals that do not appear on that database.

For those correspondence editions in which each letter is numbered, those numbers (as well as page numbers) have been included in citations. They are designated by 'lt.' ('ltt.' for plural) to avoid confusion with page numbers.

URLs for works cited in the footnotes can be found in the Bibliography.

In addition, the following abbreviations are used in the footnotes:

Add. MS.: Additional Manuscript
BL: The British Library, London
Bod: The Bodleian Library, Oxford
***CTB**: Calendar of Treasury Books: 1660–1718*, 32 vols
(London: PRO, 1904–1958)
***CR**: The Critical Review*
Dryden, *Works*: John Dryden, *The Works of John Dryden*,
ed. H. T. Swedenberg et al. (20 vols, Berkeley, Calif., 1956–2002)
Gray Correspondence: Thomas Gray, *Correspondence of Thomas Gray*,
ed. P. Toynbee and L. Whibley, 1st edn reprinted with corrections and
additions by H. W. Starr (3 vols, Oxford, 1971). Volume I for pp. 1–453,
II for pp. 455–909, III for pp. 911–1194
HO: Home Office
LC: Lord Chamberlain's Department
***MR**: The Monthly Review*

ODNB: *Oxford Dictionary of National Biography*
SP: State Papers
Spence, *Observations*: Joseph Spence, *Observations, Anecdotes, and Characters of Books and Men: Collected from Conversation*, ed. J. M. Osborn (2 vols, Oxford, 1966)
TNA: The National Archives, London
***Warton Correspondence*:** Thomas Warton, *The Correspondence of Thomas Warton*, ed. D. Fairer (London, 1995)
'Whitehead Memoirs': William Mason, 'Memoirs of the life and writings of Mr. William Whitehead', in William Whitehead, *Poems, Vol. III*, ed. William Mason (York, 1788), pp. 1–129

Introduction

The office of poet laureate was instituted in 1668 for John Dryden, and underwent its most dramatic changes following the appointments of Thomas Shadwell in 1689 and Robert Southey in 1813. Its history therefore aligns well with that flexible period of study, 'the long eighteenth century', whether it be bounded by the Restoration and the Great Reform Act, by the Glorious Revolution and Waterloo or, as here, by Dryden and Southey (1668–1813). But the symmetry is more than a coincidence. The poet laureateship of the long eighteenth century is an eminently characteristic feature of the period, and highly illuminating of some of the central issues in long eighteenth-century scholarship.

The long eighteenth century has tended to be understood as the period in which 'Britain' came into being: not just in terms of the Act of Union being signed in 1707, but in terms of the more intangible measures by which a modern nation-state distinguishes itself from the traditional, hierarchical kingdom that existed before it. Thus Britain in the long eighteenth century transitioned from a society in which king and court were paramount in all matters political, administrative, social and cultural, to one in which a nationally conscious public, powered by commercial practices and the energies of the middle class, gained the overriding agency in each of these areas.[1] Against this understanding of an essentially modernizing Britain,

---

[1] J. Barry, 'Consumers' passions: The middle class in eighteenth-century England', *The Historical Journal*, xxxiv (1991), 207–16; *The Middling Sort of People: Culture, Society and Politics in England, 1550–1800*, ed. J. Barry and C. Brooks (Basingstoke, 1994); J. Brewer, *The Pleasures of the Imagination: English Culture in the Eighteenth Century*, 2nd edn (London, 2013); *Protestantism and National Identity: Britain and Ireland, c.1650–c.1850*, ed. T. Claydon and I. McBride (Cambridge, 1998); R. O. Bucholz, *The Augustan Court: Queen Anne and the Decline of Court Culture* (Stanford, Calif., 1993); T. Claydon, *Europe and the Making of England, 1660–1760* (Cambridge, 2007); L. Colley, *Britons: Forging the Nation 1707–1837*, revised edn (London, 2009); B. Hammond, *Professional Imaginative Writing in England, 1670–1740: 'Hackney for Bread'* (Oxford, 1997); L. Lipking, *The Ordering of the Arts in Eighteenth-Century England* (Princeton, N. J., 1970); *The Birth of a Consumer Society: The Commercialization of Eighteenth-Century England*, ed. N. McKendrick, J. Brewer and J. H. Plumb (London, 1983; first published 1982); R. Terry, *Poetry and the Making of the English Literary Past: 1660–1781* (Oxford, 2001); H. D. Weinbrot, *Britannia's Issue: The Rise of British Literature from Dryden to Ossian* (Cambridge, 1994); R. Wellek, *The Rise of English Literary History*, 2nd edn (New York, 1966); K. Wilson, *The Sense of the People: Politics, Culture, and Imperialism in England, 1715–1785* (Cambridge, 1995).

voices of dissent have been raised, emphasizing either the slowness of these developments or the persistent importance of traditional institutions, ideas, practices and social groups among them.[2] The significance of this monograph, then – in its widest sense – regards how we are to make sense of this long-eighteenth-century Britain. As will be seen throughout the following pages, an interdisciplinary study of the laureateship is important in that it advances a conceptualization of the period hitherto undernourished.

There are two particular thematic threads that a study of the office engages with. The first is the role of the court vis-à-vis the emerging idea of the British nation. The predominant view – and certainly the assumption that scholars have found more useful to work with, in terms of carrying out their research – is that the court lost its practical and symbolic role at the apex of society, and was superseded by the institutions and ideologies of a new British nation. The second thread is the relationship between the court and literature (along with high culture in general). Again, the predominant view is that the more highly esteemed forms of literature, having traditionally been produced for and consumed by the court, moved from that courtly environment to a new home in the public marketplace, where they were produced for and consumed by a wider, more national and more middle-class audience. Both of these threads are associated with the idea of an emergent or newly important public.

A study of the laureateship is of crucial importance to these two threads, and to the wider picture outlined above. The office was a court office, but one which also, especially as the long eighteenth century wore on, positioned its holder in a prominent place with regard to the reading public and demanded of the laureate that they say something to the nation whose most prominent official cultural position they held. The office was a product of the traditional, courtly-patronal mode of literature, being appointed for (if not by) the highest patron in the land so as to glorify and entertain him. Yet most of the laureate's works were his own independent, commercially minded productions, and even his *ex officio* poems were widely printed in periodicals and sold as standalone publications. By 1813, the office was considered by some observers to be a flagrant anachronism,

---

[2] J. C. D. Clark, 'On hitting the buffers: The historiography of England's Ancien Regime. A response', *Past & Present*, cxvii (1987), 195–207; J. C. D. Clark, *English Society, 1660–1832: Religion, Ideology and Politics During the Ancien Regime*, 2nd edn (Cambridge, 2000); H. Greig, *The Beau Monde: Fashionable Society in Georgian London* (Oxford, 2013); D. Griffin, *Literary Patronage in England, 1650–1800* (Cambridge, 1996); H. Hoock, *Empires of the Imagination: Politics, War, and the Arts in the British World, 1750–1850* (London, 2010); *Stuart Succession Literature: Moments and Transformations*, ed. P. Kewes and A. McRae (Oxford, 2018). See also works on the court cited below.

worthy only of abolition; yet for others it remained a viable, important office, appropriate for a British genius like Walter Scott or Robert Southey. In short, despite being a manifestation of courtly patronage, it remained a conspicuous element in the literary world and in public life throughout the long eighteenth century, adapting to developments rather than being submerged by them. It can therefore be studied with a view to illuminating the place of the court, and of patronal ideas and practices, with regard to the modern British nation that was then taking shape.

This book's main argument is that the significance of the laureateship and of the court were greater than has generally been recognized. It will show that the poets laureate were not merely figures to be mocked or ignored – their office universally considered an anachronism – but that they enjoyed a continuing prominence, and even respectability, throughout the period. Moreover, the court did not lose out to the public in terms of cultural production and consumption; in fact, it came to be viewed as a public, national forum. Hence this book will argue that the court remained central to British society throughout the long eighteenth century, both as an institution and, especially, as a concept.

In doing so, this book will pay particular attention to questions of space. Its approach will be part of a significant trend, particularly evident over the last three decades, of studying eighteenth-century Britain using a spatial approach, an urban history approach or with some concern for the theme of geography.[3] As the foregoing description has indicated, the cultural history of eighteenth-century Britain has commonly been understood by reference to locations, whether actual, metaphorical or some combination of the two: locations such as the court, the nation, the public sphere and the marketplace. In analysing the laureateship's role, it is therefore necessary to ask where the office was located in the cultural landscape. Here, this book will focus on how eighteenth-century Britons themselves conceptualized

---

[3] Eg P. Borsay, *The English Urban Renaissance: Culture and Society in the Provincial Town, 1660–1770* (Oxford, 1989); *Transports: Travel, Pleasure, and Imaginative Geography, 1600–1830*, ed. C. Chard and H. Langdon (New Haven, Conn., 1996); *Geography and Enlightenment*, ed. D. N. Livingstone and C. W. J. Withers (Chicago, Ill., 1999); *The Oxford Handbook of British Poetry, 1660–1800*, ed. J. Lynch (Oxford, 2016), especially 'Part I: Poems in social settings'; R. J. Mayhew, *Enlightenment Geography: The Political Languages of British Geography, 1650–1850* (Basingstoke, 2000); M. Ogborn, *Spaces of Modernity: London's Geographies, 1680–1780* (London, 1998); *Georgian Geographies: Essays on Space, Place and Landscape in the Eighteenth Century*, ed. M. Ogborn and C. W. J. Withers (Manchester, 2004); J. Stobart, A. Hann and V. Morgan, *Spaces of Consumption: Leisure and Shopping in the English Town, c.1680–1830* (London, 2007); R. H. Sweet, 'Topographies of politeness', *Transactions of the Royal Historical Society*, xii (2002), 355–74; *Women and Urban Life in Eighteenth-Century England: 'On the Town'*, ed. R. H. Sweet and P. Lane (Aldershot, 2003).

that landscape. It will view their conceptual geography both as a subject that is illuminated by the history of the laureateship, and as a framework by which to understand what the laureateship and court meant to eighteenth-century Britons. This framework will be denoted 'the conceptual geography of culture'. The delineation of this conceptual geography, and of the laureateship and court's place within it, will be the basis for wider conclusions about British society, as well as comprising an important historiographical contribution in its own right.

This Introduction will describe the idea of a conceptual geography in more detail. It will then give a narrative and historiographical survey of the poets laureate. Lastly, it will outline the book's structure.

The conceptual geography of culture

Between 1668 and 1813, Britons routinely made reference to a number of locations in their discussions of the production and consumption of culture: the court, the church, the playhouses; coffeehouses, pleasure gardens, aristocratic country seats; London, the town, the city; England, Britain, Europe; the nation, the country, the world; the temple, the temple of fame, the closet, and so on. These locations tended to be at least partly metaphorical or ideal, but based on some actual, physical location or type of location. Britons used these locations as a way of contextualizing cultural products so as to give them meaning. They did not do so dogmatically; references to spaces were often casual and inconsistent, and coexisted with various other ways of evaluating cultural products. Nonetheless, the tendency was widespread. Writers, in particular, posited their works as existing in a certain space, with at least vague physical characteristics and at least a vague sense of producers and consumers standing visible to each other. The particular space that was being imagined had a significant bearing on the nature, purpose and value of the work.

It is therefore no surprise that historians have tended to study eighteenth-century culture by reference to spaces, even independently of the historiographical trends noted above concerning space, geography and urban history.[4] Most influential from a theoretical point of view has been Jürgen Habermas's *The Structural Transformation of the Public Sphere*

---

[4] Eg *The Pleasure Garden: From Vauxhall to Coney Island*, ed. J. Conlin (Philadelphia, Penn., 2013); H. Hoock, *The King's Artists: The Royal Academy of Arts and the Politics of British Culture 1760–1840* (Oxford, 2003); L. E. Klein, 'Coffeehouse civility, 1660–1714: An aspect of post-courtly culture in England', *Huntington Library Quarterly*, lix (1997), 30–51; D. H. Solkin, *Painting for Money: The Visual Arts and the Public Sphere in Eighteenth-Century England* (New Haven, Conn., 1993).

(first published in 1962 in German and in 1989 in English),[5] while the definitive historical work on eighteenth-century British culture has been John Brewer's *The Pleasures of the Imagination* (1997). These two works defined a narrative of eighteenth-century cultural transformation that has become widely accepted (even if the details of Habermas's original arguments have been repeatedly challenged and changed).[6] According to this narrative, culture moved from a single, central, physical location (the court) to an abstract, metaphorical location, in which vast numbers of people, each of them located anywhere, were joined together by the power of print: a location variously known as 'the public sphere', 'the public', 'the nation' or 'the marketplace'. The midpoint or the means of this transformation was provided by an archipelago of physical locations (quintessentially coffeehouses) within which small numbers of people could gather in discussion, and which together constituted a metaphorical whole (quintessentially 'the town'). As Brewer summarized it,

> in the late seventeenth century high culture moved out of the narrow confines of the court and into diverse spaces in London. It slipped out of palaces and into coffeehouses, reading societies, debating clubs, assembly rooms, galleries and concert halls; ceasing to be the handmaiden of royal politics, it became the partner of commerce.[7]

His work also acknowledged that the spatial conceptualization of culture was common among contemporaries:

> Arts and literature were discussed not in the abstract but as activities associated with special places – Grub Street, the home of the impoverished writer; Covent Garden, with its theatre and whores; the Haymarket, where there was opera; Smithfield, the centre of summer theatricals; Drury Lane, like its Covent Garden rival, a place of low life and theatre; Vauxhall Gardens, a site of summer pleasures; and St Paul's Churchyard, centre of London publishing.[8]

---

[5] J. Habermas, *The Structural Transformation of the Public Sphere: An Enquiry into a Category of Bourgeois Society*, trans. T. Burger and F. Lawrence (Cambridge, 1989).

[6] For usage of and engagement with Habermas's conceptual framework, see eg T. C. W. Blanning, *The Culture of Power and the Power of Culture: Old Regime Europe 1660–1789* (Oxford, 2002), pp. 2–14; M. Knights, *Representation and Misrepresentation in Later Stuart Britain: Partisanship and Political Culture* (Oxford, 2005), pp. 48–52, 67, 94–9; *The Politics of the Public Sphere in Early Modern England*, ed. P. Lake and S. Pincus (Manchester, 2007); J. Raymond, 'The newspaper, public opinion, and the public sphere in the seventeenth century', in *News, Newspapers, and Society in Early Modern Britain*, ed. J. Raymond (London, 1999), pp. 109–40.

[7] Brewer, *Pleasures*, p. 15.

[8] Brewer, *Pleasures*, p. 51.

However, although there has been some correspondence between contemporary and historical conceptualizations of space, it has not been thoroughgoing. Contemporaries spoke of 'public(k)' matters and of 'the public(k)'; they did not speak of 'the public sphere', or postulate that any such space had emerged in the manner or timeframe postulated by Habermas. Similarly, while historians' descriptions of a cultural 'marketplace' do bear some resemblance to processes that contemporaries would have recognized – such as Samuel Johnson's famous comment that booksellers had become the new literary patrons – contemporaries did not often use 'market' or 'marketplace' in this abstract way, or conceptually position cultural products within a 'market(place)' in the ways that they positioned them in courts, coffeehouses and playhouses. In his dictionary, Johnson gave fairly short and literal-minded definitions for 'Market' and 'Market-Place', the latter being defined as 'Place where the market is held' and illustrated by quotations in which single, particular marketplaces were denoted.[9] Even with those terms that show greater consistency of usage between contemporaries and historians – 'the public', 'the town', 'Britain' – scholars have been more concerned to use such terms as frameworks for historical analysis, rather than to study them as contemporary frameworks of analysis, or to follow the contemporary usage with any great scrupulousness. Contemporary usage has served as a jumping-off point, rather than as a pathway in and of itself. Of course, this is unavoidable. A historian who merely followed the notions entertained by the people whom they were studying would be no historian at all; they would be a writer of historical pastiche. But it does mean that our understanding of the conceptual geography of culture used by contemporaries is incomplete, and has the potential to be confused with the notions of space that scholars have put forward in their own works.

This book does not seek to map out those contemporary conceptualizations in full. However, it will attempt to treat the conceptual geography of culture as a subject in its own right, and to contribute some part of the map. This will mean analysing contemporary usage of certain words and notions at any one time; it will also mean analysing how such usage changed between 1668 and 1813. Broadly speaking, it will argue that there was a shift in conceptual geography over the course of the period, which does correspond in many ways to that which has been drawn by historians: from Britons tending to conceptualize culture by reference to physical locations, to them preferring more metaphorical ones. In the late seventeenth century, court, church

[9] S. Johnson, *A Dictionary of the English Language* (2 vols, 1755–6), ii. 'Market', 'Market-Place'.

and the two London playhouses loomed large, and there was an obsession, especially among those who produced and consumed theatrical works, with a tripartite distinction between town, court and city.[10] Producers and consumers explicitly situated plays in the physical space of whichever playhouse they were being performed in, and, only slightly less immediately, in the social world of this tripartite London. This is seen, for example, in title pages, which usually stated the theatre and acting company of the original performance, and in the invariable printing of prologues and epilogues, which comprised explicit, familiar addresses to audiences who were defined by their situations in the playhouse and their social lives in London.[11] Meanwhile, lyric poems were often published with, and blurred into, 'songs' and 'odes', and framed by reference to how they had been received in performance or in manuscript at court or in town.[12] It was this physical orienteering that gave plays (especially) and other cultural products their meaning.

By the start of the nineteenth century, this was far less the case. Cultural products tended to be conceptually situated in those larger, more metaphorical spaces that no one person, or body of people, could literally inhabit. Producers pitched their work to a hypothetical public, spread throughout England or Britain. At the same time, even those more specific, physical locations became increasingly metaphorical in the way that they were conceived. For example, the ways in which London was imagined and experienced, and was used to give meaning to cultural products (and other forms of activity), became less to do with physical presence and more to do with print circulation. London news was read across the country, often in periodicals whose title included the name 'London'. While the distinction between town and city became less meaningful, the conceptualized metropolis was increasingly used to house ideological distinctions which were entered into by readers who may never have set foot in London.[13]

It is by reference to these evolving spatial concepts that this monograph will analyse the poet laureateship. In particular, it will situate the laureateship within the dynamic of the public and the court. Of course, the first of

---

[10] T. Shadwell, *The Sullen Lovers* (1668), p. 97; A. Behn, *The Amorous Prince* (1671), 'Prologue' (unpaginated); J. Dryden, *Marriage a-la-mode* (1673) in *Works*, xi. 226.

[11] Elkanah Settle, *The Empress of Morocco* (1673), title page, sig. A3r–A4r, p. 73; A. Behn, *The City-Heiress* (1682), sig. A3v–A4r, pp. 62–3; N. Rowe, *Tamerlane* (1702), title page.

[12] T. Flatman, *Poems and Songs* (1674); Thomas D'Urfey, *A New Collection of Songs and Poems* (1683); Thomas D'Urfey, *New Poems, Consisting of Satyrs, Elegies, and Odes Together with a Choice Collection of the Newest Court Songs Set to Musick by the Best Masters of the Age* (1690), especially sig. A6r–A7r.

[13] J. Black, *The English Press: 1621–1861* (Stroud, 2001), pp. 107–8, 132–4; J. Brewer, *Party Ideology and Popular Politics at the Accession of George III* (Cambridge, 1976), p. 158.

those elements was not itself a conceptual space. Mark Knights, in his study of later Stuart political culture, viewed the public as 'a collective fiction', understood by contemporaries 'as voters, as readers, as a legitimating authority, as umpires and judges of state and church' and as 'a reading public'.[14] T. C. W. Blanning viewed it as 'a cultural actor' created by private individuals coming together in the public sphere 'to form a whole greater than the sum of the parts'.[15] However, as will be evidenced over the course of this book, the public as a contemporary concept held an important place in the conceptual geography of culture, and in the way that that geography changed over time.[16] It did so in two main ways. First, it partially superseded, and partially collapsed, an older distinction in the conceptual geography of culture. Up to 1700, writers rarely invoked the public as a forum or audience for their products.[17] Where the word 'public(k)' was used at all, it tended to be used as an adjective, and to denote matters of state or national well-being. Thus in Dryden's translation of the *Aeneid* (1697), Aeneas described a Greek who was supposedly going to be sacrificed to please the gods as 'the Wretch, ordain'd by Fate,/The Publick Victim, to redeem the State'.[18]

'Public(k)' affairs were more serious than plays and poetry; in their dedicatory epistles to patrons, writers would even sometimes contrast the seriousness of their patrons' 'publick' services with the triviality of the publication that was being offered to the patron as a diversion.[19] Against such notions, the combative Charles Gildon asserted that 'POETS' ought to be considered as bringing 'Benefit to the *Public*'. But he made this argument no earlier than 1694, clearly felt himself to be advancing an unusual opinion and only portrayed 'the *Public*' as an abstract, passive entity, rather than as an audience with a will and an opinion of its own.[20] Among seventeenth-century writers, usage of 'the public(k)' in the meaning that would later become common was rare and partial. Instead, they would present their work as having emerged from, being offered to and being

---

[14] Knights, *Representation*, pp. 5, 52, 99.

[15] Blanning, *Culture*, p. 2.

[16] The following discussion summarizes the arguments of an article on changes in the conceptual geography of culture 1660–1800 which I am currently working on. However, some citations are given here, and more supporting evidence will be given over the course of this monograph, especially in ch. 2.

[17] Though for an early example of this exact usage, see Dryden, *The Spanish Fryar* (1681) in *Works*, xiv. 99.

[18] Dryden, *Works*, v. 384.

[19] Tate, *Poems* (1676), sig. A4r–v.

[20] C. Gildon, *Miscellaneous Letters and Essays on Several Subjects* (1694), sig. A2r–A3r (sig. A3r for quotation).

received by spatially conceptualized audiences: the playhouse, coffeehouses, the court, the town.

Alongside this, writers would conceptualize a different sort of audience, albeit in a vaguer and less frequent fashion: 'the world'. The world was not necessarily separate from or contrasted with those smaller locations, but it was generally viewed as a more impartial, widespread forum which would receive a work primarily in its printed form and judge that work according to abstract criteria of quality.[21] When a distinction was explicitly drawn (which was not often), it was between the town as a physical forum, whose topography and social dynamics conditioned every aspect of a work's production and consumption, and the world as either a faceless generality or a shorthand for an abstract determination of literary quality. Occasionally, one of two other, more specific locations would be used instead of 'the world' to denote similar or overlapping ideas: 'the country' beyond London and 'the closet' within people's homes.[22]

These conceptualizations changed between 1700 and 1730. At around the turn of the century, increasing numbers of writers began to use 'the public(k)' to denote a judging audience, often interchangeably with other terms; by 1720, the new usage was widespread, and by 1730, it was commonplace. Although the world and the smaller locations preferred in the seventeenth century were still referenced, the public became writers' favourite, or even default, conceptualization of their audience.[23] But the public had not simply replaced any of the older terms, and its ascendancy did not mean that the generalized audience denoted by 'the world' had become prioritized over the particularized audience(s) denoted by (for example) 'the town'. In fact, the public was built upon both concepts: the world, on the one hand, and the conceptualization of London, especially of

---

[21] T. Otway, *Venice Preserv'd* (1682), sig. A2r; T. Southerne, *The Fatal Marriage* (1694), sig. A2r; C. Cibber, *Love's Last Shift* (1696), sig. A2r–v; G. Farquhar, *The Constant Couple* (1700), sig. A2r–v.

[22] Both used in Cibber, *Xerxes* (1699), dedication (unpaginated). Both 'the country' and 'the closet' had possible political implications: 'the country' as the antithesis of 'the court', of supposedly corrupt courtly values or of the government; 'the closet' as the royal closet, denoting the court, the monarch or the monarch's close confidants and ministers. But these political implications were generally not much present when the words were used about cultural products, especially not for 'the closet', which almost always denoted the private spaces in which every individual reader would consume the work.

[23] Dryden, *Cleomenes* (1692) in *Works*, xvi. 73, 77; R. Steele, *Poetical Miscellanies* (1714), sig. A3r–A4r; S. Centlivre, *A Bold Stroke for a Wife* (1718), pp. i, iv; L. Theobald, *The Rape of Proserpine*, 3rd edn (1727), pp. iv–vii; L. Theobald, *Double Falshood* (1728), sig. A3v, A5r–v; W. Pattison, *The Poetical Works of Mr. William Pattison, Late of Sidney College Cambridge* (1728), pp. 1, 22–3, 51–2; H. Fielding, *The Historical Register, For the Year 1736* (1737), sig. A3r–A7v.

the town, on the other. The public was London-centric and most visible in London, but it also transcended London, and could be imagined in a way that had nothing to do with the metropolis. Though in geographical terms it was therefore a more capacious concept than the town, it was a more specific concept than the world, and different from the town, in terms of the people it was denoting. This public was not just the fashionable upper classes of London, whose lives revolved around the court, coffeehouses, playhouses and soirees, but nor was it a faceless general opinion; it was the body of people who thought, bought, read and wrote, wherever they might be located in the nation. Their capital was London, but they were bound together by print.

Indeed, references to the public often give some indication of the slippages and complexities of its position. As late as 1772, Richard Cumberland published *The Fashionable Lover* with the advertisement, 'I commit this Comedy to the press with all possible gratitude to the Public for the reception it has met: I cannot flatter myself that the same applause will follow it to the closet; for … it owed much to an excellent representation [on stage].'[24] Cumberland's advertisement did not make clear whether the play's readers would also become 'the Public' now that the play was published; but, in any case, it is significant that he was using 'the Public' to exclusively denote Londoners who had viewed the play at Drury Lane, and contrasting them with readers. Perhaps, given that the published form of the play was being read by individuals in closets, readers were too atomized a group to form 'the Public'; paradoxically, the fact of publication made for a private, individual experience, whereas theatrical performances, held in crowded, sociable spaces, created a public.

Of course, for those writings that were not performed – such as most forms of lyric poetry – the public could only be composed of readers. But even here, the public often took its lead from the town. Thomas Warton's *Five Pastoral Eclogues* (1745) was prefaced thus:

> How the ideas of fields and woods, and a poetry whose very essence is a rural life, will agree with the polite taste of the town, and of gentlemen who are more conversant in the fashionable ornaments of life, is a question: but I hope as they relate to that war, which is at present the most general topic of conversation, this unpoliteness will in some measure be excused … How the author of these pieces has succeeded in the performance of this, is humbly submitted to the censure and judgment of the public.[25]

---

[24] R. Cumberland, *The Fashionable Lover* (1772), p. v.

[25] T. Warton, *Five Pastoral Eclogues* (1745), pp. 3–4.

Warton situated his work primarily in the context of 'the town', which context he feared would be to the detriment of his work's relevance and reception; yet, by the same token, he hoped that his work would be valued as a contribution to the current topic of town-based 'conversation'. He then referenced 'the public', perhaps using the term as a synonym for 'the town', perhaps alluding to a more transcendent audience whose judgement was not determined by the partialities of town life. Thus in the mid and later eighteenth century it was still normal to conceive of the public as being based in, or looking to, the physical spaces of London.

Moreover, the public's powers of judgement were more flexible than those ascribed to the town or the world. Its judgement was purer, more abstract and less hurried than the town's, but not as vague, impersonal or passive as the world's. Yet it had the potential to slide towards either extreme, both in the sense that any given writer might conceive of it in such a way and in the sense that, according to many writers, the public could be guided towards either correct or corrupt principles by writers, critics, statesmen and even kings. In 1746, Joseph Warton advertised his *Odes on Various Subjects* with the claim,

> The Public has been so much accustom'd of late to didactic Poetry alone, and Essays on moral Subjects, that any work where the imagination is much indulged, will perhaps not be relished or regarded. The author therefore of these pieces is in some pain least certain austere critics should think them too fanciful and descriptive. But as he is convinced that the fashion of moralizing in verse has been carried too far, and as he looks upon Invention and Imagination to be the chief faculties of a Poet, so he will be happy if the following Odes may be look'd upon as an attempt to bring back Poetry into its right channel.[26]

In Joseph Warton's view, the public's taste was conditioned by the fare put in front of it. A poet could bring its tastes back towards correct principles, but would have to battle against critics and other writers in order to do so.

Thus the definition of the public was looser than the town and the world in some ways – especially geographically – but tighter in others. It was an audience that existed across the nation but had relatively focused characteristics. It was constituted in the abstract space of text, but centred on the physical space of London. It could judge, but was not as partial as the audience of a London playhouse, and would have to be entered into dialogue with via print, rather than by conversation in a coffeehouse. It gave writers an audience that fitted the circumstances of eighteenth-century writing: the increasing volume of print and of the money to be made from

[26] J. Warton, *Odes on Various Subjects* (1746), sig. A2r.

it; the increasing size of London, and the fact that London was stretching its tendrils across the rest of the country via print and via improved travel facilities, which reduced London's coherence and comprehensibility as an actual community while increasing its importance as an idea; and the fact that playwriting became proportionately less conspicuous and plausible a career as the century wore on, compared to other forms of writing.

The second main way in which the public relates to the conceptual geography of culture is that, over the course of the long eighteenth century, as the spaces within which culture was conceptually situated moved from physical to metaphorical, the public served as the appropriate audience to inhabit those metaphorical spaces. This worked on a number of different levels. On one level, the development of the public as an audience for cultural products went hand in hand with the increasingly sophisticated conceptualization of Britain as a forum. In the late seventeenth century, references were routinely made to 'England', 'Britain', 'the nation' and 'the country', to specifically English and British characteristics such as Protestantism and liberty and even to the greatness of English and British literature. But the eighteenth century undoubtedly saw developments in all of these areas, and perhaps especially in the cultivation and promulgation of the literary canon.[27] As the public became established as a concept, it became established as the body of people that inhabited, and were most conscious of inhabiting, this British nation.[28] On a second level, the public was conceived as inhabiting the capital city. As mentioned above, London became increasingly potent and widespread as a metaphor, in political as much as in cultural affairs; it became the forum for the activities and opinions of people across Britain who read London newspapers, read about London, read texts that vicariously placed them in London and identified with London-based identity groups. Insofar as London was a metaphorical space for cultural production and consumption, the public was that space's audience, before whom the creator of the cultural product stood.

On a third level, the public was capable of conceptually inhabiting locations that were yet smaller in their physical referents. These locations had previously been conceived of purely in terms of their physical existence and of the audience that was physically capable of fitting inside them. However, by the turn of the nineteenth century, they were more likely to be conceived of as metaphorical locations, and it was in this sense that they played a role in cultural production and consumption. Scholars have shown one example of this in periodicals, such as the *Gentleman's Journal*

---

[27] See works on national identity and canon formation cited above.

[28] See ch. 4.

and *The Spectator*. With their contents, tone, and attitude to readers and correspondents, periodicals such as these recreated (sometimes explicitly) clubs, coffeehouses and courtly coteries, but in a printed form, meaning that they were able to be spread across Britain. This trend was evident at the turn of the eighteenth century, although Addison seems to have conceived of *The Spectator*'s readership as 'Disciplines in *London* and *Westminster*';[29] thereafter, it became increasingly pronounced, with various types of writing, including poetry, creating imagined, nationwide clubs of different sorts.[30] The public was the audience that inhabited the metaphorical locations constituted by print.

This development – a physically grounded conceptual geography evolving into a more metaphorical one, occupied by the public – obviously harmonizes well with the narrative of cultural transformation established by Habermas, Brewer and other scholars. However, this book's approach and arguments will differ from that narrative in one important respect: it will emphasize the continuing importance of the court. Here, it will be following the path laid down by such scholars as Clarissa Campbell Orr, Matthew Kilburn and especially Hannah Smith, who have argued that the court adapted to eighteenth-century developments, rather than being sidelined by them.[31]

As mentioned above, a study of the laureateship is ideally placed to forward these arguments, and to reveal the changing nature of the court's role; but the emphasis on contemporaries' conceptual geography is also highly relevant in this respect. The standard historical narrative posits that cultural change happened at the expense of the court; and the argument given above, that contemporary understandings of culture moved from specific, physical locations to wider, metaphorical ones, might be assumed to entail that a specific, physical location like the court would lose out. Likewise, it

---

[29] *The Spectator* 10 in *The Spectator*, ed. D. F. Bond (5 vols, Oxford, 1965), i. 44.

[30] M. J. Ezell, 'The "Gentleman's Journal" and the commercialization of restoration coterie literary practices', *Modern Philology*, lxxxix (1992), 323–40; D. Fairer, *English Poetry of the Eighteenth Century 1700–1789* (London, 2003), p. x; M. Haslett, *Pope to Burney, 1714–1779: Scriblerians to Bluestockings* (London, 2003), especially pp. 1–6, 17–25, 50–4; M. Haslett, 'The poet as clubman', in *The Oxford Handbook of British Poetry, 1660–1800*, ed. Lynch (Oxford, 2016), pp. 127–43.

[31] M. Kilburn, 'Royalty and public in Britain: 1714–1789' (unpublished University of Oxford DPhil thesis, 1997); *Queenship in Britain 1660–1837: Royal Patronage, Court Culture and Dynastic Politics*, ed. C. C. Orr (Manchester, 2002); *Queenship in Europe 1660–1815: The Role of the Consort*, ed. C. C. Orr (Cambridge, 2004); H. Smith, *Georgian Monarchy: Politics and Culture, 1714–1760* (Cambridge, 2006). For affirmations of the importance of particular monarchs' courts, see eg T. Claydon, *William III and the Godly Revolution* (Cambridge, 1996); J. Marschner, *Queen Caroline: Cultural Politics at the Early Eighteenth-Century Court* (New Haven, Conn., 2014); J. A. Winn, *Queen Anne: Patroness of Arts* (Oxford, 2014).

might be assumed that the laureates would suffer a similar fate: they were anchored at court, trapped under their monarchs' gaze, and therefore had no place in the Habermasian public sphere, Brewer's cultural marketplace or the increasingly diffuse conceptual geography of culture posited here. However, this monograph will demonstrate that court and laureateship remained highly important in contemporary conceptualizations of culture, evolving along similar lines to those delineated above for London as a whole, and for clubs, coffeehouses and playhouses. In proportion as the conceptual geography of culture became more abstract, the court developed from a physical to a metaphorical location, in which the public was the proper audience.

Nor was it a coincidence that the court's transformation should have proceeded in step with that of London as a whole. The court was an integral part of London; the palaces of St James's, Kensington, the Queen's House and (until it burned down in 1698) Whitehall were all located in the metropolis, and Windsor Castle and Hampton Court were nearby. Greig has pointed out that, after the huge Whitehall palace was destroyed, the court 'consisted of a constellation of smaller residences dispersed across a wider metropolitan map'.[32] Rather than diminishing its importance, this actually 'integrated the court more substantially into the London landscape', especially given that 'the royal household occupied buildings that were comparatively open to the public gaze'.[33]

As mentioned above, late seventeenth-century writers, particularly dramatists, constantly situated their works in a tripartite London, comprising a rich body of notions about court, town, city and the relations between the three. In this scheme, it was actually the city that was presented (and mocked) as the outlier, whereas the court and the town were grouped together in physical and social intimacy.[34] The town was probably the cultural space that later Stuart and early Hanoverian writers cited most frequently, and their successors continued to reference it with some frequency even into the nineteenth century; it was the fashionable part of London, home to the social elite, to the leading writers and artists and to the small number of theatres that most plays and operas were written to be performed in. Yet the town had intentionally been constructed on the doorstep of the royal palaces and parliament, and its conceptual identity was dependent upon this proximity, especially to St James's Palace. As late as 1755 (and in

---

[32] Greig, *Beau Monde*, p. 104.

[33] Greig, *Beau Monde*, p. 106.

[34] Dryden, *Marriage a-la-mode*, in *Works*, xi. 316; N. Tate, *A Duke and No Duke* (1685), sig. a2r; Cibber, *Love Makes a Man* (1701), sig. A2r–A3r.

the revised fourth edition of 1773), Johnson's dictionary defined the 'Town' area of London as 'The court end of London'.[35] The town was not a rival to the court; if anything, it was a hinterland. Likewise, as London became increasingly present and important to readers across the country, but more abstract as a result, the court was very much a part of this metropolis. And as the court became transcendental, so too did the laureate transcend the physical space of the court. He became the representative of a more diffuse, national, public court: a court that thus remained integral to the cultural landscape.

It is primarily in this sense that the court will be analysed here: as a contemporary concept. Of course, it was also a physical place, or places, being understood by contemporaries and historians alike as the several palaces in which the monarch was or might be present. Not least because the court's metaphorical potency was rooted in this physical existence, the court will sometimes appear in the following chapters in the physical sense: as the palace at which the monarch was resident, and particularly as St James's Palace, where the laureate odes were normally performed. It will also be mentioned sometimes, particularly in Chapter One, as an institution, in the sense of there being a departmental structure, a body of officials and financial resources and apparatus that together can be classed as an institution. Where the context of discussion makes it necessary to distinguish between these different senses, the terms 'conceptual court', 'institutional court' and 'physical court' will be used.[36] However, the last term will not be used often; the analytical emphasis will be on a conceptual court that included the physical court in the same way that a 'person' includes a skeleton and owes much to that skeleton in the way that they are constituted, but also comprises and connotes much more than just bones. As for the public, it too will primarily be analysed as a concept held by contemporaries: more as Knights's 'collective fiction' than Blanning's 'cultural agent'. However, there will be times, especially in Chapter Four, where the general body of readers who were conceived of and conceived themselves as the public becomes a subject of discussion in its own right, albeit with due appreciation of the difficulties of defining this generalized body, let alone defining its views. At these times, it will be distinguished from the conceptual public by the term 'the reading public'. This term is common in eighteenth-century scholarship but was not common among

[35] Johnson, *Dictionary*, ii, 'Town'.

[36] This distinction owes something to Smith's distinction between the court as an institution and the court as a forum. H. Smith, 'The court in England, 1714–1760: A declining political institution?' *History*, xc (2005), 23–41.

contemporaries, and hence serves well to distinguish the public as an object of historical, rather than contemporary, concern.[37]

It may be objected that this is a random, narrow perspective, or that it might distract in some way from the laureateship. The first objection would be supported by the admission made above, that spatial concepts were not the only way that contemporaries understood cultural production and consumption, and were not even used in an especially consistent, wholehearted or sophisticated manner. However, three defences can be made against this objection. First, even if contemporaries' use of spatial concepts was not exclusive or comprehensive, that use was widespread and shows significant consistencies, patterns and developments. It therefore warrants appreciation as a subject in its own right. Second, as is generally recognized, even a society's most casual word choices reveal a great deal about that society, and about the changes that it was going through; as will be seen, the ways in which Britons used such concepts as the public and the court in the long eighteenth century can furnish significant wider conclusions. Third, as it is by concepts that people understand their experience and surroundings, it is concepts that determine people's behaviour. Insofar as producers and consumers conceptualized culture spatially, and by reference to the public and the court, their individual and group behaviour can only be comprehended by understanding those concepts.

As for the second objection, this book will show that the history of the laureateship fits perfectly with the focus on contemporary conceptualizations. It reveals how contemporaries conceptualized the court's role with regard to culture and the public. By the same token, a consideration of these wider themes helps to make sense of the office's own role. This is true both of the laureateship as an institution, and of the laureates as individual cultural figures. Studying the laureateship as an institution, with a particular place as part of the court, allows us to better appreciate contemporary uses of spatial concepts. Studying the laureates as individuals allows us to see how and why this conceptual geography existed in the first place, and why it changed in the ways it did. As will appear in the following chapters, this geography gave individuals something to navigate as they sought advantages for themselves and their associates. Throughout this monograph, we will see the laureates, and other figures who had some concern in the laureateship, appraising the cultural landscape, identifying the place where it would be most advantageous for them to be, plotting the best route to get there and

---

[37] Eg a keyword search for 'reading public' on *Eighteenth Century Collections Online* brings up various texts in which the words 'reading' and 'public' are used in close proximity to each other, and others in which the term 'public reading' (that is, a public recital) is used, but virtually none in which the specific term 'reading public' appears.

giving utterance or action to their appraisals. Each of the individuals shown in this monograph gives some indication of the conceptual geography that existed at the time, what factors determined its shape and where court and laureateship stood within it.

Thus the usage of the terms 'public', 'court' and other terms denoting locations will primarily refer to the conceptual geography of culture as described above; this will be the main framework of analysis. Spatial terms that have proven useful in modern scholarship, but that were not used by contemporaries, such as 'the public sphere' and 'the marketplace', will generally be eschewed, although convenience and context will sometimes require exceptions. Certain other key terms will be used entirely in disregard of eighteenth-century usage. One is 'culture'. Johnson defined it as, 'The act of cultivation; the act of tilling the ground; tillage' and the 'Art of improvement or melioration'.[38] Its definition is now very different, but it is a notoriously capacious or slippery term; Ludmilla Jordanova has even argued that 'all history is cultural history'.[39] In comparison, this book's focus will perhaps seem disappointingly unambitious, and disappointingly unrelated to farming. 'Culture' will here be shorthand for 'high culture', or for what is sometimes called 'the arts' or 'arts and literature'. However, as mentioned above, it will be argued that wider conclusions about the nature of British society can be drawn from an analysis of culture so defined. As for 'literature', it will be used in its modern, somewhat anachronistic sense: creative or imaginative writing, mostly of a high-brow, fictional inclination. This is not how the term was understood in the early eighteenth century, when it tended to mean something more like 'learning' or 'book-based learnedness'. The modern definition of literature came into being in the latter half of that century, and even then, Johnson, for example, was happy to switch between usages.[40] However, as Terry has shown, this modern definition took the place of older, largely synonymous terms that were current throughout or even before the seventeenth century; ultimately, some concept of creative, fictional writing, and of its potential importance, went back to the ancient world.[41]

[38] Johnson, *Dictionary*, i, 'Culture'.

[39] Quoted as part of a discussion of definitions of 'culture' by T. Harris, 'Problematising popular culture', in *Popular Culture in England, c.1500–1850*, ed. T. Harris (Basingstoke, 1995), pp. 1–27, at pp. 10–11.

[40] Brewer, *Pleasures*, pp. 1–4, 33–54; Hammond, *Hackney*, pp. 198–200.

[41] Terry, *Literary Past*, pp. 11–34.

The office and scholarship

The laureateship, especially in its eighteenth-century form, has not been much studied by historians or literary scholars. The standard account is E. K. Broadus's *The Laureateship: A Study of the Office of Poet Laureate in England, With Some Account of the Poets* (1921), which devoted a chapter each to the later Stuart period and to the eighteenth century. This was a well-researched and insightful history, with helpful information on each of the laureates. But it does not engage with the same themes, questions and concerns as this monograph, and it is nearly a century old. General narrative histories of the office were also published in 1853, 1879, 1895, 1914 and 1955; but none are very analytical, none come close to the scholarship of Broadus and none offer much new information (if any).[42] In 2014, Ewa Panecka published a study that was predominantly focused on the laureate poems themselves. It devoted most of its attention to the twentieth and twenty-first centuries and, in its treatment of the eighteenth-century laureateship, was based on those earlier narrative histories.[43] Other than Broadus's work, the most original contribution to the field has been Rosamond McGuinness's *English Court Odes: 1660–1820* (1971). Although primarily a study of the musical trends and traditions of the biannual court odes for which the laureates wrote most of the words, it included a rigorous, comprehensive attempt to identify all of the odes and trace the history of the form.[44]

The origins of the office of poet laureate, and the rationale behind its conferral upon John Dryden in 1668, will be discussed in Chapter One. However, it should be noted here that, after several decades in which prominent English poets had bandied around the idea of 'poets laureate' and had sporadically associated this idea with the pensions that were sometimes bestowed upon favoured poets by the Stuart court, Dryden was the first man for whom the laureateship was a genuine, salaried office. William Davenant, who had received a pension from Charles I, died in 1668, and Charles II issued a royal warrant making Dryden his poet laureate shortly after. Neither Charles nor Dryden, nor (it seems) any other contemporary, viewed Dryden's appointment as a novelty or invention. The recent currency of the idea of 'poets laureate' had caused people to believe not

---

[42] W. S. Austin Jnr and J. Ralph, *The Lives of The Poets-Laureate* (London, 1853); W. Hamilton, *The Poets Laureate of England* (London, 1879); K. West, *The Laureates of England, from Ben Jonson to Alfred Tennyson* (London, 1895); W. F. Gray, *The Poets Laureate of England: Their History and Their Odes* (London, 1914); K. Hopkins, *The Poets Laureate* (London, 1954).

[43] E. Panecka, *Literature and the Monarchy: The Traditional and the Modern Concept of the Office of Poet Laureate of England* (Newcastle, 2014).

[44] R. McGuinness, *English Court Odes: 1660–1820* (Oxford, 1971).

only that Davenant had been holding a particular, official position that had now passed to Dryden, but that a long succession of other poets must have been holding the same position too. Any poet who had been pensioned by the English court, or whose work seemed associated with it, was yoked into this spurious laureate tradition, the highlights of which were Geoffrey Chaucer, Edmund Spenser and Ben Jonson. Dryden became England's first poet laureate, yet was imagined to be the latest in a long, distinguished line. At this stage, the office was honorific, with no attendant responsibilities. In 1689, due to his Catholicism and implicit loyalty to the deposed king, James II, he was himself deposed.

Dryden has received more scholarly attention than all of his long eighteenth-century successors put together (possibly excepting Southey), with all his various works having attracted at least some generous ration of academic interest. As well as dedicated monographs, biographies and essay collections, he finds his way into almost every more general publication on his period.[45] Because of the profuseness of his oeuvre, and his keenness to discuss virtually everything that was going on in his lifetime, he has proved to be the academic's friend. However, his role as laureate – which was ambiguous and ill defined – has received only a small portion of all this scholarly attention. That portion has mainly taken the form of a debate about the early years of his salary.[46]

Dryden's successor was Thomas Shadwell (PL 1689–92), with whom he shared more in common than the respective natures and copiousness of scholarly publications on the two men would suggest. Dryden and Shadwell knew each other well, having been two mainstays of the Restoration stage, and having long been professional and political rivals. But Shadwell's tenure as laureate was brief. He wrote some odes and other forms of panegyric for William and Mary, enjoyed a few years as the most successful playwright in the country, then died in 1692. The existing Shadwell scholarship reflects both the relative brevity of his tenure and the general lack of scholarly concern

---

[45] For dedicated works, see eg P. Hammond, *John Dryden: A Literary Life* (Basingstoke, 1991); P. Hammond, *Dryden and the Traces of Classical Rome* (Oxford, 1999); D. B. Kramer, *The Imperial Dryden: The Poetics of Appropriation in Seventeenth-Century England* (Athens, Ga., 1994); J. A. Winn, *John Dryden and His World* (New Haven, Conn., 1998); *The Cambridge Companion to John Dryden*, ed. S. Zwicker (Cambridge, 2004). For general publications that include substantial discussion of Dryden, see eg P. Kewes, *Authorship and Appropriation: Writing for the Stage in England, 1660–1710* (Oxford, 1998), pp. 54–63; Terry, *Literary Past*, pp. 145–67; S. Zwicker, *Lines of Authority: Politics and English Literary Culture, 1649–1689* (Ithaca, N.Y., 1996), pp. 90–199.

[46] Summarized and apparently settled in E. L. Saslow, '"Stopp'd in other hands": The payment of Dryden's pension for 1668–1670', *Restoration: Studies in English Literary Culture, 1660–1700*, xxx (2006), 31–42.

for the office. It also manifests the posthumous potency of Dryden's hatred. For a long time, Shadwell was known only as Dryden's 'dull' antagonist. But a multi-volume *Complete Works* was published in 1927 by the eccentric Montague Summers, who also provided, in the long introduction, a detailed study of Shadwell's life and times.[47] Then, over the latter half of the twentieth century, Shadwell was rehabilitated as a major Restoration playwright. There has been a fairly ample smattering of articles on various aspects of his plays; A. S. Borgman published a biography of him in 1969; and he now tends to feature prominently in any general dramatic history of the period, partly on account of being the foremost exponent of 'humours' comedy.[48] However, his work as a satirist and controversialist has been far less studied, and his brief but important tenure as laureate has been entirely neglected.

Following Shadwell was Nahum Tate (PL 1692–1715), who has proven neither the academic's friend nor the revisionist's bounty. The scant scholarly attention he has received has tended to focus on his work as a Shakespeare adaptor.[49] His other, more original plays have been largely ignored; likewise his vast reams of poetry, his attempt to write a poetic and religious version of *The Spectator* and his successful translation of the psalms into English. Purcell scholars know him as the librettist to *Dido and Aeneas*.[50] But there was a 1972 biography of him produced under the imprint of Twayne Publishers, who for several decades were publishing critical biographies of a wide range of English writers.[51] There have also been a short article on the vicissitudes of Tate's laureate salary (1957); an obscure but strangely effusive study of Tate's laureate panegyrics (1999); and a handful of other anomalous articles.[52]

---

[47] T. Shadwell, *Complete Works*, ed. M. Summers (5 vols, London, 1927).

[48] J. M. Armistead, 'Scholarship on Shadwell since 1980: A survey and annotated chronology', *Restoration: Studies in English Literary Culture, 1660–1700*, xx (1996), 101–18; R. D. Bevis, *English Drama: Restoration and Eighteenth Century, 1660–1789* (London, 1988), pp. 71–98; A. S. Borgman, *Thomas Shadwell* (New York, 1969).

[49] Eg O. Johnson, 'Empty houses: The suppression of Tate's "Richard II"', *Theatre Journal*, xlvii (1995), 503–16; T. G. Olsen, 'Apolitical Shakespeare: Or, the Restoration *Coriolanus*', *Studies in English Literature, 1500–1900*, xxxviii (1998), 411–25.

[50] A. Welch, 'The cultural politics of *Dido and Aeneas*', *Cambridge Opera Journal*, xxi (2009), 1–26.

[51] C. Spencer, *Nahum Tate* (New York, 1972).

[52] S. L. Astor, 'The laureate as Huckster: Nahum Tate and an early eighteenth century example of publisher's advertising', *Studies in Bibliography*, xxi (1968), 261–6; S. A. Golden, 'The late seventeenth century writer and the laureateship: Nahum Tate's tenure', *Hermathena*, lxxxix (1957), 30–8; P. F. Heaney, 'The laureate dunces and the death of the panegyric', *Early Modern Literary Studies*, v (1999), 4.1–4.24 [+ notes].

However, it is highly appropriate that work on Tate's laureate salary and panegyrics should bulk comparatively large in the diminutive field of his academic afterlife. Tate's tenure was a transformative period for the office. By the time of his death in 1715 – a year after Queen Anne's – the laureateship had become associated with formal expectations that had not existed for Dryden, and had passed firmly into the lord chamberlain's department in the court establishment. The laureates would henceforth be formally appointed by the lord chamberlain, and would have to write two odes a year, for New Year's Day and for the monarch's birthday, which would be set to music by the king or queen's master of music and performed as part of the festivities on those days. It also became customary for those odes to be published, as individual publications, in periodicals or both. For the rest of the eighteenth century, the office would be heavily identified with, and even defined by, this duty.

To some extent, this development was a result of Nahum Tate's own activities. Neither he himself nor anyone else regarded him as an equal of Dryden's, or even of Shadwell's. Although his early literary career had overlapped with theirs, he had never become as prominent as either of them. Nor had his name ever been firmly associated with any particular genre, as Shadwell's had been with drama, and as Dryden's had been with both drama and satire. He had written several plays, ranging from farces to topical adaptations of Shakespeare's tragedies, and one of those adaptations, *Richard II*, had even been banned from the stage for its depiction of a king being dethroned. Despite this setback, Tate's sympathies were initially with the Tories; he wrote most of the sequel to Dryden's anti-Whig satire, *Absalom and Achitophel*. He also spent the 1670s and 1680s writing lighter, more occasional poetry, which was published in *Poems* (1676) and an enlarged second edition (1684). However, his loyalties fixed firmly upon William and Mary after the Glorious Revolution. Having always been something of a political naïf, he rarely evinced any partisan leanings thereafter, with his only controversial pronouncements coming in favour of certain policies being espoused by his monarchs. In this respect, his appointment as laureate seems to have been both cause and effect, hardening his pre-existing tendencies to shy away from political controversy and cleave to the court. After he became laureate, the nature of his output became more restricted. Although he wrote occasional translations and a couple of mildly humorous poems, most of his productions were concerned with the depiction of virtuous figures and enumerations of their virtues.

Tate died a year after George I's accession, and a very different sort of writer, Nicholas Rowe, was appointed to succeed him. Rowe (PL 1715–18) was the leading tragedian of the day, a highly respected writer and an inveterate Whig office-holder. He had already served the Whig government in a fairly serious fashion under Queen Anne, and, in the few years of his life lived under George I, was to accumulate both sinecurial and non-sinecurial positions, of which the laureateship was but the most conspicuous. In terms of his work and reputation, he was almost the polar opposite of Nahum Tate. Yet he was enjoined with continuing Tate's habit of writing the biannual courtly odes: having only been a habit during Tate's tenure, it was now formalized into an official responsibility. On at least two occasions, Rowe farmed the task out to his friends.

Rowe is another figure who has attracted much attention for his theatrical work, but not much for anything else. In fact, the situation of Rowean scholarship is almost identical to that of Shadwellian. Rowe appears in general dramatic histories as the foremost exponent of a certain type of play: the softer, sentimental tragedy of the early eighteenth century, best exemplified by his three 'she-tragedies'.[53] His individual plays have, like Shadwell's, been addressed in various articles.[54] But two things set him apart from Shadwell. One is his edition of Shakespeare, which, being the first 'modern' edition, has inevitably attracted a lot of interest.[55] The other is that he was active in the reign of Queen Anne, which means that scholars have been particularly interested to tease out the political content of his work. 2017's multi-volume *Plays and Poems of Nicholas Rowe* is a good example of this. It is a comprehensive and impressive edition, providing everything that students of Rowe could possibly want; but the introductory matter to each play is dominated by party-political considerations to a greater extent than is justified by the content of those plays themselves.[56]

The next laureate was Laurence Eusden (PL 1718–30), who is the most neglected of the lot. He does not seem to have inspired a single monograph

[53] Bevis, *Drama*, pp. 123, 129–33.

[54] J. DeRitter, '"Wonder not, princely Gloster, at the notice this paper brings you": Women, writing, and politics in Rowe's *Jane Shore*', *Comparative Drama*, xxxi (1997), 86–104; A. W. Hesse and R. J. Sherry, 'Two unrecorded editions of Rowe's *Lady Jane Gray*: The early editions', *The Papers of the Bibliographical Society of America*, lxxii (1978), 220–6; P. Kewes, '"The state is out of tune": Nicholas Rowe's Jane Shore and the succession crisis of 1713–14', *Huntington Library Quarterly*, lxiv (2001), 283–308; B. Wilson, 'Jane Shore and the Jacobites: Nicholas Rowe, the pretender, and the national she-tragedy', *ELH*, lxxii (2005), 823–43.

[55] J. Candido, 'Prefatory matters in the Shakespeare editions of Nicholas Rowe and Alexander Pope', *Studies in Philology*, xcvii (2000), 210–28; R. B. Hamm, Jr, 'Rowe's Shakespear (1709) and the Tonson house style', *College Literature*, xxxi (2004), 179–205; P. Holland, 'Modernizing Shakespeare: Nicholas Rowe and *The Tempest*', *Shakespeare Quarterly*, li (2000), 24–32.

[56] R. Bullard and J. McTague, 'Introduction to *The Ambitious Step-Mother, Tamerlane*, and *The Fair Penitent*', in *The Plays and Poems of Nicholas Rowe*: i, *The Early Plays*, ed. S. Bernard, R. Bullard and J. McTague (Abingdon, 2016), pp. 35–55.

or article until 2020, when Leah Orr published an article on his reception and afterlife.[57] His *ONDB* entry is several short paragraphs in length.[58] Because he was not a playwright and was not very active in politics, he is likewise missing from more general works; but he was mentioned several times in *The Dunciad*, and Valerie Rumbold therefore touched upon him at the appropriate points in the notes to her edition of the four-book version.[59] He is the extreme version of Nahum Tate (who was also mocked in *The Dunciad*), except for the fact that Tate's characteristics as a writer included prolixity and profuseness, whereas Eusden did not write (or at least publish) very much over the course of his lifetime (contrary to Pope's characterization of him as prolix and profuse).[60] He spent much of that life at Trinity College, Cambridge, and then, between 1724 and his death in 1730, was engaged with the twin demands of clerical work and clerical drinking. (The drinking had probably begun earlier.) His appointment to the laureateship had come at a young age, and is most obviously attributable to an epithalamium he wrote for the marriage of the duke of Newcastle, who was then lord chamberlain. Although Eusden diligently wrote panegyrics (both within and without the remit of his office), he was even more diligent in his alcoholism, and he died at forty-two years old.[61]

Colley Cibber (PL 1730–57) came next. Again, he was a very different kind of appointee to Eusden. He was probably the most famous theatrical figure of the time, having acted, managed Drury Lane theatre and written plays (some of them hugely successful and enduring) for several decades. His work had not been especially political, but *The Non-Juror* (first performed 1717, first published 1718) had comprised an explicit attack on supporters of the Stuarts. As well as enjoying massive popular success, it had earned him a £200 gift from George I. He was also known to be close to leading Whig statesmen, including Robert Walpole, and was associated with government Whiggism to a greater extent than would be suggested by a perusal of his writings. Some observers considered the appointment a disgrace, and Cibber's activities as laureate only increased the numbers and the hostility of these critics; his biannual odes were the most widely mocked of the century, for reasons discussed in Chapter Five.

---

[57] L. Orr, 'Patronage and commercial print in conflict: Laurence Eusden's reception and afterlife', *Journal for Early Modern Cultural Studies*, xx (2020), 32–57.

[58] J. Sambrook, 'Laurence Eusden', *ODNB*.

[59] A. Pope, *The Dunciad in Four Books*, ed. V. Rumbold (Harlow, 1999), pp. 92, 98, 108, 111, 136–7, 194, 199, 212, 259, 287.

[60] For Tate in *The Dunciad*, p. 112.

[61] Leah Orr is sceptical about the accusation of drunkenness, but it is supported by manuscript evidence relating to his time as rector of Coningsby. See Lincolnshire Archives ANC 5/D/15/q, ANC 5/D/15/v, ANC 5/D/15/t, MON 7/13/249.

In terms of scholarship, if Eusden belongs with Tate, then Cibber is firmly in the camp of Shadwell. Indeed, he is to Pope what Shadwell is to Dryden: a 'dull' antagonist, condemned to centuries of notoriety and neglect by his opponent's hostile wit. Only in the latter half of the twentieth century did scholars begin to reappraise Cibber. Now, he is recognized as one of the major playwrights of the eighteenth century.[62] To what extent he should be identified with 'sentimental comedy', and whether such a genre even existed, are subjects of debate.[63] Whatever the case, he was certainly a popular and imaginative playwright, who was well attuned to eighteenth-century tastes. Helene Koon published a biography of him in 1986.[64] In 2001 came *The Plays of Colley Cibber: Volume 1*, edited by William J. Burling and Timothy J. Viator; but no following volumes were ever published. There have been a significant number of articles published on various aspects of his plays and on his relationships with other literary figures of the time;[65] recently, there has been emphasis on his stature as an early 'celebrity'.[66] In 2016, Elaine McGirr published a study of Cibber rebutting the literary histories that have been constructed at his expense and asserting his centrality to eighteenth-century culture.[67] The autobiographical *Apology for the Life of Colley Cibber* has long been recognized as a valuable guide to the theatrical world of the early eighteenth century. But his non-dramatic poetry has been entirely ignored, despite how much attention his laureate odes attracted at the time.

His successor, William Whitehead (PL 1757–85), has been considered a talented and interesting poet by those who have read his work, but their number is small and their voices are quiet. He has been studied even less

---

[62] Bevis, *Drama*, pp. 154–61; W. Burling and T. J. Viator, 'General introduction', in *The Plays of Colley Cibber: Volume 1*, ed. W. Burling and T. J. Viator (London, 2001), pp. 11–24, at p. 13.

[63] Bevis, *Drama*, pp. 154–5; R. D. Hume, 'Drama and theatre in the mid and later eighteenth century', in *The Cambridge History of English Literature, 1660–1780*, ed. J. Richetti (Cambridge, 2005), pp. 316–39, at pp. 323–4; H. Love, 'Restoration and early eighteenth-century drama', in *English Literature, 1660–1780*, ed. Richetti, pp. 109–31, at pp. 127–8; H. Koon, *Colley Cibber: A Biography* (Kentucky, 1986), pp. 24–9.

[64] Koon, *Cibber*.

[65] J. Fuller, 'Cibber, *The Rehearsal at Goatham*, and the Suppression of *Polly*', *The Review of English Studies*, xiii (1962), 125–34; B. K. Wallace, 'Reading the surfaces of Colley Cibber's "The Careless Husband"', *Studies in English Literature, 1500–1900*, xl (2000), 473–89.

[66] J. H. Fawcett, 'The overexpressive celebrity and the deformed king: Recasting the spectacle as subject in Colley Cibber's "Richard III"', *PMLA*, cxxvi (2011), 950–65; J. H. Fawcett, *Spectacular Disappearances: Celebrity and Privacy, 1696–1801* (Ann Arbor, Mich., 2016), pp. 23–60.

[67] E. M. McGirr, *Partial Histories: A Reappraisal of Colley Cibber* (London, 2016).

than Tate, and little more than Eusden. Other than a German-language monograph published on him in 1933 and an entry in *ODNB,* no book or article seems to have been written on him.[68] His dramatic works are referenced in *English Drama: Restoration and Eighteenth Century, 1660–1789,* where Richard D. Bevis notes that his *Roman Father* entered the repertory for a while.[69] Scholars of Charles Churchill know Whitehead as one of that satirist's repeated targets.[70] But he is mostly invisible in eighteenth-century literary scholarship.

This is partly because he has been left isolated from such important scholarly narratives as preromanticism, graveyard poetry and Gothicism. His output, which was almost entirely in verse, was initially circumscribed by the twin examples of Pope and Matthew Prior; but he had started to widen his compass just before his appointment, writing ABAB elegies and a blank verse effusion on the landscape around Bristol. Shortly after becoming laureate, he wrote a semi-official poem addressing the nation, and another addressing the poets of the nation in the manner of a bishop to his clergy. Thereafter, he published little other than his laureate odes; but those odes were highly prominent exemplars of the same poetic trends that have been located in the work of Gray, Collins and the Wartons, and they deserve to be integrated into wider studies of eighteenth-century poetics. He also produced four plays over the course of his life, with decent success; and he avoided party and political matters, while nonetheless drawing the hatred of the satirical attack-poet Charles Churchill and the opposition newspaper press. Whitehead generally enjoyed a far more positive reputation than Cibber, and was probably the most celebrated laureate *qua* laureate since Dryden.

His successor as laureate was Thomas Warton (PL 1785–90), who enjoyed even greater literary esteem, and who, for his literary scholarship and poetic innovations, was to be more enduringly esteemed, too. He was a lifelong fellow of Trinity College, Oxford, and in 1785 he was best known for his *Pleasures of Melancholy* and 'The suicide' (quintessential graveyard poems) and for his *History of English Poetry,* the only three completed volumes of which had appeared in 1774–81. He has been much studied, especially with regard to the questions of canon formation and Gothicism.[71] However, his role and work as laureate – a position he only held for five years – have not generated much interest.

[68] A. Bitter, *William Whitehead, Poeta Laureatus* (Halle, 1933); R. Scott, 'William Whitehead', *ODNB.*

[69] Bevis, *Drama,* p. 204.

[70] W. C. Brown, *Charles Churchill: Poet, Rake, and Rebel* (New York, 1968), pp. 87–8, 107.

[71] Eg Terry, *Literary Past,* pp. 293–320.

In 1790, William Pitt the Younger, then prime minister, seems to have taken the appointment decision upon himself, and gave the office to Henry James Pye (PL 1790–1813). Pye was a well-known, fairly well-respected poet, having written a number of long poems in couplets and shorter lyrics in a variety of forms; and he had served as an MP for Berkshire between 1784 and 1790, as well as serving long stints as a magistrate. While laureate, Pye turned out copious amounts of verse and prose, his name becoming a byword for bad poetry in certain quarters but being celebrated in others. He also set about diligently quelling any potential Jacobin activity, both through his powers as a magistrate and through his writings (which included two anti-Jacobin picaresque novels).[72]

Pye has been treated by academia in much the same way as Tate, Eusden and Whitehead. As a prolific writer spanning many forms and genres, he has managed to find his way into a couple of general works; his long poem *Faringdon Hill*, for example, has been discussed as an example of topographical poetry by Donna Landry and David Fairer, and the recent interest in anti-Jacobin novels has led to reinvestigations and reprintings of his *The Democrat* and *The Aristocrat*.[73] But no publication has ever been devoted specifically to him. He was generally despised by the canonical Romantic writers (among others), and no one has attempted to reverse that judgement. Like Whitehead, his poetry has been deemed insufficiently experimental or exciting to warrant study.

Pye's death in 1813, just as the Peninsular War was reaching its triumphant conclusion, gave rise to the best-documented selection process of the long eighteenth century.[74] The prince regent, prime minister and lord chamberlain, as well as various other government figures, involved themselves in the question of who should succeed Pye, united in their opinion that the role should go to the greatest poet in the land. After a certain amount of confusion, the laureateship was offered to Walter Scott, who declined it,

---

[72] For mockery of Pye, see eg Thomas Lawrence to William Godwin, Bod MS. Abinger c. 15, fo. 40.

[73] For *Faringdon Hill*, see Fairer, *English Poetry*, pp. 204–7; D. Landry, 'Poems on place', in *British Poetry, 1660–1800*, ed. Lynch, pp. 335–55, at pp. 341–51. For his anti-Jacobin novels, M. O. Grenby, 'The anti-Jacobin novel: British fiction, British conversation and the revolution in France', *History*, lxxxiii (1998), 445–71, at pp. 458–60; M. O. Grenby, *The Anti-Jacobin Novel: British Conservatism and the French Revolution* (Cambridge, 2001); H. J. Pye, *Anti-Jacobin Novels*: i, *Henry James Pye, The Democrat and The Aristocrat*, ed. W. M. Verhoeven (Abingdon, 2005).

[74] For a full account and an exploration of its implications, see Leo Shipp, 'Appointing a poet laureate: National and poetic identities in 1813', *The English Historical Review*, cxxxvi (2021), 332–63.

and then Robert Southey, who accepted. Upon his appointment, Southey (PL 1813–43) discovered that he was still expected to write the biannual odes – which he believed was contrary to a promise he had received beforehand – but eventually, in the course of his thirty-year tenure, he managed to have the task permanently dispensed with. Because Southey was generally held to be a great poetic genius by contemporaries, and because he had freed the laureateship of its duties, the position finally settled down into comfortable honourability. Southey's successors were William Wordsworth and then Alfred Tennyson. Although subsequent holders have rarely been lauded as highly as those two, the office has remained quietly respectable ever since.

Southey's tenure lies beyond this book's remit; he will only feature in the discussion of appointments (briefly) and in the Conclusion. Dryden's and Southey's appointments thus mark the two boundary stones of the eighteenth-century laureateship, one representing its creation, the other its transformation into something else. In terms of scholarly attention, too, they are good bookends, because a colossal amount of work has been carried out on both of them (although Dryden's is the more colossal). Lynda Pratt and Tim Fulford have been particularly active in restoring Southey to something like the position of prominence he occupied in his own day, leading two projects to make widely available his complete correspondence and poetic works.[75] In addition, they and others have published various chapters, articles and monographs on all manner of Southey's (very diverse) body of work, and he has become one of those stock writers often discussed in more thematic-based monographs and edited collections.[76] Whereas Dryden has proven a favourite of older and newer generations of literary scholarship alike, Southey, although somewhat neglected by the older, has been found newly relevant to the newer.[77] However, the laureateship has

[75] R. Southey, *Poetical Works, 1793–1810*, ed. L. Pratt et al. (5 vols, London, 2004); R. Southey, *Later Poetical Works, 1811–1838*, ed. L. Pratt, T. Fulford et al. (4 vols, London, 2012); R. Southey, *The Collected Letters of Robert Southey*, ed. L. Pratt, T. Fulford, I. Packer et al.

[76] Eg D. M. Craig, *Robert Southey and Romantic Apostasy: Political Argument in Britain, 1780–1840* (Woodbridge, 2007); *Romanticism and Millenarianism*, ed. T. Fulford (Basingstoke, 2002); C. Mahoney, *Romantics and Renegades: The Poetics of Political Reaction* (Basingstoke, 2003); M. O'Neill, 'Southey and Shelley reconsidered', *Romanticism*, xvii (2011), 10–24; L. Pratt, 'Revising the national epic: Coleridge, Southey and Madoc', *Romanticism*, ii (1996), 149–64; *Robert Southey and the Contexts of English Romanticism*, ed. L. Pratt (Aldershot, 2006); W. A. Speck, *Robert Southey: Entire Man of Letters* (London, 2006).

[77] Eg E. A. Beshero-Bondar, 'Southey's gothic science: Galvanism, automata, and heretical sorcery in *Thalaba the Destroyer*', *Genre*, xlii (2009), 1–32; M. Leporati, '"Authority from heaven": Robert Southey's *Madoc* and epic Christian imperialism', *European Romantic Review*, xxv (2014), 161–80.

not loomed very large in this corpus, the exceptions being volume three of the *Later Poetic Works*, the introductions of which discuss Southey's appointment and poetic practice as laureate, and Michael Gamer's work on the poet's motivations for accepting the post.[78]

Scholarship on the eighteenth-century laureates, then, comprises a patchy body of work. A great deal has been written on some of the laureates, not much on some of the others, and there are great discrepancies between the kinds of work that have been done on each figure. Moreover, insofar as the eighteenth-century laureateship has been paid attention to at all, it has been dismissed and disparaged. Broadus and other scholars of the office's entire history have routinely depicted the period between Dryden and Southey as the low point;[79] they have also assumed that this was the general and uniform opinion of contemporaries. Broadus's observation 'that Warton's appointment had turned a good poet into a bad laureate', and thus 'crystallized' public opinion against the office and the odes, is typical.[80]

Even those scholars who have devoted attention to any individual laureate, and who have therefore taken a more sympathetic view of that poet and his official work, have set up an explicit, contemptuous contrast to the office itself and to its other holders. Koon, for example, argued that Cibber's odes were not as execrable as his critics made out. However, to support her point, she insisted that Whitehead's efforts 'were no better than Cibber's and considerably duller, but they were not attacked' – an observation mistaken on both counts.[81] Daniel Ennis, in his discussion of the laureateship as one of the eighteenth century's poetic 'Honours', lumped Whitehead together with Eusden as 'obscure but politically reliable poetasters whose undistinguished verse did nothing to raise the prestige of the position'.[82] Fairer was respectful (in passing) to Warton's laureate odes, calling them 'effective and dignified', but then went on to say, 'It was generally held that Warton, whose tenure fell between those of William Whitehead and Henry James Pye, raised the reputation of the post at a difficult moment in its history.'[83]

---

[78] M. Gamer, 'Laureate policy', *Wordsworth Circle*, xlii (2011), 42–7; M. Gamer, *Romanticism, Self-Canonization, and the Business of Poetry* (Cambridge, 2017), pp. 156–96; main introduction and section introductions in Southey, *Later Poetical Works*, ed. Pratt and Fulford, iii.

[79] E. K. Broadus, *The Laureateship* (Oxford, 1921), pp. 135–63; Hopkins, *Poets Laureate*, pp. 62–113.

[80] Broadus, *Laureateship*, p. 154.

[81] Koon, *Cibber*, pp. 128, 180 (for quotation).

[82] D. J. Ennis, 'Honours', in *British Poetry, 1660–1800*, ed. Lynch, pp. 732–46, at p. 733.

[83] D. Fairer, 'Introduction: The achievement of Thomas Warton', in *Warton Correspondence*, pp. xvii–xxxvi, at p. xxxiii.

The foregoing description has already indicated some of the reasons why the eighteenth-century laureateship has been viewed in this way: its holders tended to be writers who have not become canonical figures of British literature, whereas those eighteenth-century writers who are now deemed canonical were not appointed, and in some cases even set themselves against the laureates. This relates to the second major reason why the office has been neglected: a handful of critiques of the laureateship were made by eighteenth-century figures that, due to their wittiness or to the canonical status of the persons making them, have proven popular and enduring. Pope's four-book *Dunciad*, private comments by Gray, a footnote in Gibbon's *The History of the Decline and Fall of the Roman Empire* and the *Probationary Odes for the Laureatship* have been taken as representative samples of contemporary opinion on the office, and as absolute damnations of it, rather than as the partial, partisan or idiosyncratic comments that they generally were.[84] However, the most fundamental reason for the office's neglect is that it was a courtly, patronage-based office. It has therefore been taken as anachronistic, ill-fitting and uninteresting in relation to those ideas about changes in eighteenth-century culture and society that have dominated the relevant scholarship.

New contributions to scholarship

By the same token, a study of the laureateship can provide a fuller, more nuanced picture of this period than has hitherto appeared. This monograph will argue that, as certain scholars cited above have asserted, the extremity of eighteenth-century developments has tended to be exaggerated. In particular, it will demonstrate that the laureateship was considered a relevant and respectable office to a greater extent than is supposed, and that, far from being anachronistic, it was actually representative of certain court-orientated ideas and practices of cultural production that persisted and adapted throughout the long eighteenth century. This argument is located at the interstices of literary and historical scholarship, and will both continue, and take advantage of, the trend in eighteenth-century studies towards interdisciplinarity. The types of evidence and approaches here employed are variously rooted in the traditional practices of each separate discipline, but will be used in conjunction so as to illuminate each other. Ultimately, of course, this monograph is written by a historian and published by the Royal Historical Society. Its core audience is historians of eighteenth-century Britain, especially cultural historians. Nonetheless, interdisciplinarity is its guiding principle, and – as could hardly be otherwise, given the subject matter – it is very much aimed at literary scholars too.

[84] For descriptions of these canonical critiques, see Broadus, *Laureateship*, pp. 128–9, 135–6, 148–9, 155.

Hence this book makes three major contributions to eighteenth-century scholarship. They are especially significant for the cultural historiography of Britain in the long eighteenth century, where this book aims to set a new agenda. But they have a broader significance for our understanding of how eighteenth-century British society was structured and functioned, and will therefore engage scholars of eighteenth-century Britain in general. Moreover, these contributions may encourage scholars of earlier periods and of other European and Atlantic countries to take on similar perspectives.

The first major contribution is the most obvious: to reinstate the laureateship to a position of great importance in eighteenth-century Britain. By proving that the office and its holders mattered to contemporaries, it will prove that scholarship on eighteenth-century British culture and literature must henceforth take heed of them. Moreover, this reinstatement has wider ramifications: it will emphasize the multifaceted importance of institutions in eighteenth-century British culture and the validity of the laureate-style model of cultural producer (as opposed to, for example, the Romantic model) throughout the long eighteenth century.

The second major contribution is to place the court and its relationship with the public in a more central place in our understanding of eighteenth-century Britain. Of course, as described above, this is not an unprecedented contribution. Certain scholars have established something similar before, and in recent scholarship it has become a vague truism that tradition coexisted with modernization in the eighteenth century.[85] However, there remains much to explore and prove in terms of what this meant in practice. This monograph will provide a detailed, thoroughgoing case study of the court's relationship with the public, and will show that this relationship was vital to the workings of British culture and society. It will also demonstrate how the interaction of tradition and modernization actually functioned, thus turning a vague truism into a concrete, complex truth. These dynamics are denoted by the book's subtitle, 'Courting the Public'.

The book's third major contribution is that it advances a new paradigm for eighteenth-century cultural history: the conceptual geography of culture. Although partially foreshadowed by scholars in the ways suggested above, this is a topic that has not hitherto received dedicated study even *as* a topic, let alone as a paradigm of research and analysis. If accepted, it will mean a movement away from the Habermasian public sphere paradigm that has dominated the field for so long. Hopefully, this book will draw other scholars' attention to the conceptual geography of culture too, filling in more parts of the map, and will encourage them to see it as

---

[85] Smith, *Georgian Monarchy*, p. 12.

a valid, fruitful framework by which to study cultural history, not just in eighteenth-century Britain but in earlier periods and other countries. Even if it is not taken up widely, it will nonetheless show that there are paradigms other than the Habermasian one, and concepts other than that of the public sphere, by which to approach eighteenth-century British culture.

Overall, then, this book sets out a fresh vision of how British society and culture functioned. It shows Britons acting according to a conceptual geography that changed over time, and that became increasingly shaped by print and by the metaphorical spaces that print constituted, but in which London and its court remained enduringly central. The laureate – a court poet, usually successful in London society before and after becoming laurelled – was a figure whose appointment, works and reception testify to this state of affairs, and who also held an important role in maintaining it.

Structure

The structure of this book is partly chronological, partly thematic. This structure has been chosen as giving the best representation of the way in which the office changed and developed over time, while also allowing the key aspects and themes of the office to be properly discussed and analysed and showing how certain aspects and themes became more or less prominent over time. Chapter One focuses on the later Stuart period, investigating the formation, early fluidity and transformation of the laureateship in those years. By examining court archives and those of Charles Sackville, sixth earl of Dorset, along with contemporary publications on the court and the writings of the first three laureates, this chapter shows that the office was instituted as a vague, honorific position, before becoming fixed with a certain function by the early years of George I's reign. The laureate gained a distinct place within the royal household and its cultural life, which it occupied for the next hundred years.

Chapter Two then focuses on George I and George II's laureates, and especially on Nicholas Rowe. Investigating the dichotomy of courtly values and commercial values as it manifests in the printed works of these laureates, that dichotomy is shown to be a false one, with the laureateship being both a symbol and an organ of their mutuality. Rowe, Eusden and Cibber pitched their work to court, town and public, and used the validation gained from each to sell their work to the other. Nor were they atypical in their practices; in a sense, the laureateship to which they were appointed formed the pinnacle of a system in which literature was produced and consumed in various interrelated spaces, including the court.

Chapter Three, taking a view of the entire Hanoverian period, returns to more behind-the-scenes matters. It discusses the practicalities of appointing a new laureate, looking at the roles of the different agents: king, royal family, lord chamberlain, politicians and others. Although this Introduction has indicated that there was no overwhelming consistency in terms of what kinds of writers were appointed laureate, Chapter Three shows that a number of significant patterns can be identified. The laurel was used to strengthen and legitimise various networks and to establish how those networks connected with the court. Behind each selection process, there was a complex relationship between the exigencies of patronage and ideas of merit; in this respect, the court-centred patronage that encompassed the laurel was used to determine the value and meaning of writers who had hitherto been working outside the forum of the court.

Chapter Four broadens the thematic scope, bringing the related topics of national identity, partisan politics and ideas concerning literature more directly into focus. Using a large amount of contemporary printed material (predominantly newspapers), this chapter seeks to establish the reception of George III's laureates among the reading public. It shows that, in the reign of George III, the laureate became a public figure to an unprecedented extent. George III's laureate held a unique and important place in contemporary literature, and his office was clearly of much greater prominence, and much greater diversity of reception, than has been previously recognized. This pre-eminence demonstrates how contemporaries conceived the court, the public and the relationship between the two.

With the first four chapters having covered the long eighteenth century in a vaguely sequential fashion, Chapter Five then takes the entire period as its timeframe and explores the corpus of biannual laureate odes. It studies the odes as deliberate attempts to present an image of the monarch, the national community and the relationship between the two. It argues that the laureate ode format was highly sensitive to that relationship, and increasingly responsible for mediating it to the reading public. Although the odes were constantly evolving, these issues remained consistently important to the ode format. In the later Stuart period, the odes were explicitly situated in the physical space of the court; in published form, they appealed to readers by allowing them to vicariously enter the court and witness the ode's performance. The court was thus presented as standing at the head of society; all readers would wish to physically come there. By the turn of the nineteenth century, the odes were doing something very different. They now portrayed the court as an abstract, metaphorical space, at one with the nation.

Lastly, the Conclusion summarizes the main arguments of each chapter, discusses once more the importance of the laureateship, and indicates possible future directions of research.

1. Patronage asserted: The formation of the laureateship, 1668–1715

The eighteenth-century laureateship was very different from that which was conferred on John Dryden in 1668. Dryden's laurel was akin to the unofficial laurels of Ben Jonson and William Davenant, being a mark of nothing more than a pension and poetic honour, both stemming from the person who was supposedly best placed to judge of such matters, the king. The eighteenth-century laureateship, on the other hand – the office that formed under William III and Anne, and was formalized at the accession of George I – was an office that could be located in a distinct place within the court establishment, and which was defined by its function: the writing of biannual odes for performance at court. This chapter will investigate how and why such a transformation occurred. It will consider a range of different evidence: archival material generated by the court, and particularly by the lord chamberlain's office; the private papers and accounts of Charles Sackville, sixth earl of Dorset, who was lord chamberlain in the crucial transformative years of 1689–95; contemporary printed material on the court; and the laureates' own writings.

These issues have important ramifications for the wider themes of this monograph: the court's place in the conceptual geography of culture, and in British society as a whole. The laureateship's formation was a highly significant aspect of the court's position, but the process was necessarily uncertain. During a half-century of continual ruptures between one monarchical regime and the next, with each successive monarch burdened by rival claimants rather than legitimate heirs, and with the putative Golden Age of Charles I's court separated from touching distance by the interregnum, there was a constant need for monarchs and their court officials to work out their ceremonial role afresh, and to try to create a compelling representation of the ideal of courtly rule. This heightened awareness of the importance of ceremony, and the ruptures in courtly practice, manifested strongly in the realm of high culture. Contemporaries portrayed the court as occupying a patronal role in literary, artistic and musical production, characteristic of the past and of successful foreign monarchies. But they also looked to alternative forms of financial and ideological stimulus for such production, or cast doubt on the court's patronal role. Due to the increasing extent of print and the continuing development of non-court institutions, the conceptual rubrics of the town, the world and the public became increasingly important in cultural production and consumption. Thus for those who had some form of attachment to the institutional court, or who sought to benefit from it in some way, it became increasingly necessary to define the court's position towards the town and the world, and eventually towards the public.

Hence the formalization of a pension into an office of poet laureate; hence the office eventually taking on the fixed form that it would keep for the next hundred years; but hence also the continual uncertainties of the process. The laureateship went from a vague position to a fixed position with set duties specifically because the court's cultural role was being worked out and defined. The settling of the laureateship's position was symptomatic of this: by bringing the laureate securely into a position related to the court, paying him more regularly and giving him a set role, the court was given a clear manifestation of its cultural role, and of its relationship to the town, the world and the public. That role also allowed for court ceremonial to co-opt the poetic talents of an esteemed writer. In all these respects the process was highly successful. The laureateship that was fixed into place in 1715 was to endure for a century, and, as will be seen in the following chapters, was to play an increasingly important part in literary affairs.

This chapter will begin its investigation of these matters with a short survey of the relevant scholarship, which will also serve to flesh out the situation summarized above. It will then proceed to a discussion of the uncertainties of the laureate's initial position, especially during Dryden's tenure, by reference to the works and correspondence of the later Stuart laureates (Dryden, Shadwell and Tate). The next section will explore archival evidence relating to the lord chamberlain's department to show how and when the laureate's position became defined. The earl of Dorset's records will be brought in to complete the picture, and lastly the printed works of Shadwell and Tate will be used to demonstrate their own instrumentality in these processes.

Settings of the scene

The later Stuart period was a time of constant reinvention for the institutional court.[1] From the outbreak of the Civil Wars in 1641 to the Restoration in 1660, there had existed only various thin semblances of Charles I's monarchical

---

[1] For the court's history, fragility and ruptures, see R. O. Bucholz, *The Augustan Court: Queen Anne and the Decline of Court Culture* (Stanford, Calif., 1993), pp. 12–35; H. Smith, 'The court in England, 1714–1760: A declining political institution?' *History*, xc (2005), 23–41, at pp. 26–7; K. Sharpe, *Rebranding Rule: Images of Restoration and Revolution Monarchy, 1660–1714* (New Haven, Conn., 2013), pp. 3, 7–8.

court: his wartime court at Oxford, Oliver Cromwell's regime and Charles II's court in exile. When Charles II was restored to the throne in 1660, he was therefore seeking to re-establish his court upon a model from which it was disconnected by twenty years of abeyance. He (and the officials and associates concerned in the endeavour) did so with the memories of the Civil Wars, regicide and interregnum still fresh. He needed to assert a legitimacy that was based on immemorial tradition but responsive to recent developments.

Charles II's successor, his brother James II, came to the throne in 1685 having survived an attempt to have him excluded from the line of succession only a few years earlier, and immediately had to defeat an armed attempt upon the throne by Charles II's illegitimate son, the duke of Monmouth. In 1688–9 he fled to the continent in the face of the Glorious Revolution, which installed his daughter Mary II and her Dutch husband William III as joint monarchs, but in circumstances that were controversial at the time and continued to be so thereafter. They were not the legal successors under any law that had existed prior to that point, especially given that James II remained alive until after Mary's death and just before William's. The issue of how to justify (or deny) their legitimacy therefore came to the fore of British political debate. Their court was distinguished from recent courts by centring on two monarchs rather than one, and by William's foreignness in nationality and religion. William and Mary's accession also saw the later Stuart period's greatest purge in terms of court personnel, effecting a huge loss of experience and continuity, and filling court positions with Whigs who perhaps felt little loyalty to the institutional court.

Mary's death came several years before William's, and it was her sister, Anne, who acceded to the throne in 1702. But Anne had lost her only living child, the duke of Gloucester, shortly beforehand. Her court differed from William's in that, for the first time in a century, the sole monarch was a woman, and also in that she was an Englishwoman and a devout Anglican. Her reign was overshadowed by the issue of the succession, which had been settled upon her distant relative, the dowager Electress Sophia of Hanover, but which was still claimed by James II's son. Sophia's and Anne's deaths in 1714 saw the relatively untroubled accession of George I, another foreign, non-Anglican male. Unlike William, he brought with him neither armed soldiers, nor a wife, nor even competence in the English language. But he did bring a solid brood of legitimate children and grandchildren, meaning that, after seventy-five years of discontinuities and ersatz successions, the British court was able to take on a relatively settled form.

Among the issues that have most interested recent scholars of the later Stuart period, the court has loomed increasingly large, especially for the reign of Charles II. The issue of the court's relationship to culture has become especially important, and has been treated in various insightful ways, revealing the issue's wider implications for the court's place in society and the role of the monarchy.[2] The related themes of formality, ceremony and representation are critical here; historians have often been concerned to plot their material with relation to one or more of these themes, and to suggest whether the court's formality, ceremonial role and representative efforts were growing or diminishing over their chosen period of study. Historians have also sought to work out how the court's cultural role changed in response to the wider societal changes of the time, from the impact of the Civil Wars, to the emergence of a public sphere; and literary scholars have explored how those changes manifested in literature.[3]

There remains much to explore in terms of how successive monarchs and court officials responded to the uncertainties of their courts' inceptions, how they responded to the public and what cultural role they played. However, some of the works cited above have indicated a line of argument that will prove significant for this chapter's argument. R. O. Bucholz believed that Charles II's 'real cultural achievement' was to resurrect the court's 'traditional leadership as an artistic patron', making widespread again the assumption 'that cultural innovation and patronage depended on the court'. Charles achieved this, despite financial difficulties and the emergence of the public sphere, by a wide yet discriminating patronage, by making his court attractive on a personal level and by encouraging innovation. For William III's reign, Tony Claydon's work stressed the manner in which the court of William and Mary developed a coherent ideology that legitimized their unusual rule and distinguished them from their predecessors' courts. Both historians presented these activities as occurring in deliberate, targeted interaction with the public.[4] Similarly, Kevin Sharpe showed successive courts structuring and enacting their authority by reference to traditional conceptions of monarchy and to somewhat mythical notions of how the court operated

[2] Eg T. Claydon, *William III and the Godly Revolution* (Cambridge, 1996), pp. 1–4, 73–88, 228–9; E. Corp, 'Catherine of Braganza and cultural politics', in *Queenship in Britain 1660–1837: Royal Patronage, Court Culture and Dynastic Politics*, ed. C. C. Orr (Manchester, 2002), pp. 53–73; A. Barclay, 'Mary Beatrice of Modena: The "Second Bless'd of Woman-kind?"', in *Queenship in Britain 1660–1837*, ed. Orr, pp. 74–93; J. A. Winn, *Queen Anne: Patroness of Arts* (Oxford, 2014).

[3] R. Hutton, *Charles II: King of England, Scotland, and Ireland* (Oxford, 1989), p. 453; M. Jenkinson, *Culture and Politics at the Court of Charles II, 1660–1685* (Woodbridge, 2010), especially pp. 5, 11–20; A. Keay, *The Magnificent Monarch: Charles II and the Ceremonies of Power* (London, 2008), especially pp. 2, 22–4; Sharpe, *Rebranding Rule*, especially pp. 7–8, 202–14, 343–50, 482–4, 502–6, 510–14; B. Weiser, *Charles II and the Politics of Access* (Woodbridge, 2003).

[4] Bucholz, *Augustan Court*, pp. 16–17; Claydon, *Godly Revolution*, pp. 64–88.

prior to the Civil Wars, but using those ideological resources in a manner that was appropriate for a new context in which the public not only exerted its own social, political and cultural authority, but was increasingly vocal in asking questions of both the institution and the occupants of monarchy.[5]

This idea of a court responding to the challenges and pressures of its situation, and doing so by defining its cultural role and enacting that role in engagement with audiences outside of the court, is something that fits well with the history of the laureateship. In turn, the history of the laureateship will prove greatly illuminating as to how the various parties interested in the court as a concept went about this. This chapter will argue that the laureateship was created, and progressively defined, due to the need for those parties to present successive courts as legitimate and pre-eminent, which need was enacted in between a traditional, ideal conception of the monarchical court on the one hand, and an increasingly sophisticated cultural apparatus outside the court on the other. This required the court to be presented as exerting patronal and ceremonial leadership over cultural production, but doing so in interaction with audiences outside of the court. The laureateship was the result.

The birth pangs of the office

Prior to Dryden's appointment, the office of poet laureate did not exist. Contemporaries with any interest in the matter assumed that there was such an office, and that William Davenant had been its most recent holder. But Davenant – the poet, playwright and stage manager whose death in April 1668 precipitated Dryden's appointment – had never occupied any such office.[6] Instead, he had held a pension from Charles I. Having written a number of masques for the entertainment of Charles's court, and a number of poems in praise of the royal family, Davenant had become the beneficiary of Charles's patronage, receiving £100 a year from 1638 onwards. During the Civil Wars, Davenant fought for the king, and endured both exile and imprisonment under the interregnum regime. But his pension lapsed, and was not renewed by Charles II. The idea that he had been poet laureate – an idea apparently cultivated to some degree by Davenant himself – was not based on any official appointment.[7]

In a similar way, it was widely thought that Ben Jonson had preceded Davenant as poet laureate. He too had written masques and poems for and

---

[5] Sharpe, *Rebranding Rule*, pp. 7–8, 202–14, 343–50, 482–4, 502–6, 510–14.

[6] E. K. Broadus, *The Laureateship* (Oxford, 1921), pp. iv, 51–64; A. M. Gibbs, 'Introduction', in W. Davenant, *The Shorter Poems, and Songs from the Plays and Masques*, ed. A. M. Gibbs (Oxford, 1972), pp. xvii–xciii, at pp. xx, xxiv–xxv, lvi.

[7] Broadus, *Laureateship*, pp. 51–8; Gibbs, 'Introduction', pp. xx, xxiv–xxvi, xxxii–xxxviii, lvi.

in honour of Charles I; he too had been rewarded with a pension; he too had sometimes been informally thought of, by others and by himself, as a 'poet laureate' or as 'the king's poet'.[8] Jonson had once requested his friend John Selden, a scholar, to investigate the tradition of crowning poets with laurel, which went back to ancient Greece and Rome. Selden had duly done so, and published the results in the second edition (1631) of his *Titles of Honor*. The practice of crowning poets, he found, appeared sporadically across European history, and had honoured such great poets as Petrarch and Tasso. Laurel leaves were the standard and hoariest material used for this crown.[9]

The laurel wreath had been a mark of glory in ancient Greece, and the association of laurel with greatness had persisted in European iconography ever since. The actual practice of crowning with laurel therefore found a metaphorical analogue in poetry itself. Poets would regularly depict other poets, and also generals and statesmen, as being crowned with laurel in recognition of their greatness. This iconographical trope, combined with the research of Selden and the pensioning of Jonson and Davenant, made for a muddled understanding as to what a poet laureate actually was and who had officially been designated thus. By the time of Davenant's death, it was generally thought that not only he and Jonson, but also Spenser, Chaucer and certain others, had been appointed and paid as official poets laureate.[10]

However, if the institution of the laureateship in 1668 involved a reconceptualization of certain past poets' relationships with the court, in practical terms this meant that the laureate was little more than a court pensioner in the manner of Jonson and Davenant. He did not have any duties, and there was no explicit definition of his role. He was a poet whom the king had favoured with a regular stipend to be paid from the treasury, and the dignity of his appointment was signalled by the formal letters patent with which the king appointed him. According to the letters patent appointing Dryden laureate,

> wee [Charles II], for and in consideration of the many good and acceptable services by John Dryden ... to us heretofore done and performed, and taking notice of the learning and eminent abilities of him the said John Dryden, and of his great skill and elegant style both in verse and prose, and for diverse other good causes and considerations us thereunto especially moving, having nominated, constituted, declared, and appointed ... him the said John Dryden, our Poet Laureat and Historiographer Royal;

[8] Broadus, *Laureateship*, pp. 40–51; R. McGuinness, *English Court Odes: 1660–1820* (Oxford, 1971), pp. 5–6.

[9] John Selden, *Titles of Honor*, 3rd edn (1672), pp. 333–42.

[10] Broadus, *Laureateship*, pp. 15–23, 33–9.

giving and granting unto him the said John Dryden all the singular rights, privileges, benefits, and advantages, thereunto belonging, as fully and amply as Sir Geoffrey Chaucer, Knight, Sir John Gower, Knight, John Leland, Esquire, William Camden, Esquire, Benjamin Johnson, Esquire, James Howell, Esquire, Sir William D'Avenant, Knight, or any other person or persons having or exercising the place or employment of Poet Laureat or Historiographer, or either of them, in the time of any of our royal progenitors, had or received, or might lawfully claim or demand, as incident or belonging unto the said places or employments, or either of them. And for the further and better encouragement of him the said John Dryden, diligently to attend the said employment, we are graciously pleased to give and grant [a pension of £200 and a butt of canary wine].[11]

There are several things of note in this patent. The first is that all power and responsibility for the appointment was assigned to Charles II personally, who had 'nominated, constituted, declared, and appointed' Dryden. The second is the vague but comprehensive message as to why Dryden was appointed, with the only specific reasons stated being his talent for verse and prose, but with a general assertion that Dryden had in some way served the king already (presumably in his writings). Lastly, the office was not defined at all except by vague reference to the past. Dryden's 'employment', which he was encouraged to attend to 'diligently', was not described, and must be presumed to be merely a continuation of the sorts of 'services' he had already been providing. His office allowed him certain 'rights, privileges, benefits, and advantages', but, instead of describing what these might be, the patent simply referred to a spurious list of honourable predecessors, and to other unnamed 'person or persons' who may have held the office under Charles's 'royal progenitors'. It then granted a £200 pension and butt of canary wine as *additions* to these undefined historical 'rights, privileges, benefits, and advantages'.

Essentially, then, the office of poet laureate (as it appeared in this patent) was created as an attempt to connect Charles II with his 'royal progenitors', Dryden with the great poets of the past and the patronage between Charles and Dryden with the patronage that was believed to have existed in past ages of great kings and great poets. This conceptualization of the past, and this conceptual link between Charles II's court and the courts from which it was separated by the interregnum, was more important than the logistics of the new office. The definition of the office was provided by the idea that there was a natural link between the king of a nation and that nation's greatest poet. Chaucer, Jonson and (although passed over in the patent)

---

[11] Patent printed in Dryden, *The Critical and Miscellaneous Prose Works of John Dryden*, ed. E. Malone (4 vols, 1800), iv. 553–9.

Spenser all proved this link. They were kings of verse, whom their monarchs had acknowledged as such and supported. In turn, they had celebrated their monarchs: not simply out of gratitude, but because it was a poet's duty and privilege to celebrate great men.

However, the connection being expressed here went beyond the laureateship and its spurious line of succession. It was a connection that had been inherent to the poetic vocation, or at least to certain ideas of the poetic vocation, since ancient times, and likewise inherent to certain conceptualizations of what good rulers and good courts ought to be. Poets in general (it was often posited) were ideally situated under the patronage of a monarch, from whence they would transmit the glories of that monarch's reign through their writings. But the patronal relationship was nonetheless often phrased, or at least felt to exist in its most important form, in terms of a one-to-one relationship between one great monarch and one great poet. The prime model for this ideal relationship was that of Augustus and Virgil. This was a relatively distant relationship, but one of symbiotic necessity, whereby Augustus was known to favour his poet (sometimes financially), grant him the political and intellectual conditions needed to flourish, and set an example of greatness and heroism by his own princely actions. In turn, the poet would glorify the monarch by producing great works, some of which would specifically acknowledge and praise that monarch. Dryden and William Soames gave one of the clearest expressions of these notions in their *Art of Poetry* (1683), a translation of Boileau's recent *L'Art poétique* (1674), which was itself based heavily on Horace's *Ars Poetica*. The Dryden–Soames poem celebrated the patronage of 'a sharp-sighted Prince', who 'by early Grants/Rewards [poets'] Merits, and prevents [their] Wants'. It exhorted poets to 'Sing then his Glory, Celebrate his Fame;/Your noblest Theme is his immortal Name ... But where's a Second *Virgil*, to Rehearse/ Our Hero's Glories in his Epic Verse?'[12]

These ideas had become newly significant upon Charles II's accession. This was partly due to the example of France under Louis XIII and Louis XIV, where a programme of court patronage had been developed and where poets routinely sang the king's praises.[13] Charles II had spent part of his time in exile in Paris, and had witnessed the magnificence of Louis XIV's

---

[12] Dryden, Works, ii. 155. See also Dryden, *Threnodia Augustalis*, in *Works*, iii. 102–3; C. Gildon, *Miscellaneous Letters and Essays on Several Subjects* (1694), pp. 9–10; B. A. Goldgar, *Walpole and the Wits: The Relation of Politics to Literature, 1722–1742* (Lincoln, Neb., 1976), pp. 8–16.

[13] P. Burke, *The Fabrication of Louis XIV* (New Haven, Conn., 1992), pp. 49–59.

patronage;[14] and English poets of the Restoration were highly aware of their French counterparts' work.[15] The Restoration itself was also important in emphasizing the connection between court and poets. Many post-1660 writers, including Dryden, portrayed the interregnum as a time of cultural catastrophe, and, accordingly, celebrated the Restoration as a renaissance. Public theatre, which had been suppressed under Oliver Cromwell, quickly became the major proof and emblem of this change. The London stage was legally duopolized by two theatre companies, one of which was run by Davenant, each owing their existence to a royal patent. Charles was a regular theatregoer and, in addition, frequently had his favourite plays acted at court. He was known to have given ideas for original and translated plays to certain playwrights, and even allowed Dryden (prior to his appointment as laureate) to publish *Secret-Love* as 'His [Charles's] Play' on account of his favour for it.[16]

Partly due to the money in drama, and partly due to its cultural prestige, the stage attracted men and women of literary ambition to an unprecedented extent.[17] The word 'poet' became virtually synonymous with, yet more common than, the word 'playwright'.[18] Most plays were published in book form after performance, and these publications were usually prefaced with a dedicatory epistle to the playwright's patron. Generally, this patron would be a nobleman – perhaps a prominent figure at court, like Rochester or Buckingham – who would in turn reward the playwright financially and in certain more miscellaneous ways.[19] It was not atypical for the dedicatory epistles to note the patron's loyalty or service to the crown, to praise the king as well as the patron himself or to emphasize the fact that all plays ultimately rested under the king's patronage.[20] Thus most literary figures of the time – including Dryden, Tate and (until the Exclusion Crisis) Shadwell – were bound up in networks of patronage and systems of literary production that reached their apex with the court. This was because, as stated previously,

[14] McGuinness, *Court Odes*, pp. 8–9.

[15] P. Kewes, *Authorship and Appropriation: Writing for the Stage in England, 1660–1710* (Oxford, 1998), pp. 36–7, 43.

[16] Kewes, *Authorship*, pp. 26–8, 36–7; J. Munns, 'Theatrical culture I: Politics and theatre', in *The Cambridge Companion to English Literature 1650–1740*, ed. S. Zwicker (Cambridge, 1998), pp. 82–103; Winn, *Dryden*, pp. 145–51; for *Secret-Love*, see Dryden, *Works*, ix. 114–203 (p. 115 for quotation).

[17] Kewes, *Authorship*, pp. 2–3.

[18] Kewes, *Authorship*, pp. 29–30.

[19] Kewes, *Authorship*, pp. 25–6.

[20] Eg A. Behn, *The Feign'd Curtizans, or, A Nights Intrigue* (1679), sig. A2r–A3v; Dryden, *All for Love*, in *Works*, xiii. 3–9; T. Otway, *Venice Preserv'd* (1682), sig. A2r–v.

contemporaries were not overly concerned with the public as an audience for cultural products at this time; instead, they were concerned with those persons and activities who operated within, and constituted, what was conceived as the town, the physical identity and conceptual existence of which were bound up with the court.

When Davenant died in 1668, it was therefore fitting and logical for all involved that Dryden should be appointed poet laureate. By that point, he was England's leading playwright, and his plays were known to have pleased the king. He was already patronized by certain prominent courtiers.[21] With his publications, he had also achieved success with the world: the audience of readers that went beyond, and could be conceived as standing at one remove from, the court and town. This audience was not as physically immediate, socially prestigious or financially lucrative as that of the court and town, but neither was it entirely distinct from them or negligible in its own right. Moreover, the apparatus of Dryden's publications (title pages, dedicatory epistles, prologues, epilogues) sought favour with the world by advertising their positioning in, and success with, the court and town. Thus the laureateship definitively consolidated the relationship between court and poetry. It proved the pre-eminence of the court in cultural matters by extending a symbolic and financial patronage over the poet who was most highly esteemed by a court-centric nobility, by the town and by the world. At the same time, it cast into a more well-defined form the links between Charles II's court and that of his 'royal progenitors'.

For over a decade following his appointment, Dryden continued with his literary career in the same manner as he had before, unburdened by any official demands. Sporadically receiving his official salary, he focused mainly on writing plays, many of which were premiered or subsequently performed at court, and he enjoyed the recognition of being 'the Kings Poet Laureat'.[22] No court official or minister made any apparent effort to direct Dryden's activities. This state of affairs changed slightly with the Exclusion Crisis, during and after which Charles II entered into fierce political disputes and attempts to propagate his political message. Dryden did then write certain disputational writings that seem to have received some official instigation, and his writings became more broadly identified with his position as laureate; it became increasingly commonplace for him

---

[21] Winn, *Dryden*, pp. 191–2.

[22] *True Domestick Intelligence*, 23 Dec. 1679 (for quotation); E. L. Saslow, '"Stopp'd in other hands": The payment of Dryden's pension for 1668–1670', *Restoration: Studies in English Literary Culture, 1660–1700*, xxx (2006), 31–42, at p. 33; Winn, *Dryden*, pp. 191–2, 208–9, 221, 243–55, 314.

to be attacked as a mercenary hireling of the court.[23] Dryden's laureateship came to be defined – at the time and subsequently – by his occasional, partisan, pro-court writings.

However, looking at the more direct evidence of Dryden's relationship with the institutional court, it becomes apparent that it was neither very close nor very active, even after he started writing his disputational works. Throughout his tenure, he had great difficulty in securing the courtly favour that he was supposedly entitled to. Dryden's salary was perpetually in arrears, and he often had to solicit high-placed courtiers and ministers to help him have just a portion of those arrears paid.[24] In 1677 he wrote a letter to the twenty-two-year-old Lord Latimer, son of Lord Chancellor Danby, pleading for the former to plead to the latter to have 'My Sallary from Christmasse to Midsummer, last' paid. The letter went on to mention one of Dryden's more attentive patrons, 'My Lord Mulgrave', who, the letter suggested, had also been interceding on Dryden's behalf, presumably with mixed results.[25] A similar letter of 1683, this time addressed to the lord of the treasury, Lawrence Hyde, told a similar story. It began, 'I know not whether my Lord Sunderland has interceded with your Lordship, for half a yeare of my salary,' and went on to justify his request by reference to his work on behalf of both the king and Hyde's late father.[26] Dryden reminded Hyde, 'The King is not unsatisfyed of me, the Duke [of York, the future James II] has often promisd me his assistance; & Your Lordship is the Conduit through which their favours passe.'[27] He ended the letter on the pitiful note, 'You have many petitions of this nature, & cannot satisfy all, but I hope from your goodness to be made an Exception to your generall rules.'[28]

It would therefore seem that Dryden's role as laureate gave him no particularly direct channel to the king. The evidence of the letters (and also of the dedicatory epistles) shows Dryden as being scarcely any different, in terms of royal attention, from any other professional poet. He was still bound up in the lower strands of the patronage network that culminated

[23] T. Shadwell, *The Medal of John Bayes* (1682), pp. 1–2, 5, 7–10; P. Harth, *Pen For A Party: Dryden's Tory Propaganda in Its Contexts* (Princeton, N. J., 1993); Sharpe, *Rebranding Rule*, pp. 194–222; Winn, *Dryden*, pp. 209, 371–80, 395–405, 420–3.

[24] J. Dryden, *Discourse Concerning the Original and Progress of Satire*, in *Works*, iv. 23; Saslow, 'Dryden's pension'; Winn, *Dryden*, pp. 191–2.

[25] J. Dryden, *The Letters of John Dryden: With Letters Addressed to Him*, ed. C. Ward (Durham, N. Car., 1942), p. 12.

[26] Dryden, *Letters*, p. 20.

[27] Dryden, *Letters*, p. 21.

[28] Dryden, *Letters*, pp. 21–2.

in the crown. He still had to cast about for any and every patron he could find, hoping that they would pay him on their own account and present his petitions to the king's government. And he still had to accept that his petition was one among many, and would often go ignored. Charles, he said, was 'not unsatisfyed' with him. It was a cautious and negative phrase, but justified. Likewise his reference to James's frequent promises of favour, which, he implied, had not borne fruit. His royal masters showed him little positive attention. Even as laureate, he was still just a struggling poet, making his own way in the world of letters, and using his laureateship as just one more lever in the common system of patronage.

It is even possible that he was not the only poet to have been granted some form of courtly position. In 1674, Dryden joined forces with Shadwell and another playwright, John Crowne, to publish *Notes and Observations on The Empress of Morocco*, attacking a young newcomer, Elkanah Settle. Settle's tragedies *Cambyses* (1671) and *The Empress of Morocco* (1673) had been hugely successful with audiences both in the town theatres and at court; the latter had in fact received its first performance at court, and Rochester and Mulgrave (prominent aristocratic courtiers) had each contributed prologues to it. In 1672, Settle had been made 'Sewer in ordinary to His Matie being one of the poettes in His Mats Theatre Royall', and Samuel Holt Monk has speculated that although the position was probably a sinecure, 'Settle may have had some part in the staging of plays at court'.[29] The title page to *The Empress of Morocco* certainly designated Settle as 'Servant to his Majesty', a designation usually confined to Dryden, provoking Shadwell to grumble in the preface to *The Libertine*, 'he is no more a Poet than Servant to his Majesty, as he presumes to write himself'.[30] It clearly rankled with Settle's rivals that he should claim to have a special, official relationship with Charles II, and they were keen to weaken the validity of this relationship; and Dryden may have been provoked to co-author the *Observations* because he felt that his own special, official position in the patronage network was being compromised by Settle's pretensions. But again, the main point to make here is the uncertainty of Dryden's position. The laureate had no fixed pre-eminence in the network of courtly patronage, and no official recourse by which to assert his pre-eminence. If another poet pleased the king and his courtiers sufficiently, that poet might well be appointed to a courtly position that would place him above Dryden in the nebulous hierarchy, at least until that poet's fortunes waned too.

Shadwell's surviving letters are fewer than Dryden's, and Tate's are non-existent. But it appears that under William, Mary and Anne, the laureates

[29] S. H. Monk, 'Commentary', in Dryden, *Works*, xvii. 327–484, at pp. 390–1.
[30] T. Shadwell, *The Libertine* (1676), sig. br.

faced similar struggles to Dryden's. Shadwell received nothing for the first two years of his tenure, and his salary was still in arrears when he died.[31] The lord chamberlain who had appointed him laureate – Charles Sackville, earl of Dorset – had been a friend and patron of Shadwell's long before that appointment, and (as will be explored in more detail below) had even paid him a private pension.[32] In 1691, Shadwell attempted to have a friend's play performed, and was scorned and rebuffed by the theatre company concerned, despite his laureate status. He wrote to Dorset – whose position as lord chamberlain gave him authority over the London stage – requesting intervention. Nothing happened; Shadwell wrote once more. This time, Dorset intervened and had the play performed.[33] Like Dryden before him, Shadwell's office seems to have given him no special privileges in literary affairs. He was frustrated in his attempts to exert theatrical influence; he wrote to Dorset because Dorset was a long-time friend and patron; and Dorset, on that account, rendered Shadwell assistance. Shadwell's laurel crown granted him neither authority of his own, nor any special connection to royal or governmental authority.

The case of Tate is even more unfortunate. Unlike Dryden and Shadwell, he did not receive the office of historiographer along with that of laureate, meaning his salary was only £100.[34] It is unclear how reliably this was paid over the course of the 1690s. Samuel Golden noted that Thomas Rymer, who had been made historiographer, had to petition regularly for the money that was due to him, whereas Tate did not seem to petition at all; and Golden extrapolated from this that Tate *was* paid.[35] Yet it is more likely, in view of Dryden and Shadwell's difficulties, that Tate's payments were

---

[31] Broadus, *Laureateship*, p. 85.

[32] A. S. Borgman, *Thomas Shadwell* (New York, 1969), p. 25; Broadus, *Laureateship*, pp. 77–8; B. Harris, *Charles Sackville, Sixth Earl of Dorset, Patron and Poet of the Restoration* (Urbana, Ill., 1940), p. 75; 'A letter from Shadwell to the earl of Dorset' (24 Jan. 1682) in T. Shadwell, *Complete Works*, ed. M. Summers (5 vols, London, 1927), v. 401.

[33] Borgman, *Shadwell*, pp. 86–7; 'A letter from Shadwell to the earl of Dorset' (19 Jan. 1691) in Shadwell, *Works*, v. 403; 'A letter from Shadwell to the earl of Dorset' (2 May 1692) in Shadwell, *Works*, v. 404.

[34] The office of historiographer was nominal until this separation, serving only as an adjunct to that of laureate. Broadus, *Laureateship*, pp. 59–64. For the separation and Tate's subsequent salary, see Broadus, *Laureateship*, pp. 63–4; 'Thomas Rymer Esq Historiographer' (8 Dec. 1692), TNA, SP 44/341, fo. 452; 'Nahum Tate Esq Poet Laureat' (8 Dec. 1692), TNA, SP 44/341, fo. 453. For the office of historiographer, see 'Historiographer c.1662–1782, c.1807–1837' in *Office-Holders in Modern Britain: Volume 11 (Revised), Court Officers, 1660–1837*, ed. R. O. Bucholz (London, 2006), p. 179.

[35] S. A. Golden, 'The late seventeenth century writer and the laureateship: Nahum Tate's tenure', *Hermathena*, lxxxix (1957), 30–8, at pp. 33–5.

as unreliable as Rymer's, and that Tate was either too modest to make a fuss (which would have been in keeping with his character), or made his petitions in some way that has left no evidence.

From 1700 onwards, however, certain evidence of Tate's penury begins to appear. In February of that year he petitioned the king, complaining that he needed to print a new edition of his translation of the psalms, but was too poor to supply the advance required by the printer. He ascribed this poverty to the fact that he had 'already been at much expense, and his salary of poet laureate [was] £100 *per ann.*, of £300 which his predecessors enjoyed'. (He was mistaken as to the value of his predecessors' salaries.) He therefore requested an addition to his salary or a one-off payment.[36] In 1703, his privations led him to have his yearly butt of wine (which had been a perk of the office since Dryden's appointment) commuted into an extra £30 per year.[37] He requested more money in 1704 to meet the printer's advance for a supplement to his psalms, and in 1712 the Treasury Minutes reveal a discussion on Tate's arrears.[38] Like Dryden and Shadwell, Tate found it more worthwhile to cultivate alternative or subsidiary patrons than to rely directly on the monarch. Dorset had been the one to appoint Tate, having been a patron of his for some time already, and he continued to patronize Tate thereafter.[39] Robert Harley was also an important patron.[40] Beneath these two eminences were a brood of lesser noblemen and statesmen to whom Tate dedicated works and who presumably paid him some subsistence in return.[41]

For all of his efforts, the final years of Tate's life were wretched. He was forced to take refuge in the Mint on at least two occasions – apparently

[36] *Calendar of State Papers Domestic: William III, 1699–1700*, ed. E. Bateson (London, 1937), p. 372.

[37] *CTB xviii, 1703*, p. 225. There is some uncertainty as to when this commutation actually occurred; many scholars follow Southey in blaming Pye, but Southey was certainly mistaken. Warton believed that the wine was 'never taken in Kind, not even by Ben [Jonson]; but in Money', yet he too seems to have been mistaken, and Tate seems to have been the laureate responsible. *Warton Correspondence*, lt. 577, at p. 629; editorial notes, pp. 629–30.

[38] *CTB xix, Jan. 1704–March 1705*, p. 60; *CTB xxvi, 1712 (part 2)*, p. 33.

[39] See N. Tate, *A Poem Occasioned by William III's Voyage to Holland* (1691), p. 7; *Elegies etc.* (1699), pp. 71–9; 'To William Broughton, Esq; Marshall of the Queen's-Bench', in M. Smith, *Memoirs of the Mint and Queen's-Bench* (1713), pp. 5–8 (p. 6); and his dedications to *Brutus of Alba* (1678), *A Poem on the Late Promotion of Several Eminent Persons in Church and State* (1694), and J. Davies, *The Original, Nature, and Immortality of the Soul*, ed. N. Tate (1697).

[40] N. Tate, *The Muse's Memorial, Of the Right Honourable Earl of Oxford, Lord High Treasurer of Great Britain* (1712); *The Muse's Bower an Epithalamium* (1713).

[41] N. Tate, *A Present for the Ladies*, 2nd edn (1693), to the countess of Radnor; *Panacea: A Poem upon Tea* (1700) to 'the Right Honourable Charles Montague, *Esq*; One of his Majesty's most Honourable Privy Council'.

hiding from his creditors – and died there in 1715.[42] The poetry and prefatory material he wrote over the course of Anne's reign tells of his collapse into dearth and desperation. He felt that he had spent his life serving the court, the church and the cause of virtue, but that it had only been to his cost.[43] Golden observed that Tate was no longer petitioning the crown by this point, and suggested that he 'must have been out of favour'.[44] Again, it may be that Tate *was* appealing for money, but in a way that left no record. Or it may just be that Tate had learned how little he could expect from the court. He was not 'out of favour', as such. He had simply never been *in* favour.

However, the case for courtly negligence towards the laureateship can be overstated. Arrears of payment were standard for all court officials and pensioners, with payments becoming more reliable under Anne but never catching up with the deficit.[45] Moreover, some of Tate's appeals did result in aid. The request for an addition to his salary or a one-off payment, made in 1700, received the latter response to the sum of £200.[46] In 1705, a royal warrant paid him £50 for his psalms supplement;[47] and in 1712 Harley (as lord treasurer) and Robert Benson (as chancellor of the exchequer) directed the exchequer to pay Tate's deficit 'from time to time'.[48] Tate convinced William to make a proclamation in favour of his psalms translation, and he set up his short-lived periodical, *The Monitor*, with the approval or even the express command of Anne.[49] Finally, as will be detailed below, Shadwell and Tate as laureates were becoming increasingly responsible for the biannual odes that were set to music by the master of the king's or queen's music and performed at court on the monarch's birthday and on New Year's Day.

Moreover, when attention is turned from the plight of the individual laureates to other forms of evidence, it becomes clear that the reigns of William III and Anne marked not a continuation of Dryden's laureateship,

---

[42] C. Spencer, *Nahum Tate* (New York, 1972), pp. 37–40.

[43] Eg Tate's dedication to Davies's *Immortality*, sig. A4v; N. Tate, *The Muse's Memorial of the Happy Recovery of the Right Honourable Richard Earl of Burlington from a Dangerous Sickness in the Year 1706* (1707), p. 1; 'Broughton', p. 6; *A Poem Sacred to the Glorious Memory of Her Late Majesty Queen Anne* (1716), pp. 1–2.

[44] Golden, 'Tate's tenure', p. 36.

[45] Bucholz, *Augustan Court*, pp. 115–44.

[46] *CTB xv, Aug 1699–Sep 1700*, pp. 51–2, 290, 315.

[47] *CTB xx, 1705–6 (part 2)*, p. 229.

[48] *CTB xxvi, 1712 (part 2)*, p. 33.

[49] T. Cibber [and Robert Shiels], *The Lives of the Poets* (4 vols, 1753), iii. 260 (stating that Anne commanded Tate to write *The Monitor*); N. Tate, *A New Version of the Psalms of David* (1700), sig. Av; N. Tate, Mr Smith, et al., *An Entire Set Of The Monitors* (1713), sig. Ar.

but a time of transition. Dryden's laureateship had been an anomalous, ill-defined position: an attempt to formalize certain vaguer, pseudo-mythological ideas about the poetic vocation and to elevate the traditional practice of bestowing court pensions on worthy poets, but an attempt that was lacking in formal definition. The laureate was therefore left adrift with regard to the court – the body from which his ideological prestige and remunerative recognition was supposed to flow – and unable to fulfil the ideals that underpinned his office. Shadwell and Tate, following on from Dryden, were still to suffer somewhat from these issues. But at the same time, their tenures saw the office adapting, and moving from a position of unsatisfactory anomalousness to one of functional and institutional definition. The need for successive courts to be presented as legitimate, and proven as viable courts in accordance with the traditional model by increasingly formalized ceremonial and cultural activities, doing so in interaction with the town and the world, was recurrent and growing. As a result, the laureateship was becoming better defined and being given greater prominence and purpose. Tate may never have quite grasped the courtly acknowledgement that his financial straits necessitated, but he bequeathed to his successors an office that now had a fixed place vis-à-vis both the institution and the concept of the court.

The lord chamberlain's department

The best place to start an investigation of the way in which the laureateship transformed over the later Stuart period, and solidified in its new position under the early Hanoverians, is in the documents produced by the court at the time, and particularly by the lord chamberlain's department. The first three laureates – Dryden, Shadwell and Tate – were all appointed by formal letters patent, indicating the original idea behind the office: that it represented the king's choosing of a certain great poet to be his laureate. Yet when Tate's office was reconfirmed at Anne's accession, it was by warrant from the lord chamberlain's department. From George I's accession onwards, all new appointments followed this process.[50] However, although this alteration in the appointment process highlights the transference of the office into the lord chamberlain's care, it is somewhat misleading about how and when that transference occurred. Other records from the lord chamberlain's department tell a more exact story.

The lord chamberlain's department was the largest and most diffuse in the royal household, concerned with court ceremonial in its widest sense. It included the household above stairs, and a more anomalous grouping

50 Broadus, *Laureateship*, pp. 89–90.

of courtly officers and temporary employees concerned with revels, artisanship and such matters. If the laureate was to be found in any court department, it would have most logically been this one.[51] However, the earliest records of the staff falling under the lord chamberlain's remit – of which the most useful are the comprehensive establishment books – do not include the laureateship. An establishment book for 1671 (three years after Dryden's appointment) contains no trace of either the poet laureate or the historiographer.[52] The next existing establishment book, running from 1674 to 1685, is similarly lacking.[53] A precedent book from about the same period, containing 499 pages and several lists of places within the lord chamberlain's disposal, finds no place for the laureateship either. Although the information in the book generally dates to between 1660 and 1689, there is even a note from May 1693 written by the then lord chamberlain, Dorset, solemnly setting out that none of the above positions are to be given without his consent or warrant; and the list of positions in question, titled 'places in ye Lord Chamberlains disposall', finds place for an 'Embroider' and a 'Drum Major and Drummers', but none for a poet laureate.[54]

The sequence of establishment books, which is somewhat patchy, resumes in 1695. Here the poet laureate is finally accounted for, but is not treated with much attention. The contents page directs the reader to almost the back of the book, where is to be found, after the 'Kettle Drum[m]er for Ireland' and before a tacked-on scrawl about the 'Maker & Repairer of the water engines at Kensington' and a section for 'Vocall Musick', a poet laureate going by the name of 'Nathaniel Tate'. Since Tate's forename was actually 'Nahum', he was clearly not being treated as an important part of the court establishment. However, he did at last belong to the lord chamberlain's jurisdiction. A couple of pages after Tate comes a closing, reiterative list of 'Places in the Disposall of the L[ord] Chamberlain of His Ma[jestie]s Household', registering the poet laureate and the historiographer.[55]

The next establishment book, 1700–2, is even more telling. Here the laureate and the historiographer are placed on the final page of the establishment list, and Tate is again re-christened as 'Nathaniel'. He and the historiographer precede only the Kensington water engineer and 'Vocall

[51] J. M. Beattie, *The English Court in the Reign of George I* (Cambridge, 1967), pp. 17–18, 23–52; Bucholz, *Augustan Court*, pp. 37–9; 'Chamber administration: Lord Chamberlain, 1660–1837', in *Court Officers, 1660–1837*, ed. R. O. Bucholz, pp. 1–8.

[52] TNA, LC 3/27.

[53] TNA, LC 3/28.

[54] TNA, LC 5/201, p. 181.

[55] TNA, LC 3/3, pp. 26, 30.

Musick' staff, which latter positions are appended with dates but no salaries, indicating them to have been occasional positions, recorded at some point after the establishment list had first been compiled. As for the laureate's and historiographer's salaries, they are included in the 'Treasury Chamb[e]r' column – this particular establishment book specifying whether each salary came from that source or from the 'Cofferer' – but then, in a different, hastier hand, a note has been made underneath the salaries: 'Excheq[ue]r'.[56] This note is found in many other places throughout the establishment book, and is part of more far-reaching organizations of court finances and payments. But its appearance next to the laureate's name reinforces the impression that his exact place in the department was uncertain.

According to the establishment books, it was in Anne's reign that the poet laureate's situation began improving. The 1702–13 establishment book included him (with the historiographer) on a much earlier page than usual, among more estimable company: the page begins with 'Master of ye Revels', then reads 'Yeomen of ye Revels', then laureate and historiographer.[57] This was the beginning of an association between the laureate and the revels staff, and is especially notable in the light of the office's changing function (detailed below). However, while the contents pages of this and following establishment books clearly group together the revels staff, they just as clearly leave the laureate out of that grouping; and the books in general, while tending to place the laureate near to the revellers, do not indicate the master of revels's authority to extend to the laureateship.[58] The association was based on similarity of function, rather than on any official relationship.

It was also in the 1702–13 establishment book that Tate's name was finally treated with due courtesy, 'Nahum Tate Esqr', and his payment was listed in the treasury chamber column, rather than in the new 'Exchequer' column. A precedent book for 1697–1739 gives further evidence of the financial reorganizations affecting the laureateship, with an establishment account dated to June 1702 attributing all expenses to 'the Office of Treasurer of our Chamber', and a note next to Tate specifying his payments to be 'in lieu of the like Salary or allowance which was also payable to him at Our said Exchequer'.[59] But by the end of Anne's reign, these financial reorganizations were winding up, and the laureate's position had almost been worked out. The next two establishment books (for 1714 and 1714–27) are, in respect of

---

[56] TNA, LC 3/4, p. 34.

[57] TNA, LC 3/5, p. 8.

[58] See especially TNA, LC 3/8 (1717–24), contents page and p. 9.

[59] TNA, LC 5/202, p. 125.

the laureateship, almost identical to that of 1702–13.[60] The sole remaining development, witnessed in the various (and overlapping) establishment books of the 1720s and 1730s, was for the laureate, historiographer and revellers to start being more closely grouped with the master of ceremonies. They sometimes even appeared on a dedicated 'Ceremonies' page or section.[61] But this was just a cosmetic neatening of a situation that had been developed over the course of William's and Anne's reigns and fixed at the accession of George I. The revels staff had generally been understood as pertaining to ceremonial matters anyway, even before they became friends with the laureate.

Before analysing these developments, it is worth taking a look at some different evidence that concerns itself with the same subject matter: publications on the court establishment. The most useful and prominent is Edward Chamberlayne's *Angliae Notitia, Or The Present State of England*, in which Chamberlayne attempted to give a general picture of contemporary England. His work included a section on the court, comprising various catalogues enumerating every single member of the court establishment. Twenty-two separate editions of the work were printed between 1669 and 1707, each with various alterations, at which point the work passed to Chamberlayne's son, John, and became *Magnae Britanniae Notitia*, continuing until 1755. Its successive editions therefore can be used to explore the changes in the laureateship's position.

The first edition did not record the laureate at all, either in the list of places at the lord chamberlain's disposal or anywhere else. However, the second edition (also 1669) complicates matters. Here, the poet laureate appeared in a long section on '*His Majesties* Servants *in Ordinary* above Stairs'. He appeared towards the end, and in miscellaneous company, coming after '*Messengers of the Chamber in Ordinary*', 'One Library Keeper' and 'One Publick Notary', and just before '*Musitians in Ordinary*' and such figures as '*Apothecaries*', '*Chirugeons*', '*Printers*' and a '*Hydrographer*'. This time, the historiographer was nowhere in sight (though the position, of course, was at this point held jointly with the laureateship. The fact that the hydrographer's position remained one below the laureate's in all future editions suggests that Chamberlayne may have mixed up 'historiographer' with 'hydrographer').[62] The holders of neither the laureateship nor the other surrounding positions were named. Earlier in the book, the lord chamberlain's office was described as bearing jurisdiction over 'all Officers belonging to the Kings Chamber,

---

[60] TNA, LC 3/6, 3/7.

[61] Eg TNA, LC 3/14 (1735).

[62] E. Chamberlayne, *Angliae Notitia*, 2nd edn (1669), p. 265.

except the Precincts of the Kings Bed-Chamber, which is wholly under the Groom of the Stole; and all above Stairs; who are all sworn by him (or his Warrant to the Gentleman Ushers) to the King. He hath also the over-sight of … [various positions, including] Apothecaries, Surgeons, Barbers, &c.'[63] The laureate was not specifically named as coming under his authority, and the section on offices above stairs included the bedchamber staff, who had earlier been specified not to be part of that authority, but instead to answer to the Groom of the Stole. Moreover, the above-stairs section was long, sprawling and often subdivided, and the laureate only appeared towards the end of it.

Nonetheless, it cannot be ignored that Chamberlayne (the author) had suggested that the laureateship formed part of the lord chamberlain's remit, in contrast to the contemporary establishment records emanating from the chamberlain's office. Chamberlayne's remark that all positions above stairs were sworn by the chamberlain or his warrant, and his listing of the poet laureate in the above-stairs section, is also contradicted by the fact that Dryden, Shadwell and Tate were all appointed by formal letters patent, without reference to the lord chamberlain's office. Perhaps Chamberlayne was simply uncertain of where to place the laureate in his account of the state of England, and, judging him to pertain to the court in some capacity, decided that he must be some form of above-stairs official, since he could certainly not be located below stairs, and since other artistic and artisanal officials tended to answer to the lord chamberlain.

The seventeenth edition (1692) was the first to be published after the Glorious Revolution. The material on the court had been gradually reorganized over the years, but the position of the laureate, while being given slightly more clarity, had not been much changed. Here, it appeared towards the end of '*A List of their Majesties Officers and Servants in Ordinary above-stairs*', in a small, miscellaneous grouping headed, 'Also among his *Majesties Servants in Ordinary* are reckon'd'. This group – which was separated from the master of revels by several pages and subsections – comprised a '*Principal Painter*', 'One *Poet Laureat*', 'One *Hydrographer*', 'One *Library-keeper*' and then a few other positions.[64] There was no historiographer, despite the position having parted from the laureateship by this time. All the positions were named and had their salaries given; the laureateship was correctly identified as '*Thomas Shadwell* Esq; 200*l. per An.*' However, in the following, eighteenth edition (1694), Chamberlayne mistook both the name

---

[63] Chamberlayne, *Angliae Notitia*, pp. 247–9.
[64] Chamberlayne, *Angliae Notitia*, 17th edn (1692), p. 134.

and the salary, 'Mr. *Nathanel Tate.* 200 *l. per An.*'[65] Clearly, Chamberlayne still did not know where to locate the poet laureate. He was not basing his understanding of the laureateship on a very sure grasp of the facts; but then, there were not many facts to be grasped. After all, even Tate and his paymasters had never known how large a poet laureate's salary ought to be.

The nineteenth edition (1700) boasted on its title page that it was issued 'with great Additions and Improvements'. However, Chamberlayne's treatment of the laureateship witnessed neither. It was lumped at the end of the above-stairs officers again, in between the principal painter and the hydrographer, and its salary was once again listed wrongly as '200 *l. per An.*'[66] Chamberlayne actually retracted his earlier innovation of naming the holders of the laureateship and its neighbouring offices. The mistake was repeated in the twentieth edition (1702), and then with the twenty-first edition (1704) came a further diminution, the laureate's salary being erased entirely.[67] The final edition (1707) repeated this very cursory notice of the laureateship, and, as testament to the care with which *Angliae Notitia* was being revised by this stage, it even repeated the designation of the relevant chapter as pertaining to the '*Government of the King's Houshold*'.[68] By this point, Anne had been on the throne for five years.

With the 1707 Act of Union came the new title *Magnae Britanniae Notitia*, and John Chamberlayne, the new author, finally began to get things right (although the book still remained inconsistent as to whether Britain was now ruled by a king or queen). At the end of a cramped, grubby, generally uninformative list of '*The Queen's Officers and Servants in Ordinary above Stairs, under the Lord* Chamberlain' appeared '*Poet Laureat*, Nahum Tate, *Esq*; Sal. 100 *l. per Ann.*', followed by the Hydrographer and the Historiographer ('T. Rimer, *Esq*; Sal. 200 *l. per Ann.*').[69] The 1718 edition then had '*Poet Laureat*, Nicholas Rowe, *Esq*; *Sal.* 100 *l.* per Ann.' in a list of '*Other Servants to the King*' at the end of the section on the lord chamberlain's department.[70] In these successive editions, often apparently compiled in a rush and with the materials being continually rearranged, it would therefore appear that

---

[65] Chamberlayne, *Angliae Notitia*, 18th edn (1694), p. 241.

[66] Chamberlayne, *Angliae Notitia*, 19th edn (1700), p. 175.

[67] Chamberlayne, 20th edn (1702), p. 180; 21st edn (1704), p. 178.

[68] Chamberlayne, 22nd edn (1707), pp. 163, 178.

[69] J. Chamberlayne, *Magnae Britanniae Notitia* (1707), p. 614. The title page advertised this as the twenty-second edition, but it was in fact different from the twenty-second and final edition of *Angliae Notitia*, though published in the same year.

[70] Chamberlayne, *Magnae Britanniae Notitia*, 'The five and twentieth edition of the *south* part call'd *England*, and fourth of the *north* part call'd *Scotland*' (1718), p. 93.

the Chamberlaynes were gradually, uncertainly finding an appropriate place for the laureate as a semi-unique servant in ordinary above stairs, answering to the lord chamberlain and being paid £100 a year. There were also other sources of information for readers interested in the staffing of the court, and they generally treated the laureateship in a similar way.[71] The compilers of these sorts of publication were evidently unreliable in their treatment of the laureateship. But they did recognize that the laureateship pertained to the lord chamberlain's jurisdiction, even, in Edward Chamberlayne's case, expressing this recognition before it was accurate.

Taking the foregoing evidence as a whole, then, the picture that emerges is one of confusion, but nonetheless of significant developments in the positioning and definition of the office over time. The Hanoverian succession set these developments in stone. For the next hundred years, the only major change in the courtly positioning of the laureateship was the cosmetic one of emphasizing the closeness of the laureateship (and the revellers) to the ceremonies staff. The reason, nature and implications of these developments will be explained in due course, when the changing function of the laureateship is discussed below. But before then, the transition of the office into the lord chamberlain's keeping must be investigated in more detail. The lord chamberlain at the time was the earl of Dorset. It is on his private accounts that the investigation will be founded.

Dorset's accounts

Dorset was famous in his own day and subsequently for his literary patronage, which was variously (and sometimes conjointly) described as discerning and universal.[72] The first three poets laureate all benefitted from his patronage over significant stretches of time, and duly dedicated some of their works to him. Although he was personally close to Charles II, he opposed James II's policies and fell from favour, and then supported William and Mary's accession to the crown. For this support he was rewarded at the Glorious Revolution, including by being made lord chamberlain. He held the post from 1689 until 1695, overseeing the dismissal of Dryden from the laureateship (due to Dryden's refusal to renounce Catholicism) and the appointment of Shadwell in his place. As lord chamberlain, he was known for his greedy and aggressive practices, exhibiting a general desire to expand and solidify the powers of his department and an attendant desire that he and his favoured underlings should reap all the financial benefits that

---

[71] Eg Anon., *The Present State of the British Court* (1720), pp. 33–7.

[72] For Dorset as literary patron, politician and lord chamberlain, see Harris, *Charles Sackville*, pp. 31, 101, 117–36, 173–204.

they could. The late 1680s and 1690s were in some ways an ideal time for such practices, with constant shifts and squabbles over the jurisdictions of the various court departments.[73] In one of the precedent books referred to above, there is a detailed description of a dispute that the lord chamberlain's department was involved in over who had the right to appoint the court's Lenten preachers.[74] All these points are significant in considering what happened to the laureateship around this time.

As has been discussed above, when Dorset became lord chamberlain, it was by no means the case that the laureateship should have had anything to do with him. Dryden had not been appointed by a lord chamberlain, nor did he answer to one; and the establishment records of the lord chamberlain's office took no notice of any poets laureate before Tate. Yet when Dorset became lord chamberlain, he busied himself with the laureateship and made decisions regarding its occupant. It was Dorset who dealt with Dryden, trying to convince him to change religion and stay on as laureate, and who was responsible for Shadwell's and Tate's appointments, both men thanking him for this in dedicatory epistles.[75] Looking further ahead, Dorset's successors as lord chamberlain enjoyed the formal prerogative of choosing a laureate; and the first establishment book of the lord chamberlain's department to have been written during Tate's tenure, although coming a couple of years after Tate's appointment, includes the laureateship as one of the offices in the lord chamberlain's disposal. Evidently, Dorset was fixing the laureateship in the lord chamberlain's firmament. Given his keenness to make the most of his position, and the fact that he was acknowledged as a great patron and a man of eminent literary taste, it would not have been unnatural for him to act in such a way; and given that the king who had installed him as lord chamberlain had no knowledge of English literature, and had more pressing business on his hands, it would not have been difficult. A consideration of Dorset's personal accounts provides further evidence of his instrumentality in the repositioning of the laureateship. It also reveals why Dorset acted towards the laureateship as he did.

In the accounts, Dryden, Shadwell and Tate all appear recurrently as beneficiaries of Dorset's financial patronage. Although Dryden had had to be ejected from the laureateship for his religious and political unsuitability, it was well known by the end of the seventeenth century that Dorset had

---

[73] Bucholz, *Augustan Court*, pp. 39–44.

[74] TNA, LC 5/201, fo. 48.

[75] T. Shadwell, *Bury-Fair* (1689), sig. A2r–v; Tate, dedication to Davies, *Immortality*, sig. A4r–v.

personally recompensed him for this loss.[76] Dryden seems to have viewed Dorset as his greatest patron until the end of his life despite their political differences, and he duly shows up in Dorset's account books (which begin in 1671) a number of times, for (usually large) one-off payments.[77] Shadwell, meanwhile, was first paid in July 1684 (£10), and, after several more such payments over the years, was last paid on 23 December 1689.[78] There is no appearance of regularity to the payments; they come at fairly random intervals and are described in differing ways. But the final payment is (uniquely) described as being 'for a quart[er]', indicating that Shadwell was in receipt of a £40 pension paid in quarterly sums by the end of 1689, and flagging up the deficiencies of the account books: it seems that they do not cover all the payments that Dorset was making to poets.[79] Dorset was known for giving out money in spontaneous and irregular ways that would have escaped even the most diligent of accountants, and his accounts must therefore be considered as an incomplete record of his financial patronage. On the other hand, there is evidence that his private pension payments were sometimes in arrears, suggesting that there may be more omissions of payments than of records in the account books.[80]

Tate's recorded payments are more numerous than Shadwell's, and are more routinely identified as constituting the quarterly payments of a £40 annuity.[81] His first recorded payment came in July 1689, and his last in May 1694. But his last £10 annuity payment came in October 1692, and the only payment after that – the May 1694 payment – had nothing to do with the annuity, being a gift of £5 10s, paid by specific order and probably relating to a poem that Tate dedicated to Dorset around this time.[82] Again, the recorded annuity payments do not add up to the four per year that would be expected, suggesting negligence in either the payments or the account keeping. The account books continue until Dorset's death in January 1706,

---

[76] Harris, *Charles Sackville*, pp. 121–3; D. Griffin, *Literary Patronage in England, 1650–1800* (Cambridge, 1996), pp. 50–1.

[77] Kentish History and Library Centre, U269, A7/23, A7/26, A7/28.

[78] Kentish History and Library Centre, U269, A7/6, A7/12, A7/13 (two payments), A7/17, A7/18.

[79] There is a separate set of receipts in Dorset's accounts, but they do not pertain to any payments that are not also identifiable in the account books. Kentish History and Library Centre, U269, A189–90, passim.

[80] Harris, *Charles Sackville*, pp. 124, 196–7.

[81] Kentish History and Library Centre, U269, A7/17, A7/18 (two payments), A7/19, A7/20, A7/23 (two payments), A7/24, A7/25, A7/26 (last to be identified as a quarterly payment), A7/28.

[82] Tate, *Late Promotion*.

but with no more appearances from Dryden, Shadwell or Tate, other than a subscription payment for Dryden's Virgil translation in July 1694.[83] It is also worthwhile noting that after Shadwell's death, Dorset paid Shadwell's son £20 by specific order (in December 1692).[84]

Of course, it is unsurprising to find Dorset granting payments to Dryden, Shadwell and Tate, given his reputation as a general benefactor of poets. But these payments are noteworthy in two respects. The first is that, in spite of his reputation, Dorset actually seems to have been concentrating his favour on these specific three poets, and especially Shadwell and Tate. Nathaniel Lee's widow was also in receipt of a fairly long-running annuity, but there is otherwise not much trace of Dorset's much-vaunted literary patronage.[85] As mentioned above, the accounts do not give a complete picture of Dorset's largesse; but it is nonetheless hard to escape the conclusion that Dryden, Shadwell and Tate were his three favoured poets.

More striking still is the dating of Dorset's payments. As mentioned above, Shadwell can be identified as having been paid from July 1684 to December 1689, and Tate from July 1689 until May 1694. Dorset's patronage of (and friendship with) Shadwell had started well before 1684, but it was around this time that Shadwell started suffering financially due to his political opposition to the court; Shadwell was later to thank Dorset for saving him in these barren years. Still more significant is the year that Shadwell was appointed poet laureate: 1689. It was in this same year that, according to the accounts, he ceased to receive a private pension from Dorset. Tate, who seems to have first started receiving his own pension in the same year, succeeded Shadwell as laureate at the end of 1692; there are no more recorded annuity payments for him after this appointment, with the only subsequent gift being the £5 10s of May 1694. The pattern is unmistakable. Dorset stopped paying out annuities to Shadwell and Tate at about the time that they were each made laureate. Moreover, his payments generally seem to have been motivated by the desperation of the recipients: Dryden was given a financial safety blanket after being jettisoned from the laureateship; Shadwell's payments began when his Whig partisanship had reduced him to penury; and Tate's constant financial problems have been documented above. Even in the case of Nathaniel Lee, Dorset seems to have been more concerned with supporting his widow with an annuity than paying Lee himself while he was still alive, and the Lees' case was especially piteous, given Lee's descent into madness and poverty in the latter years of his life.

---

[83] Kentish History and Library Centre, U269, A7/28.

[84] Kentish History and Library Centre, U269, A7/26.

[85] For Lee's widow, eg Kentish History and Library Centre, U269, A7/40.

Dorset's payments to this small band of poets, then, correlate firmly with two things: their desperation, and the laureateship. He paid them when they needed it, and he stopped paying them when they were appointed laureate. Dorset's approach to the laureateship thus becomes clear. He was not bestowing it as Charles II had bestowed it on Dryden, only as a mark of royal distinction and as proof that the court did indeed patronize great poetry (although Dorset, as a great patron himself and as a key member of the Williamite regime, would presumably have recognized the continuing importance of establishing the cultural patronage of the court, too). More immediately, he was using it to support a couple of poets, Shadwell and Tate, whom he liked or pitied above all others. By so doing, he transferred the financial burden of his patronage from his personal coffers to the court. This was entirely in keeping with his attitude to the lord chamberlain's department as a whole, and with the more general disregard that office-holders tended to have for the borderline between their own private means of patronage and the patronage opportunities attached to their office.

It would therefore appear that Dorset's time as lord chamberlain was crucial in the development of the office of poet laureate. Widely known and respected for his taste in literature and for his patronage, he was appointed lord chamberlain by a king and queen who had little interest in the laureateship; therefore, armed with an expansionist zeal and a small troupe of starving poets, he decided to annex that office to his own department and to bestow it in the same manner as he had previously been bestowing his private funds. He was encouraged in this endeavour by the general disorganization that existed in the court at this time, and by the particular state of the laureateship, which, while being an anomalous office, also seemed to have just the sort of character that – as Edward Chamberlayne had felt in 1669 – could justify its coming under the lord chamberlain's jurisdiction. He was so successful that, by the time of Tate's death in 1715, the laureateship had become naturally regarded as an office in the lord chamberlain's gift, disposed by his department's warrant. Officially speaking, it no longer had anything to do with the crown, which had previously been used to appoint 'the king's poet laureate' according to formal letters patent. The heir to Virgil would no longer float about in vague communion with his latter-day Augustus. He had been redefined as a court functionary, and fitted into a niche under the remit of the lord chamberlain.

Finding a role

However, these developments were not purely organizational. They were bound up with the functional transformation that the office was undergoing. The eighteenth-century poet laureate was not to be a Drydenic figure, either in the early sense of enjoying an honour that conferred no responsibilities, or in the later sense of writing disputational works on the king's behalf. Instead, he was to be a panegyric functionary. The job of the eighteenth-century laureates was to centre on the writing of biannual odes, scheduled for the monarch's birthday and for New Year's Day. The odes would be set to music – usually, and with increasing exclusivity, by the master of the king's or queen's music – and performed at court on the set date. The texts would often be published soon after. By the mid century, a large and growing number of periodicals were making it their habit to print the words of the odes immediately after their performances at court, and this widespread practice was to persist until the odes were discontinued.[86]

The odes and their history will be explored in Chapter Five, but there are a couple of things worth drawing attention to here. Firstly, they were highly suited to the manner in which the regimes of William, Mary and Anne presented themselves and were presented to the public.[87] Whereas Charles II's regime had entered into a furious debate over monarchical power and legitimacy, post-1688 regimes attempted to make their case without appearing to make any case at all, and to avoid being associated with the disputes between Whigs and Tories. Instead, the ideology of rule that emanated from and focused on the courts of William, Mary and Anne was that they (and especially William) had been providentially ordained to rescue England from Catholicism and sin. These monarchs would overturn the popish oppression beneath which England had laboured; they would then reform the nation's morals and manners, through both example and action.[88] In line with this, Sharpe showed how pro-court poetry in these years tended to favour emotive assertion over argument, thus making the court's case by appealing to the emotions and suggesting all matters of dispute to have been already settled.[89] What Sharpe did not observe is that the characteristics of the ode format were particularly amenable to such a tendency, being ecstatic, sublime, emotive and celebratory in tone, whereas rhyming couplets (the most common form of verse) had a more logical and argumentative bent.

---

[86] McGuinness, *Court Odes*, pp. 1, 10–11. See chs 4 and 5.

[87] An interesting, nuanced exploration of this suitability for the reign of Mary II, albeit focused more on non-laureate ode writers, has recently been given in H. Smith, 'Court culture and Godly monarchy: Henry Purcell and Sir Charles Sedley's 1692 birthday ode for Mary II', in *Politics, Religion and Ideas in Seventeenth- and Eighteenth-Century Britain: Essays in Honour of Mark Goldie*, ed. J. Champion, J. Coffey, T. Harris and J. Marshall (Woodbridge, 2019), pp. 219–37.

[88] Claydon, *Godly Revolution*, pp. 1–4, 22, 46–63, 72–3, 79–88, 90, 126–59, 228–9.

[89] Sharpe, *Rebranding Rule*, pp. 373–82.

The second thing to note is that it was during the tenures of Shadwell and especially Tate that the existence of the biannual courtly odes became firmly established and the association of the poet laureateship with those odes took shape. Some form of song or ode had tended to be performed at court on festive occasions prior to 1681, and performances became increasingly routine thereafter, with a host of different poets supplying texts for the performances up to 1715. But Shadwell and Tate, when laureates, were increasingly responsible for their production; and when Tate died a year after the Hanoverian succession, this informal practice hardened into a formal demand. It was actively expected of Rowe that he would provide two odes a year for the designated occasions, and it was expected of him purely because he had been laureated. Rowe occasionally subcontracted the odes out to friends and associates.[90] During Tate's laureateship, if another person had written an ode, then that ode would have been ascribed to that other person. But for Rowe, the arrangement was different; even if he was not to write the odes himself, he was responsible for sourcing them, and they would be formally ascribed to his pen. By the reign of George I, the laureates had thus been exclusively identified with the function of providing the biannual odes. This identification was to remain into the early nineteenth century.[91]

As to why this identification came about, part of the answer lies with Shadwell and Tate themselves. Upon the arrival of William and Mary, Shadwell immediately published several works of panegyric celebration, seemingly of his own volition, which predated his appointment as laureate.[92] Once appointed, he produced a batch of seven further panegyrics, some of which were avowed as odes for specific occasions (such as William's return from Ireland), and some of which were performed at court as part of the birthday and New Year festivities.[93] Tate was to continue and expand this panegyric trend. Although his output had been relatively diverse in the early part of his career, he showed a marked trend in his later years – starting even before his appointment as laureate – towards writing panegyric poetry. His panegyrics were written in couplets as well as odes, and, although he regarded

[90] J. Hughes, *The Correspondence of John Hughes, Esq* (2 vols, 1773), i. 84–5.

[91] See ch. 5.

[92] *A Congratulatory Poem on His Highness the Prince of Orange* (1689); *A Congratulatory Poem to the Most Illustrious Queen Mary upon Her Arrival in England* (1689).

[93] *Ode on the Anniversary of the King's Birth* (1690), *Poem on the Anniversary of the King's Birth* (1690), *Ode to the King on His Return from Ireland* (1691), *Ode on the King's Birth-Day* (1692), and *Votum Perenne: A Poem to the King on New-Years-Day* (1692) were all published around the time of their performance. A 1689 birthday ode to Mary and a New Year's ode for 1690 do not seem to have been, though the former appeared in Anon., *Poems on Affairs of State, The Second Part* (1697), pp. 223–4. For performances, see McGuinness, *Court Odes*, pp. 19–20.

his reigning monarch as his prime and most glorious theme, he also wrote panegyrics for a wide group of other figures, from bishops, to beauties, to personal friends. None of this was accidental on Tate's part; on several occasions he articulated his belief that a poet's highest calling was to serve religion and virtue, and that the best manner of doing this was to set forth glorious instances of virtue which would serve as stimuli for emulation.[94]

Most tellingly in the context of the laureateship, he linked his role as laureate to his panegyric poetry. Writing a dedication to Dorset, he thanked him for:

> placing me in His Majesty's Service; a Favour which I had not the Presumption to seek. I was conscious how short I came of my Predecessors in Performances of Wit and Diversion; and therefore, as the best means I had of justifying Your Lordship's Kindness, employ'd my Self in publishing such Poems as might be useful in promoting Religion and Morality. But how little I have consulted my immediate interest in so doing, I am severely sensible. I engaged in the Service of the Temple at my own Expence, while Others made their profitable Markets on the Stage.[95]

By way of spatial concepts, Tate here made several clear distinctions. One was between his activities before and after being appointed laureate. He claimed to have 'employ'd my Self … in promoting Religion and Morality' as a direct and considered response to being made 'His Majesty's' laureate. The second distinction was between himself-as-laureate and his fellow, non-laureated poets. While Tate was 'engaged in the Service of the Temple', others were making money from the immoral stage. His location, 'the Temple', was abstract and transcendental, serving the good of the nation as a whole; their location, 'the Stage', was a specific, partial location, in which certain poets selfishly made money, and theatregoers gained transitory pleasure. Lastly, Tate distinguished between himself and his predecessors. Dryden and Shadwell had been celebrated writers, known for their 'Performances of Wit and Diversion'. Tate claimed that he could not compete with them in this respect, and so intentionally took the laureateship in a different direction. If he could not 'justify' his appointment by literary greatness, he would do so by religious and moral utility.

It is likely, then, that the increasing identification between the laureates and the biannual odes was due in part to Shadwell's and Tate's volitions.

---

[94] Eg N. Tate, *Characters Of Vertue and Vice* (1691), sig. A2r; 'To The Reader' (unpaginated) in *An Elegy In Memory Of the Much Esteemed and Truly Worthy Ralph Marshall, Esq;* (1700); *Happy Recovery*, pp. 21–2; *A Congratulatory Poem to His Royal Highness Prince George of Denmark* (1708), p. 4.

[95] Tate, dedication to Davies, *Immortality*, sig. A4r–v.

Because of Shadwell's political inclinations and his career as a Whig polemicist, and Tate's belief in the importance of panegyric verse both for poetry in general and for his own personal distinction, it suited them to assume responsibility for the songs or odes that had already started to be performed on festive occasions at court. They thereby elevated the status of those odes and created an identification between them and the laureateship. Undoubtedly, this emergence of a function for the laureateship was also bound up with the contemporaneous formal developments in the office's positioning. From Nicholas Rowe's time onwards, the laureates would be more fixedly placed and more securely paid than had been the case in the later Stuart period, and would be tasked with a specific ceremonial function, which would often entail the publication of the laureate's text.

The laureateship therefore became formalized in line with the urge to present successive courts as courtly and legitimate, an urge felt and acted upon by various figures who had some connection to the court as an institution or some interest in the court as a concept. After 1688, this meant the assertion of a particular, godly kind of courtliness, and after 1714 it meant the formal affirmation of practices that seemed, in retrospect, to have been commonplace prior to the Hanoverian succession. The identification of the laureates with the odes was part of this, because it bolstered the ceremonial activities associated with the court and gave the court and laureate a clearer role vis-à-vis those audiences comprised within the town/world/public concepts. Moreover, the odes proved useful for propagating to the town/world/public a certain image of the court that was in keeping with each regime's wider ideology of legitimation. Yet the role of Shadwell and Tate in bringing this about flags up an issue that has not yet been explored in this chapter. So far, the pressures on successive regimes, and their court-centric responses to them, have mostly been discussed in macro terms, and not firmly related to the evidence under discussion. How those macro issues operated has been left unclear.

After all, though from a macro perspective it could be stated that the later Stuart court progressively defined its ceremonial life and cultural role, and that it did so by the formation and formalization of the laureateship, it is obviously the case that none of this was the result of a long-term plan. The institutional court was not a sentient being, and its history was marked by continual ruptures. It therefore remains to be explained how these macro changes operated, focusing on the pressures and opportunities that were presented to various individuals, and how those individuals' actions in response to those pressures and opportunities constituted the process of macro cause and effect. This chapter's argument is that monarchs and their court officials did play a part, but that developments in the court's institutional and conceptual role in cultural affairs were not simply a matter of policy, or leadership, from those individuals. Instead, the court-as-patron was a concept towards which various individuals worked and which various individuals sought to tap into, in pursuit of their own objectives.[96] The court's cultural role was defined as much by those whose interest it was to create that role from the outside as by those within; it was created by the very acts that sought to benefit from its creation.

This can be seen in the activities of all the persons discussed in this chapter. Firstly, it can be seen in the laureates themselves. In different ways, Dryden, Shadwell and Tate all felt that it was incumbent upon them to foster a relationship with the court, and to present themselves to their readers in terms of their court-centric identity. Dryden did this before his appointment in his *Astraea Redux* and *Annus Mirabilis* (long, ambitious poems celebrating Charles II, published for general retail), and in publishing *Secret-Love* as 'His [Charles's] Play'. Then, as laureate, he portrayed himself as serving the court by way of his disputational writings. Shadwell greeted the arrival of William and Mary with panegyrics, and continued to write panegyrics when laureate, as well as advertising his status as poet laureate. Tate had written the follow-up to Dryden's *Absalom and Achitophel*, and, like Shadwell, wrote panegyrics for monarchs; but when he was appointed laureate, he realized that he could not rival Dryden or Shadwell as a pre-eminently celebrated writer, and therefore defined his relationship with the court in a new way, presenting the court as a supremely moral and religious institution which he was serving through his moral, religious writings, and seeking to engross responsibility for the production of the biannual courtly odes. This self-presentation also identified him with the rhetoric of courtly reformation that was promulgated by William's, Mary's and Anne's regimes, further reinforcing the commercially advantageous notion that he enjoyed a firm association with the court, while also allowing him to make a better claim on the favour and finances of the court establishment. All three men (or their printers) made sure to designate them(selves) as 'servant to his majesty' or 'king's poet laureat' on their published title pages.[97]

---

[96] The importance of considering how individuals outside the court bought into monarchical culture and the monarchical image, and used it for their own ends and as a negotiation with the crown, has been stressed by historians working on eg the reigns of Georges I, II and III. L. Colley, *Britons: Forging the Nation 1707–1837*, revised edn (London, 2009), pp. 221–33; H. Smith, *Georgian Monarchy: Politics and Culture, 1714–1760* (Cambridge, 2006), pp. 123–4.

[97] Eg *The State of Innocence, and Fall of Man* (1677), in Dryden, *Works*, xii. 80, 'By John Dryden, Servant to His Majesty'; *The Scowrers* (1691), 'Written by Tho. Shadwell, Poet Laureat, and Historiographer-Royal'; *An Elegy on the Most Reverend Father in God* (1695),

Thus these writers found it advantageous to validate their own literary practice by reference to the court. In doing so, they validated the court's own cultural role, while also necessitating that they define what that role was. The diverse profusion of their own writings, and the breadth of their audiences, meant that it would not have been immediately obvious how they stood in relation to the court, and what role the court played in their writings; but by defining their own positions as poets laureate, they made it more likely that their salaries would actually be paid, and they emphasized to their readers the nature and importance of their status as prime beneficiaries of court patronage. Thus the macro situation, of a court under pressure to define itself by reference to its traditional ceremonial and cultural role, and having to do so in engagement with the town/world/public, operated through the micro activities of individual agents. Each poet laureate sought to take advantage of the traditional ideal of the court's ceremonial and cultural role, and to do so on the basis of his own former success with theatregoers and readers, while also attempting to use his position as court poet to increase that success. Collectively, they thereby affirmed the court's cultural role and its relationship with the town/world/public, causing the macro pressures to translate into a macro response from the non-sentient court: the creation and the increasing formalization of the office of poet laureate at the interface of court and town/world/public.

Aristocratic patrons played their part too. Whether these patrons were closely associated with the court or not, they were part of a system that was bound up with the institutional and conceptual court, in social and political terms as much as in cultural; without due regard for the crown, there could have been no due regard for those persons placed just below the crown in the social hierarchy, whose authority and status derived from the crown. The court also held out the best opportunities for aristocrats' own statuses and material benefits, encouraging them to have a strong presence there. It was therefore in their interests to bring 'their' writers to court, to argue their case at court and to encourage writers to work within the framework of courtly patronage, because by doing so they would increase their own prestige as patrons.[98] This is seen, for example, in Dryden's intercessions with various courtly and aristocratic figures to have his salary paid; and it is seen in the patronage activities of Dorset.

Indeed, Dorset provides the clearest evidence of what is being described here: the functioning of individual agency within macro developments.

'By N. Tate, Servant to His Majesty'; *The Kentish Worthies* (1701), 'By Mr. Tate. Poet – Laureat to His Majesty'.

[98] On the court's importance to the aristocracy, see H. Greig, *The Beau Monde: Fashionable Society in Georgian London* (Oxford, 2013), pp. 100–30.

Dorset contributed massively to the definition of the court's cultural role, and of the laureateship within it, by seeking to benefit himself, his favoured poets and his monarchs. Even his endeavours to benefit those poets and those monarchs were ultimately beneficial to him, since those poets gave him his reputation as a patron and those monarchs had appointed him lord chamberlain. To help his own finances, Dorset removed the patronal burden from himself to a higher sphere, the court. To burnish the idea of himself as a great patron, he brought the laureateship firmly within the lord chamberlain's department and gave it to two poets with whom he had good relationships. To help out Shadwell and Tate, he made sure that their position within the royal household structure would be more robust than Dryden's had been. And to buttress the Williamite regime against its enemies, he helped define the poet laureate as someone who would write on behalf of the court and contribute to its ceremonial life. Thus the wider changes of the time manifested in the pressures and opportunities that presented themselves to one individual, and, by responding to them, he contributed to those wider changes. Dorset, along with a number of individuals both within and without the court, thus created and defined the court's role as a cultural patron, and fixed the laureateship as a critical element within it.

Conclusion

The laureateship had gone from being an honorific, informal position which was not firmly placed in the institutional court structure, to one firmly under the lord chamberlain's auspices, grouped with the revels and ceremonies staff, and defined by its exclusive and comprehensive relationship with the writing of biannual odes. Looking onwards through the eighteenth century, this formalization of the laureateship into a functional manifestation of courtly patronage was to be advantageous, in that it gave the laureate a distinct role and prominence with the reading public and meant that his courtly position and payment of salary were fixed and regular, but was also to entail problems when competing ideas about the poetic vocation began gaining currency. As will be seen in the following chapters, the laureateship did not simply become obsolete or ridiculous, but certain observers would eventually describe it in this way.

The questions now are why these developments occurred and how they relate to the wider issues described at the start of this chapter. Essentially, they manifested the urge to formalize the cultural role and ceremonial life of successive courts, and to fix their position towards literature through the creation of a literary office. There was a pressure to do so even at the start of Charles II's reign, because the Civil Wars had ruptured his court from that of his predecessors, and that pressure was renewed with the start of each new reign, due to the repeated turbulences that marked each succession and due to the new questions about monarchical rule and monarchical legitimacy that each succession created. Moreover, as will be explored further in the next chapter, new activities of cultural production and consumption were emerging, conceptualized under the rubrics of town, world and public. At the start of Charles II's reign, a patronage network that centred on the court and reached its apex with the king still appeared to form the prevailing cultural framework. Poets pitched their work to well-placed patrons, and strove against each other for the attention of the royal family. Though it was the two town theatres of London that promised the best hopes of money, those two theatres were intimately connected with the court, and courtly patronage was a key factor in whether a playwright would succeed there, as well as offering occasional fixed pensions or employments to figures who initially made their name on the stage. Conceptually, the town overlapped with the world, and would come to be partially subsumed by the public, but its primary intimacy was with the court: it was 'the court end of London'.

Even at this point, though, the court's position needed to be determined more clearly and formally, as achieved through the institution of the laureateship; and the wider situation was changing, making such definition increasingly necessary. Just as audiences outside the court were becoming more willing and able to scrutinize the conduct of the monarch, so too were the finances and inclination necessary for cultural consumption burgeoning among them, tempting poets (and others) to seek fame and fortune with what would come to be conceived as the public. There was pressure on the court to respond to these developments. Its response ties in with the historiographical themes discussed above: formality, ceremony and representation. A laureateship was formed and formalized, held by a writer who had found success outside the court but who would now take a leading role in courtly ceremony, and who would represent the court to the town, the world and the public.

The last thing to stress is how important the laureateship was, and how successfully its position was fixed. The laureateship became important partly because it *was* so well defined and *did* have the potential for definition. If Elkanah Settle had occupied a rival courtly role to Dryden's in the 1670s, that role did not make much of a mark beyond the court's walls, and had no staying power in comparison to the laureateship; it faded away, while the laureateship became an ever more fixed and prominent part of the cultural landscape. Settle's putative role had neither a present definition, nor past or future potential; the laureateship, on the other hand, had a name and an official salary as well as a heritage that stretched back to ancient Greece and Rome (encompassing Chaucer, Spenser and Jonson), and was found capable of being put to new uses in response to new circumstances (first in the Exclusion Crisis, then with the biannual odes). The laureateship was something that writers, nobles, court officials and monarchs could fix onto. It thus served an important function in defining or even proving the court's cultural role, and it became more important and more fixed in this regard as the later Stuart period wore on. It was a distinct but flexible concept, hence its utility at the interface of the concepts of court and town/world/public. The office that had become fixed by 1715 was then to remain unchanged for a century, and was highly prominent and much discussed throughout that time.

Clearly, then, a successful position had been found for it. Acting inadvertently in concert, various individuals had defined the court's role as a cultural patron, and had worked out answers to the issues of formality, ceremony and representation, in which the newly (trans)formed office of poet laureate played a central part. This had occurred not just because there existed a traditional courtly ideal in which cultural patronage was a crucial element, which could be asserted by anyone associated with the institutional court, but because of the political scrutiny and commercial practices of audiences outside the court. The next chapter will examine those audiences.

2. Loyalty marketed: The works of the early Hanoverian laureates, 1700–30

The court does not much feature in scholarship on early eighteenth-century cultural production and consumption, and nor does the laureateship. This chapter seeks to redress the balance. It argues that while in this period the prevailing norms of cultural production certainly became more associated with the concepts of the town and the public, the court retained a significant role, coexisting and interacting with them. The laureateship is evidence of this. It was an office based conceptually in the court, proving the importance of the court as a space of cultural production and consumption, but it faced outwards to the town and the public.

The central issues of this chapter will be framed by a two-sided question. On one side is the question of what involvement contemporaries conceived the court as having in high culture, and particularly literature, in the early eighteenth century. It is generally supposed that culture underwent a great change between the early Stuart and early Hanoverian periods, going from 'courtly' to 'commercial'. Having been produced in a court-based system, by patronized artists, for an audience centred on the court, they came to be produced (according to this narrative) in a marketplace system, by independent professionals, for an increasingly middle-class public. The marketplace (and, to some extent, political parties) therefore supplanted the court, becoming central to the production and consumption of culture. In this chapter, this narrative of cultural transformation will be questioned.

On the flipside is the second question: what was the role and status of the laureateship in this period? In considering the extent to which culture was characterized by reference to the court, and the conceptual relationships between court, town and public, it is reciprocally necessary to consider the laureates' works, and how contemporaries perceived the laureates. This chapter will focus on the laureates Nicholas Rowe (appointed 1715, died 1718), Laurence Eusden (died 1730), and Colley Cibber (died 1757), especially the former. Whereas subsequent chapters will examine the Hanoverian laureate appointment processes, the public standing and the official odes of the laureates, this chapter will start from a thematically earlier position, focusing primarily on the works that the laureates wrote *before* becoming laureate. It was on the basis of their pre-laureate works that Rowe, Eusden and Cibber made their names, gained their success within the particular cultural geography that will be elaborated in this chapter and eventually earned their appointments to the laureateship. In a sense, their appointments signalled royal patronage over their entire oeuvres, and symbolically confirmed that they had spent their careers working to make themselves the most eminent and serviceable poets in the eyes of the supreme arbiter of such things, the monarch. It is therefore vital to analyse their pre-laureate writings.

Moreover, there is an important dynamic at play between these writers' pre-laureate reputations, mostly established under Queen Anne, and their appointments as laureate, under Georges I and II: the establishment of the Hanoverian regime on pre-existing foundations, and the relatively smooth rapprochement effected between the Hanoverian court and the metropolis. As argued previously, the court's location within the town, and within London, was highly significant; and the public that was being conceived at this time was London-centric, overlapping with and partially building upon the concept of the town. The most important geographical distinction in eighteenth-century society was between a court-centred metropolis on the one hand and the nation beyond London on the other, rather than between the court and the town, or the court and the public. This was perhaps never more evident than during George I's reign: the early Hanoverians nestled into London, only ever leaving it to return to Hanover, and Londoners embraced them. Hence this chapter's apparently oxymoronic title: the early Hanoverian laureates were those who had achieved success with the court and town during the later Stuart period.

In terms of the conceptual geography of culture, the approach here will be different to the previous chapter's. Chapter One focused on the conceptual spaces employed by Britons to understand the production and consumption of culture, how those spaces related to each other and where and why the laureateship was positioned among them. Here, the emphasis will fall rather on what those concepts denoted, and on how they determined meaning. Each concept – court, town, world, public, playhouse, coffeehouse and so on – was associated with its own particular group of people, who constituted the creators and especially the audience of cultural products. Each concept was also associated with its own particular set of values, as determined by its physical nature, the types of people who inhabited or constituted it and the types of activities engaged in by those people. In turn, these values determined the meaning of the cultural products that related to that concept, both as the values that motivated their creation and as the values by which they were judged. There was nothing rigidly consistent about any of this; as mentioned in the Introduction, the usage of these concepts was varying and undogmatic. It is informative rather for its extent and general patterns than for its intellectual sophistication. By studying how the poets laureate positioned their work, and the values by which they recommended it and expected that it would be judged, we can see more clearly how Britons of the early eighteenth century conceived of the cultural landscape and of the court's place within it.

Because of the emphases found in the scholarship with which it will engage, this chapter will focus on the concepts of the town and the public, but not the world, even though the latter was still regularly referred to by early eighteenth-century Britons. Here, until the final section, the world will be elided with the public, despite the relationship between the concepts of world and public being more complex than such an elision would suggest.

Courtly to commercial?

Nicholas Rowe (1674–1718), appointed poet laureate a year after George I's accession, was one of the most respected literary figures of his time, and several of his plays remained repertory staples throughout the eighteenth century. In current scholarship, he tends to be defined in three ways: as a professional playwright who was expertly catering to new, middle-class audiences; as a party-political figure, ardently serving the Whig cause; and as Shakespeare's first 'modern' editor.[1] In each of these respects, Rowe is depicted as characteristic of his period and of the triumph of the public as an entity. Because his literary work was produced in line with the prevailing trends of literary value, and excelled according to the criteria of those trends, he enjoyed critical esteem and popular success. To understand this three-pronged characterization, the way in which Rowe's society – the Britain of William III, Anne and George I – is understood by scholars must be looked at in more detail. It will be shown that scholars have often implied or stated a certain dynamic between spaces, audiences and values, which will feed into this chapter's analysis of the laureates' work.

The first salient point regards the state of drama around the turn of the eighteenth century. As outlined in Chapter One, when the playhouses

---

[1] Bernard, editor of the recent *Plays and Poems of Nicholas Rowe*, also emphasizes Rowe's translation of Lucan's *Pharsalia*, but that was (mostly) published after Rowe's death, and does not tend to feature in Rowean scholarship. S. Bernard, 'General introduction', in *The Early Plays*, ed. Bernard, Bullard and McTague, pp. 1–28, at pp. 2–4; Bullard and McTague, 'Introduction to *Step-Mother*, *Tamerlane*, and *Fair Penitent*', in *The Early Plays*, ed. Bernard, Bullard and McTague, pp. 35–55.

had been restored by Charles II, drama had been closely bound up with the court: the two theatre companies held royal patents and were named after the king and his brother; a court-based coterie had written many of the new plays in the 1660s and a lesser number thereafter; king and courtiers frequently visited the playhouses or had plays acted at court; playwrights and actors (such as Dryden and Nell Gwynn) often ended up with court connections; and literary patronage was centred on the king and a court-centric aristocracy. With this court-based patronage system thus dominating the production and consumption of drama, plays were written according to the interests and ideals of the king, aristocracy and upper gentry. Playwrights' appeal to this audience was an important factor in their success, and the highest form of success was conceptualized as having a play performed at court or gaining the king's personal approval. This meant a preponderance of heroic dramas, aristocratic wit-based comedies and refined, cosmopolitan plays translated from French and Spanish originals.[2]

By the end of the seventeenth century, however, drama was undergoing radical changes. Audience complexion was changing. There were an increasing number of people who had the inclination and resources to visit the theatre, and an increasing proportion of them were not gentry or courtly. Theatre thus became more orientated towards what scholars generally describe as 'the middling sort', 'the (new) middle class', 'the public' or 'the town'.[3] There is a certain overlap between these formulations: they comprise the notion of a literate, numerous, expanding set of persons who were fairly prosperous, but who were not aristocratic, and who were to have an increasing impact on all areas of public life over the course of the eighteenth century. But these terms also have more specific applications. The 'new' or 'rising' middle class of the eighteenth century has long been a truism of historiography and of literary and theatre scholarship, gesturing vaguely towards the modern, transhistorical definition of that class. Recent decades, however, have seen social historians attempting to recreate a

---

[2] S. L. Archer, 'The epistle dedicatory in Restoration drama', *Restoration and Eighteenth-Century Theatre Research*, x (1971), 8–13; R. D. Bevis, *English Drama: Restoration and Eighteenth Century, 1660–1789* (London, 1988), pp. 39–42, 71–90; B. Hammond, *Professional Imaginative Writing in England, 1670–1740: 'Hackney for Bread'* (Oxford, 1997), pp. 69–77; P. Kewes, *Authorship and Appropriation: Writing for the Stage in England, 1660–1710* (Oxford, 1998), pp. 36–7; H. Love, 'Restoration and early eighteenth-century drama', in *The Cambridge History of English Literature, 1660–1780*, ed. J. Richetti (Cambridge, 2005), pp. 109–31, at pp. 112–28; D. C. Payne, 'Patronage and the dramatic marketplace under Charles I and II', *The Yearbook of English Studies*, xxi (1991), 137–52, at pp. 138–40, 147–52.

[3] Bevis, *Drama*, pp. 67, 117–20; Hammond, *Hackney*, pp. 69–79, 249–51.

more historically exact middle class, often using the contemporary term, 'middling sort'.[4] They have defined this 'middling sort' as 'independent trading households', where 'trade' stretches from lower artisanship to well-educated professionalism, and where bureaucrats are permitted 'independence'.[5] And they have argued that this group was indeed on the rise, and was indeed exercising an ever more prevalent role in public life; its numbers, economic heft, social prominence, ideological character and political voice were inexorably gaining ground, especially in London. Crucial to its identity and power was its relationship with commerce: the rise of the middling sort was a phenomenon that was symbiotic with the commercialization of Britain.[6]

As for 'the public' and especially 'the town', they are both often held to contain significant gentry elements; the gentry, although numerically small, exercised a disproportionate influence over taste and fashion.[7] But 'the public' had a fundamentally middle-class identity, while 'the town' held a mixture of social classes: there the middle class confidently rubbed shoulders with the upper.[8] Especially in cultural matters, the basic novelty and substance of 'public' and 'town' were that they were an impersonal mass of paying consumers. As Cibber put it, ''Tis dangerous to Quarrel with a whole Town … their Will is Law, and 'tis but reasonable it shou'd be so, since they pay for their Power.'[9] Moreover, the lower gentry were

---

[4] Eg J. Barry, 'Consumers' passions: The middle class in eighteenth-century England', *The Historical Journal*, xxxiv (1991), 207–16; *The Middling Sort of People: Culture, Society and Politics in England, 1550–1800*, ed. J. Barry and C. Brooks (Basingstoke, 1994); P. Borsay, *The English Urban Renaissance: Culture and Society in the Provincial Town, 1660–1770* (Oxford, 1989); P. Earle, *The Making of the English Middle Class: Business, Society and Family Life in London 1660–1730* (London, 1989); M. R. Hunt, *The Middling Sort: Commerce, Gender, and the Family in England, 1680–1780* (Berkeley, Calif., 1996); H. Mui and L. H. Mui, *Shops and Shopkeeping in Eighteenth-Century England* (London, 1989); L. Weatherill, *Consumer Behaviour and Material Culture in Britain 1660–1760* (London, 1988).

[5] J. Barry, 'Introduction', in *Middling Sort*, ed. Barry and Brooks, pp. 1–27, at pp. 2–3; S. D'Cruze, 'The middling sort in eighteenth-century Colchester: Independence, social relations and the community broker', in *Middling Sort*, ed. Barry and Brooks, pp. 181–207, at pp. 181–3.

[6] Barry, 'Introduction', p. 3; Hunt, *Middling Sort*, pp. 1, 6, 15–20; J. H. Plumb, 'Commercialization and society', in *The Birth of a Consumer Society: The Commercialization of Eighteenth-Century England*, ed. N. McKendrick, J. Brewer and J. H. Plumb (London, 1983; first published 1982), pp. 263–334, at p. 284.

[7] Barry, 'Introduction', p. 19; Hunt, *Middling Sort*, p. 16.

[8] For discussion of this particular point, and a partial refutation, see H. Greig, *The Beau Monde: Fashionable Society in Georgian London* (Oxford, 2013), pp. 11, 63–94.

[9] Cibber, *Woman's Wit* (1697), sig. A2r.

not very distinct from the upper middling sort, and indeed are sometimes still included in broad definitions of an eighteenth-century middle class, while the richest members of the middling sort rivalled the peerage for wealth.[10] Finally, whatever else might be said about these formulations, it is usually the case that scholars hold them in contradistinction to the court.[11] Lawrence Klein (though not inclined to make much of the middle class) perhaps put the case most dogmatically, arguing that a town or public based in coffeehouses developed an ideology of politeness as part of 'the larger process' by which a 'cultural regime centred on a court was transmuted into a post-courtly one'.[12] Nor was this accidental; according to Klein, Whig writers, especially Joseph Addison, were intentionally undermining the court (and church), and intentionally replacing them with coffeehouses in particular and the town in general as spaces of cultural authority.

Because theatre was now financed, enjoyed and criticized by this new audience, its values changed accordingly. Plays became more sentimental, feminine, didactic and moralizing; less cynical and witty; looser in genre; more reflective of contemporary, middle-class life. Although determinations of the genres of this period are problematic, it is instructive to note some of the designations that have sometimes been employed: sentimental comedy, crying comedy, humane comedy, reform comedy, domestic tragedy, she-tragedy. Meanwhile, heroic drama was falling into abeyance by the turn of the century (albeit with occasional revivals later on).[13]

There is much that might be objected to in these generalizations. Theatre scholars, it might be argued, have drawn too simplistic a connection between the characteristics of eighteenth-century drama and the supposed values of a supposedly middle-class audience. However, recent scholarship has generally served to shore up this picture, and to bestow evidential rigour on what were once vague assumptions. Historians of the middle class have

---

[10] Hunt, *Middling Sort*, pp. 15–20.

[11] R. O. Bucholz, *The Augustan Court: Queen Anne and the Decline of Court Culture* (Stanford, Calif., 1993), p. 242; M. Haslett, *Pope to Burney, 1714–1779: Scriblerians to Bluestockings* (London, 2003), pp. 1–25, 50–4, 86; M. Knights, *Representation and Misrepresentation in Later Stuart Britain: Partisanship and Political Culture* (Oxford, 2005), p. 273; N. McKendrick, 'Commercialization and the economy', in *Consumer Society*, ed. McKendrick, Brewer and Plumb, pp. 7–194 (p. 43).

[12] L. E. Klein, 'Coffeehouse civility, 1660–1714: An aspect of post-courtly culture in England', *Huntington Library Quarterly*, lix (1997), 30–51, at pp. 44–51 (p. 50 for quotation).

[13] Bevis, *Drama*, pp. 117–20, 123, 129–33, 154–61; Hammond, *Hackney*, pp. 105–25, 144; R. D. Hume, *Henry Fielding and the London Theatre, 1728–1737* (Oxford, 1988), p. 20; R. D. Hume, 'Drama and theatre in the mid and later eighteenth century', in *The Cambridge History of English Literature, 1660–1780*, ed. J. Richetti (Cambridge, 2005), pp. 323–4, 328; H. Koon, *Colley Cibber: A Biography* (Kentucky, 1986), pp. 24–9, 178; Love, 'Drama' pp. 112–28.

found that this group did indeed generate and follow a distinct structure of values, and that these values broadly correlate with the tendencies identified by theatre scholars in later Stuart and early Hanoverian drama.[14] Various reasons have been advanced to explain this middle-class attitude. Hunt suggests that there was a 'middling urge to understand and better control the social world in which commerce was conducted',[15] and that ideals of morality, virtue, sociability and sympathy were manifestations of this 'urge'; they would bring stability and trust to a commercial world that had a short supply of both. Similarly, Brewer observed that the middle class faced problems of economic volatility and debt, and sought to deal with them by placing a premium on certain relevant personal qualities. It was important to show reliability, candour, affability, generosity, politeness and civility, and to encourage these qualities in others.[16] Middle-class persons thus had material reasons to care about other middle-class persons and to show sympathy towards them, as well as to demonstrate their own feelings, but within careful constraints of morality and politeness.

Jonathan Barry, meanwhile, pointed out that the middle-class life cycle was more variable than that of the higher and lower social groups, in terms of both the changes that would occur over an individual life span and the differences between individual middle-class persons' experiences. This, he argued, gave the middle class a strong sense of the importance of personal qualities, which would be crucial in determining each person's fortunes. Success or failure was dependent on 'the classic virtues'. 'These moral evaluations thus came to play a major part in the self-classification of the middling sort,' being used both to distinguish this group from those above and below it, and to distinguish individuals within the group.[17] It might also be argued (although Barry did not extend his observation this far) that this concern with stereotypically middle-class qualities, and with their importance in determining an individual's fortunes, would have fuelled a middle-class interest in drama based on domestic, relatable, middle-class family stories. Whether or not these reasons are found convincing, the important point here is that the middle class were indeed committed to values of politeness, sociability, virtue, morality, domesticity and sentiment.

[14] Barry, 'Introduction', pp. 4–18; J. Barry, 'Bourgeois collectivism? Urban association and the middling sort', in *The Middling Sort of People*, ed. Barry and Brooks, pp. 84–112, at pp. 95–103; J. Brewer, 'Commercialization and politics', in *Consumer Society*, ed. McKendrick, Brewer and Plumb, pp. 195–262, at pp. 214–15, 217, 229–30; Hunt, *Middling Sort*, pp. 14, 16, 101–24; Plumb, 'Commercialization and society', p. 269.

[15] Hunt, *Middling Sort*, pp. 102 (for quotation), 121.

[16] Brewer, 'Commercialization and politics', pp. 214–15, 229–30.

[17] Barry, 'Introduction', pp. 14–16.

It seems fair, then, that theatre scholars have linked the changes they see in drama of the late seventeenth and early eighteenth centuries with the increasingly middle-class character of audiences.[18]

The wider literary scene was changing, too. Because of the expansion of a literate, middle-class reading public, who were confident enough to want to have their voice heard and had sufficient leisure time to read imaginative writing, literature was no longer produced by the economic and ideological impetus of a patronizing court and aristocracy, but by that of this new readership. It was therefore produced and consumed in a literary marketplace.[19] Again, this had far-reaching ramifications for the kind of literature that was produced. When literature had been produced for (and to some extent by) a court-based coterie, dramatic forms had been the most highly valued. Of the non-dramatic forms, the most heavily practised and valued had been harsh satire and fulsome panegyric.[20] Now, both forms were subject to a growing number of objections: the panegyric was sometimes considered too obsequious, the satire too rude.[21] The preferred writing was softer, politer and more accessible; it was based on contemporary life. Humble prose also became more commercially viable and (in some instances, especially as the early eighteenth century wore on) more respectable: for example, *The Spectator* and Samuel Richardson's novels.[22] Drama did not suffer much in absolute terms; even the two most high-profile writers of the eighteenth century, Pope and Johnson, harboured ambitions of being a playwright at certain points in their careers.[23] But

[18] For a good, recent exploration of this topic, see A. E. Hernandez, *The Making of British Bourgeois Tragedy: Modernity and the Art of Ordinary Suffering* (Oxford, 2019). However, Hernandez focuses on the half-century after Rowe's death, and explicitly discounts Rowe's she-tragedies from the genre of bourgeois tragedy (p. 10).

[19] Brewer, *Pleasures*, pp. 1–4, 7–11, 15–71; Hammond, *Hackney*, pp. 2–6, 13, 69–77, 104–44, 249–51; Haslett, *Pope to Burney*, pp. 1–25, 50–4; J. P. Hunter, 'Political, satirical, didactic and lyric poetry (1): From the Restoration to the death of Pope', in *English Literature, 1660–1780*, ed. Richetti, pp. 160–208, at pp. 202–4.

[20] Hunter, 'Restoration to Pope', pp. 183–7.

[21] J. Butt, *The Mid-Eighteenth Century*, ed. G. Carnall (Oxford, 1979), pp. 114–24; Hunter, 'Restoration to Pope', pp. 202–4; A. Marshall, 'Satire', in *The Oxford Handbook of British Poetry, 1660–1800*, ed. Lynch (Oxford, 2016), pp. 495–509, at pp. 495–99.

[22] T. C. W. Blanning, *The Culture of Power and the Power of Culture: Old Regime Europe 1660–1789* (Oxford, 2002), pp. 147–8; Brewer, *Pleasures*, pp. 89–107; Hammond, *Hackney*, pp. 69–79, 104–44, 178–91, 249–51, 266–75; J. Keith, 'Lyric', in *British Poetry, 1660–1800*, ed. Lynch, pp. 579–95, at pp. 580–2; W. B. Warner, 'Novels on the market', in *English Literature, 1660–1780*, ed. Richetti, pp. 87–105, at pp. 87–92, 100–5.

[23] For the assertion of theatre's continuing cultural importance throughout the 18th century in recent scholarship, see B. Orr, *British Enlightenment Theatre: Dramatizing*

literary ambition was no longer as heavily concentrated upon the stage as it had been during the Restoration period, and the careers of Pope and Johnson flag up the point that a lessening proportion of high-profile writers wrote primarily for the stage.[24]

For all the sentiment, mildness and politeness of this period, however, these were also the years of 'Rage of Party'. Undoubtedly, this 'Rage' was a more restrained affair than had been the Exclusion Crisis and Tory Reaction. Under Charles II, those who had lost the political game had sometimes paid with their lives. By the time of Anne's reign, this was no longer the case. Nevertheless, the political nation was split into two partisan camps.[25] Party needs and party principles fuelled the production and consumption of literature. Parties also served to heighten, but to some extent fragment, the value accorded to literary works. It was widely recognized by contemporaries that any work that came evidently from one side would be hyperbolically lauded by its sympathizers and hyperbolically damned by its opponents. Yet a work that could bridge the gap between the parties, like Addison's *Cato*, was all the more valued as a result.[26]

The final salient point to make about early eighteenth-century society is that it saw a slowly increasing interest in the works of the British past. The middle-class public was patriotic, and was interested in an incipient national canon. Milton came of age with Addison's *Spectator* essays; Spenser enjoyed a minor boost in popularity, foreshadowing his later triumphs; and Shakespeare's reputation was, for the first time, elevated beyond that of any other modern writer. Pope wrote imitations of Waller, Cowley, Spenser and even Chaucer; Prior had great success with a poem in Spenserian stanzas (1706). The first two decades of the eighteenth century were still very different to the 1760s and 1770s in terms of appreciation of the nation's literary heritage, but it was nonetheless the case that a firm notion of that heritage was being formed, and that it was much to a contemporary writer's advantage to craft some sort of personal relationship with it.[27]

Difference (Cambridge, 2020), p. 14.

[24] Spence, *Observations*, i. 235, at p. 103; Hammond, *Hackney*, pp. 48–50; P. Rogers, 'Samuel Johnson', *ODNB*; E. M. McGirr, *Partial Histories: A Reappraisal of Colley Cibber* (London, 2016), pp. 83–6; D. Nokes, 'John Gay', *ODNB*.

[25] T. Harris, *Politics Under the Later Stuarts: Party Conflict in a Divided Society 1660–1715* (London, 1993); G. Holmes, *British Politics in the Age of Anne*, 2nd edn (London, 1987); Knights, *Representation*, pp. 3–10, 18–25.

[26] Knights, *Representation*, pp. 354–60.

[27] Brewer, *Pleasures*, pp. 33–54, 371–82; Butt, *Mid-Eighteenth Century*, pp. 4–6, 58–78, 94–114; A. Rounce, 'Scholarship', in *British Poetry, 1660–1800*, ed. Lynch, pp. 685–700;

This was the literary landscape of the early eighteenth century as it generally appears in the relevant scholarship. The town and public had superseded the court. Those persons who constituted the town and public wanted literature in keeping with their own values. The activities through which they produced and consumed literature formed a new commercial system, replacing the old courtly-patronage system. Writers, readers and theatregoers, in conceptualizing the town as the forum for cultural products and the public as the consumers of those products, created and judged literary works by reference to these values. And this was the context in which Rowe and Cibber, arguably the two most successful and genre-defining playwrights of the early eighteenth century, were working. They understood the forum, audience and values that were dominant, they positioned their work adroitly and their writings chimed well with the values in question. Thus they enjoyed critical and popular success.

Meanwhile, the court is generally assumed to have been insignificant.[28] It is held that, at the Hanoverian succession, the newly triumphant Whigs gave the laureateship to Rowe as a reward for his commercial success and party-political service, bypassing a king who, after all, did not even understand English. But the laurel (in this interpretation) was not very material to Rowe's standing at the time or to later scholarly assessments of him. It was a small additional emolument for an inveterate place-seeker. The works that he produced in fulfilment of its function – the biannual panegyrical odes – were ignored by contemporaries because they were anachronistic; they were not characteristic of or valued by his age in the way that his plays (and his Shakespeare edition) were.[29]

As mentioned in the Introduction, however, there is a body of scholarship that strikes a different note. Historians such as Hannah Smith and literary scholars such as Dustin Griffin have sought not to overturn the novel, commercial and public characterization of the early eighteenth century, but rather to show both the persistence and adaptability of traditional

---

R. Terry, *Poetry and the Making of the English Literary Past: 1660–1781* (Oxford, 2001), pp. 2–8, 287–323; H. D. Weinbrot, *Britannia's Issue: the Rise of British Literature from Dryden to Ossian* (Cambridge, 1994), pp. 115–41; H. Wilkinson, *Edmund Spenser and the Eighteenth-Century Book* (Cambridge, 2017).

[28] Brewer, *Pleasures*, pp. 15–33, 137–9; Bucholz, *Augustan Court*, pp. 11, 228–42; Hammond, *Hackney*, pp. 69–79.

[29] For the idea that neglect (at best) or scorn (at worst) constituted the invariable reception of laureate odes, and the public attitude towards the laureateship, from Shadwell's appointment to Pye's death, see Introduction and ch. 5, but also Broadus, *Laureateship*, pp. 84–8, 102–3 (for Rowe), 113, 119, 123, 133–5, 144–5, 154–63.

practices, and to reintegrate the court. This chapter will do likewise. It will do so by analysing how Rowe, and then Eusden and Cibber, positioned their work, and what values their work embodied and appealed to for success. This analysis will show that the three men did indeed write commercially, position their work within the town and before the public, and seek to succeed by the values relevant to this positioning. At the same time, though, they were solicitous to place their work in the court, for the attention and patronage of royal, aristocratic and other courtly figures. More significantly still, they sometimes envisaged their courtly and non-courtly audiences as overlapping, and sometimes as symbiotic, but rarely as rivals. By appealing to the court, they hoped to appeal to the town and public; by appealing to the town and public, they hoped to appeal to the court. Again, the town's situation as 'the court end of London' becomes relevant; again, the public's centring on a London world comprising both court and town becomes clear.

Rowe's plays as commercial

Rowe's plays (which are all tragedies, except for the never-revived *Biter*) are justly understood as being 'sentimental', 'domestic', 'moralizing' and 'she-tragedies'. They were produced specifically for consumption by the new kinds of audience delineated above, whose principles and practices of consumption they ably serviced. This is best seen in Rowe's first play, *The Ambitious Step-Mother* (1701). In its dedication, Rowe explained his theory of tragedy. Noting that 'Terror and Pity are laid down for the Ends of Tragedy' by Aristotle, Rowe pronounced his inclination towards the latter. The audience 'should … always Conclude and go away with Pity, a sort of regret proceeding from good nature, which, tho an uneasiness, is not always disagreeable, to the person who feels it. It was this passion that the famous Mr *Otway* succeeded so well in touching, and must and will at all times affect people, who have any tenderness or humanity.'[30] Thus he recast Aristotelian tragedy in a mould that was determined by, on the one hand, an audience of 'tenderness' and 'humanity', and, on the other, by recent English practice, exemplified by Thomas Otway. Pity stemmed from, and satisfyingly reminded viewers of, their 'good nature'; it was even a sort of pleasure, being 'not always disagreeable'.

---

[30] Rowe, *The Ambitious Step-Mother* (1701), sig. A3r.

The prologue (which followed in the printed work, but of course would have initiated the performative experience) gave such ideas in a more artful, less theoretical form.[31] It began:

> If Dying Lovers yet deserve a Tear,
> If a sad story of a Maids despair,
> Yet move Compassion in the pitying fair,
> This day the Poet does his Art employ,
> The soft accesses of your Souls to try.[32]

In these opening lines – the consonants of which imparted a soft, delicate air – the play was configured around tears, sadness, compassion and pity. The female element was heavily emphasized: Rowe appealed to the 'pitying fair' in the audience, and emphasized 'a Maids despair'. The titular subject of the play – *The Ambitious Step-Mother* – became immediately sidelined. She could not function as an object of pity or female identification, and therefore had to give way to 'Dying Lovers' and despairing maids.

The relationship between playwright and audience was set out as an emotive, intimate one. The 'Art' of the 'Poet' was 'The soft accesses of your Souls to try'. Rowe thus envisioned the playwright's task as touching his audience's sensibilities. In so doing, he would 'try' – and potentially confirm – both his and their capacities for passionate sensitivity. Tragedy was thus a profoundly moving and open experience, in which both playwright and audience bared their souls to each other, and, ideally, came away confirmed in their humanity. The prologue continued in the same vein, referencing Otway and 'humane nature' again, and equating 'Grief', particularly that of 'the weeping fair', with 'niceness of Taste' and 'the Tragick Muse'. Finally, Rowe made a rousing demand: 'Assert, ye fair ones, who in Judgment sit,/Your Ancient Empire over Love and Wit;/Reform our Sense, and teach the men t'Obey.'[33] Even allowing for

---

[31] Prologues were often not written by the playwrights themselves. There is no evidence that this was the case here, although Rowe is known to have sometimes had prologues or epilogues written for him by others (contrary to Johnson's statement in his biography of Rowe that it was 'remarkable that his [Rowe's] prologues and epilogues are all his own, though he sometimes supplied others'). Even if this prologue was not written by Rowe, it is nonetheless significant, because it was presumably endorsed by Rowe and formed an essential part of the read and performed experience. S. Johnson, 'Rowe', in *The Lives of the Poets*, ed. J. H. Middendorf (3 vols, New Haven, Conn., 2010), ii. 576–95, at p. 584. 'Nicholas Rowe to Alexander Pope, 1713', and editorial note by George Sherburn, *Electronic Enlightenment Scholarly Edition of Correspondence*. On prologues and epilogues, C. Wall, 'Poems on the stage', in *British Poetry, 1660–1800*, ed. Lynch, pp. 23–39, at pp. 24–7.

[32] Rowe, *Ambitious Step-Mother*, sig. A6r.

[33] Rowe, *Ambitious Step-Mother*, sig. A6r–v.

the tongue-in-cheek tendencies of eighteenth-century prologues, it is clear that Rowe here presented a theory of tragedy that emphasized the humane, the sentimental and the feminine.

While *Step-Mother* concerned high politics in an eastern kingdom, Rowe's later plays evinced a desire to bring the action ever closer to contemporary life. The cardinal quotations here are from *The Fair Penitent* (1703), in the prologue to which Rowe promised that he would not give the audience a tale of kings and queens, because such tales took place in 'a higher Sphere./ We ne'er can pity what we ne'er can share.' Therefore, 'an humbler Theme our Author chose,/A melancholy Tale of private Woes'. Here, 'you shall meet with Sorrows like your own'.[34] The play itself was an adaptation of Philip Massinger's *The Fatal Dowry* (published 1632), but with Massinger's emphasis on the bridegroom transferred to the eponymous 'penitent' bride. Eighteenth-century audiences viewed her as a realistic, relatable female character, whose story aroused both pity (in her favour) and moral considerations (at her expense).[35]

After *The Fair Penitent*, Rowe actually strayed back towards 'higher Sphere[s]'; but he always tried to make his characters relatable, domestic and relevant to modern concerns. For example, *Ulysses* (1706) began with a jaunty prologue in the 'mock-epic' style that Brean Hammond has identified as being characteristic of this period. According to Hammond, writers of the late seventeenth and early eighteenth centuries, having been brought up on the classics and desirous of writing epics, found themselves pulled towards contemporary, realistic and middle-class life by their audiences. Thus a 'credibility gap' opened up between the classical and the contemporary urges. Writers found that the only way to bridge this gap (and, at the same time, a brilliant way of achieving comic effect) was by developing a 'mock-epic' style in which modern life and classical literature were ironically, jarringly melded.[36] Rowe's *Ulysses* prologue was a manifestation of this phenomenon. It began, 'A Lady, who, for Twenty Years, withstood/The Pressing Instances of Flesh and Blood' was 'Left at ripe Eighteen' by her husband, Ulysses, who had gone to 'Battel for a Harlot at *Troy* Town'. Penelope (the 'Lady') was inundated with 'fresh Lovers … Much such as now a-days are *Cupid's* Tools,/Some Men of Wit, but the most part were Fools./They sent her *Billets doux,* and Presents many,/Of ancient Tea and *Thericlean* China.' Happily, though, Penelope was 'Coxcomb

[34] N. Rowe, *The Fair Penitent* (1703), sig. a2r.

[35] For reception, see below.

[36] Hammond, *Hackney*, pp. 105–44.

Proof'.[37] Then, Rowe abruptly abandoned this tongue-in-cheek jauntiness so typical of contemporary prologues, and stated, in all seriousness, that 'Our *English* Wives shall prove this Story true', by remaining chaste while their husbands fought and died abroad.[38] Rowe ended with a celebration of British heroism, on show at that time in the War of the Spanish Succession, and exhorted 'Ye beauteous Nymphs': 'with open Arms prepare/To meet the Warriors, and reward their Care'.[39]

The play itself confirmed this switch to seriousness. Ulysses was modern in both a realistic and an exemplary sense. He became agitated at the thought that Penelope might be cheating on him, and at one point even cursed her infidelity, before being reproved by his friends for his overreaction.[40] But he was also chaste, pious and virtuous; it was these qualities, rather than his classically heroic prowess, that most distinguished him from the villainous suitors, and that guaranteed his eventual success. Whereas the suitors were constantly 'Immerst in Riot, and defying/The Gods as Fables',[41] Ulysses was restrained and good, and made repeated appeals to the gods.[42] Eventually, he was reunited with Penelope. Having warmed up his audience with a typically mock-heroic prologue, Rowe therefore revealed his prevailing inclinations even before that prologue was finished, and carried them sombrely through the rest of the play. Distant and classical subjects could indeed be made incongruous by comparing them to modern life; but that incongruity was neither necessary nor urgent. For Rowe, the *Ulysses* story was affective, moral and relevant. Ulysses and Penelope could easily function as a realistic couple, sharing the concerns and experiences of their audience, and giving an ideal for modern domesticity.

Indeed, although Rowe's subsequent plays all concerned royal subjects, his emphases remained domestic, sentimental and modern. The plays were uniformly geared towards questions of love and lust. Questions of state and narratives of heroism were present, but marginal. However much the plays initially seemed to be about politics and principles, they always turned out to be convoluted love affairs. The various romantic and sexual desires of each character were (almost always) the sole agents and motivators of the plot and (almost) the sole concern of the dialogue. *The Royal Convert* (1708) was on one level an allegory in favour of Protestantism and the 1707 Union

[37] N. Rowe, *Ulysses* (1706), sig. A3r.

[38] Rowe, *Ulysses*, sig. A3r.

[39] Rowe, *Ulysses*, sig. A3v.

[40] Rowe, *Ulysses*, pp. 31–2.

[41] Rowe, *Ulysses*, p. 41.

[42] Rowe, *Ulysses*, p. 62.

between England and Scotland; yet the play was mostly concerned with the various personal loves and lusts of each character. As the despairing Seofrid put it: 'What is the boasted Majesty of Kings,/Their Godlike Greatness, if their Fate depends/Upon that meanest of their Passions, Love?'[43]

In many respects, Rowe was following the model made definitive by Pierre Corneille: a plot confined by the three dramatic unities; each character 'loving' and/or 'loved by' another character; some presiding issue of politics and/or government; that presiding issue brought into tension with, or subjected to the test of, or riven by the demands of, *amour*.[44] In *The Royal Convert*, the (female) character Rodogune even started shrieking about her 'injur'd Glory',[45] calling to mind the 'gloire' tediously insisted upon by the characters in such Corneille plays as *Le Cid*. But whereas Corneille always at least intended love to be a subordinate issue, and imagined himself to be exploring questions of state, Rowe's plays were unashamed in placing love at the forefront. Rowe's female characters were also stronger, and far more vocal about female oppression, than Corneille's. The injuredly glorious Rodogune, for example, ranted at some length about the sufferings of women and the unfairness of male dominance.[46] She hoped one day for women to be in charge, and to subdue and oppress men; but she herself actually spent most of the play controlling and oppressing two of the other characters, Aribert (a man) and Ethelinda (a woman). In *Jane Shore*, the titular character herself (who, unlike Rodogune, was an object of sympathy) made a similar complaint, although without Rodogune's hopes of revenge.[47] Neither complaint was refuted by any of the other characters. Indeed, Shore's complaint was given the extra impact of being allowed to close out the play's first act. In Rowe's hands, then, the neoclassical model of tragedy was adapted to become modern and affective. Whereas Corneille was concerned with creating poetic masterpieces, and wrote in a theatrical context dominated more overtly by the court, Rowe was giving his middle-class, paying audiences a spectacle of relevance and sentiment.

Party-political matters loom larger in Rowean scholarship than do elaborations of his middle-class sentimentality, but the latter actuates the plays far more than does the former.[48] As a corrective against this tendency,

---

[43] N. Rowe, *The Royal Convert* (1708), p. 22.

[44] P. Gaillard, 'Introduction', in P. Corneille, *Horace*, ed. P. Gaillard (Paris, 1976), pp. 3–20, at p. 10.

[45] Rowe, *The Royal Convert*, p. 27.

[46] Rowe, *The Royal Convert*, p. 55.

[47] Rowe, *The Tragedy of Jane Shore* (1714), pp. 11–12.

[48] R. Bullard and J. McTague, 'Introduction to *The Ambitious Step-Mother*, *Tamerlane*, and

only a brief analysis of partisan politics will be given here; a more searching interrogation of the nature of political parties will be given in Chapter Three. For the most part, Rowe's plays did not contain political messages and references, and their overall designs were not determined by political intentions. However, Rowe may have hoped that their sentimentality, politeness and conscious modernity, and the fact that they were written by a known Whig, would in some way have advanced the party cause.[49] Several of his plays, meanwhile, did carry scattered political references. *Jane Shore* seemingly contained some overtly partisan lines, although these, and the overall design of the play itself, have been debated.[50] *The Royal Convert* contained an overt celebration of the 1707 Act of Union and, in its narrative, offered a more extended endorsement of that Act, showing Saxons and Britons joining together.[51] *Jane Gray* was an explicit and thoroughgoing attack on Jacobites and popery.[52] Rowe's second play, *Tamerlane*, was a celebration of William III, mainly depicting him in conflict with Louis XIV, but also casting attendant invective on William's domestic malcontents, and making William the mouthpiece of Whiggish religious doctrine. The dedication, prologue and epilogue of *Tamerlane* set out these applications, but were hardly necessary to reveal so blatant a parallel.[53] It seems, then, to have been Rowe's general practice to make his political references unmissable. He was not subtle in either *Tamerlane*, *The Royal Convert* or *Jane Gray*. This fact renders unlikely the more speculative assertions of scholars on his other plays. If Rowe had wished to make them politically relevant, the evidence would probably not be hard to find.[54]

The Fair Penitent', in *The Plays and Poems of Nicholas Rowe*: i, *The Early Plays*, ed. S. Bernard, R. Bullard and J. McTague (Abingdon, 2016); J. DeRitter, '"Wonder not, princely Gloster, at the notice this paper brings you": Women, writing, and politics in Rowe's *Jane Shore*', *Comparative Drama*, xxxi (1997), 86–104; P. Kewes, '"The state is out of tune": Nicholas Rowe's *Jane Shore* and the succession crisis of 1713–14', *Huntington Library Quarterly*, lxiv (2001), 283–308; B. Wilson, 'Jane Shore and the Jacobites: Nicholas Rowe, the pretender, and the national she-tragedy', *ELH*, lxxii (2005), 823–43.

[49] For more on these ideas, discussed in connection with other contemporary Whig writers, see L. E. Klein, 'Liberty, manners, and politeness in early eighteenth-century England', *The Historical Journal*, xxxii (1989), 583–605, at pp. 584–7, 603–5; Klein, 'Coffeehouse civility', pp. 44–51; A. Williams, *Poetry and the Creation of a Whig Literary Culture 1681–1714* (Oxford, 2005), pp. 15, 159–63, 204–27, 239–40.

[50] DeRitter, 'Politics in *Jane Shore*'; Kewes, '*Jane Shore* and the succession crisis'; Wilson, '*Jane Shore* and the Jacobites'.

[51] Rowe, *The Royal Convert*, pp. 55–6.

[52] Eg Rowe, *The Tragedy of the Lady Jane Gray* (1715), pp. 2, 5, 33–4.

[53] Rowe, *Tamerlane* (1702), dedication (initially unpaginated, then sig. b2r–v).

[54] For discussion of the difficulties and complexities of looking for political content in

In fact, when Rowe addressed the issues of parties directly, he evinced a commonplace strain of distaste for them.[55] In the dedication to his 1714 *Tragedies*, Rowe complained that parties were selfish, factional groups, pursuing their own interests at the expense of the nation's. Parties worked for the 'Subversion of the established Government', and were 'Enemies' of George I, Protestantism and 'our Libertys'. Against this, Rowe contrasted the 'honest Man, and … good Subject', who would write and act 'in Defence of the Legal Constitution'.[56] On a related note, Rowe claimed that his own plays furthered the cause of virtue and morality, which was linked to the cause of Protestantism, Hanoverianism and liberty. This was most evident in *Jane Gray*, where Jane was idealized as a character (pious, virtuous, meek, self-sacrificing) to represent the purity and goodness of the cause she represented (the Protestant succession). By making his audience love and feel pity for Jane, Rowe believed that he was inculcating Whiggish principles in the nation, and thus assisting the patriotic causes of George I, Protestantism and liberty. Thus in his final play, the sentimental side of Rowe's practice became synonymous with the partisan side. But again, Rowe did not see himself as making a 'party' argument. In fact, by using Lady Jane Grey, he was emphasizing the supposedly patriotic and non-partisan nature of his principles. Jane was a historical figure who had lived long before Whiggism and Toryism; a spotless and celebrated Protestant heroine; a founding figure in Anglican mythology; an innocent young girl, rather than an intellectual or controversialist; she was also wedded to an Englishman, unlike her successor, whose marriage left England at Spain's mercy. Rowe was thus making Whiggism synonymous with national identity.

Of course, Rowe's anti-party analysis would have been recognized by contemporaries as Whiggish.[57] Although his distaste for parties was undoubtedly genuine, it was this genuine distaste that gave his argument force. He was claiming that Whiggism was synonymous with the national interest, and so could not be considered partisan, whereas Jacobites (and indeed all Tories, insofar as they could be tarred with the same brush) represented a partial, partisan and unpatriotic interest. At the same time, this partisan/anti-partisan attitude is characteristic of a culture that was

---

18th-century plays, see Hume, *Fielding Theatre*, pp. 77–86.

[55] On early 18th-century distaste of parties, *The Spectator* 125, in *The Spectator*, ed. D. F. Bond (5 vols, Oxford, 1965), i. 509–10; I. Kramnick, *Bolingbroke and His Circle: The Politics of Nostalgia in the Age of Walpole* (London, 1968), pp. 26–32, 153–9.

[56] Dedication to Rowe's *Tragedies* (1714), reprinted in Rowe, *The Dramatick Works of Nicholas Rowe* (1720), sig. A5r–v.

[57] Knights, *Representation*, pp. 337–48; Kramnick, *Bolingbroke*, pp. 153–5.

actuated by both commercial and party-political values. Rowe was a Whig, for whom there was cultural authority in the party cause; the furtherance of that cause was thus a factor that made a literary work valuable. But politics was only one consideration, and only one source of value. For Rowe, it was not to override such values as sentimentality, sociability, politeness, humaneness and contemporaneity, which values were appropriate for a commercial, middle-class culture. Rowe's plays might therefore have been designed and celebrated on account of their partisan worth, but only occasionally and secondarily. Party concerns were sometimes mixed with sentimental, moralizing and contemporary concerns, but were usually excluded by them. Indeed, it seems likely that Rowe and his audiences shared a conviction that had his plays been too party-motivated, their value would have been fatally compromised. Rowe's ideal was expressed towards the end of his 1714 dedication. 'I could not but congratulate the Publick, upon seeing Men of all sides agree so unanimously as they did upon … the Applause of Mr. *Addison's Cato*, and the Encouragement given to Mr. *Pope's* Translation of *Homer* … I hope it is an Omen of their Unanimity in other Matters.'[58] For Rowe, the greatest value was in *uniting* 'the Publick'.

Rowe himself was familiar with uniting 'the Publick' in 'Applause', because his own plays were huge and enduring successes. He appears to have made an impact with his debut, *Ambitious Step-Mother*;[59] *Tamerlane* and *The Fair Penitent*, although destined to become repertory staples, initially had moderate but not extraordinary success;[60] his comedy, *The Biter*, had a decent, six-night first run;[61] *Ulysses* appeared ten times in its first season, and *The Royal Convert* had a five-night run followed quickly by two further performances;[62] *Jane Shore* proved Rowe's greatest immediate success, being staged eighteen times in its first month and a half;[63] and *Jane Gray* enjoyed decent popularity, but not as much as *Shore*.[64] When Jacob Tonson published Rowe's *Shakespear*, he made sure that the advertisements and title page featured Rowe's name prominently, hoping to create interest in the work by playing on Rowe's reputation. Tonson was also creating a link between two great playwrights, past and present, which, due to the incipient energies of patriotic canon formation, boosted Rowe's reputation

---

[58] Rowe, *Dramatick Works*, sig. A6r.

[59] Bernard, 'General introduction', p. 12.

[60] Bernard, 'General introduction', p. 13.

[61] Bernard, 'General introduction', p. 14.

[62] Bernard, 'General introduction', p. 16.

[63] Bernard, 'General introduction', p. 19.

[64] Bernard, 'General introduction', p. 21.

further. The popularity of Rowe's *Shakespear* duly fed into the feverish popularity of Rowe's next play, *The Tragedy of Jane Shore. Written in Imitation of Shakespear's Style*, which, in turn, fed back into the popularity of Rowe's *Shakespear* (with Tonson capitalizing on *Jane Shore* by expanding *Shakespear* to include Shakespeare's non-dramatic verse).[65] The production of *Jane Gray* was accompanied by a storm of opportunistic publications, with publishers rushing out fictional and non-fictional works on Jane Grey to take advantage of Rowe's appeal.[66] Nor did that appeal diminish quickly. *Tamerlane* and *Jane Gray* remained repertory staples until almost the end of the century, and *The Fair Penitent* and *Jane Shore* well into the nineteenth. Excluding Shakespeare, *The Fair Penitent* was the sixth most frequently performed tragedy of the 1700s.[67] In terms of publication, these four plays were to be printed some 140 separate times between them, prior to modern editions. Rowe was widely esteemed as one of the great literary figures of his time. Over fifty years later, Johnson admitted to him having many great qualities, especially admired his command of blank verse and was able to quote sections of his plays from memory.[68]

It seems just, therefore, to view Rowe as a characteristic figure of his age: someone whose work held a particular appeal for contemporary consumers of literature. It is likewise natural that, looking at the content of his work, and looking at the conditions of the time, a correlation has been drawn between sentimental, middle-class, patriotic plays and sentimental, middle-class, patriotic audiences. Equally, Rowe was the perfect playwright for a time of party rage, being able to both stoke that rage and calm it. Thus a play like *The Fair Penitent* could appeal to spectators' sense of humaneness and sympathy, while *Tamerlane* could be celebrated by Whigs as a partisan piece. Indeed, *Tamerlane* was played throughout the eighteenth century on 4 and/or 5 November, serving as a Whiggish commemoration of William's arrival. Rowe's work was esteemed highly in the early eighteenth century, and this esteem was at least partly due to its ability to meet the demands of a commercial and party-political culture. Critical pamphlets on *Jane Shore* and *Jane Gray* both described the plays in question as having received 'the Applause

---

[65] R. B. Hamm, Jr, 'Rowe's "Shakespear" (1709) and the Tonson house style', *College Literature*, xxxi (2004), 179–205, at pp. 190–3.

[66] A. W. Hesse and R. J. Sherry, 'Two unrecorded editions of Rowe's *Lady Jane Gray*: The early editions', *The Papers of the Bibliographical Society of America*, lxxii (1978), 220–6, at pp. 220–1.

[67] M. Goldstein, 'Introduction', in N. Rowe, *The Fair Penitent*, ed. M. Goldstein (Lincoln, Neb., 1969), pp. xiii–xxi, at p. xiv.

[68] However, Johnson's overall estimation of Rowe is difficult to define. Johnson, 'Rowe', p. 594; *Johnsonian Miscellanies*, ed. G. B. Hill (2 vols, London, 1966; reprint of the 1897 edn), ii. 197.

of the Town'.[69] This 'Town' was where Rowe, theatregoers and readers alike conceptualized the plays and themselves as being situated. It was Klein's town, a rival to the court, superseding it as the prime forum of cultural production and consumption. Likewise, it was the middle-class public, neither located nor interested in the court, that funded, enjoyed and celebrated Rowe's plays.

Rowe's plays as courtly

Up to this point, the discussion has been intentionally confined to the two standard interpretations of Rowe's work. It has demonstrated the nature of Rowe's appeal to a middle-class paying public based primarily in a non-court town, and shown how his works were celebrated according to the standards of just such an audience. It has also shown how Rowe's works derived value from the party-political situation, by giving political comment, advancing a party cause, and yet encouraging an end to party strife; but it has argued that this party element was not as important to Rowe's work as recent scholarship has claimed. Taken together, these two interpretations would suggest that Rowe was characteristic of an age of post-courtly culture, and that Rowe's success resulted from his ability to meet the standards created by a new system of cultural production and consumption, based physically and conceptually outside of court. But it is now time to change this picture. It is time to consider, once again, how contemporaries conceived of the court's involvement in culture. This chapter will not examine the practicalities of such an involvement, which are investigated elsewhere in the monograph. Instead, emphasis will fall on what literary works themselves can tell us about the role the court was conceived to have in literary production, and about how fair it is to characterize early eighteenth-century culture as 'commercial' and 'post-courtly'.

The starting point is Rowe's first play, *Ambitious Step-Mother*. The dedication to this play was quoted above as an illustration of how Rowe's tragedic theory centred on pity. But Rowe's dedication was not just a manifesto; it was also, of course, a dedication. The dedicatee was the earl of Jersey, who was specified as being 'Lord Chamberlain of his Majesty's Houshold, &c'.[70] Rowe had many, conventional praises to offer to Jersey, and explicitly solicited his patronage. Particularly telling is the passage in which he praised Jersey's 'Taste and Judgement', and said that 'all men that I have heard speak of your Lordship' had encouraged him to 'hope every thing from your Goodness. This is that I must sincerely own, which made me extremely Ambitious of your Lordship's Patronage for this Piece.' He then admitted that his play had

---

[69] Anon., *A Review of the Tragedy of Jane Shore* (1714), p. 3; C. Gildon, *Remarks on Mr. Rowe's Tragedy of the Lady Jane Gray, And Other Plays*, 2nd edn (1715), p. 5.

[70] Rowe, *Ambitious Step-Mother*, sig. A2r.

faults; but, 'since the good nature of the Town has cover'd, or not taken notice of 'em', he would not worry about them too far himself.[71] Thus Rowe begged a traditional patron–client relationship of Jersey, hoping for financial and other less tangible forms of beneficence. And for all that he acknowledged the authority of the town – an authority that had even encouraged him to think his play better than it was – that authority was secondary to the 'Taste and Judgement' of Jersey. Indeed, the 'good nature' of the town, which was elsewhere portrayed as an authoritative humaneness, here became a benign failing: a cheery disregard for the exact standards of true judgement. In this dedication, then, Rowe recognized a predominantly patronage-based system of literary production and consumption. The fact that he had chosen the 'Lord Chamberlain of his Majesty's Houshold' implied the same notion revealed so often in Restoration dedications: that the patronage system was centred on the court, and reached its apex in the king.

The play itself, although rife with love and sentiment, was a heroic tragedy, and would not have been too out of place in the 1660s or 1670s. Likewise *Tamerlane*, which, although generally studied for its relation to political parties, was, most immediately, a panegyric to the king. *Tamerlane*'s dedication, to the marquis of Hartington, was an explicit example of the idea that the playwright should appeal to a noble patron who was himself a direct servant of and link to the king. Although Hartington was highly praised for his own sake, his 'crowning good quality' was deemed to be 'your Lordship's continual adherence and unshaken Loyalty to His present Majesty'. Rowe 'cannot help distinguishing this last instance very particularly'.[72] Rowe then springboarded from Hartington into a 'Panegyrick' on William.[73] After panegyrizing at some length, he said, 'If your Lordship can find any thing in this Poem like [William] … I persuade my self it will prevail with you to forgive every thing else that you find amiss.'[74] Of course, this was typical panegyric rhetoric, and should not be read in too wide-eyed a fashion; but it was nonetheless significant that Rowe claimed the entirety of his play's value to rest in its ability to represent the monarch (and, by extension, the monarch's qualities and glory). Rowe finished by noting that his dedication to Hartington had given him 'the pleasure of expressing those Just and Dutiful Sentiments I have for his majesty, and that strong Inclination which I have always had to be thought … Your Lordships most Obedient, Humble Servant'.[75] Once again,

---

[71] Rowe, *Ambitious Step-Mother*, sig. A3r.

[72] Rowe, *Tamerlane*, dedication (unpaginated).

[73] Rowe, *Tamerlane*, dedication (unpaginated, then sig. br).

[74] Rowe, *Tamerlane*, sig. bv.

[75] Rowe, *Tamerlane*, sig. bv.

Rowe cast the playwright as servant to the noble courtier, and expressed the idea that through that patronal relationship, the playwright could satisfy the more abstract patronage he received from the king by offering him praise.

The dedication was always the first thing to appear in a printed work, and would therefore have framed and conditioned the work itself. On stage, the prologue came first; and, in *Tamerlane*'s prologue, Rowe delivered a similar message to that which he gave Hartington, but in a form appropriate for the setting. He told his crowd that

> Of all the Muses various Labours, none
> Have lasted longer, or have higher flown,
> Than those that tell the Fame by ancient heroes won ...
> Like [Virgil to Augustus] (tho' much unequal to his Flame)
> Our Author [Rowe] makes a pious Prince his Theme.[76]

Again, it was asserted that the highest form of poetic value came from representing a glorious monarch. This assertion was supported not by some reference to Otway making English audiences cry, but by one made to the classical, timeless image of Virgil and Augustus. This was in keeping with a courtly-patronal mode of literary production: a prince eternally re-enacting the ideal of Augustus, held in a relationship of reciprocal glory with a poet who re-enacted the role of Virgil; the poet entirely dependent on the prince; the prince dependent on the poet for the transmission of their reputation to posterity. Rowe then gave a panegyric on William in artful rhyming couplets.[77] The play that followed was a panegyric in the form of a heroic tragedy, although, like all of Rowe's plays, its generic model was primarily Cornelian and its spirit was primarily sentimental. This mixing of forms and values – the courtly and heroic with the sentimental and middle-class – was significant, as will be demonstrated below.

All of Rowe's plays had dedications, and they all fitted the values associated with the court-centred patronage system. *The Fair Penitent*, though famous for offering the middle-class audience 'Sorrows like your own', was dedicated to the duchess of Ormond, who, like Hartington, was used as a springboard to her monarch (Anne). Indeed, the duchess was 'the Noblest and Best Pattern' of Anne's 'own Royal Goodness, and Personal Virtues'.[78] The prologue itself, which began by disavowing 'the Fate of Kings and Empires', nonetheless ended with a brief encomium to the queen. Rowe was attempting to 'shew [the audience] Men and Women as they are'; and, 'With Deference to the

---

[76] Rowe, *Tamerlane*, sig. b2r.

[77] Rowe, *Tamerlane*, sig. b2r.

[78] Rowe, *The Fair Penitent*, sig. av.

Fair', he had to admit that 'Few to Perfection ever found the Way'. But 'This Age, 'tis true, has one great Instance seen,/And Heav'n in Justice made that One a Queen.'[79] He asserted the contemporary realism of his play; he gave a smile to 'the Fair'; then he bowed his tragedy onto the stage with a tribute to Anne. Although she was far distant from the world of the play, she stood over it as a positive ideal of womanliness, in contrast to the shortcomings of the titular penitent. The modest tale of everyday passions was placed under the presiding spirit of a perfect queen and set before the appreciative eyes of a courtly authority. Rowe hoped that 'the Misfortunes and Distress of the Play ... may be not altogether unworthy of [the duchess]'s Pity. This is one of the main Designs of Tragedy, and to excite this generous Pity in the greatest Minds, may pass for some kind of Success in this way of Writing.' The duchess's praise would have meant 'much more to me than the general applause of the Theatre'.[80] For Rowe, drama was best appreciated by the great, courtly figures, whatever principles it was composed upon. Courtly figures were not distinct from the theatregoing audience, but crowned it, and represented its qualities and ideals in their highest forms. Anne was the perfect woman and patroness. The duchess of Ormond, who was a link to and stand-in for Anne, was the perfect sentimental theatregoer.

As mentioned above, Rowe's subsequent plays returned to the world of courts and princes. He may have treated his subjects in a way that appealed to a middle-class, paying audience, but they were princes and courtiers all the same. And although (as mentioned above) *The Royal Convert* included a pro-Union message, the explicit articulation of that message only came as a subsidiary part of a long closing panegyric to Anne. Ethelinda ended the play with a recitation of a prophecy, beginning, 'Of Royal Race a *British* Queen shall rise,/Great, Gracious, Pious, Fortunate and Wise.' This went on for a total of twenty-one lines, explaining that 'this happy Land her Care shall prove,/And find from her a more than Mother's Love ... most in peaceful Arts she shall delight,/And her chief Glory shall be to Unite.'[81] The Union thus appeared as but an aspect of Anne's own 'Glory', and an emblem of the greatness of her reign.

None of this is to say that Rowe was writing the sort of material that was written under Charles I or Charles II, or that the conditions of cultural production and consumption had not changed since the mid seventeenth century. The situation had certainly changed since then; but the conceptual role of the court, and the practical agency of a patronage system centred

---

[79] Rowe, *The Fair Penitent*, sig. a2v.

[80] Rowe, *The Fair Penitent*, sig. A4r.

[81] Rowe, *The Royal Convert*, p. 56.

on the court, had not lapsed. Instead, Rowe's work shows that the court was conceived as being intimate with, and important to, middle-class theatregoers and readers. He was positioning his plays not simply within the town, or on a stall for a paying public, but also in the court. The traditions, themes and values characteristic of the courtly production and consumption of culture were mixed with those characteristic of audiences and activities situated outside the walls of the court.

For example, Rowe's dedications were ostensibly private epistles to individual patrons. Yet they were invariably printed at the beginning of each of his publications (as was conventional). Every single reader who bought one of Rowe's publications would not only have been confronted with, but also to some extent had their reading of the play conditioned by, a dedicatory epistle that was not actually addressed to them personally. Therefore, the dedication was functioning as an essential aspect of commercial publication. Rowe was broadcasting his position within a court-based patronage system so as to increase his profitability. The fact that he came under the patronage of some great, courtly nobleman served as a recommendation to middle-class, paying consumers, who were thus encouraged to buy his wares and finance his writing. The particular use that Rowe made of his dedications conferred a further profitability to his product. By the artistry of his praise, he was showing off both his literary ability and the strength of his relation to his patron; by extending that praise to the reigning monarch, he suggested a patronal relationship with the crown itself, and emphasized his loyal monarchist sentiments; and by the values he exhibited in the dedication – for example, a polite distaste for partisan rage, or a tragic theory centring on pity – he turned a private dedicatory epistle into an advertisement for his readers. In all these ways, then, courtly patronage was marketable. On opening the publication, buyers would have seen that Rowe was validated by the patronage system, and, in reading through the dedication, they would have assessed the strength of his position within that system, and found his credentials glowingly contextualized within a semi-mythical private dialogue between him and his patron. Thus Rowe's commercial and critical success with paying customers was built upon the idea that his play had a position at court, as well as in the town playhouses.

At the same time, court and patron benefitted too, and Rowe's own position within the patronage system was strengthened by his success with paying customers. In his dedications, patron and court had an idealized picture of themselves promulgated to all of Rowe's readers. Their putative good qualities were trumpeted through the marketing of mass-produced texts. In particular, they were shown to be great patrons, who had enabled Rowe to produce such great works of art. The individual patron, the court and the patronage system itself had created Rowe's tragedies. Thus a literary work was produced through the ideological and financial agency of court-based and town-based audiences and the public working in conjunction: indeed, working through each other. As a result, cultural value was understood in accordance with the ideals that pertained to each of these forums and audiences. To a lesser extent, political partisanship was involved as well. Rowe's most direct discussion of party matters was usually found in his dedicatory epistles and in connection with the various royal figures in his plays. The Whig cause operated within and by means of the court, the town and the public.

This chapter has already demonstrated some of the manifestations of all this in Rowe's work. One was the *Step-Mother* dedication to the lord chamberlain, in which Rowe justified his play to the dedicatee by reference to the judgement of 'the Town', while justifying it to his readers by reference to the patronage of a great courtly figure in possession of 'Taste and Judgement'. Another was *Tamerlane*, where Rowe offered his audience a dramatized panegyric of William, complete with Whiggish proselytizing and sentimental subplots. *The Fair Penitent* provided the image of an idealized courtly patron and viewer, the duchess of Ormond, who both stood in for Queen Anne and exemplified the sentimental humaneness that Rowe sought from his paying audience. And *Ulysses* and *The Royal Convert* created an ideal of sentimental, contemporary, patriotic, middle-class monarchy, many decades before George III would famously embody the same. Indeed, the prophecy at the end of the latter presented Anne as the apotheosis of three separate strands of cultural value: courtly, party-political and paying public. She was a great classical prince, a forger of Whiggish Union and a loving mother to her nation. Each strand of her identity was dependent upon the others.

However, the best example came in Rowe's final drama, *Jane Gray*. Performed and published just after the Hanoverian succession, *Jane Gray* was dedicated to Caroline, the new princess of Wales, and immediately identified her with England's Protestant martyr-queen. 'A Princess of the same Royal Blood to which you are so closely and happily ally'd, presumes to throw her self at the feet of YOUR ROYAL HIGHNESS for Protection,' Rowe announced. He had drawn his Jane Grey in approximation to the actual historical figure, but had also somewhat 'improv[ed]' her, to make her worthier 'of those Illustrious Hands to which I always intended to present her'.[82] The identification was further strengthened when Rowe then celebrated Caroline's own Protestantism and patriotism. She chose the British rather than the Imperial crown, because

---

[82] Rowe, *Jane Gray*, p. iv.

doing the latter would have required her to convert to Catholicism;[83] and she had now become 'the brightest Ornament' and 'the Patroness and Defender of our holy Faith'.[84] But she was not just a religious paragon. She was 'the Best Daughter to our KING, and Best Wife to our PRINCE',[85] a model of touching domesticity. Caroline thus appeared not just as Rowe's patron, but as a great royal figure who had given the poet his subject and inspired him in his art, as Virgil was held to have done by representing Augustus as Aeneas. Moreover, she protected and exemplified the values of Rowe's readership: love of Britain, devotion to Protestantism and domestic femininity. The last theme in Rowe's dedication was the obligation that Britain owed to its new princess. Since the Hanoverians had saved Britain from popery, 'every particular Person amongst us ought to contribute' to 'discharg[e] that Publick Obligation'.[86] *Jane Gray* was Rowe's own 'Offering'.[87] Again, though, the dedicatory epistle was not sent in private; it was published with every copy of the play. The reminder of 'Publick Obligation' therefore worked in two ways. On the one hand, it informed readers of how obliged they were to their magnificent new princess; on the other, it allowed them to buy into Rowe's 'discharging' of 'that Publick Obligation'. By purchasing and reading *Jane Gray*, they could give Rowe's offering their endorsement, and thereby register their own loyal gratitude.

In the prologue, Jane Grey herself was focused upon. It was shown that she was both a great prince and a humble exemplar of sentimental values. She was 'A Heroine, a martyr, and a Queen'; irrespective of Rowe's 'Art', his choice of subject 'shall something Great impart,/To warm the generous Soul, & touch the tender Heart'.[88] She shone with royal resplendence, yet she had an affective relationship with her audience, based on a sympathetic humaneness. 'To you, Fair Judges, we the Cause submit,' Rowe continued. 'If your soft Pity waits upon our Woe,' then 'the Muse's Labour' would have been successful.[89] Rowe was again appealing to his favourite constituency: the female, deep-feeling audience. But in this instance the 'Sorrows like your own' were those of a queen. The relatable, sympathetic, sentimental heroine was Jane Grey. By activating his audience's pity for her, Rowe created an affective bridge between the patriotic identity of Protestant Britain and the real-life character of Princess Caroline.

[83] See H. Smith, *Georgian Monarchy: Politics and Culture, 1714–1760* (Cambridge, 2006), pp. 32–7.

[84] Rowe, *Jane Gray*, p. v.

[85] Rowe, *Jane Gray*, p. iv.

[86] Rowe, *Jane Gray*, p. iv.

[87] Rowe, *Jane Gray*, p. vii.

[88] Rowe, *Jane Gray*, p. xi.

[89] Rowe, *Jane Gray*, p. xi.

These themes were all emphasized throughout the play as a whole. For example, the legitimacy of Jane's rule was explained to be based on the realm's consent (including parliament's approval), making Jane a symbol of the Hanoverian succession. Jane herself was depicted as patriotic, Protestant, self-sacrificing, meek and humane. At one stage, she spoke of the difficulty of being queen; she had only taken on the royal burden 'To save this Land from Tyranny and *Rome*'.[90] This was a reminder of both the Jacobite threat and the gratitude Britons owed to their new royal family. Just before Jane died, she prayed that Heaven would raise up a 'Monarch of the Royal Blood,/Brave, Pious, Equitable, Wise, and Good', and that this 'Hero' would save Britain from Rome, then leave behind a son who would 'guard that Faith for which I die to-day'.[91] With these words, Jane created a transcendental royal line, carried across dynasties, united by its virtues and its Protestantism, but also valid on the basis of 'Royal Blood'. She emphasized that her own story – a sentimental she-tragedy – was synonymously a story of party struggle (against the Tories of Jacobite inclination) and of courtly greatness. The epilogue then gave a similar message to that found in the dedication, making the Caroline–Jane parallel clear for spectators. It emphasized that Caroline was 'the Fairest of her Sex', and that the audience owed her 'Gratitude'.[92] Rowe also warned against 'vile Faction', and said that 'If you are taught to dread a Popish Reign,/ Our Beauteous Patriot has not dy'd in vain.'[93] Again, the various priorities appropriate to different conceptual spaces were here working in tandem. The relatable, sympathetic female character served as a celebration of Whiggism and of the court *because* she was a relatable, sympathetic female character. The Whig cause was revealed to animate both the sentimental, identifiable story and the court *because* it was the Whig cause. And the court presided over both the story and Whiggism *because* it was the court. The product itself – *Jane Gray* – was a work not of patronage, or of party, or of professionalism alone, but of all three coexisting in synonymity.

The work of Nicholas Rowe, then, presents a challenge to the conventional modern picture of eighteenth-century culture. It is not simply the case that culture was produced for the public, town, marketplace and/or political party. In fact, Rowe's work suggests that the court was still a central concept in understandings of culture, and that those audiences and activities that were contained within that concept – royals, aristocrats, court officials, patronage – were still of vital importance to cultural production and consumption.

---

[90] Rowe, *Jane Gray*, p. 37.

[91] Rowe, *Jane Gray*, p. 65.

[92] Rowe, *Jane Gray*, p. 67.

[93] Rowe, *Jane Gray*, p. 67.

The concepts of the town and the public, which denoted middle-class and non-courtly audiences, and commercial and party-political modes of production and consumption, did not supersede the court; they worked in conjunction with it. It is because Rowe's work satisfied the attendant values so adeptly that he was so highly esteemed by contemporaries. He was commercially successful with both theatregoers and readers, critically lauded and valued both as a strident Whig and as someone whose work appealed across the party divide. Finally, he was made poet laureate by his Hanoverian king, in operation with the new parliamentary and ministerial Whig regime. His appointment was the supreme and appropriate honour for a man who succeeded according to a particular set of values, determined by a conceptual geography of culture in which the court coexisted with town and public. The laureateship was not an anachronism. In fact, it was highly characteristic of early eighteenth-century culture.

Eusden and Cibber

Upon Rowe's death in 1718, he was replaced by Eusden, later to become notorious as a drunken clergyman, but then a Cambridge Fellow, young poet and member of the Addison–Steele nexus of writers.[94] Eusden had just written a poem on the marriage of the duke of Newcastle. Newcastle was lord chamberlain, and a pugnacious one; later, as a leading figure in successive ministries, he gained a reputation for pettiness, defensiveness and jealousy over his prerogatives. It therefore seems highly likely that the 1718 appointment decision was his. When Eusden eventually died in a stupor of provincial booze, he was replaced by Cibber. Cibber was a famous playwright and actor, a firm Whig and one of the managers of Drury Lane theatre. He was a friend and associate of many of the leading governmental figures, including Walpole himself, and contemporaries sometimes or partially credited his appointment to this closeness.

In the work of Eusden and Cibber, a similar case to that of Rowe is revealed. It was commercial, courtly and (sometimes) party-orientated; it sought success with town and public, traditional forms of patronage and (sometimes) party advantage. The poem that apparently gained Eusden the laurel – *A Poem on the Marriage of His Grace the Duke of Newcastle* (1717) – is a good example. It was a panegyric and an epithalamium, praising Newcastle and his bride. Eusden aspired to 'reach transcendent Worth with Praise', and to depict 'A *British Pollio* … More bright, than *Pollio*, whom a *Virgil* drew'.[95] The poem was classical and courtly, invoking the timeless

---

[94] See ch. 3.

[95] L. Eusden, *A Poem on the Marriage of His Grace the Duke of Newcastle to the Right*

examples of Virgil and his patrons, and using them to praise Newcastle and to re-enact the Virgilian patronal model (Pollio being one of Virgil's patrons). But it also included themes that were more specifically typical of early eighteenth-century poetry, and that were present across all kinds of poems that seem more directed to the public than to a patron. For example, Eusden represented Venus and Minerva having a civil, high-society sort of debate, in which Venus announced her concern for Britain's welfare, and designated it 'that blest Isle' where 'Triumphant Beauty reigns,/And willing Youth wears Love's delightful Chains./Not ev'n *Augustus* dares to disobey,/ His *Carolina's* Looks confirm my Sway'.[96] Thus the prince of Wales and his wife were held up as epitomes of the polite, loving spirit that apparently animated Britain; the monarchy was the crown of a sentiment that was here cast as patriotic. But Minerva insisted that *she* was more concerned for Britain: 'My Pow'r shall *Brunswick's* [i.e. George I's] lawful Crown protect,/ And still his Councils, and his Arms direct.'[97] She then cited Newcastle as the greatest and most patriotic Briton, and boasted that he did not feel Venus's powers. Venus retaliated by causing Newcastle to fall in love with Henrietta Godolphin and marry her. '*Britannia's* Welfare is my great Design,' she announced; by inducing Newcastle and Henrietta to marry, she had guaranteed Britain a 'num'rous Line' of patriotic progeny.[98] There was also, at the start of the poem, a warning against 'baneful Faction', which 'would its Pow'r advance/By Popish Chains, and *Vandal* Ignorance'.[99] This was contrasted with the bright glories and patriotism of Newcastle.

The whole performance was delivered in typically refined couplets, and it sold so well that a second edition was published in the same year, before Eusden had even been made laureate.[100] Thus Eusden enjoyed commercial success, struck a minor blow for his party and received the patronage of a great courtly figure, all of which factors contributed to his rise to the laureateship. Again, cultural production and consumption appear not simply as commercial, or party-political, or even courtly, but mixed. Paying readers liked Eusden's courtliness; court-based figures presumably liked Eusden's popular appeal and his ability to write competent, modern verse. Both sets of people also liked his party spirit, and the party faithful liked his courtly and popular appeal. By satisfying the needs and ideals of

---

Honourable the Lady Henrietta Godolphin (1717), p. 4.

[96] Eusden, *Marriage*, p. 6.

[97] Eusden, *Marriage*, p. 7.

[98] Eusden, *Marriage*, p. 14. In fact, the couple were to be childless.

[99] Eusden, *Marriage*, p. 3.

[100] Eusden, *Marriage*, 2nd edn (1717).

these different constituencies, Eusden's poem was exemplary of the then prevailing conditions of cultural production.

As laureate, Eusden continued in this vein, writing panegyric poetry that was designed to appeal to the individual addressee, the court more generally, the paying public and (sometimes) the party of (governing) Whigs. It appealed to them not as separate constituencies, but by way of each other. The court as formulated in Eusden's poetry was not distinct from the public; it stood at the head of it, epitomizing its values and concerns and leading it in taste. The Walpolean Whigs, meanwhile, were solidly identified with the court. In *An Epistle to Walpole* (1726), Eusden celebrated the addressee's elevation to 'the Most Noble *Order* of the *Garter*',[101] and felt no hesitation in offering his verse to him, confident that 'On whom GEORGE smiles, a WALPOLE will not frown'.[102] Walpole was deemed the 'Delightful Wonder of each *British Tongue*',[103] and his chief quality was his 'em-bosom'd Care' for '*Albion*'.[104]

Cibber did not write much in the way of non-dramatic verse, but this did not mean that his appointment was incongruous. He was a hugely successful dramatist, some of whose plays were among the century's most popular. Although he was most well known for his prose comedies, he wrote verse tragedies too, one of which, his adaptation of *Richard III*, remained a popular favourite well into the nineteenth century.[105] Most of Cibber's plays debuted around the same time as Rowe's (from the late 1690s into the 1710s), and were in fact the comedic analogues to Rowe's; they have often been seen as typifying the sentimental and middle-class inclinations of the time, just as Rowe's did in tragedy.[106] Like Rowe, Cibber was a Whig, and his plays sometimes delivered overt party messages.[107] But, again like Rowe, Cibber's work was also orientated towards a courtly audience and its attendant values. The best example of how these strands operated in conjunction is *The Non-Juror* (1718). This play was an adaptation of Molière's *Tartuffe*, given a heavily anti-Jacobite design. This anti-Jacobitism identified the play as Whiggish, but it also identified it as a paean to George I and the Hanoverian monarchy. Suitably enough, the play ended with the

---

[101] L. Eusden, *An Epistle To the Noble, and Right Honourable Sir Robert Walpole, Knight of the Most Noble Order of the Garter* (1726), p. 3.

[102] Eusden, *Walpole*, p. 4.

[103] Eusden, *Walpole*, p. 4.

[104] Eusden, *Walpole*, p. 12.

[105] Bevis, *Drama*, pp. 154–61; Burling and Viator, 'General introduction', pp. 13–14; Koon, *Cibber*, pp. 36–9, 44–50, 178.

[106] Koon, *Cibber*, pp. 24–9, 178.

[107] Koon, *Cibber*, pp. 86–97.

observation that 'no Change of Government can give us a Blessing equal to our Liberty', followed by the couplet, '*Grant us but this and then of Course you'll own,/To Guard that Freedom,* GEORGE *must fill the Throne.*'[108] It might be argued that Cibber's praise of George I was not very meaningful in and of itself; it was simply a stock doctrine of Whiggism. But even if that argument has some merit, it actually highlights the point being made here. The court interest was not separate from the party interest, but was bound up with it; dictates of court and party coexisted, cooperated and maintained each other. The play was also an enormous commercial success, delighting audiences and being published in a fifth edition before the year was out.[109] Cibber made an unprecedented sum of money from the copyright (£105), and was given a huge gift of £200 by the king, to whom the dedicatory epistle was addressed.[110] Again, the persistence and nature of the court as a cultural forum is evident.

In the works of the three poet laureates of the early Hanoverian period, then, literary figures are revealed to have been working within a conceptual geography of culture in which court, town and public were each important and were interrelated. The question now is this: were the laureates anomalous? Was it because they were unique (in the respects demonstrated above) that they were appointed to the laureateship, and, as laureates, did they continue to behave in unique ways because they were encouraged to do so by their office? Is it wrong to draw wider conclusions from a study of them?

Testing the laureate paradigm against the wider literary scene suggests that, in fact, the laureates' situation was far from abnormal. For example, the institutional court still practised direct financial patronage, and still conferred fixed employments, even upon non-laureate poets. George I gave an enormous patronal gift of £500 to Richard Steele for his *Conscious Lovers*, a popular, sentimental, moralizing, reforming comedy by a stalwart, vigorous Whig.[111] For his services to the Walpolean Whigs, Edward Young was recommended by Walpole for a court pension, which he duly received.[112] Queen Caroline's patronage of Stephen Duck was famous among contemporaries. She granted him a series of courtly employments, ensured that his publications were financially successful by encouraging her acquaintances to subscribe to them,

---

[108] C. Cibber, *The Non-Juror* (1718).

[109] C. Cibber, *The Non-Juror*, 5th edn (1718); Koon, *Cibber*, pp. 86–9.

[110] Hume, *Fielding Theatre*, p. 26.

[111] Hume, *Fielding Theatre*, p. 26.

[112] D. Griffin, *Literary Patronage in England, 1650–1800* (Cambridge, 1996), pp. 155–63.

which would in turn have increased their popular sales appeal.[113] Meanwhile, Richard Savage dubbed himself a 'Volunteer Laureate', and published an annual panegyric for Caroline.[114] Not only did this secure him a pension from her, but it also gave him a marketable identity, and allowed him to publish a regular, royally authorized product each year.[115]

Indeed, on every occasion of note for the royal family – accessions, marriages, returns from abroad, recoveries from illness, births, deaths – the nation would be convulsed by poetical activity. Poets of every stripe and pedigree would compose something suitably panegyric, and publish it for retail: sometimes with a politically partisan bent, sometimes with a dedicatee (distinct from the subject or addressee of the poem itself), sometimes in an imagined dialogue with another poet.[116] Oxford and Cambridge would commonly produce an entire volume of such poems on these occasions, written by current dons and undergraduates, in English, Latin, Greek and other languages (albeit not with retail in mind).[117] Many of these poems were 'odes', either sharing the pseudo-Pindaric form of the laureate odes, or written in some other 'ode' form.[118] The Prior poem mentioned priorly – his Spenserian ode – was in fact *An Ode, humbly inscrib'd to the Queen*.[119] As late as 1789, the now-canonical poet William Cowper wrote a poem in response to George III's recovery from illness, and had it presented to Princess Amelia, in the hope that it would be shown to the queen. He said of the poem that 'though it be praise it is

---

[113] B. Rizzo, 'The patron as poet maker: The politics of benefaction', *Studies in Eighteenth-Century Culture*, xx (1991), 241–66, at pp. 244–8.

[114] Griffin, *Patronage*, pp. 169–88.

[115] Not that Savage's savvy deserves any emphasis. See S. Johnson, 'Savage', in *Lives of the Poets*, ii. 848–968.

[116] See eg the instructively named, Anon., *Albina, the Second Part. Or, The Coronation. A Poem on Her Present Majesty's Happy Accession to the Crown. By the Author of Albina: Or, A Poem on the Death of King William the Third* (1702); S. Duck, *A Poem On the Marriage of His Serene Highness the Prince of Orange, with Ann Princess-Royal of Great Britain* (1734); L. Eusden, *A Letter to Mr. Addison on the King's Accession to the Throne* (1714); P. Turner, *Augustus. A Poem on the Accession of His Majesty King George. Humbly Dedicated to the Right Honourable Charles, Lord Hallifax, One of the Lords Justices Appointed by His Majesty* (1714).

[117] H. Forster, 'The rise and fall of the Cambridge muses (1603–1763)', *Transactions of the Cambridge Bibliographical Society*, viii (1982), 141–72, at pp. 143–5, 147–9, 151–2; H. Power, 'Eyes without light: University volumes and the politics of succession', in *Stuart Succession Literature: Moments and Transformations*, ed. P. Kewes and A. McRae (Oxford, 2018), pp. 222–40.

[118] See ch. 5.

[119] M. Prior, *An Ode, Humbly Inscrib'd to the Queen. On the Late Glorious Success of Her Majesty's Arms* (1706).

truth', and 'it seemed necessary that I, who am now a poet by profession, should not leave an event in which [George and Charlotte's] happiness and that of the nation are so much concerned, uncelebrated'.[120] It was specifically because he was a 'poet by profession' that he should give vent to his devotion to the king and queen, and should mark an occasion that was equally of royal and patriotic importance. Such poems were not the products of any one simple system of literary production and value; they were commercial, they were patronized, they were courtly, they were political, they were professional, they were nationally conscious. They understood poetic worth, and potential reward and advancement, as being conferred by a set of values that related to multiple sources, among which was the court.

The theatre, meanwhile, presents a similar picture. While it is certainly the case that it was not as closely associated with court-based personnel as in Charles II's reign, the Hanoverian theatre nonetheless retained associations with the court that were both functionally and ideologically vital. For one thing, public theatre still operated under the system of royal patents. This situation became somewhat confused in the first few decades of the eighteenth century, when theatres began to operate under licences, temporary patents or under no official authorization at all; but the 1737 Licensing Act returned the system to something like its original purity, for the most part eliminating all but two patented companies.[121] Moreover, as Smith and Harry William Pedicord have demonstrated, the relationship between the Hanoverian family and London theatres was not just regulatory and negative, but was active, patronal and mutually beneficent.[122]

The spaces in question

The last point that needs to be made concerns the terminology used by the three laureates in their assessments of the conceptual geography of culture. As set out in the Introduction, late seventeenth-century writers predominantly conceptualized the cultural landscape in terms of the town and the world, rather than the public; but this situation changed between 1700 and 1730, such that writers, although still making reference to the town and the world, were primarily concerned with the public, which bore a complex and variable relationship to the concepts of the town and the world. The triumph of the public as a concept in cultural production was part of a significant shift in the

[120] R. Southey, 'A life of the author', in W. Cowper, *The Works*, ed. R. Southey (15 vols, London, 1835), iii. 3.

[121] Hume, *Fielding Theatre*, pp. 3–14, 239–53.

[122] H. W. Pedicord, *'By Their Majesties' Command': the House of Hanover at the London Theatres, 1714–1800* (London, 1991), pp. 2, 41; Smith, *Georgian Monarchy*, pp. 232–8.

conceptual geography of culture, from the dominance of specific, physical locations to that of transcendent, metaphorical locations. This came about as a result of three factors: the increasing extent and importance of print culture; the expansion of London, in terms of its physical size, its dominance of print culture and its improved transport links to the rest of the country; and the increasing viability of non-dramatic forms of literature.

However, for many writers the older terms of the town and the world remained the preferred expressions until at least 1720, and, for perhaps most writers who had started their careers before Anne's accession, until their deaths. Between 1696 and 1718, Cibber published some seventeen plays, most of them full length and most of them with dedicatory epistles. In these plays' dedicatory epistles and other paratexts, Cibber consistently identified his main audience as 'the Town'; and, in contrast to that strain of later Stuart rhetoric that had held theatregoers' taste to be partial and degraded, portrayed himself as an autochthonous creature of the playhouse, servicing a theatregoing audience whose taste was the highest and purest imaginable, specifically because it operated within the playhouse. Meanwhile, he used the word 'publick' only rarely, only as an adjective, and only in reference to serious matters of national weal. Eventually, in 1719, he used the term 'the Publick' as an audience of cultural products, interchangeably with 'the Town'. Thereafter, he published few further plays; but, when he did, his paratexts employed both terms.[123]

With Nicholas Rowe, the case was similar: throughout his career, he used the term 'the Town' rather than 'the Publick' to identify his main audience. When he used the word 'publick', it was as an adjective, referring to the ways in which his aristocratic dedicatees served the nation. There were only two uses of 'the Publick' as a noun in his paratexts. The first was in the *Tamerlane* dedication (1702), in which he explicitly contrasted Hartington's and William's work, 'so necessary to the Publick', with his own work, 'the entertainment of leisure Hours only'.[124] The second was towards the end of his life, in the dedication to the volume of his collected tragedies (1714). This was the usage quoted above: 'I could not but congratulate the Publick, upon seeing Men on all sides agree so unanimously as they did' in applauding *Cato* and Pope's Homer translation. In both cases, therefore, writers who had begun their careers at the turn of the eighteenth century tentatively started using the word 'the Publick' in the 1710s. Yet Cibber's usage of 'the Publick' came as part of a discussion in which he surveyed his career as a whole and

---

[123] See dedicatory epistles, other forms of preface, prologues and epilogues to all plays between *Love's Last Shift* (1696) and *Papal Tyranny in the Reign of King John* (1745). For his 1719 use of 'the Publick' and 'the Town', see 'To Sir Richard Steele' and 'To the Reader' prefacing *Ximena* (1719), sig. A3r–p. xliv.

[124] Rowe, *Tamerlane*, sig. A2r–v.

explained that he would be ceasing to write plays from now on, while Rowe's also came in relation to political partisanship and as part of a retrospective of his writing career. On the whole, 'the Town' remained the primary concept that they used to situate, and make sense of, their playwriting.

This is important, because the town was the specific physical location that was 'the court end of London'. In social terms, it was defined by its aristocratic and gentry inhabitants, whereas the neighbouring city was defined more by middle-class elements: shopkeepers, artisans, aldermen, citizens.[125] Both before and after the Hanoverian succession, it therefore remained standard for writers in general, and playwrights in particular, to conceptually position their work in the midst of the particular section of metropolitan society that congregated around, and passed in and out of, the walls of the court. This, ultimately, is why Rowe's, Eusden's and Cibber's works looked both ways, to court and to public. Those works were being situated in a town that was not simply a precursor to the public, but constituted the interface of court and public. It was the hinterland of the former and the heartland of the latter.

Conclusion

When the Hanoverian royal family arrived, it was swiftly accepted into the arrangement elaborated above, and in turn made itself comfortable within it. The town needed a court and the court needed a town. Hence, just as various individuals acting for their own gain had brought about the formation of the laureateship and the formalization of the court's cultural role in the later Stuart period, various individuals acting for their own gain effected something similar after 1714. Playwrights like Cibber and Rowe, successful purveyors of cultural products for the town in which they were based, immediately turned their attention to the new royal family and court establishment, welcomed its leading figures, and sought success with the town by celebrating the new regime. In turn, court and government officials placed the cultural authority of the new court upon the foundations of the old, one aspect of which was the appointment of Rowe as poet laureate. For the next two reigns, the court remained closely identified with London. Georges I and II did not leave London to visit other parts of Britain; Jacobitism (as seen in Fielding's *Tom Jones*, and in the Oldmixon letter discussed in the next chapter) was a feature of places like the West Country, rather than of London. This physical reality underlay the conceptual geography by which cultural products were produced, consumed and given meaning. George III would glory in the name of Britain; George IV would visit Scotland; but the physical court of Georges I and II was physically nestled in London.

[125] Greig, *Beau Monde*, pp. 1–11, 100–30.

3. Merit rewarded: The Hanoverian appointments, 1715–1813

Chapter One showed that in the decades following its establishment, the office of poet laureate underwent significant changes, moving from a vague, honorific position to a more specific and functionary role. By the time of the Hanoverian succession, it had become fixed in a particular niche within the lord chamberlain's department, tasked with providing the biannual odes that would be performed at court on the royal birthday and on New Year's Day. This chapter will investigate related matters for the century following George I's accession, focusing on how and why each laureate was appointed. On this basis, it will make wider points about the laureateship's role, situation and significance.

To begin with, this chapter will survey the appointments of the Hanoverian period as a whole, from Nicholas Rowe in 1714 to Robert Southey in 1813. It will then identify patterns, and use the evidence relating to each individual appointment to shed light on the others. Lastly, it will use three case studies to explore the wider questions about how the laureateship was conceived and what significance it had. It will emphasize two particular themes: the networks that underlay each laureate's appointment, and the purpose that the laureateship was expected to fulfil. Each laureate was appointed by the will of a single person or small group of people in informal discussion, and each appointment came after a brief but intense period of activity in which various self-appointed candidates promoted their claims and besought their friends to intercede for them. It is therefore worthwhile to explore what sorts of network were coming into play in each case, and where those networks were physically and conceptually situated. As for the purpose of the laureateship, it will be shown that the rationale behind each appointment consists in the complex relationship between the exigencies of patronage and ideas of 'merit'.

Because the second section of this chapter will attempt to make sense of the appointments that have been surveyed in the first section, and because the case studies that constitute the third section all fall within the wider period explored in the first and second sections, some of the information presented here will be mentioned in more than one place. This repetition will hopefully be excused as necessary. The approach taken in this chapter is essentially that of a snowball which, rather than being rolled downhill so as to gather momentum, is rolled continually around the same wide field of snow, steadily gathering mass. To have adopted a different approach, in which thematic arguments, comparisons and case studies were inserted at the chronologically appropriate moments within the descriptive overview of the appointments, would have compromised the nature of the overview, disrupted the coherence of the analysis and confused the themes of the case studies.

Overview of the appointments

There is no direct evidence as to who selected Nicholas Rowe for the laureateship in 1715. He was famous for the strength of his Whig politics, and, throughout his life, he managed to accumulate sinecurial and non-sinecurial public offices during periods of Whig ascendancy; but he was also an eager place-hunter during the years of Tory dominance at the end of Anne's reign.[1] Alexander Pope later told a story in which Robert Harley, the Tory first lord of the treasury, hinted to Rowe that it might be worth his while to learn Spanish, whereupon Rowe spent many months diligently learning the language, expecting that he was to be appointed to a position responsible for dealings with Spain, only for Harley to tell him, 'Then, sir, I envy you the pleasure of reading *Don Quixote* in the original.'[2] Whether or not in connection with this, Jonathan Swift claimed (also many years after) that he used to intercede with Harley on behalf of Rowe and other Whigs, trying to get them government places in spite of their politics.[3] Clearly, then, Rowe was no stranger to place-hunting, and, as a genial man who enjoyed a wide and well-placed circle of friends (including Pope), he may well have put himself forward for the laureateship when it became vacant in 1715.[4] He would certainly have known how best to advance his claim.[5] Joseph Addison seems to have distrusted him somewhat, on account of his superficiality and glibness;[6] but even these were the qualities of a seasoned courtier and place-hunter, and they would have done him no harm in

[1] A. Sherbo, 'Nicholas Rowe', *ODNB*; A. Pope, *The Correspondence of Alexander Pope*, ed. G. Sherburn (5 vols, Oxford, 1956), i. 27, 102–3; Spence, *Observations*, i. 214, at p. 93.

[2] Spence, *Observations*, i. 221, at p. 96.

[3] J. Swift, *The Correspondence of Jonathan Swift*, ed. H. Williams (5 vols, Oxford, 1963–5), ii. 369.

[4] On Rowe's geniality, Spence, *Observations*, i. 249, at p. 109.

[5] On patronage and place-hunting, R. O. Bucholz, *The Augustan Court: Queen Anne and the Decline of Court Culture* (Stanford, Calif., 1993), pp. 64–114; J. M. Beattie, *The English Court in the Reign of George I* (Cambridge, 1967), pp. 152–61; and the third case study, below.

[6] O. Ruffhead, *The Life of Alexander Pope, Esq.* (1769), p. 493.

gaining such offices as were to be gained through court attendance, seeking favours of great men and calling upon friends for timely intercession.

Whether the laureateship was indeed such an office remains to be established. But, if it was, Rowe was the ideal man to acquire it; and, since he did acquire it, and there is no other evidence as to how, it seems reasonable to put forward these particular means as a possibility. But he was also the foremost tragic playwright of his day, and was a famously ardent Whig. Therefore, without yet exploring the relationship between these three potentially key recommendations of his (place-hunting prowess, publicly recognized poetic merit and famous Whiggery), each of these three qualities can be provisionally suggested as having, in his case, determined the bestowing of the laureateship.

There was a great bustle among the literary community upon Nahum Tate's death, with many writers trying to gain the laureateship.[7] But only two or three of Rowe's competitors are now identifiable. One was John Dennis, another Whig man of letters, whose popularity and reputation as an imaginative writer were lesser than Rowe's. He would certainly have made a better controversialist and disputational writer, if that had been what court and government officials were looking for, because he was primarily known for his literary criticism and his generally trenchant prose; but on the other hand, his politics were idiosyncratic, and he had been known for public discords with other Whig writers.[8] Although he was already one of the king's waiters at the Customs House, he was not as personally endearing or well connected as Rowe.[9]

Dennis's candidature is known only from contemporary newspapers, as is that of a man named William Ellis, whose candidature seems to have been a hoax or joke.[10] Some newspapers even reported that Dennis had been made laureate, suggesting that his candidature proceeded quite far.[11] The last candidate to note is John Oldmixon, who did not appear

[7] Eg *Weekly Packet*, 30 July–6 Aug. 1715; *Weekly Journal with Fresh Advices Foreign and Domestick*, 13 Aug. 1715.

[8] A. Williams, *Poetry and the Creation of a Whig Literary Culture, 1681–1714* (Oxford, 2005), pp. 125–7.

[9] *Weekly Packet*, 30 July–6 Aug. 1715.

[10] *Weekly Packet*, 30 July–6 Aug. 1715; *Weekly Journal with Fresh Advices Foreign and Domestick*, 13 Aug. 1715. 'William Ellis' does not appear in the *ODNB*, *The London Stage* or other relevant databases. However, there is an *ODNB* article on a 'Jacobite politician' named Sir William Ellis who held office at the Jacobite court at this time; he does not seem to have been a published writer. P. Wauchope, 'Sir William Ellis', *ODNB*.

[11] *Weekly Journal with Fresh Advices Foreign and Domestick*, Saturday, 13 Aug. 1715; *Weekly Packet*, 30 July–6 Aug. 1715; *Weekly Packet*, 6–13 Aug. 1715; *British Weekly Mercury*, 6–13 Aug. 1715.

in the newspapers, but, in a letter of 1718, claimed that he would have been appointed to succeed Tate if it had not been for Rowe, to which fact (Oldmixon stated) Samuel Garth could testify.[12] The tenor and context of Oldmixon's letter (which will form this chapter's first case study, below) give reason to believe that he was exaggerating on this point, particularly given his non-appearance in contemporary newspapers, but he was presumably at least known to have a claim on the office. The nature of this claim would have rested on his tenacious Whig politics and his standing as a man of letters; by 1715, he was primarily known for Whiggish prose tracts and more miscellaneous non-fiction writings. But he was somewhat lacking in connections, living in Somerset and linked to London chiefly through his communications with Jacob Tonson.[13]

In 1715, then, the laurel was gained by a pre-eminent tragic playwright with impeccable Whig credentials and the means and abilities to acquire court patronage. As well as an indeterminate number of now-invisible competitors, he defeated two fellow Whig writers who lacked his courtliness and connections and whose writings were not only less celebrated than his, but had come to centre on non-fiction prose. There is no evidence as to who may have made the appointment decision, although Oldmixon believed Samuel Garth, the poet, physician and Kit-Cat Club stalwart, to have infallible knowledge on the matter. The lord chamberlain at the time was the duke of Bolton, who had only just taken up the position and was widely regarded by contemporaries as a buffoon.[14] He was, however, a staunchly pro-Hanoverian Whig and former Junto follower, and his correspondence shows that he was concerned with favouring those who were known to be loyal to the new regime.[15] Although he technically had the office in his gift, he perhaps would not have exerted much agency over the matter, or would have bowed to the arguments and intercessions of others. But any preference he did show would have surely been for someone known to be a strong Whig, like Rowe.

[12] BL Add MS. 28275, fo. 46. Printed in J. Oldmixon, *The Letters, Life and Works of John Oldmixon: Politics and Professional Authorship in Early Hanoverian England*, ed. P. Rogers (Lampeter, 2004), pp. 54–7, and J. Tonson the Elder et al., *The Literary Correspondences of the Tonsons*, ed. S. Bernard (Oxford, 2016; first published 2015), pp. 184–6; the two publications give essentially the same transcription, but the Rogers publication has more extensive notes.

[13] J. A. Downie, 'Foreword', in *Oldmixon*, ed. Rogers, pp. iii–v; P. Rogers, 'Life', in *Oldmixon*, ed. Rogers, pp. 13–27.

[14] M. Kilburn, 'Charles Paulet [Powlett], second duke of Bolton', *ODNB*.

[15] 'Charles Paulet, 2nd duke of Bolton to Joseph Addison, Monday, 4 October 1717 – [a fragment]', *Electronic Enlightenment Scholarly Edition of Correspondence*; 'Charles Paulet, 2nd duke of Bolton to Joseph Addison, Sunday, 21 November 1717', *Electronic Enlightenment Scholarly Edition of Correspondence*.

For 1718, although there is likewise no direct evidence, the case is clearer. Laurence Eusden, the Cambridge Fellow and budding poet, had already been forging a small place for himself in the Addison–Steele nexus of literary London, contributing to Steele's *Poetical Miscellanies* (1714) and to *The Spectator* and *The Guardian*, and addressing poems to Halifax and Addison.[16] In 1717, he published a reasonably popular epithalamium on the wedding of the duke and duchess of Newcastle, at a time when Newcastle was not only lord chamberlain and a prominent member of the Kit-Cat Club, but was also trying to establish himself as a great literary patron in the mould of Dorset (one of his forebears as lord chamberlain, and another Kit-Catter) and Halifax (also a Kit-Catter).[17] In 1718, the laureateship became vacant, and Eusden was promptly appointed. The unreliable Cibber–Shiels biographical compendium of the mid century, *The Lives of the Poets*, was to attribute this appointment to Newcastle, and was also to offer its opinion that Eusden deserved the honour, being morally unblemished and a not inconsiderable versifier.[18]

The only other known candidate was Oldmixon, whose aforementioned letter dates from this time, and consists of a plea to Tonson to intercede on his behalf with Newcastle. However, Oldmixon made vague reference to Thomas Tickell, John Hughes and John Dennis, seeming unsure as to whether or not they would contend with him;[19] and Garth had apparently written to Newcastle encouraging him to favour Leonard Welsted.[20] Pat Rogers, in a note to his transcription of Oldmixon's letter, states, 'There were indeed alleged to be many candidates for the vacant post.' But he bases this claim on John Sheffield's poem 'The Election of a Poet Laureate in 1719', which was simply a new, topical iteration of the 'Session of the Poets' tradition of poems, and included depictions of most major writers of the time vying for the laurel crown, at least several of whom were evidently never in contention for the laureateship.[21] Rogers does admit as much, and then adds, more plausibly, 'the poem may perhaps reflect a degree of excitement and charged interest in quarters of literary London somewhat remote from

[16] J. Sambrook, 'Laurence Eusden', *ODNB*.

[17] O. Field, '"In and Out": An analysis of Kit-Cat Club membership' (Web Appendix to *The Kit-Cat Club* by Ophelia Field, 2008); O. Field, *The Kit-Cat Club* (London, 2009; first published 2008), pp. 308–9, 330, 334, 350.

[18] T. Cibber [and Robert Shiels], *The Lives of the Poets* (4 vols, 1753), iv. 193–5.

[19] Oldmixon letter, pp. 54–5. References are to the printing in *Oldmixon*, ed. Rogers.

[20] R. Steele, *The Correspondence of Richard Steele*, ed. R. Blanchard (Oxford, 1941), p. 111.

[21] J. Sheffield, *The Election of a Poet Laureat* (1719), reprinted in J. Sheffield, *Works* (2 vols, 1723), i. 195–200.

Grub Street'.[22] In any case, beyond Oldmixon and Eusden (and perhaps Welsted), it is impossible to find any other definite contenders.

It seems almost certain that Newcastle made the appointment decision. Given his later activities as a patronage magnate, and his later reputation for jealousy, pettiness and paranoia, it is probable that he made this decision alone.[23] However, one of Addison's biographers has speculated that Addison may have advanced Eusden's claim.[24] Moreover, there were certainly times during Newcastle's tenure that George I (or someone close to him) selected someone for a position in the lord chamberlain's jurisdiction, with Newcastle required to do no more than rubber-stamp the decision. Similarly, there is evidence of Newcastle deciding upon an appointment to a different office and then seeking the king's ratification for it.[25] In the case of a poetic office, though, it seems improbable that George I would have been overly concerned with the decision, given his incomprehension of English and dislike of ceremony.[26]

For the 1730 decision, the evidence is much better. The newspaper press had developed substantially, and a greater number of letters from the time have survived.[27] Colley Cibber, Lewis Theobald and Stephen Duck were the main candidates, perhaps along with Matthew Concanen; and Richard Savage was in some sense involved as well.[28] Cibber was appointed. The claim made in his autobiographical *Apology* (1740) that 'Part of the Bread I now eat, was given me, for having writ the *Nonjuror*' has generally been taken to refer to the laureateship.[29] He also wrote there, 'In the Year 1730,

[22] Rogers, Note 2 to Oldmixon letter, p. 55.

[23] R. Browning, 'Thomas Pelham-Holles, duke of Newcastle upon Tyne and first duke of Newcastle under Lyme', *ODNB*; P. Langford, *A Polite and Commercial People: England, 1727–1783* (Oxford, 1992), pp. 14, 18, 43, 54, 188–9, 195, 206–12, 217–20, 223–32.

[24] P. Smithers, *The Life of Joseph Addison* (Oxford, 1954), p. 209.

[25] Beattie, *English Court*, pp. 132–8.

[26] J. Black, 'Foreword to the Yale Edition', in R. Hatton, *George I*, with new foreword by J. Black (New Haven, Conn., 2001), pp. 1–8, at pp. 1–3; Hatton, *George I*, pp. 132–42.

[27] For more on the appointment and reaction to it, B. A. Goldgar, *Walpole and the Wits: The Relation of Politics to Literature, 1722–1742* (Lincoln, Neb., 1976), pp. 89–98; H. Koon, *Colley Cibber: A Biography* (Kentucky, 1986), pp. 125–6.

[28] *The Weekly Register*, 31 Oct. 1730; *The St. James's Evening Post*, 29–31 Oct. 1730; Swift, *Correspondence*, iii. 421; R. M. Davis, *Stephen Duck, The Thresher-Poet* (Orono, Maine, 1926), pp. 40–50; D. J. Ennis, 'Honours', in *The Oxford Handbook of British Poetry, 1660–1800*, ed. J. Lynch (Oxford, 2016), pp. 732–46, at p. 738; J. H. Middendorf, editorial note in S. Johnson, 'Savage', in *Lives of the Poets*, ed. J. H. Middendorf (3 vols, New Haven, Conn., 2010), ii. 184–968, at p. 885.

[29] C. Cibber, *An Apology for the Life of Colley Cibber* (2 vols, 1756; first published 1740), ii. 58; K. Hopkins, *The Poets Laureate* (London, 1954), p. 68.

there were many Authors, whose Merit wanted nothing but Interest to recommend them to the vacant *Laurel*.'[30] Certainly, he was on good terms with various high-ranking Whig peers and politicians, and was recognized as a firm adherent to, or even oblique bulwark of, the Walpole ministry. The *Non-Juror* had played a significant part in this, while also being hugely successful among theatregoers and eliciting the hefty financial favour of George I. The duke of Grafton, lord chamberlain 1724–57 and close friend of George II, esteemed Cibber both socially and (although apparently not much interested in books)[31] as a playwright, as did Walpole, Henry Pelham and Newcastle.[32] Cibber had also recently dedicated his and Vanbrugh's comedy, *The Provok'd Husband* (1728), to Queen Caroline.

Cibber's biographer Koon has further adduced, as a reason for his appointment, that by 1730, his plays enjoyed more popularity on the stage than any other living playwright's.[33] But Swift, Pope and their circle of correspondents had something to say on the subject too. Lady Elizabeth Germain wrote to Swift over two months after Cibber's appointment, 'if it was the Q. and not the Duke of G: that picked out such a Laureat she deserves his Poetry in her praises'.[34] Pope reported, in a letter of 1728, 'I am told the Gynocracy are of opinion, that they want no better writers than Cibber and the British Journalist.'[35] Germain's suggestion came in the same sentence as her admission that she was not well acquainted with Pope, so it may be the case that Swift had merely passed Pope's report on to her, and that she was responding to it, rather than having had the testimony from another source; but in any case, this suggestion of the influence of Queen Caroline (and her female entourage) is noteworthy, and will be discussed as the second case study. Swift's own analysis was more mercurial:

> as to Cibber if I had any inclination to excuse, the Court I would alledge that the Laureats place is entirely in the Lord Chamberlain's gift; but who makes Lord Chamberlains is another question. I believe if the Court had interceded with D. of Grafton for a fitter Man, it might have prevailed.[36]

However, it was widely felt at the time that the favourite poet of Queen Caroline was Stephen Duck, and that, whether or not everyone else was

---

[30] Cibber, *Apology*, i. 35.

[31] J. Black, *George II: Puppet of the Politicians?* (Exeter, 2007), p. 127.

[32] Goldgar, *Walpole*, pp. 189–96; Koon, *Cibber*, passim, especially p. 125.

[33] Koon, *Cibber*, pp. 125–6.

[34] Swift, *Correspondence*, iii. 441.

[35] Swift, *Correspondence*, iii. 265.

[36] Swift, *Correspondence*, iii. 459.

simply following her lead, Duck was in fashion at court. Both before and after the matter of the laureateship, Caroline showered bounties on Duck, and they did not slip off his back. He was given offices, a home, a wife and a pension. But he had no politics to speak of and no connection with Walpole's ministry, and his writings (all lyric poetry), though fairly popular in publication, were something of a novelty act, being rooted in his background as a rustic labourer who had taught himself to read and write.[37] Furthermore, Duck was away from court around the time of Eusden's death, attending the deathbed of his first wife, and Hopkins has suggested that this absence was the critical factor in his failure.[38]

Theobald, meanwhile, was solidly present at court at this time, attending daily and wearing himself out specifically so as to acquire the laureateship. But although he had a wide-ranging literary output, he was not as distinguished a writer as Cibber, and, by his own admission, he had no powerful patrons.[39] Neither was Richard Savage as distinguished or well connected as Cibber, and he would probably have been considered too unreliable for the laureateship anyway (although he later became Caroline's 'Volunteer Laureate', writing her birthday poems in exchange for a pension).[40] Matthew Concanen was a solid Whig and journeyman poet who, at some point around 1730, attracted the patronage of Newcastle, but who was never especially successful or well respected; he does not loom large in the competition for the office.[41] Surprisingly, then, it would seem that Colley Cibber – the most reviled man in the history of the laureateship – was appointed because, unlike any other writer of the day, he had every possible recommendation for the job. His backers were potentially legion.

At one point during his tenure, when he feared himself to be dying, Cibber wrote to Grafton (whose time as lord chamberlain was almost entirely coeval with Cibber's as laureate) requesting that his successor be Henry Jones, an Irish poet. However, Cibber recovered. By the time that he sank into an illness from which he could *not* recover (1757), Jones had become obscurer, and less dear to Cibber, than he had been at the time

[37] For more on Duck, see Davis, *Duck*, especially pp. 40–93; B. Keegan, 'The poet as labourer', in *British Poetry, 1660–1800*, ed. Lynch, pp. 162–78; L. Stephens, revised by W. R. Jones, 'Stephen Duck', *ODNB*.

[38] Hopkins, *Poets Laureate*, pp. 73–4.

[39] P. Seary, 'Lewis Theobald', *ODNB*; Lewis Theobald to William Warburton, Dec. 1730, in *Illustrations of the Literary History of the Eighteenth Century*, ed. J. Nichols (8 vols, Cambridge, 2014; first published 1817–58), ii. 616–18.

[40] D. Griffin, *Literary Patronage in England, 1650–1800* (Cambridge, 1996), pp. 169–88; Johnson, 'Savage', pp. 910–15; F. Johnston, 'Richard Savage', *ODNB*.

[41] J. Sambrook, 'Matthew Concanen', *ODNB*.

of Cibber's sickly, but not mortally sickly, endorsement. Nonetheless, he did appear in an early and ill-informed newspaper report on the contest to become laureate, in *Lloyd's Evening Post*: 'The following Gentlemen are talked of as Candidates … Mr. Mason, Mr. Henry Jones, Mr. Lockman, Mr. Boyce, and Mr. Hackett.'[42] For the most part, these names do not show up elsewhere. 'Mr. Boyce' may have been a reference to a writer named Thomas Boyce, but the candidacy of a 'Boyce' for the laureateship was more likely a misunderstanding: the musician and composer William Boyce had been appointed master of the king's music in December 1755, and was not officially sworn in until June 1757, a few months before Cibber's death.[43] Since the master of the king's music was responsible for composing the music for the laureates' annual odes, it would have been easy to assume he was involved with the laureateship. The most that can be said for 'Mr. Hackett' is that he was very obscure.[44] John Lockman, like many of the writers mentioned so far, had a wide-ranging, miscellaneous body of work to his name, and his greatest successes were in prose; he had also been appointed secretary to the council of the Free British Fishery in 1750, inspiring him to publish prose and verse works about fish.[45] None of these men seem to have been particularly known for their politics.

William Mason, poet, clergyman, polymath and busybody, regarded himself as a fervent 'old Whig'.[46] This designation meant different things at different times, and even to different people, but Mason believed his principles to have been '*in* fashion' in the latter years of George II's reign, and '*out* of fashion' thereafter.[47] Yet political works were never very prominent in

[42] *Lloyd's Evening Post and British Chronicle*, 12–14 Dec. 1757.

[43] R. J. Bruce, 'William Boyce', *ODNB*.

[44] A search of 'Hackett' as author on *ECCO* for the dates 1740–1760 brings up only two publications: a collection of epigrams and a two-volume collection of epitaphs, both dated 1757, both edited by John Hackett ('Late Commoner of Baliol-College, Oxford' according to the epitaph volume).

[45] J. Sambrook, 'John Lockman', *ODNB*.

[46] On Mason, J. W. Draper, *William Mason: A Study in Eighteenth-Century Culture* (New York, 1924).

[47] *Warton Correspondence*, lt. 348, at pp. 386–7. He was also involved in the Yorkshire Association movement, keeping up a regular correspondence with Christopher Wyvill until the two of them fell out in the 1790s. Mason–Wyvill correspondence in North Yorkshire County Record Office, ZFW 7/2/45/1, 7/2/45/11, 7/2/53/5, 7/2/66/6, 7/2/66/10, 7/2/66/19, 7/2/66/23, 7/2/66/24, 7/2/66/26, 7/2/71/16, 7/2/84.9, 7/2/89/25. For more on the varieties and evolution of 18th-century Whiggism, see J. G. A. Pocock, *Virtue, Commerce, and History: Essays on Political Thought and History, Chiefly in the Eighteenth Century* (Cambridge, 1985), pp. 215–310; '*Cultures of Whiggism': New Essays on English Literature and Culture in the Long Eighteenth Century*, ed. D. Womersley (Newark, Del., 2005).

Mason's sprawling, interdisciplinary oeuvre, and, when his politics fell '*out* of fashion', he turned to pseudonyms and anonymity as a vehicle for his political publications.[48] He was one of the most well-connected men of his day, and an assiduous seeker of patronage (for himself and for others).[49] He was the private tutor, and afterwards lifelong friend, of Lord John Cavendish, whose older brother William, duke of Devonshire, served as lord chamberlain between 1757 and 1762. Through this connection with the Cavendishes, Mason was made a royal chaplain in 1757, and held the post until 1772, most of his tenure thus coming under George III and the kinds of ministries that Mason disliked.

The year of his appointment to the royal chaplaincy – a year when Mason's politics were still '*in* fashion' – was also the year of Cibber's death. In the event, Mason did play a part in the appointment process, though he was not (as Horace Walpole believed) offered the laureateship himself.[50] As he later explained in his memoirs of Thomas Gray (1775) and Whitehead (1788), the lord chamberlain, Devonshire, told his brother, Lord John Cavendish, to offer the laureateship to Gray, whereupon Lord John, being busy elsewhere, passed on the commission to Mason.[51] Gray was a lifelong Cambridge Fellow, and had few contacts among writers, nobles or statesmen; nor had he ever publicly expressed or been identified with any political persuasion. But he was close friends with Mason and with Lord John, and, as well as having published his massively popular *Elegy* several years before, had recently published his two *Odes*, provoking widespread fascination. The laurel came to him unsolicited, and he rejected it.

It was then offered to Whitehead, another non-political and somewhat reclusive figure who was best known for *The Roman Father*, a repertory play of the second half of the eighteenth century. Along with Gray, Mason and 'Warton' (and also Young, Armstrong and Akenside), Whitehead had recently been commended by the *Critical Review* as one of the great poets of the age, 'not inferior to *Pope himself*, and who might have vied with him in reputation, had they been as properly introduced into the temple of Fame'.[52]

---

[48] Eg *Heroic Epistle to Sir William Chambers* (1773). See *Warton Correspondence*, lt. 348, at pp. 386–7.

[49] *Warton Correspondence*, ltt. 347–8, at pp. 385–7.

[50] H. Walpole, *Memoirs of King George II*, ed. J. Brooke (3 vols, New Haven, Conn., 1985), ii. 294.

[51] W. Mason, 'Memoirs of the life and writings of Mr. Gray', in T. Gray, *The Poems of Mr. Gray*, ed. W. Mason (2 vols, 1775), ii. 1–159, at p. 18; 'Whitehead Memoirs', pp. 86–8.

[52] *CR* 1.3, April 1756, p. 276. For *The Roman Father* (1750), see Chapter Four. For Whitehead's distaste of politics, see eg Whitehead letters to George Simon Harcourt, Bod MS., Eng misc d. 3844, fos. 41–42b, 112; but for his private political convictions, see eg Eng misc d. 3845, fos. 91–b; Eng misc d. 3846, fos. 10–b, 13, 92b.

Whitehead did not know the Cavendishes, but he was the tutor of the scions of the aristocratic Jersey and Harcourt families. Their intercessions had already procured him the position of secretary and registrar to the Order of the Bath, and Earl Harcourt had once been governor of the prince of Wales (the future George III).[53] It is generally thought that this connection was what determined the appointment in Whitehead's favour.[54]

However, there is some reason to doubt this. When Whitehead had been appointed secretary and registrar, he had profusely thanked Lord and Lady Jersey for their endeavours on his behalf. Evidently, he had therefore known who was responsible for the favour, despite having been in Germany at the time.[55] Yet the laureateship, he later claimed, came to him 'Unask'd … and from a friend unknown': a comment which Mason endorsed.[56] The Jerseys had been seeking places for Whitehead for several years by this point; in one letter of 1753, Lord Jersey pointed out to Newcastle that a place in the Wardrobe had just become vacant, and said, 'I need not repeat to your Grace how much it is incumbent on us to serve Mr Whitehead; or how greatly we should think ourselves obliged if you could obtain it.'[57] It is possible, therefore, that Devonshire or someone close to him remembered Whitehead's needfulness and decided to have the laureateship given to him without any direct prompting by the Jersey family (or by the Harcourts). Yet if this were so, the unknown agent would probably still have informed the Jerseys or Harcourts of the favour that they had done them, and on what remembrance they had done it. Another relevant consideration is that since the Jersey family had previously been assiduous in seeking positions for Whitehead, it seems unlikely that they would have been completely inactive when such an obviously applicable post as that of poet laureate became available (unless they believed his position as secretary and registrar sufficient).[58]

---

[53] This position placed intermittent responsibilities on Whitehead. Bod MS., Eng misc d. 3845, fos. 99–b, 110; George the Third, *The Correspondence of King George the Third: From 1760 to December 1783*, ed. J. Fortescue (6 vols, London, 1927), ii. lt. 794, at p. 148, lt. 909, at p. 217, lt. 910, at p. 218.

[54] Eg E. K. Broadus, *The Laureateship* (Oxford, 1921), p. 136.

[55] William Whitehead to Lord Jersey, 7 June, 16 Sept. and 29 Nov. 1755. London Metropolitan Archives, Acc. 510/242, 510/245, 510/246.

[56] 'Whitehead Memoirs', p. 87.

[57] Lord Jersey to Newcastle, 29 Nov. 1753. BL Add MS. 32733.

[58] Orr claims that Whitehead gained the post due to Lady Jersey's influence on the duchess of Newcastle, who, Orr says, was a friend of Lady Jersey's and the wife of the lord chamberlain. But she gives no evidence for this claim, which must be at least partly mistaken: the duke of Newcastle had not been lord chamberlain for a few decades, and, although he was now prime minister, he had left behind his literary interests long before

Perhaps, then, it was the case that the Jersey family (or perhaps the Harcourts) did intercede on Whitehead's behalf, and successfully, but either they did not inform Whitehead on this occasion, or he feigned ignorance in public as to who had interceded for him. Perhaps it was the Jerseys' wont to be silent about their favours to him, and he had only heard of their intercession in the case of the Bath position through another channel. But it is an equally likely scenario that on the occasion of Cibber's death, the Jersey family was too predisposed or unaware to intercede in time, and the laureateship was offered to Whitehead of Devonshire's own volition, or on the prompting of another, mysterious agent. As for Mason, he was apparently told by Lord John that he had been considered for the office, but that it had been thought improper to bestow it upon someone in holy orders: which, Mason told his readers, was a reason 'I was glad to hear assigned; and if I had thought it a weak one, they who know me, will readily believe that I am the last man in the world who would have attempted to controvert it'.[59] One biographer of Gray has asserted that Mason had 'wished for' the office, and 'raged with disappointment' not to get it.[60] A more recent biographer, Robert Mack, mentions this assertion doubtfully, but with no outright disagreement, and further suggests that Gray's letter to Mason explaining why he turned the post down may entail a 'thinly veiled attack on Mason's own vanity'.[61] But there are no grounds for either suggestion. The most pertinent questions are whether Mason was given this explanation by Lord John before or after Gray's refusal (the chronology is unclear in Mason's account), and whether Lord John's stated reason for rejecting Mason was sincere, or was merely a sop to Mason's rageful, thinly veiled vanity.

The laureateship, then, had been offered to two rather reclusive men, neither of whom had any apparent connection with political affairs, but who were both friends with Mason and who were each on intimate terms with a couple of (different) well-placed peers. They were both respectable

---

1757. Orr is probably speculating on the basis of Mason's comment that Whitehead owed his Bath appointment to Lady Jersey's influence, or is confusing that comment with Mason's subsequent description of Whitehead's laureate appointment. Even Mason's ascription of Whitehead's Bath appointment to Lady Jersey's influence is arguably mistaken, since Whitehead's letters, and the 1753 letter from Lord Jersey to Newcastle, show Lord Jersey taking the lead in interceding for Whitehead; Lady Jersey, who was often very ill, seems to have had a more background role. 'Whitehead Memoirs', pp. 86–7; C. C. Orr, 'Queen Charlotte, "scientific queen"', in *Queenship in Britain 1660–1837: Royal Patronage, Court Culture and Dynastic Politics*, ed. C. C. Orr (Manchester, 2002), pp. 236–66, at p. 255.

[59] 'Whitehead Memoirs', pp. 87–8.

[60] E. Gosse, *Gray* (London, 1895), p. 138.

[61] R. L. Mack, *Thomas Gray: A Life* (New Haven, Conn., 2000), pp. 498–9.

poets who had not dabbled much in prose. However, when the office became vacant in 1785, it was passed on to Thomas Warton, who was in most respects a different kind of figure. He was an Oxford Fellow, and, like Gray and Whitehead, had not exerted himself for the laureateship; but he was far more closely connected with the London-based world of arts and literature than either of those men, and was known more for his work as a literary historian than for his lyric poetry. He seems to have inspired a fairly disinterested zeal of intercessory generosity in those who knew him; his campaign for the Oxford Regius Professor of History post in 1768–71 had, for example, been taken to heart by William Warburton (then bishop of Gloucester).[62] Likewise in 1785, Warton was informed by Edmond Malone, 'Some of your friends here have spoken of you for the Laureat, and wish you to think of it for yourself.'[63]

At least one of those friends had spoken very much to the point. Already, the previous day, Warton had written to Joshua Reynolds, offering 'Many, many thanks for your most friendly exertions in my favour. How can I refuse what you have so kindly procured? The laurel was never more honourably obtained.'[64] Reynolds was at this time president of the Royal Academy, and enjoyed a testy, sporadic communication with George III, in addition to being close to many other well-placed politicians, peers, artists and writers.[65] However, the newspapers of the time also mentioned rumours that the king himself had intervened to have Warton made laureate, and Joseph Warton wrote to his and Thomas's sister, 'the King has sent to offer it Him in the Handsomest manner'.[66] Around this time, the antiquary Michael Lort wrote to a correspondent that there was disagreement as to whether Reynolds or George III had been responsible.[67] Newspaper evidence from the next several years suggests that George III's preference and intervention became the generally accepted reason for Warton's appointment.[68]

[62] D. Fairer, 'Introduction: The achievement of Thomas Warton', in *Warton Correspondence*, pp. xvii–xxxvi, at p. xxvi; *Warton Correspondence*, lt. 263, at pp. 293–4.

[63] *Warton Correspondence*, lt. 482, at p. 529.

[64] *Warton Correspondence*, lt. 481, at p. 527.

[65] H. Hoock, *The King's Artists: The Royal Academy of Arts and the Politics of British Culture 1760–1840* (Oxford, 2003), pp. 136–79; J. Reynolds, *The Letters of Sir Joshua Reynolds*, ed. J. Ingamells and J. Edgcumbe (New Haven, Conn., 2000), lt. 25, at p. 32, lt. 38, at p. 49, lt. 172, at p. 183, lt. 195, at pp. 202–3, lt. 227, at p. 227.

[66] *General Advertiser*, 25 April 1785; Joseph Warton to Jane Warton, 29 April 1785, Bod, MS. Don. c. 75, fos. 39–40b.

[67] *Illustrations*, ed. Nichols, vii. 468.

[68] *General Evening Post*, 28–30 April 1785; *Public Advertiser*, 2 June 1790.

A few decades later, John O'Keeffe mentioned in his *Recollections* (1826) that he had gone to see Lord Salisbury (lord chamberlain, 1783–1804) upon Whitehead's death and asked to be made poet laureate, to which Salisbury had replied that 'he had not the smallest objection; but that he had previously given his promise to another'.[69] Yet there is no indication of whether, on this occasion, Salisbury's 'promise' represented a rubber-stamping of someone else's decision, or whether it had been motivated by either Reynolds or George III. Despite the titles and positions that Reynolds accrued under George, and the intermittent communications between the two men, their relationship was not a smooth one, so it is unlikely that Reynolds gained Warton the office by interceding with George himself. Perhaps Reynolds suggested Warton to Salisbury, who passed on the suggestion to George; perhaps Reynolds and George both decided upon Warton independently. Reynolds did not know Salisbury well, but was in occasional, distant interaction with him.[70] Whatever Reynolds's involvement, it therefore seems likely that George had the decisive say on this occasion.

Other than O'Keeffe, the only identifiable competitor to Warton was Robert Potter, who was described by the newspaper that mentioned him as 'the Translator, of Aeschylus'.[71] However, there is no further evidence of his candidacy, and he was not as prominent a public figure as Warton. In any case, the translator of ancient Greek literature lost out to the redeemer of England's own literary past. Rumours connected Mason with the post on this occasion and again in 1790; for example, one newspaper in 1788 referred to Hayley and Mason as 'disappointed candidates for the Laureatship'.[72] But that newspaper was almost certainly wrong about Hayley, and Mason's twentieth-century biographer has expressed doubt as to the truth of these rumours. Mason himself always insisted that he had no such wish.[73]

In 1790, it was stated that 'Many persons have been spoken of as being intended to fill the vacant place of Laureate.'[74] However, the only genuine candidates now identifiable are William Hayley, Henry James Pye and (perhaps) Robert Merry. The former was a popular, fashionable poet, primarily on account of his didactic poem to women, *The Triumphs*

---

[69] J. O'Keeffe, *Recollections of the Life of John O'Keeffe* (2 vols, 1826), ii. 132–3.

[70] Reynolds, *Letters*, lt. 121, at pp. 126–7, lt. 180, at p. 189.

[71] *General Advertiser*, 25 April 1785.

[72] *Morning Chronicle and London Advertiser*, 10 Nov. 1788.

[73] Draper, *William Mason*, pp. 106–7, 114–15. Ennis asserts that Mason was offered the laurel in 1785 and refused it, but gives no evidence, and is probably repeating rumour or speculation from elsewhere. Ennis, 'Honours', p. 734.

[74] *Diary or Woodfall's Register*, 7 June 1790.

of Temper (1781), which was perhaps the most popular English poem of George III's reign until the emergence of Scott and Byron. He had many prominent acquaintances, including a crew of fellow Williams: Pitt the Younger, Cowper and Blake. Indeed, he was later to acquire a government pension for Cowper from Pitt, whom he had met and befriended when Pitt was only fourteen.[75] Upon Warton's death, Pitt, who was then prime minister, apparently offered the laureateship to Hayley, who turned it down, thanking him in verse for the offer.[76] The post was then offered to Pye, who accepted. Pye and Hayley were both prolific poets, and Pye had been a loyal Pittite MP from 1784 until just before Warton's death; his initial election campaign had been supported by a large grant from the government's secret service fund.[77] He and Hayley also had a great mutual respect for each other's work, with commendatory verses to each other published in Pye's 1787 *Poems on Various Subjects*.[78] When Pye complimented Cowper in a prose work, Hayley wrote to Cowper to draw his attention to it, and Cowper expressed gratification at receiving praise from such a source.[79] Perhaps, then, Hayley put a word in for Pye to Pitt in 1790.

In any case, Pye exploited his own connection to Pitt as rigorously as possible, continually courting him, both in person and by letters, in search of places. It was probably primarily by these means that he gained the office (as shall be investigated in the third case study, below). Meanwhile, the candidacy of Robert Merry is known only by a single newspaper report: 'Mr. Merry, who was a *Cambridge Man*, should he be chosen Laureat, will, in turn, vindicate the honours of that University.'[80] It is not clear how much weight should be placed on this testimony, since the paper in question, *The World*, enjoyed a friendly working relationship with Merry, and had been regularly publishing his Della Cruscan poetry for several years by this time. Moreover, in 1790, Merry's sympathies were already turning in favour of the French Revolution, which would not have endeared him to the government.

---

[75] William Hayley, *Memoirs of the Life and Writings of William Hayley Esq.* (2 vols, 1823, i. 127–8.

[76] Hayley, *Memoirs*, ii. 35; V. W. Painting, 'William Hayley', *ODNB*.

[77] TNA, PRO 30/8/169, fos. 256–b; George III, *The Later Correspondence of George III*, ed. A. Aspinall (5 vols, Cambridge, 1962), i. lt. 62, at p. 50, lt. 158, at p. 157.

[78] H. J. Pye, *Poems on Various Subjects* (2 vols, 1787), i. 45–9.

[79] W. Cowper, *The Letters and Prose Writings of William Cowper*, ed. J. King and C. Ryskamp (5 vols, Oxford, 1979–86), iv. 123–4.

[80] *The World*, 7 June 1790.

Last of all was the 1813 appointment.[81] Although various poets hoped for the office, the only men who could ever have been offered it were Walter Scott (who had first refusal) and Robert Southey. In this decision, both the prince regent (the future George IV) and the prime minister, Lord Liverpool, were in agreement. The lord chamberlain was then the marquess of Hertford, who was seventy years old. He favoured Scott, and was cagey about Southey due to the latter's former reputation as a radical. Throughout the decision process, though, Hertford was keenly solicitous of Liverpool's opinion, and set his compass primarily by this reference point. Scott did not make any request for the office, but the historiographer and royal librarian James Stanier Clarke probably agitated on his behalf, whereas Southey's claim was pushed by, among others, John Wilson Croker (secretary to the Admiralty) and certain members of Hertford's own family. Liverpool seems to have been the prime decision-maker, but with the prince regent greatly important too, and the lord chamberlain was not much more than a rubber-stamper on this occasion. As for the reasons behind Scott and then Southey's selection, all of the men involved in the selection process avowed a desire to appoint the best poet in the kingdom. It was also significant that both poets were strongly associated with the *Quarterly Review*. This journal, which enjoyed a huge readership, was pro-ministerial, and a belligerent advocate for the war that Lord Liverpool's government was prosecuting.

Now that the individual laureateship appointments for the Hanoverian period have been examined in turn, it is time to cast a critical look over the evidence as a whole, so as to answer the questions raised in the introduction to this chapter.

Patterns and consistencies

The first question is what wider trends can be identified across these appointments, especially with regard to who made the decision, what kind of people were considered for the post and the reasons for a laureate's appointment.

On at least one occasion (1757), the lord chamberlain (Devonshire) can be seen to have chosen the laureate, probably in discussion with his brother, possibly in response to intercessions from elsewhere, but with no evidence of his being directed from above. Similarly, in 1718, it cannot seriously be doubted that the lord chamberlain (Newcastle) selected the laureate. There are suggestions that certain people interceded with him: the literary men, Tonson, Addison, Garth and certain 'Illustrious Persons' speculated on by Oldmixon. However, for the reasons already given, it seems likely that

---

[81] On this appointment process, L. Shipp, 'Appointing a poet laureate: National and poetic identities in 1813', *The English Historical Review*, cxxxvi (2021), 332–63.

Newcastle's personal preference was strong from the beginning and that he determined the choice himself. In 1730, the lord chamberlain (Grafton) appointed the laureate in a formal sense, but contemporaries believed that his decision had been influenced by others, or that others could have contravened it, had they so wished. It should also be remembered that Grafton was notoriously boorish and illiterate. For the later appointments, the lord chamberlain Salisbury was involved in 1785 but not attributed any agency by contemporaries, and was then overshadowed (if not ignored) by the prime minister, Pitt, in 1790, while in 1813 the lord chamberlain simply ratified the decisions of others. Given that the laureateship remained, throughout this period, an office that was technically in the lord chamberlain's gift, the evidence as a whole would point to the conclusion that the lord chamberlains could and did select the laureates in the reigns of George I and George II, and that, even under George III, the default procedure was that the lord chamberlain should select the laureate and offer that person the post without recourse to anyone else. However, there was always room for other powerful voices to exert themselves on the matter, if they so chose; and, in George III's reign, the selection of the laureate became seen as a matter which went beyond the lord chamberlain's remit. It became a valid object of concern for kings, prince regents and, especially, prime ministers, any of whom would expect their opinion to be carried if they put it forward.

A comprehensive view of the appointments would therefore suggest that in 1715 – when Rowe was appointed, but by an unknown agency – it was probably the lord chamberlain, the duke of Bolton, who made the decision, but that he probably acted on advice and intercession rather than according to any great personal preference. Likewise, in 1730, a comparison with other appointments encourages an emphasis on Grafton's role in the decision, but also flags up the importance of the lord chamberlain's personality, as this particular one showed little interest in posts such as the laureateship. As for 1785, when Pitt was not yet established in power or as assertive as he was in 1790, it seems valid to suggest that Salisbury, while fairly indifferent as to who should be poet laureate, was the person with whom Reynolds interceded to have Warton made laureate (if Reynolds's contribution was key), and that he either passed on this suggestion to George III, or was the initial and major recipient of George's own suggestion as to Warton being made laureate. Therefore, it was probably only in 1790 and 1813 that the lord chamberlain was not much involved in the decision-making process and that an assertive prime minister took the laureate selection mostly upon himself.

However, this pattern also indicates the importance of royalty in the decision-making. In 1785, George III clearly had some role in the appointment. If he played no part in the 1790 appointment, then it should be remembered that he had only recently recovered from his first bout of madness, and was now beginning to leave the direction of national affairs securely in the hands of Pitt. By 1813, he was fully incapacitated; but, in his absence, Southey's appointment did see heavy involvement from the prince regent.

As for the appointments under George I and II, there is no hint of those kings having had any involvement. This too is what would be expected on the basis of their personalities. George I did not speak English and George II's first language was German, and, while their general attitude to matters of high culture has been debated by historians, they undoubtedly had no interest in English-language literature.[82] It is highly instructive that, across their two reigns, the only appointment to have been connected by contemporaries with the royal family was that of 1730. This was the only appointment between George I and George III's accessions to occur when England had a queen, and the queen in question was George II's wife Caroline. Recent decades have seen an increasing appreciation for Caroline, who is now regarded as having turned the court into a vibrant, flourishing social venue and having had a highly significant role as a patron of artistic and intellectual matters.[83] Whereas the courts of George I and George II are supposed to have been relatively dull and philistine, Caroline, during her period on the throne (1727–37), brought splendour and vitality to the court, as well as colouring it with her own particular personality.[84] It is therefore no coincidence that her pet poet, Duck, was Cibber's main competitor for the laureateship in 1730, or that Pope and others then believed her influence to have been paramount in the selection of Cibber.

In fact, then, the Hanoverian period sees the laureate appointments matching the history of the royal family and of court life exactly.[85] In the reigns of George I and II, the kings had nothing to do with the laureateship because it was not among their interests. However, in that decade in which Caroline presided over the court, she had a significant, perhaps

---

[82] Black, 'Foreword', *George I*, pp. 1–8; Black, *George II*, pp. 108–29.

[83] H. Smith, *Georgian Monarchy: Politics and Culture, 1714–1760* (Cambridge, 2006), pp. 32–7; J. Marschner, 'Queen Caroline of Anspach and the European princely museum tradition', in *Queenship in Britain*, ed. Orr, pp. 130–42; Marschner, *Queen Caroline: Cultural Politics at the Early Eighteenth-Century Court* (New Haven, Conn., 2014); C. Gerrard, 'Queens-in-waiting: Caroline of Anspach and Augusta of Saxe-Gotha as princesses of Wales', in *Queenship in Britain*, ed. Orr, pp. 143–61.

[84] Black, *George II*, p. 137.

[85] On the royal family and court life, Smith, *Georgian Monarchy*, pp. 73–104, 193–243; G. M. Ditchfield, *George III: An Essay in Monarchy* (Basingstoke, 2002), pp. 7, 49–76, 138–68; E. A. Smith, *George IV* (New Haven, Conn., 1999), pp. 65, 81, 87, 142–3, 146–8, 206–7.

even overwhelming, influence on who was made laureate. When George III became king, the situation changed. George III was more assertive in English affairs than either of his predecessors had been; he was a lover and connoisseur of English literature, and he was eager to become a significant patron of the arts. Thus, for the one appointment predating George III's descent into illness and retreat from public affairs, he became the first reigning monarch since Charles II to exert himself in the appointment of a laureate. In 1813, still in alignment with the wider history of English royalty, the appointment saw the involvement of a cultured and well-read prince regent. As for whether any of these observations can help shed light on the individual laureateship appointments, the answer is probably negative. Where there is evidence of royal involvement, royalty was indeed involved, and probably with significant influence; where there is no such evidence, it is because royalty had no interest in being involved at that time, except perhaps in 1790.

Finally, on the subject of decision-makers, there are the littler interceders to be considered. Not too many of these are now visible, although the evidence from both the laureateship appointments in particular and the workings of patronage in general suggest that they potentially would have been numerous and influential. As well as the peers and government figures involved in, for example, Southey's appointment, various cultural figures appear to have exerted themselves across the period. Given the nature of the office, they probably could have had significant influence. Clearly, the likes of Tonson, Reynolds and Hayley could not have decided on the appointee themselves, as a lord chamberlain, monarch or prime minister could; but they could have had a powerful voice in articulating a poet's claim and merits for the office.

Who were those poets, though, and what were their merits? Were the criteria for a laureate as arbitrary and inconsistent as they seem on the surface, and was the poet's selection merely a result of having the right backers? The laureates and their competitors were patently a mixed bunch, some of them (like Rowe) being seasoned place-hunters, others (like Gray) being college recluses; some of them were primarily known as playwrights, some of them as lyric poets, some of them for their prose. But certain patterns can nonetheless be identified. Firstly, the obvious and cynical qualities do hold true: it helped to have connections and to be politically well disposed towards the government. Most of those who became or almost became laureate were well connected, and those who were not – Gray and Whitehead – nonetheless had one or two key connections, Gray being close friends with Lord John Cavendish and on reasonably good terms with Devonshire (who hosted Gray in his own box on George III's coronation), Whitehead being intimately bound up with the Harcourt and Jersey families.[86] Rowe was a bastion of Whiggism, Eusden was a willing Whig and Cibber was associated with both the general Whig defence of the Hanoverian succession and the particular ruling band of Whigs. Dennis and Oldmixon, laureate candidates in the early years of George I's reign, were also firmly Whiggish.

It is tempting to suggest that politics became less important in the reign of George III. Contemporaries were certainly less inclined to see the appointments *as* political appointments during his reign, and it is generally the case that historians and literary scholars find slightly less political matter to study in the later eighteenth century than they do in the early eighteenth. In addition, as the thrones and successions of Georges I and II were under greater threat than those of George III, it would make sense that there was a greater need for a politically reliable laureate in the early than in the late eighteenth century. Nonetheless, George III's laureates did tend to be politically amenable. Warton may not have partaken of much in the way of overtly political activity, but he was a firm supporter of the king; Pye was a loyal Pittite MP; and Southey, although his politics were idiosyncratic, was writing for the *Quarterly Review* in favour of government policies by 1813. Scott was known to be Tory, pro-Pitt and pro-government, while Hayley was friendly with Pitt but not much involved in political activities. The only laureate-elects who had no association with a party or government were Gray and Whitehead, in 1757 (towards the end of George II's reign); but even they were dealt with through Mason, a staunch 'Old' Whig.

The laureateship appointments also show some correlation with another broader trend: the lessening dominance of plays over other forms of imaginative writing, and the increasing prominence of non-dramatic poetry. Broadly speaking, the earlier laureates (going back to the later Stuart period, too) were primarily known as playwrights, while the later laureates were not. General men of letters, some of whom were primarily known for their non-dramatic prose – for example, Dennis, Duck, Theobald and Concanen – were always present as candidates, but in the first half of the eighteenth century they tended to lose out, whereas under George III they were more successful. Southey represents the culmination of this trend, being 'the only existing entire man of letters' in Britain.[87] 1757 marks the turning point: Gray was a lyric poet who never produced a play in his life, while Whitehead

[86] Thomas Gray to James Brown, 24 Sept. 1761, *Gray Correspondence*, lt. 345, at pp. 752–5. For more on the relationships of the Jerseys and Harcourts to the court, and some mention of Whitehead and Mason within this nexus, see Orr, 'Scientific queen', pp. 244–57.

[87] Lord Byron in his journal, 22 Nov. 1813: Lord Byron, *Letters and Journals*, ed. R. E. Prothero (6 vols, London, 1898–1901), ii. 331.

had had his greatest and most enduring success with a tragedy (*The Roman Father*) and remained involved with theatrical affairs thereafter, but mostly published non-dramatic poetry, and was well known for both.

However, it is somewhat misleading to distinguish dramatists from non-dramatists. The dramatists – even Cibber – also published in other forms, while the non-dramatists had usually written a play or two over the course of their career, and probably would have focused more of their energies on the stage if only the stage had accepted them, given how lucrative a successful play could be. It is therefore perhaps better to say – at least for the later Stuart and early Hanoverian periods – that *successful* writers were favoured for the laureateship, and writerly success lay principally in the theatre. Under George III, the pattern continued, but with the measures of writerly success becoming different and more diverse. The men chosen for the laureateship enjoyed more success in their field than anyone else: Gray in lyric poetry, Warton in the rediscovery of the English lyric, Hayley in gentle didactic poetry, Scott in metrical romances, Southey as an 'entire man of letters' and poetic genius. Whitehead, meanwhile, straddled a transitional period with a sort of calm mastery, leaving only Eusden and Pye as the exceptions to the pattern. But at the time of their appointments, even Eusden 'was a Person of great hopes' (as Gray later stated), and even Pye was fairly well respected for his numerous publications (as seen in Hayley's and Cowper's attitude towards him).[88]

As for the failed candidates, they were generally successful in some particular field, but were not as successful as the men who were chosen ahead of them, or had not found such a defining prominence in one particular field; on this count, it should be remembered that Whitehead was second choice after Gray, and Pye after Hayley. This flags up two features of the appointments: first, as was mentioned already, the history of the appointments represents a microcosm of wider literary developments; second, those writers offered the laureateship had almost invariably found great critical and commercial success in their careers to date. In short, the writers chosen for the laureateship were among the leading few writers of their time.

This analysis of the kind of men considered and favoured for the laureateship has already suggested some reasons for why each laureate was appointed: they deserved the office on account of their literary success, they had proven themselves politically agreeable or even politically serviceable and they enjoyed the connections to be able to advance these powerful claims. However, these are all speculations; whether any patterns can be found

---

[88] Thomas Gray to William Mason, 19 December 1757, *Gray Correspondence*, lt. 259, at p. 544.

in the identifiable reasons given for the appointing of laureates is another matter, and is hampered by lack of evidence. Party-political considerations appear, but only obliquely, in 1715 and 1730, and still more obliquely in 1790 and 1813; but they were almost certainly of no importance in 1757 and 1785. In 1718, Eusden was clearly appointed for having written a poem celebrating the lord chamberlain's marriage, but on no other occasion did the laureateship become so overt an embodiment of an individual patron–client relationship (as it had done under Dorset), except, in a very different manner, in 1790. The reasoning and processes behind each appointment therefore appear inconsistent.

However, the inconsistency that appears on an appointment-by-appointment basis was nonetheless productive of the more consistent patterns regarding the kind of people appointed laureate (as outlined above). This in itself is instructive. It suggests that underlying the successive laureateship appointments, there may have been some consistent sense of the qualifications and characteristics necessary for a laureate, or some notion of precedent – a suggestion for which there is otherwise no evidence, since no contemporary can be found avowing that such-and-such a laureate was appointed because they were similar to their predecessors. On the other hand, perhaps no one ever did have any such sense, or appeal to any such reasoning; perhaps the broader patterns identified above are not ascribable to the conscious reasoning of any of the agents involved in the appointments, but rather reflect the deeper institutional facts of the office itself, and its positioning with regard to the court and literature.

Indeed, one factor that supports this somewhat abstract conclusion is that the patterns identified above were all susceptible to an oscillating alternation. To state it plainly: Shadwell was very political; Tate was not; Rowe was very political; Eusden was not; Cibber was political; Gray and Whitehead were not; Hayley was not, but Pye was; Scott was political, but Southey was more complicated. Shadwell was a pre-eminent playwright; Tate was comparatively undistinguished; Rowe was a pre-eminent playwright; Eusden was comparatively undistinguished; Cibber was a pre-eminent playwright; Gray and Whitehead were pre-eminent in different fields; Warton was pre-eminently Wartonish; Hayley was a pre-eminent non-dramatic poet, but Pye was not massively distinguished for anything in particular; Southey and Scott were pre-eminent in their own fields. It is a similar story in terms of the distinction between university men and non-university men, and in any other identifiable pattern.[89] Admittedly, there

---

[89] There has not been space to investigate the university pattern, but, essentially, the reigns of Georges I and II saw the favouring of men associated with Cambridge, and that of

is not a very large sample size to be working with here, and the oscillation reduces under George III, as well as being mitigated throughout by the inclusion of people who were selected but not appointed (Gray, Hayley and Scott). It would be mitigated even further by some sort of weighted inclusion of the other candidates. In fact, the true alternation only exists for the time period between Shadwell and Cibber, a period comprising five names (and also including the later Stuart period, which is not even the subject of this chapter, due to the laureateship being something different at that time).

Nonetheless, it is clearly the case that few, if any, laureates were succeeded by someone who was similar to themselves (in terms of the features discussed above), and that it was more normal for a new laureate to have similarities with their laureate-grandfather than with their immediate predecessor. This observation supports the argument that those who selected the laureates were not doing so with a job specification in mind, and that the processes by which a laureate was appointed were not much dictated by a consciousness of precedent. In turn, this argument suggests that the patterns identifiable in the history of laureate appointments are ascribable to the nature of the office itself rather than to anyone's conscious decision-making.

Case study: Oldmixon

Now that this investigation of the appointments has been carried out, it is time to ask what the foregoing information and conclusions can reveal about the nature of the laureateship and about the society it was part of. This shall be done by looking at three case studies, the first two of which will focus on the networks that were coming into play in each appointment process, and how they were physically and conceptually situated.[90] These first two will also investigate how such networks produced ideas of value or merit, and the third will build on this by showing the practicalities of patronage. Those

---

George III saw the favouring of those associated with Oxford. This reflects the fact that Cambridge had a far more Whig and pro-Hanoverian identity, and Oxford a more Tory and pro-George III. In terms of oscillation, it was usually the case that a man with a strong university affiliation was replaced by one who had a weak (or no) affiliation, and so on. For the universities in the 18th century, see *The History of the University of Oxford. Volume V: The Eighteenth Century*, ed. L. S. Sutherland and L. G. Mitchell (Oxford, 1986); D. A. Winstanley, *The University of Cambridge in the Eighteenth Century* (Cambridge, 1922).

[90] For recent work drawing attention to networks, see M. J. Ezell, 'The "Gentleman's Journal" and the commercialization of restoration coterie literary practices', *Modern Philology*, lxxxix (1992), 323–40; D. Fairer, *English Poetry of the Eighteenth Century 1700–1789* (London, 2003), p. x; M. Haslett, *Pope to Burney, 1714–1779: Scriblerians to Bluestockings* (London, 2003); Williams, *Whig Literary Culture*, pp. 204–40.

ideas entailed a claim on the meaning of literature, and the appointment of a laureate constituted both a result of and a reinforcement of such a claim.

As was discussed above, many different agents were potentially involved in the appointing of a laureate, pertaining to a number of different spheres of activity and identity. At the time of the 1813 selection, the prime minister, the prince regent, the lord chamberlain, the lord chamberlain's aristocratic relatives, the historiographer and royal librarian, and several figures associated with the government (some of whom held pronounced literary interests) were all involved in determining Pye's successor. It may be that, were there as much surviving evidence for previous appointments as there is for Southey's, a similar story could be told throughout the Hanoverian period. In any case, the laureateship selection process clearly had the potential to draw in the activities of a wide and diverse cast of characters. By considering the interrelations of these characters, and the overlapping spheres that the appointment processes touched upon, this chapter will now show how the laureateship functioned with regard to the networks that comprised Hanoverian society. It will make the argument that the laureateship demonstrates something of the nature of these networks, and had an important role to play in constituting them, partly through the binding agency of patronage (as well as through other means that are explored in other chapters). The laureateship stands out as an important element in the networks of Hanoverian society – networks that show some similarities across the period, but that also changed in significant ways.

The first case study is Oldmixon's letter to Tonson, relating to the 1718 appointment.[91] The letter began:

> If you ever had Compassion for a man most unjustly Suffering for his Zeal for a Cause you always espoused which I shall most amply make appear when I come to London/If my particular Attachment to yr Interest & the Pleasure I took in Serving you If the Desire I have to return to Town & Evidence by Deeds what I can only now by Words can prevail upon a Generous Mind I flatter my self you will be so kind, as to speak to my Lord the Duke of Newcastle that I may succeed Mr Rowe in the Laureats Place which I was to have had before had it not been for him as Sir Samuell Garth knows. My Lord will be spoken to by severall Illustrious Persons. But I know, Sir, yr Opinion & Recommendation in this case will have as much Weight as any Bodies.

---

[91] Oldmixon's decision to write to Tonson was misguided and ill-informed. Tonson had recently retired from literary affairs and left London for the continent. For Tonson, Newcastle, Oldmixon and the Kit-Cat Club, see S. Bernard, 'Introduction', in *Correspondences of the Tonsons*, ed. Bernard, pp. 1–68; Rogers, 'Life'; Field, *Kit-Cat Club*; Williams, *Whig Literary Culture*, pp. 204–40.

There are several obvious points to make about this plaintive appeal. Firstly, it is a testament to the importance and workings of the Kit-Cat Club and of the Whiggish writers, politicians and peers who were not part of that Club but who had dealings with its members and shared its ethos. Oldmixon conjured up an image of Newcastle – the lord chamberlain at court, a prominent literary patron, a rich young nobleman and a Whig politician – being approached by Tonson and 'by severall Illustrious Persons' (that is, peers) to advance the claims of their favoured writers. Newcastle the patron, whose patronage to some extent operated through the medium of the Kit-Cat Club, was here imagined to be susceptible to the implorations from that Club and its associated members in terms of how he bestowed that (court) patronage. But Oldmixon believed that Tonson's 'Opinion & Recommendation' would be as powerful as any of those peers'. Tonson, as the great publisher, ex-secretary of the Kit-Cat Club and personal friend of Newcastle, was credited with an influence over Newcastle that was the equal of anyone's in the matter of the laureateship. Through this influence, Oldmixon – a small, suffering writer who lived far distant from London – imagined that he could gain Newcastle's patronage and be made laureate. He was highly aware of his competitors and of other associated writers who may have been able to speak well or ill of him; he insisted that he would have been laureate already if not for Rowe, and that Garth could vouch for this fact; then, as the letter went on, he discussed various other Whig writers, explaining why their claims were worse than his and alluding to their own connections and to the patronage that some of them had already enjoyed.

The network that Oldmixon thus articulated was one in which 'Illustrious Persons' – peers, and especially politically active and court-based Whig magnates like Newcastle – stood in leading positions, with a hierarchy of lesser peers and then literary figures beneath them, rendering them service in exchange for intercessions and patronage. Those lesser figures, as well as serving the same overall masters and working on the same page, were also competitors with each other, their loyalties more vertical than horizontal. This chimes well with Field's observation that patronage was 'the single most important constant in the Club's story – the mechanism that made it tick'.[92] Oldmixon also suggested that the system functioned according to a sense of fairness and noblesse oblige. The figures at the top of the hierarchy were defined by their lustre and lucre, those at the bottom by their hard work and neediness. Material rewards were therefore expected to flow downwards, puddling in the laps of those people who had worked the hardest and whose needs were the greatest. When explaining why he

[92] Field, *Kit-Cat Club*, p. 36.

should be preferred to his competitors, Oldmixon pointed out that he was 'the Oldest Claimer', and that 'Mr Hughes has a 500l a Year Place, So they all have, I think.' Oldmixon's long-standing need, and the fact that his competitors had already been supplied with rewards, rendered him the most appropriate recipient of the laureateship. The system had to contain an ideal of fairness, or else the vertical transactions it consisted of would break down; it was this logic to which Oldmixon appealed.

Yet there was also a sense in which the hierarchy was blurred. Tonson, a low-born literary figure, not connected with the court or government, appeared at Newcastle's elbow, equally influential with any of the 'Illustrious Persons'. Oldmixon also ended the letter with the supposition that 'if Friends will be Friends I see no Reason to despair of carrying it': a comment that seems to suggest the existence of other interceders who, from the word 'Friends' and from Oldmixon's other known relationships, were probably not 'Illustrious Persons'. He probably meant such people as Addison and Steele, neither of whom were mentioned in the letter but whose influence is well known, or people who were neither writers nor aristocrats. Whatever the case, Oldmixon was suggesting a nexus centred on Newcastle in which figures from distinctly different backgrounds, deriving their position and influence from distinctly different sources (rank, money, sociability; success in writing, or publishing, or politics, or organization) jostled about with each other, both competing and cooperating.

Moreover, Oldmixon clearly articulated the rationale that had brought this particular network into being and given it its powers of patronage; at the same time, he indicated his knowledge of the values that were important to that network, and that therefore had to be appealed to by someone who wished to profit by it, whether by gaining a leading position within it (as Newcastle had done) or by pulling the right levers to make money fall out of it (as Oldmixon wished to do). The first line of his letter was, 'If you ever had Compassion for a man most unjustly Suffering for his Zeal for a Cause you always espoused ...'. This was a highly sympathetic appeal – 'Compassion', 'Suffering' – but it was a sympathy that was activated by 'a Cause you always espoused', namely, the Whig cause (and, in some sense, the cause of the Hanoverian succession). Throughout the letter, Oldmixon maintained this mixture of personal pitifulness (designed to play upon Tonson's heartstrings) and political zeal. He turned himself into a Whig martyr, for whom personal, emotive sympathy was conflated with the great motivating cause of Whiggism. 'Hard will be my Case', he said, 'if while I am banishd in a Corner of ye Kingdom surrounded with Jacobites vilifyd insulted & having not a Minutes Ease my Friends will not endeavour that this fatal Absence of mine may not be my Ruin.' His 'Friends' had to save him from his tragic situation in the midst of Jacobites, which had been brought about by his selfless work for the cause; it was as much of an emotional necessity as a political one. What this indicates is that the network being invoked here – a network centring on Newcastle and the Kit-Cat Club – was one in which a set of personal relationships was actuated and fostered by a transcendent ideological cause, which cause, in turn, became the cause of those persons and their relationships. Oldmixon did not call it 'the Whig cause'; he called it 'a Cause you always espoused'. The nature and importance of this cause allowed it to draw together people from different walks of life who would be well suited to aid, serve and reward each other, and who, by working in unison, would be able to take hold of the means by which to benefit themselves and each other. This meant that there was an explicit and complex interplay between working for the abstract cause and working for the individuals who made up that cause – an interplay that Oldmixon appealed to, and sought to take advantage of, in his letter to Tonson.

Obviously, this is making the discussion reminiscent of the ideas of Lewis Namier. His arguments have been refuted from a number of angles, and Walcott's interpretation – which, having applied Namier's arguments to the reign of Queen Anne, impinges still more closely on 1718 – has been comprehensively discredited by the work of Geoffrey Holmes.[93] But a somewhat more recent definition of party by Frank O'Gorman does apply here. For O'Gorman,

> a party is an organized group which pursues political power and thus political office. It endeavours to cultivate popular support for its beliefs and focuses its activities upon Parliament … such a definition is sufficiently flexible to allow parties to be treated (at the same or different times) as vehicles of ideology, agencies for securing popular support, dispensers of patronage or instruments of government.[94]

Party is here defined by its pursuit of a power located in the metropole and gained by the cultivation of popular support, where ideology, patronage and government can all serve as both means to and ends of that power. O'Gorman emphasized that these different constituent elements can come into play 'at the same or different times', suggesting that different persons, interest groups or relationships might demonstrate various combinations

[93] L. Colley, *In Defiance of Oligarchy: The Tory Party 1714–60* (Cambridge, 1982), pp. 85–117; H. T. Dickinson, *Liberty and Property: Political Ideology in Eighteenth-Century Britain* (London, 1977), pp. 1–10; G. Holmes, *British Politics in the Age of Anne*, 2nd edn (London, 1987), especially pp. 6–49.

[94] F. O'Gorman, *The Emergence of the British Two-Party System, 1760–1832* (London, 1982), p. viii.

of these elements which differ in the way that they conceptualize the party cause or in their conduct with regard to it.

Moreover, it may be argued that the ideological element is sometimes emphasized too strongly in scholarship on parties. Somewhat contrary to the tenets of the Geoffrey Holmes consensus, debate in the early eighteenth century seems to have focused on personalities more often than on abstract ideological matters;[95] and there are clear continuities between the behaviour of the old-fashioned, much-maligned political cliques of the early modern kingdoms, and the political parties of the early eighteenth century. Newcastle himself later became a stalwart of the Walpolean regime and the Old Corps Whig party that followed it, both of which groups had to fend off constant accusations that they had betrayed the principles of Whiggism, and both of which emphasized their Whig identity primarily by recourse to warnings about Jacobites. Newcastle spent his entire political career worrying about the actions of his fellow politicians, wondering about the fidelity of his 'friends' and seeking to reward his followers. His primary role and expertise was in managing court and government patronage on a nationwide scale.[96] He seems to have spent a great deal less time fretting about the niceties of Whiggism, or constructing justifications of his creed. Of course, he did not need to construct any such justifications, since that was the job of men like Oldmixon; but Oldmixon had to be paid for those services, and it was services like those that kept Newcastle in the power and the money. Politics was personal. Oldmixon's letter to Tonson did not make any appeal to specifically Whig ideas or values. Instead, it offered the pitiful image of an old man, dying and miserable, having spent his life in the service of 'a Cause you [Tonson, personally] always espoused', now surrounded by a hideous band of Jacobites. The Whigs were outnumbered and oppressed; they had to stick together, and help out their own; Oldmixon had to be given the laureateship.

But they were more outnumbered in some areas than others. Oldmixon was on his own in Somerset, whereas Tonson was amid a strong core of Whigs in London. Hence the final suggestion that Oldmixon's letter provides on

---

[95] Eg periodicals tended to concern themselves primarily with the personalities and actions of public figures (such as Marlborough and Harley), historical figures (such as Thomas Wolsey) and fictional figures (such as the members of the Spectator club). For some examples of the tendency to understand politics by reference to individual persons (and their personal qualities), see eg R. Steele et al., *The Tatler* 4 (i. 44), 5 (i. 51–3), 130 (ii. 257), 193 (iii. 43–4) and *The Spectator* 174 (ii. 186–7), in *The Tatler*, ed. D. F. Bond (3 vols, Oxford, 1987) and *The Spectator*.

[96] Browning, 'Thomas Pelham-Holles'; Langford, *Polite and Commercial People*, pp. 14, 18, 43, 54, 188–9, 195, 206–12, 217–20, 223–32.

the subject of the Kit-Cat Club network: the importance of London, and of physical proximity. Again, Oldmixon emphasized this point at the very start of his letter: 'If you ever had Compassion for a man most unjustly Suffering … which I shall most amply make appear when I come to London.' Here, he appeared like the risen Jesus, thrusting himself before a doubting Tonson and showing him his wounds; those wounds would only gain credit if they were touched; and Oldmixon needed credit to pay for the laureateship. Immediately he carried on in this vein: 'If the Desire I have to return to Town & Evidence by Deeds what I can only now by Words can prevail upon a Generous Mind …' The Whig network to which Oldmixon made appeal was explicitly London-based. Its leading members and operations were in London – especially the town part – and, if a Whig was to function within it and derive benefit from it properly, he had to be present in the metropole. As well as emphasizing the importance of location to this network, and how centrally clustered it was, this rhetoric also reiterates the importance of the personal. Of course, Whiggism and Toryism were nationwide ideologies, uniting people across a vast geographical span; Oldmixon and his struggles with his Jacobite neighbours in Somerset were proof of that. Moreover, the contemporary Tory caricature of Whigs as un-English metropolitans, associated with mobile capital rather than a fixed stake in the land, was belied by Newcastle himself, an aristocrat whose power base lay in his huge landed estates outside of London. But as Oldmixon's letter demonstrates, it was nonetheless the case that Whiggism was centred on the activities and relationships of a relatively small, factional clique of men who were at their most active and powerful *as* a clique when in London, and who (especially in the person of Newcastle) were intimate with the (London-situated) court. Oldmixon knew this, and knew that he had to be present in London at least some of the time if he was to prove his service in the Whig cause and gain the benefits that he deserved. His sufferings would not have become real until he had shown the personal evidence of them to Tonson; his 'Words' would have only become 'Deeds' once he had set foot in London.

The fact that Oldmixon lived so far and so continuously away from London was therefore a severe handicap to him, and rendered him only a peripheral member of the network to which he was making appeal. But what is noteworthy is the way in which he tried to circumvent this handicap, and even extract advantage from it. Just as his physical absence from London curtailed his practical ability to forward his claims, so that absence was used to demonstrate his zeal for the Whig cause, which zeal had come at the cost of his own person. Again, the importance of personal relationships becomes evident, but here constructed in an alternative, imagined form. In the absence of his *actual* person, Oldmixon created a surrogate: an affective, ideal version of himself, placed before the Londoners so as to trigger a personal reaction in them. If he could not be in London, then his bleeding wounds could be, reminding Tonson and Newcastle of the valiant work he has been doing for them among the Jacobite hordes of Somerset. Thus he made his claim to be considered as an intimate part of a London that was Whig, Hanoverian and comprised the court and the town, even when he was physically distant.

Ultimately, this attempt to make capital from his disability was not enough; he lost out to Eusden. Whether Eusden was living more often in Cambridge or London at this time is not clear, but, whatever the case, Eusden had been much more successful over the previous couple of years in making friends and patrons among London Whigs, and had played a bigger part among them (for example, with his contributions to Steele's and Addison's productions).[97] Whether physically or imaginatively, he had done a better job of rendering himself present to the London Whigs, and to Newcastle and the Kit-Cat Club, and the court around which they were centred.

Nonetheless, Oldmixon's attempt is very telling. It reveals that this network to which he was appealing was a sort of imagined, nationwide community, bound by the abstract ideal of a Whig cause, but that it was centred on a real clique, spending significant amounts of time in London, operating according to their personal relationships and their proximity to the Hanoverian court. Again, it must be emphasized that neither Namier's, Walcott's nor contemporary Tories' depictions of the Whigs were correct; ideology mattered hugely in politics, Whiggism was a nationwide ideological cause and the differences between Whigs and Tories were not merely (or even largely) social or geographical. Yet Oldmixon's letter does testify strongly to the geographical and personal network that was inextricably bound up with the ideological

---

[97] There is not much surviving epistolary evidence of Eusden's connections, but W. Pattison, *The Poetical Works of Mr. William Pattison, Late of Sidney College Cambridge* (1728), pp. 37–8, does give some examples of the titular poet's correspondence with Eusden, with Pattison seeking subscriptions for a planned volume of his poetry and asking for Eusden's help. In 1726, Eusden offered him, 'If, either there [in London], or here [in Cambridge], I can be of any little Assistance to you, you shall not ever want it'; Pattison wrote in reply, 'If you can oblige me with your Interest in Cambridge, or Recommendations here in Town, I know you will give me leave to depend upon them.' This would suggest some belief on Pattison's part that Eusden was indeed capable of exerting influence in both Cambridge and London. Eusden then appears a few pages later having recommended a doctor in London, who came to Pattison when he fell sick with smallpox in Edmund Curll's shop in London, although it is not clear whether Eusden was present there at the time or had recommended the doctor previously (pp. 44–5). After that, he appears as one of the subscribers to Pattison's intended poetic miscellanies, designated '*Poet-Laureat*' and placed directly above Pope (p. 63); and then, further on, one of Pattison's poems is 'To Mr. *Eusden*, desiring his Corrections on a Poem' (pp. 157–8).

cause, and which rendered the Whigs a party rather than just an abstract set of ideas. The laureateship, as a piece of court patronage designed for writers, was one of the prizes that held this network together. Indeed, being designed for writers, and having a nationwide prominence, it was uniquely important in reifying this interdisciplinary network. But although it could thus function as a symbol and lubricant of the overall triumph of Whiggism, in practice its fate would be determined by a small band of metropolitan Whigs – peers, politicians, courtiers, literary figures – who would use it as a personal reward for whoever was most evidently serviceable before their eyes.

Case study: Fashion

By 1718, that London-based Whig world was already splitting, and the Kit-Cat Club was collapsing as a result. Newcastle would enter into a protracted conflict with Steele over Drury Lane theatre, Steele holding a patent to perform drama, Newcastle holding the lord chamberlain's vague powers over all matters theatrical. Newcastle eventually triumphed, and proved the authority of court and government over an independent, commercial playhouse, an authority that would eventually be confirmed and strengthened by the Licensing Act (1737).[98] By the time of Eusden's death in 1730, the Whigs were irrevocably fractured between the ruling Walpoleans (sometimes referred to by contemporaries as 'the court Whigs') and the opposition Whigs; Grafton was the lord chamberlain, and George II and Caroline were on the thrones.

To some extent, however, a similar case to 1718 is in evidence. Cibber was one of the managers of Drury Lane theatre (over which the lord chamberlain's authority had been proven during his time there). He was intimate with various Whig magnates. Both as a highly successful playwright and as one of the men who chose what plays to perform, he had great influence in London's theatrical affairs. Contemporaries often associated him with the ruling Whigs, and his massively successful *Non-Juror* had gained him the patronage of George I due to its rebuttal of Jacobitism. He can therefore be viewed as having succeeded by the same criteria as those which Oldmixon unsuccessfully made appeal to. Although there was no longer any Kit-Cat Club, his success would seem to indicate the operations of a similar network to that which had existed in 1718.

However, there is another angle on the 1730 appointment worth following, and it is relevant to subsequent appointments too. Henry Power has argued that a 'central feature of Scriblerian literature' was 'the contrast it draws

---

[98] Beattie, *English Court*, p. 26; R. D. Hume, *Henry Fielding and the London Theatre, 1728–1737* (Oxford, 1988), pp. 3–14, 239–53.

between durable classical literature, capable of communicating its message across generations, and ephemeral modern works, written to tickle the palates of fickle consumers'.[99] In the years around 1730, it was according to this contrast that Pope, Swift and their correspondents made sense of the laureateship, its holders and the prime contenders for it. It has already been touched upon that they felt the laureateship to have been primarily contested between two men, Duck and Cibber, who enjoyed favour from the women at court, chiefly the queen. But a more thorough examination of their letters reveals a wider tendency to contrast themselves with those two favoured authors, and to articulate the contrast by reference to the idea of an ephemeral fashion that was not only commercial, but equally (and connectedly) courtly and commercial. On the one hand, Pope et al. were 'unfashionable', and were isolated from court; on the other, Duck and Cibber were 'fashionable', and their fashionableness derived from a courtly, female preference.

Pope set the tone in 1728, writing to Swift (as was quoted above): 'I am told the Gynocracy are of opinion, that they want no better writers than Cibber and the British Journalist; so that we [himself and Swift, the unfashionable writers] may live at quiet, and apply ourselves to more abstruse studies.'[100] A couple of years later he wrote to John Gay, just before Eusden's death became widely known, that the 'bad taste' of the times was indicated by the fact that Eusden had the laurel, and that Duck enjoyed popularity. He went on, 'I hope this Phaenomenon of Wiltshire [Duck] has appear'd at Amesbury, or the Duchess [of Queensbury, whose seat was at Amesbury] will be thought insensible to all bright qualities and exalted genius's, in Court and country alike.'[101]

The duchess of Queensbury was a close friend of Gay, and a correspondent of Pope and Swift. She had recently been banned from court due to having argued with Grafton and George II over Gay's *Polly*, the sequel to the *Beggar's Opera*, and she thus served as a kind of anti-court patroness, contrasted with the women of court by her superior taste and disregard for 'fashion'. Indeed, the same note was then rung in a letter from Gay and the duchess to Swift, in November 1730. Gay, describing how happily isolated he was at Amesbury, wrote, 'I do not Envy either Sir Robert, or Stephen Duck, who is the favorite Poet of the Court. I hear sometimes from Mr Pope, & scarce from any body else; Were I to live here never so long I believe I should never

---

[99] H. Power, *Epic into Novel: Henry Fielding, Scriblerian Satire, and the Consumption of Classical Literature* (Oxford, 2015), p. 4.

[100] Swift, *Correspondence*, iii. 265.

[101] Pope, *Correspondence*, iii. 143.

think of London, but I cannot help thinking of you.'[102] Again, the contrast was between the isolated band of unfashionable poets, keeping up only their communications with each other – 'I hear sometimes from Mr Pope, & scarce from any body else' – and the favourites of London and the court, Walpole in politics, Duck in poetry.

However, this contrast did not tend to be phrased in terms of politics. The one exception was Gay's passing reference to Walpole, and even here the prime minister was used only as a shorthand for someone enjoying court favour and London bustle. Instead, the emphasis was on 'taste' and 'fashion', with the bad taste of the court, and especially of the court women, contrasted with the good sense and good taste of the duchess of Queensbury. Admittedly, Swift and Pope had reasons to avoid explicit political discussion in their letters;[103] but it is nonetheless significant that Pope, Swift and their correspondents wrote consistently in this way, and portrayed the matter of the laureateship through this lens. Indeed, when Swift first reported the news about the appointment to Gay and the duchess, he wrote, 'But the vogue of our few honest folks here [in Dublin] is that Duck is absolutely to Succeed Eusden in the Lawrell, the contention being between Concannan or Theobald, or some other Hero of the Dunciad.'[104] Even here, Swift could not help framing the news in such a way as to place the laureateship in opposition to Pope's satirical epic; even here, Swift could not resist using a phrase like 'the vogue' when mentioning the news of Duck's impending success.

It has already been noted that Lady Elizabeth Germain, when writing to Swift shortly after Cibber's appointment, mentioned the possibility that it was the queen who had chosen the laureate in the same sentence as she mentioned her want of acquaintance with Pope.[105] Whether or not this shows her to have been repeating news that originated with Pope, it is notable that Pope should again have been presented in immediate contrast with the laureate: Lady Elizabeth was 'sorry' for her lack of acquaintance with Pope, while the queen 'deserves' the poetry of such a laureate as Cibber. A month later came Swift's letter to Pope in which he suggested that 'the Court' either selected the laureate, or could have interceded with

[102] Swift, *Correspondence*, iii. 415.

[103] As Johnson was to observe mockingly later on, Swift and Pope were paranoid about their letters being read by the government, and tended to think of themselves as standing above the political fray. Johnson, 'Pope', in *Lives of the Poets*, iii. 1177–8. See also Goldgar, *Walpole*, pp. 28–49.

[104] Swift, *Correspondence*, iii. 421.

[105] Swift, *Correspondence*, iii. 441.

Grafton to have had someone else chosen, had it so desired. Just before this speculation came an apology from Swift; he wrote that Pope had been 'hard on me for saying you were a Poet in favour at Court: I profess it was writ to me either by Lord Bol. or the Doctor. You know favor is got by two very contrary qualitys, one is fear, the other by ill taste; as to Cibber ...'.[106] Yet again, the mention of Cibber's appointment was framed in a wider discussion about 'ill taste' and 'favour at Court'; yet again, the contrast was between Pope and Cibber, even if Swift had let the contrast lapse in a previous letter, and been reprimanded for it by Pope. Presumably, the letter in which Pope reprimanded Swift also grouped together the matters of 'ill taste' and 'favour at Court' with that of Cibber's appointment. This is the sense given by Swift's formulation: '... ill taste; as to Cibber ...'.

Lastly, in 1732, Swift wrote a letter to the duchess in which he expounded on what a bad courtier she was. Indeed, she was not even qualified to be a 'maid of honour'; there was no place for her in Pope's 'Gynocracy' of sycophantic court women spreading the fashions set by their queen. Swift, enumerating the ways in which she failed as a courtier, went on:

> you are neither a free-thinker, nor can sell bargains ... you pretend to be respected for qualityes which have been out of fashion ever since you were almost in your cradle ... your contempt for a fine petticoat is an infalible mark of disaffection, which if further confirmed by your ill tast for wit, in preferring two old fashioned Poets before Duck or Cibber; besides you spell in such a manner as no Court Lady can read, & write in such an old fashioned Style, as none of them can understand.[107]

Here, Swift presented a comprehensive depiction of the fashionable court woman and her debased taste. He thrice bantered the duchess for being 'out of fashion', in terms of her serious 'qualityes', her taste in 'wit' and, more trivially, her handwriting, and he demonstrated her 'disaffection' for the court by her taste in clothes and her taste in poets.

Thus Swift portrayed a court in which vice, irreligion and corruption were jumbled together with the ruling fashions in clothing, wit and handwriting, and where a debased female taste was characteristic of a degraded courtly ethos.[108] Again, Swift stressed the contrast between Lady Queensbury's preference for the unfashionable poets and the courtly preference for Duck and Cibber (who both, by now, enjoyed remunerative marks of court

---

[106] Swift, *Correspondence*, iii. 459.

[107] Swift, *Correspondence*, iv. 73.

[108] On Pope, Swift, Gay and anti-Walpolean views, I. Kramnick, *Bolingbroke and His Circle: The Politics of Nostalgia in the Age of Walpole* (London, 1968), pp. 56–83, 206–34.

favour). His close linking of 'petticoats' with 'wit', as well as his reference to 'Court Ladies' in the same line, indicates that he was thinking particularly in terms of a female court preference. To Pope, Swift and their friends, then, the matter was clear. While the court politicians destroyed the country with their underhand practices and misrule, the women of the court, led by the benign patroness Queen Caroline, set a fashion for (among other things) bad poets, principally Duck and Cibber. These poets were frivolous, vapid and lacking in integrity. Indeed, it was necessary and inevitable that they be so, since they were the mere trinkets of a gynocratic court fashion. As a fashion, though, they would be swept away in time, leaving serious writers like Pope and Swift to stand proud before posterity. It was as a mocking inversion of this theme that Pope, in one of the earliest letters quoted here, stated that Duck and the laureate (at that time, Eusden) would stand as monuments to 'our ancestors' of the present 'bad taste'.[109]

In this interpretation, then, the appointment of Cibber and Duck's nearness to being appointed were the result not so much of the workings of a political faction, as of a courtly fashion set by the patronage and favour of Queen Caroline, and by the spatial dynamics of cultural production and consumption. As with the Kit-Cat Club, this fashion was centred on a small nucleus of Londoners, based in and around the court. The court ladies and the lord chamberlain were at the head of it, and it was associated with London-based readers, theatregoers and politicians. By contrast, Swift was in Ireland, Gay and Lady Queensbury were in Amesbury and Pope was legally disbarred from living in London due to his Catholicism. As with Oldmixon's attempt to bridge the gap between London and Somerset in a conceptual way, and to fight for a nationwide Whiggism, the court fashion was not confined to London: Pope's usage of the term 'Court and country', quoted above, was to denote a fashion spanning both, in which Caroline and Duck were leading figures. But the fashion was based in the court and town of London – which formed a single unit – and diffused across the nation from there.

Of course, Pope and Swift's interpretation was based on a solipsistic sense of contrast in which their own independence of mind and greatness of talents were highlighted by reference to the lesser poets who enjoyed a gaudy, transitory favour in the present day but whom posterity would treat with ignominy. Yet it is nonetheless significant that Pope and his correspondents should have settled on Cibber and Duck to provide this antithetical role, or that they should have insisted on viewing Cibber, Duck and the laureateship within this framework. Although the Scriblerian contrast

---

[109] Pope, *Correspondence*, iii. 143.

identified by Power, between durable classical literature and ephemeral modern works, usually and most evidently played out by reference to a commercial, consumerist public, it was here being consistently cast with reference to court favour. As in *The Dunciad*, the modern, dull, degraded culture was presided over by a queen.

Moreover, their interpretation can be shown to be accurate in at least some particulars. Helped along by Caroline's favour for him, Duck did indeed become a 'Phaenomenon' with the reading public. It has already been noted that she gave him various material rewards; and there were perhaps ten pirate editions of his poems between 1730 and 1733. His most productive and rewarding time as a poet came between the start of Caroline's patronage of him and her death in 1737.[110] Cibber's success as a writer had different and older foundations, and his appointment to the laureateship demonstrates the overlap between commercial popularity and courtly fashion in a different way to the case of Duck. Pope, like everyone else in the eighteenth century, thought highly of Cibber's *The Careless Husband*; but otherwise he found Cibber to be a great debaucher of public taste, overseeing a theatrical diet of pantomime, farce, dross and mutilations. He was outraged at the popular, commercial success that Cibber enjoyed, finding it indicative of the bad taste of the times.[111] This success owed nothing to Caroline's patronage, but it helped carry him into the favour of the royal family. By 1730, his work would have been well known and much enjoyed by the court; he had been entertaining the royal household for years, and it had been in 1728 that Pope had claimed the 'Gynocracy' to 'want no better writers than Cibber and the British Journalist'. Cibber's final comedy, *The Provok'd Husband* (1728), was dedicated to Caroline, and began with the words, 'The *English* Theatre throws itself, with This Play, at Your MAJESTY's Feet, for Favour and Support.'[112] Here, Cibber explicitly brought the commercial theatre of the town together with courtly, queenly favour. Indeed, the royal family had attended the play for one of its first performances.[113]

Whatever Caroline's feelings of indulgence for Duck, she and the members of her household were far more familiar with Cibber, and recognized him as one of the leading figures of literary and London-based

---

[110] Davis, *Duck*, pp. 40–93; Stephens and Jones, 'Duck'.

[111] A. Pope, *The Dunciad Variorum* (1743) in A. Pope, *The Poems of Alexander Pope*, ed. J. Butt (London, 1996; first published 1963), pp. 317–459; E. M. McGirr, *Partial Histories: A Reappraisal of Colley Cibber* (London, 2016), pp. 2–5, 131–5.

[112] *The Provok'd Husband* (1728), sig. A2r. On its authorship, P. Dixon, 'Introduction', in Sir John Vanbrugh and Cibber, *The Provoked Husband*, ed. P. Dixon (London, 1975), pp. xiii–xxvii, at pp. xviii–xxv.

[113] Dixon, 'Introduction', p. xxvi.

entertainment. Like Duck, he was fashionable, and it was a fashion that encompassed Caroline and her court, as well as readers and theatregoers outside the court. In his case, the role of the 'Gynocracy' with regard to the fashion was different than in Duck's, but Cibber's dedication of *The Provok'd Husband* emphasizes the fact that it did indeed have a role, and so too does his appointment as laureate. If Pope, Swift and their correspondents are to be believed, Cibber's appointment and Duck's almost-appointment came at the hands of Caroline and her court ladies, who presided over a literary 'fashion' that originated in London and spread out across the nation. It was this fashion that Duck and Cibber were benefitting from. By bestowing the laureateship on Cibber, Caroline confirmed both the fashion itself, and the role of her court as one of its central forums.

Case study: Pye

These two case studies have shown how certain networks might carry a poet to the laureateship, and to an extent they have provided a pseudo-Namierite proof as to the importance of connections, personalities and geography. Yet they have also shown that ideals or even ideologies were bound up with the functional workings of the relevant networks. If Oldmixon was attempting to make himself appear present and serviceable to his superiors, then he was also appealing to the qualities that were important to those superiors and that gave the network its coherence and rationale: the Whig cause. Likewise, Cibber was fashionable not just because he was liked by the right people, but because his work had those qualities that made the right people like it. In the final case study – Pye's letters to Pitt – the relationship between ideal merit and the practicalities of patronage will be more specifically explored.

This chapter has already shown that there were various rationales and criteria that a poet could appeal to, or profit by, in the contest to become laureate, and that different networks operated in different ways. Throughout the period, there was generally some sense that the laureate should 'deserve' the laurel, and that it should be handed to someone who 'deserved' it. Oldmixon protested, 'Long have I been in the Service of the Muse and the Press without any Reward'; a century later, the laureateship was decided on the basis that 'Scott was the greatest poet of the day, & to Scott therefore they had written to offer it.'[114] Yet the sense in which a poet 'deserved' the laurel was neither simple nor straightforward. The notion of merit did not necessarily refer to some pure ideal of poetic merit, but it usually at least overlapped with some such ideal.

---

[114] R. Southey, *The Collected Letters of Robert Southey*, ed. L. Pratt, T. Fulford, I. Packer et al., lt. 2305. See also lt. 2307.

A good starting point in this consideration is provided by John Beattie, in his 1967 study of George I's court. Exploring the reasons behind court appointments, he observed that while a candidate's 'ability' was sometimes referred to in support of their claim for a post, it was never unmixed with patronage. He gave as an example Thomas Burnet, a loyal Whig writer, who spent several years soliciting and attending on great men in the early years of George I's reign, fruitlessly hoping for a place, and eventually receiving an unsought office that had no relation to his qualities or expertise.[115] Likewise, when Theobald was unsuccessful in his bid for the laureateship in 1730, he asked Warburton whether he ought to stay on at court, continuing to solicit great men in the hope of a place; the attempt upon the laureateship was thus potentially not the end, but the beginning of the search for court patronage, despite the fact that no other position would have suited Theobald's activities as well as the laureateship. Something similar can be seen in Pye's interactions with Pitt. The two logics – 'Merit' and 'Interest', in Cibber's terms[116] – sometimes appear in distinct, as well as in elided, operation.

The Chatham Papers in the National Archives have several letters from Pye to Pitt, and they show him constantly wheedling and badgering his political master with all the adroitness of a seasoned veteran.[117] In 1784 he wrote to Pitt, 'I am really both ashamed & hurt to trespass so often on that time which I know is so fully employed.' He went on to discuss the expenses that had been incurred in his election campaign, which he submitted 'to your own consideration'.[118] The next surviving letter is from July 1790, just after Pye's appointment as laureate. Pye wrote to inform Pitt of Salisbury's offer to him, 'which I have accepted, but as that office is by no means one of profit, I flatter myself it will not interfere with the kind intentions you had the goodness to express concerning me in regard to an application I made respecting another appointment at the close of the last session of Parliament'.[119] Here, Pye barely seemed interested in the laureateship. Pitt, having evidently been pestered for a position, decided to have Pye made laureate as a means of fulfilling the patronal obligation that was being demanded of him; and Pye, whose financial difficulties required a more substantial remedy, was keen to ensure that the laureateship would not be

---

[115] Beattie, *English Court*, pp. 152–3.

[116] Cibber, *Apology*, i. 35.

[117] For the most part, he was advancing his own cause; but he also sought patronage for another man, William Pratt, in 1785. Pye to Pratt, 27 June 1785, TNA, PRO 30/8/169, fo. 15; Pratt to George Rose, 20 Aug. 1787, TNA, PRO 30/8/169, fo. 18

[118] Pye to Pitt, 27 July 1784, TNA, PRO 30/8/169, fo. 256.

[119] Pye to Pitt, 16 July 1790, TNA, PRO 30/8/169, fo. 258.

thought a sufficient recompense for the place-hunting capital that he had built up, therefore reminding Pitt of his earlier claims as quickly as possible. His claim was couched in such unassuming terms as 'I flatter myself', and was presented as evidence of Pitt's 'kind intentions' and 'goodness', rather than of Pye's neediness; but it was a fairly blunt reminder.

In subsequent letters, Pye became more obsequious and wheedling still, and gave further evidence of how assiduously he could pester Pitt in hope of patronage. He explained in 1791:

> I did myself the honor of waiting on you yesterday. But as I am fully sensible how precious your time always is … I would by no means wish to intrude on your leisure by requesting the favour of a personal interview, but as you Sir had the goodness to think of me for a situation in the County of Berks, where I believe there is now no probability of a vacancy … I hope you will pardon the liberty I take in requesting your remembrance of me on some other occasion.

He then explained that he had come to London due to a vacancy appearing in the tax office, but he wrote 'rather from the desire of offering myself to your recollection than the presumption of pointing out any particular mode for the exercise of the kind intentions you have had the goodness to express towards me'.[120] Again, Pye's rhetoric cast the proposed transaction in terms of Pitt's goodness and superiority, and portrayed Pye himself as a supplicant worm, so wormy as to be horrified at himself for even daring to pop his head above the soil. But behind the rhetoric was another fairly blunt estimation of Pye's place-hunting capital and of what he wished to spend it on. Since he had earlier been able to acquire a promise from Pitt – that he should have a situation in Berkshire – he now wished to trade that promise in for a position of equivalent value in the tax office. A couple of weeks later, Pye, writing from a coffeehouse in London, explained that the aforementioned Berkshire situation (now identified as that of receiver of the land tax) was vacant after all.[121] Clearly, although a place-hunter was not too fussy about what places he ended up with, it helped to have a hawkish appreciation for where vacancies did or did not exist, and to be able to deal in specificities, rather than vagaries, with one's patron, even if those specificities would then be traded in for different specificities at a later date.

Pye went on to explain that he had applied to Pitt and no one else, even though some of his friends in the government had suggested that he apply elsewhere. He expressed his confidence that there was no need to apply

[120] Pye to Pitt, 3 April 1791, TNA, PRO 30/8/169, fos. 260–b.
[121] Pye to Pitt, 27 April 1791, TNA, PRO 30/8/169, fos. 262–b.

elsewhere anyway, since Mr Steele had assured him of Pitt's good intentions towards him.[122] Thus Pye managed to express his loyalty to Pitt even as he hinted at its lapsing, and he made clear which quality made the difference between loyalty and its absence: Pitt's intentions. This was an almost absurd articulation of the nature of the patronal relationship, in which the client was a paragon of loyalty, but only to the patron who secured him his just deserts. Pye's letter then continued in a stream of obsequiousness and diffidence, in the course of which he finally mentioned some personal quality of his own – namely, that he would be utterly incorrupt in the role of receiver of the land tax, and 'indeed shall be rather anxious to get the public money out of my possession'. Finally, in 1795, Pye wrote to Pitt again, telling him, 'Mr Neville having communicated to me your good wishes to assist me in general, tho' it was not possible in the particular mode which he was so obliging as to mention, I take the liberty of mentioning a small thing now vacant in the Excise.' (The previous holder had died. Pye, having been both a worm and a hawk, now became a vulture.)[123] The salary of this office was small; as with the laureateship, Pye made sure to play down the office's value. But he stated that it would be useful in accumulation with his other salaries. Of course, Pye did not want to seem to be 'grasping at any unreasonable accumulation of favours', but salaries in public office were irregularly paid, and Pye was reliant on his income from them. Further downplaying the value of the offices he had already been given, he added that the expense of living in London rendered public office more an injury than a benefit to him.[124] This was the first and last time that Pye discovered his inner Oldmixon, presenting himself as an object of pity.

Again, as with Theobald, the bestowal of the laureateship was not the end, but almost the beginning, of the quest for patronage. Although most of the letters date from after Pye's appointment, it is evident how Pye went about achieving the laurel (and his other positions too). Only once in the course of these letters did Pye appeal to his own personal qualities; only once did he appeal to his own neediness; rarely did he say anything positive about the positions he had already been granted. For the most part, Pye's emphases lay elsewhere. The key was to be persistent and rigorous, but to

[122] Pye to Pitt, 27 April 1791, TNA, PRO 30/8/169, fos. 262–b.

[123] In fairness, Pye had good reason to desire offices and money. The Faringdon estate he had inherited from his father was encumbered with £50,000 of debt, and his election and parliamentary attendance expenses eventually necessitated him selling the estate. J. Brooke, 'Pye, Henry (1709–66), of Faringdon, Berks', 'Pye, Henry James (1745–1813), of Faringdon, Berks', *The History of Parliament*. My thanks to Stephen Conway for this observation and reference.

[124] Pye to Pitt, 15 April 1795, TNA, PRO 30/8/169, fo. 264.

attribute that persistence and rigour to the bounteousness of the patron. Pye, like Oldmixon, knew that he had to be continually before Pitt's eyes in London, ideally in person, but when that was not possible, through writing. And he knew that he could not trust to vagaries or to chance; he had to construct a continuous narrative, or even a sort of balance account, of all his former dealings with Pitt, continually building up capital and then cashing it in when a worthwhile reward materialized. Like any good accountant, Pye needed to be able to cook the books, turning everything into more capital for himself; and he needed to be able to leap upon any irregularity of Pitt's, proving that Pitt had not kept up his side of the bargain properly and was still obliged to pay up. Pye lauded Pitt as a great man, a great statesman, a great benefactor and a generous mind, and he showed himself to be unendingly grateful and devoted. But he also did enough to indicate that this valuation of Pitt, and of their relationship, was bound up with the balance sheet.

It was to such a man, and for such activities, that Pitt allocated the laureateship. As with Rowe and Theobald, the appointing of a laureate here appears to have been little more than the distribution of a vacant position to a place-hunter who had been agitating for a salary. On each occasion, some great person, having been courted for some time by various importunate suitors, learned that, due to the death of the previous laureate, there was now an open, salaried position, and therefore gave it to whichever suitor had been most importunate and had built up the strongest claim to favour. The laureateship was but one more bauble in the endless round of patronage.

This, however, is only one aspect of the matter. It does not cover, or sit well with, all the various motives described throughout this chapter, or all the various people concerned with the laureateship. It certainly does not sit well with the fact that, as mentioned above, the laureates tended to be among the leading few literary figures of their day. Gray, Warton and Hayley were all selected for the laurel without making any effort to seek it for themselves, and at least two of them seem to have been offered it for little reason other than their stature as poets. Even in the case of Pye, his letter of 1790 suggests that he had not actively sought the laurel. Pitt may have offered it to him as a sop to his incessant importunities, but the offer also seems to have stood somewhat apart from the regular game of patronage transactions. Beattie's observation remains sound: it is not easy to disentangle ability/merit from patronage/interest. Generally speaking, it is not even relevant to make the attempt; and in the case of the laureateship, whenever the cause of an appointment seems to err more one way than the other, it is rather towards the ideal of pure merit than away from it.

Conclusion

To some extent, this distinction between 'Merit' and 'Interest' can be mapped onto the distinction between the commercial and the courtly, explored in the last chapter. Merit was often established away from court – in the playhouses or in publication – as with Cibber's plays and Gray's poetry. It then required interest – solicitations, attendance, friends in high places – to have the writer installed at court as laureate. The nature of the merit was a matter of variability, and depended on the particular network that was coming into play. In 1718, merit could refer to service for a Whig party cause; in 1730, it could refer to fashionableness among (apparently) the women of court. The network concerned would then use this merit as one of the raw materials of patronage, using it to acquire the office of poet laureate for whichever writer had a sufficiently convincing stock of that merit and was personally best placed with the other people who made up that network. The workings of that equation were different each time, as were the types of network and person coming into play; however, the end result was that the poets selected for the laurel tended to be among the most popular and esteemed writers of their day. Ultimately, some notion that the laurel ought to go to a worthy poet, or even (as was said explicitly in 1813) to 'the greatest poet of the day', factored strongly throughout the period. The laurel was used to strengthen and legitimize various networks, to link them more firmly to the court and to establish the court's importance to them. As a result, the court's cultural role was reinforced: the ultimate validation of a celebrated poet came in the form of courtly office.

Moreover, the foregoing analysis has shown the importance of physical and conceptual spaces more generally in bestowing value on cultural products. In fact, it can be argued that cultural products' meaning was only latent until they were positioned in a certain space. Oldmixon, Duck, Cibber and Pye all had the merit of their cultural products to refer to, but they could only use that merit by coming to the right location, and by demonstrating how that merit related to the values of the location in question. Oldmixon had to place himself conceptually in London, and explain how his writings and travails in Somerset related to the cause of the Whigs based in court and town; Duck had to travel from Wiltshire to court to become popular in London and nationwide as a poet, then lost out on the laureateship partly because he had been away from court; Cibber was more successful, having always been based in the town, and enjoying strong connections to certain courtly figures; and Pye hovered constantly around the metropolis, intermittently swooping down towards Pitt so as to collapse in the soil at his feet. Again, the importance of London, and especially that of court and town, is evident. Nor is it surprising that court and town formed a unit in this way, given that they were physically proximate to each other. It would have taken Oldmixon longer to travel from Somerset to London than it now takes us to travel from London to Australia.

In the Introduction to this book, the randomness and contingency of the laureate succession appeared to be evident. This chapter has now traced certain patterns, and it has shown that the history of the laureate appointments follows (among other things) the contours of literary history and the history of the royal family. There remained a large degree of variability in terms of who was appointed laureate, why and by whose agency. Yet even in this respect, the laureateship was representative of Hanoverian society. Poetry was not some discrete notion or institution; it did not pertain exclusively to the marketplace, the nation, the public or any such thing. It was positioned where different conceptual spaces overlapped, handled by a variety of different agents, each valuing it in different ways. Political parties, lordly families, royals, court officials, artists, publishers and writers themselves all had their own claims on its meaning, and sought to utilize and legitimate it in their own ways. Such being the case, it is unsurprising that the history of the laureateship should appear, in some ways, random and inconsistent, as if no one really knew what to do with the office, or had any fixed notion of its purpose. In fact, there were too many people who knew what to do with it, and too many purposes for it. Throughout it all, though, there remained an ideal of poetic merit, and a sense that its proper recognition came in the form of a courtly office designed specifically for poets.

4. Parnassus reported: The public laureate, 1757–1813

Throughout the long eighteenth century, the laureateship was a prominent feature of the English literary landscape. John Dryden, the most highly regarded writer of the late seventeenth century, was routinely referred to as 'the laureate', and the office played a significant part in how he and his works were perceived by others. Colley Cibber likewise became known as 'the laureate', and in this capacity was mentioned innumerable times in print. Even when held by less famous writers, the office always attracted interest and commentary. The laureateship was not forgotten about during either Tate's or Eusden's tenure; at their deaths, as at the death of every other laureate, there was a buzz of activity among the literary community, with even those writers who were not hopeful for the office themselves showing an interest in who should receive it.

The reigns of George II and George III, however, were to see the laureate become a public figure in an unprecedented manner. As the volume and sophistication of print culture developed – particularly with the flourishing of periodicals – the relationship between laureate and readers became newly familiar.[1] When the laureate had become responsible for the birthday and New Year's odes, those odes had started to appear as individual publications and in newspapers, but their circulation had been relatively limited. By the accession of George III, and over the course of his reign, it became standard for the odes to be printed prominently in newspapers, and for a lively discussion of the laureate and his odes to be carried on in this same medium. The odes also appeared in various magazines, as did other, semi-official poems by the laureates;[2] and the popular *Annual Register* series (launched by Robert Dodsley in 1759) would usually publish both laureate odes in its 'Poetry' section, moving them to the start of that section from

---

[1] On periodicals, H. Barker, *Newspapers, Politics, and Public Opinion in Late Eighteenth-Century England* (Oxford, 1998); J. Black, *The English Press in the Eighteenth Century* (London, 1987); A. Forster, *Index to Book Reviews in England 1749–1774* (Carbondale, Ill., 1990); A. Forster, *Index to Book Reviews in England 1775–1800* (London, 1997).

[2] Eg *The Gentleman's Magazine* almost always printed each laureate ode; and Whitehead's semi-official *Verses to the People of England* was printed in such places as the *Newcastle General Magazine* and *The Scots Magazine*, both Feb. 1758.

the 1775 volume onwards.[3] Meanwhile, the two leading review magazines, the *Monthly* and *Critical*, would generally give extended reviews of the laureates' more substantial works.[4] Under George III, the laureate held a unique and important place in print culture.

This chapter will provide something of a corrective to those which have preceded it. Previous chapters have looked mostly at behind-the-scenes matters, and at how the laureateship was treated and conceived of by those people who were directly involved with it. By contrast, this chapter will try to establish how the laureateship was understood by everyone else: what role the laureate was perceived to have, how much or how little the office was held in esteem and where the laureateship was situated in terms of the conceptual geography of culture. Broadly speaking, then, this chapter is concerned with the public reception of the office. It will include some discussion of private letters, but the bulk of its evidence will be published periodicals, and especially newspapers. There are two main reasons for this focus. One is that periodicals provide a copious and easily searchable body of relevant material; the office, its holders and their odes featured countless times in periodicals over the course of George III's reign. By comparison, other forms of evidence are less copious and less conveniently mineable. The second main reason is the unique nature of periodicals, and especially newspapers. More than any other body of material, the newspaper press can be claimed as the forum of the public.

As discussed previously, 'the public(k)' was a term not much used in later Stuart cultural matters. Although it started gaining ground around the turn of the eighteenth century, and became the standard term to denote the audience for cultural products by 1730, the older concepts of the world and the town were generally preferred before the Hanoverian succession, and even, by many writers, up to and beyond 1730. The town in particular remained a key concept throughout the eighteenth century, even in discussions of non-dramatic works. However, the concept of the public will come to the fore in this chapter. It will be treated in two ways: as a concept (sometimes specified as 'the conceptual public') and as an entity (sometimes specified as 'the reading public'). Thus, on the one hand, this chapter will explore how periodical writers made sense of the laureateship using the concept of the public, and where they situated laureateship and court vis-à-vis that public. But, on the other hand, this chapter will seek

[3] Eg *The Annual Register, or a View of the History, Politics, and Literature, for the Year 1777* (1778), pp. 196–7. These volumes' enduring popularity is evidenced by the fact that each one was being reprinted for years to come: eg in 1783 there were reprintings of *1775* (a 4th edition), *1758* (7th edition), *1759* (7th edition) and others.

[4] See final section of this chapter.

to assess how the laureateship was viewed by the mass of people who were conceived of and conceived of themselves as the public: hence its additional concern with the historical entity of the reading public.

Also important to this chapter's analysis will be the themes of literature, national identity and partisan politics, the relations of which to print culture in general and newspapers in particular are often evident in scholarship on the later eighteenth century. This period is generally seen as a crucial one for the establishment of literature as a concept, the development of Britishness and the creation of a patriotic literary canon. The public that came to maturity in this period, both as a concept and as an assertive, self-conscious entity constituted by print culture, was patriotic, middle-class and based as much in the provinces as in London. It was the prime mover of the period's political disputes, as the theoretical justification and practical support behind Wilkes, the Association movement and other demands for reform, as well as behind the status quo.[5] Literature, national identity and partisan politics all therefore played a part in the attitudes shown towards the laureateship in periodicals, sometimes explicitly. National identity will be especially important here. The Introduction has already argued that over the course of the long eighteenth century, Britons came to prefer larger, abstract, metaphorical spaces to smaller, specific, physical spaces as the concepts by which to frame cultural production and consumption. In this chapter, it will be seen that one of the most important spaces in the late eighteenth-century conceptual geography of culture was the nation. It was the largest and one of the most appropriate forums for the public, and it was primarily articulated by means of print culture. Yet at the same time – and arguably of greater practical significance – print culture also constituted a metaphorical London that could be entered into by individual readers everywhere. This London was not simply oppositional, or defined only by parliamentary politics and town culture; the court and loyalism were key to it.

First, this chapter will explore the nature of newspapers as evidence, and as constituents of the conceptual and the reading public. Second, it will give a wide overview of how newspapers treated the laureateship. It will then explore newspapers' treatment of three individual laureates: Whitehead,

[5] Barker, *Late Eighteenth-Century Newspapers*, pp. 1–94; J. Brewer, *Party Ideology and Popular Politics at the Accession of George III* (Cambridge, 1976); S. Conway, *The British Isles and the War of American Independence* (Oxford, 2000), pp. 103–8, 128–65; S. Conway, *War, State, and Society in Mid-Eighteenth-Century Britain and Ireland* (Oxford, 2006), pp. 165–9; S. M. Lee, *George Canning and Liberal Toryism, 1801–1827* (Woodbridge, 2008), pp. 108–18, 131; J. Parry, *The Rise and Fall of Liberal Government in Victorian Britain* (New Haven, Conn., 1993), pp. 6, 23–36; K. Wilson, *The Sense of the People: Politics, Culture, and Imperialism in England, 1715–1785* (Cambridge, 1995).

Warton and Pye. Their tenures correlated roughly with George III's reign, and hence form this chapter's timeframe. Lastly, evidence from the *Monthly* and *Critical* reviews will be brought in to supplement the evidence from the newspaper press. These investigations will give rise to further conclusions about how George III's subjects conceived of the relationship between the court and the public.

Periodicals and the public

This book has argued the laureateship to be a key institution in the way that contemporaries conceptualized the court and its relationship to other spaces and audiences. The public was one such audience. Prior to the Hanoverian succession, the spaces most often referred to in relation to culture had been: court, town and city (neighbouring and permeating each other, with the court and town being especially tightknit); the playhouses (key sites within, and microcosms of, this tripartite London); and the world (only vaguely conceptualized, and generally denoting publication and the experience of reading). The public had been a concept important to late seventeenth-century political discussion, but had not been much used in terms of culture. However, over the course of the early eighteenth century, the public became reconceptualized in cultural terms, in a way that built upon the older concepts of the town and the world but did not replace them. It was used in a variety of ways, sometimes interchangeably with the town, sometimes interchangeably with the world, but generally bridging the two: it denoted a body of opinionated persons consuming cultural products, especially in print. However, its connection with print culture was not invariable or straightforward. Sometimes, the term explicitly denoted a body of people located in, centred on or looking towards London.

The public's position straddling print culture and the capital is especially evident in newspapers. Contemporaries and historians alike have identified print culture in general, and newspapers in particular, as key to the existence of the public.[6] The newspaper press created a nationwide forum for understanding and debating all manner of affairs, including literary; the second half of the eighteenth century even saw poetry sections becoming established in many newspapers.[7] Meanwhile, newspapers assiduously made

---

[6] J. Brewer, *The Pleasures of the Imagination: English Culture in the Eighteenth Century*, 2nd edn (London, 2013), pp. 114–40; J. Raven, *Publishing Business in Eighteenth-Century England* (Woodbridge, 2014), pp. 1, 15; M. Knights, *Representation and Misrepresentation in Later Stuart Britain: Partisanship and Political Culture* (Oxford, 2005), pp. 52, 98.

[7] Black, *The English Press: 1621–1861* (Stroud, 2001), pp. 90, 106–7, 128–32. On the printing of poetry, see comment from 'Zeno' below.

reference to '(the) public (opinion)', 'the (sense of the) people' and similar terms. They sought to report on this public, keep it informed, appeal to it and be its mouthpiece. By the middle of the eighteenth century at the latest, newspapers conceived of this public as a nationwide and increasingly middle-class body. Rather than inhering in a London coffeehouse, it was to be found in the vast mass of sturdy, respectable, patriotic Britons who lived and worked all over the country, their opinions formed by nothing other than their own good sense and good values.

Nonetheless, the newspaper press was London-centric. Even by the end of the eighteenth century, it was more highly developed in London than anywhere else. Newspapers published in London, often bearing the name 'London' in their title, were distributed throughout the rest of the country. Provincial newspapers were dependent on London newspapers for much if not most of their news, and generally contained little in the way of local news or distinctively local opinion; Jeremy Black has drawn attention to the role of the provincial press as 'an intermediary between London and the localities'.[8] The events that newspaper consumers read about had mostly taken place either in London or abroad, and the political disputes that they followed were primarily being acted out in the metropolis. Even John Wilkes's disputed election was for the county of Middlesex. The conceptual public that features in this chapter, and the conceptual nation that it inhabited – the public and nation being used to make sense of the laureateship – were abstract and constituted by print; but they were centred on, and sometimes took as their main conceptual forum, London.

This emphasis served two important purposes. The physical space of London, containing the court, parliament and much else besides, had traditionally been, and continued to be, the most important site in Britain for events and processes that had some bearing on the country as a whole, and the most important source of practices and ideologies that encouraged people to see themselves as English and British. The London-centricity of the newspaper press therefore served the purpose of keeping people in touch with a location that it made sense to be in touch with. But the second purpose concerned print culture itself: print culture formed a transcendent space, which nonetheless needed some physical reference points to be able to function. As a concept, London made print culture navigable. Moreover, these two purposes worked in tandem: print culture in general, and the newspapers in particular, gained their structure from the physical, traditional importance of London, and in turn promulgated that importance to readers across Britain.

[8] Black, *English Press 1621–1861*, pp. 107–8, 132–4 (pp. 133–4 for quotation); Brewer, *Popular Politics*, p. 158.

Within the London that was thus packaged for the reading public, the court held a central importance. As Matthew Kilburn has shown, news of goings-on at court usually featured at least once a week in newspapers produced in eighteenth-century London, covering various topics; major royal occasions, such as the birthday and New Year celebrations during which the laureate odes were performed, would receive particularly extensive coverage.[9] In political news, though some newspapers endorsed opposition politicians within and without parliament, others endorsed the court and government, including ministers who were termed or conceptualized as being in some way 'court' politicians: this was used for such individuals as Walpole, Bute and North, or simply as a way of referring to all government ministers, Walpolean Whigs or supporters of George III. Culturally, the court would feature by way of the poet laureate, or institutions that held royal backing or identification, such as the Royal Academy. The London of print culture was court and town together; it was a dynamic of political and cultural activity that readers everywhere entered into, and took up positions within. They thereby validated the dynamic, and its physical referents, on a nationwide level.

However, newspapers are of course not a source material that can be read uncritically. Their position vis-à-vis the reading public is enigmatic. Contemporaries often accused eighteenth-century newspapers of articulating dishonest, distorted opinions, either because of some supposed personal animosity or predilection, or because of supposed bribery; and this view has endured into historical accounts.[10] Recent studies have provided a more nuanced picture: that, although there were political hirelings writing articles and letters for newspapers, and although politicians did give subsidies to and launch certain newspapers, the scale of political involvement was not sufficient to dictate newspaper content. Newspapers were commercial entities, whose survival and success were dependent on sales and advertising.[11] Yet it remains imperative to handle newspapers with care. The authorship of most newspaper entries is unknown; moreover, it is impossible to determine how readers interacted with newspapers, or what proportions of supply, demand and propaganda determined what was printed.[12]

---

[9] M. Kilburn, 'Royalty and public in Britain: 1714–1789' (unpublished University of Oxford DPhil thesis, 1997), pp. 10–13.

[10] Eg A. Aspinall, *Politics and the Press c.1780–1850* (London, 1949).

[11] Barker, *Late Eighteenth-Century Newspapers*, pp. 1–94; Barker, *Newspapers, Politics and English Society, 1695–1855* (Harlow, 2000); Black, *Eighteenth Century Press*; S. Burrows, *French Exile Journalism and European Politics, 1792–1814* (Woodbridge, 2000), pp. 89–142; B. Harris, *Politics and the Rise of the Press: Britain and France, 1620–1800* (London, 1996).

[12] Eg Black, *English Press 1621–1861*, pp. 93, 107; Burrows, *Exile Journalism*, pp. 9–10, 69–70.

Another issue is that when studying newspapers, historians have shown most interest in their politically minded invocations of the public; indeed, these were probably the most frequent and emphatic sorts of invocations made. Therefore, whereas this monograph has previously stressed the divergence between the political and cultural concepts of the public, it is now basing its arguments on a form of evidence where the two stand side by side, possibly distinct from each other, possibly conjoined, but certainly with the political standing taller than the cultural. However, this is a problem to be embraced rather than shunned. This book has already admitted the usage of the concepts under consideration to have been fluid and undogmatic, and seeks to understand them in whatever breadth is relevant to the laureateship. Although it is evident that newspaper commentary on the office was sometimes politically motivated, that does not make the commentary any less sincere, authentic or informative. In fact, the presence of political motivations is consistent with the previous chapter's arguments: that the meaning of poetry in general, and of the laureateship in particular, was laid claim to by a number of different agents, rather than by any pure tribunal or objective audience; and that the value of cultural products was only latent until it had been activated within some particular context. Moreover, the end of this chapter will discuss the more specifically literary views provided by the *Monthly* and *Critical* reviews, and compare them to the newspaper evidence.

Nonetheless, given the issues mentioned above, it would not be possible to simply read what the newspapers say about the laureates, and determine on that basis how the reading public viewed the laureates. Instead, this chapter will analyse the overall contours of the discourse on the poets laureate that existed in the newspaper press, in full awareness that this discourse was created, cultivated and consumed by a number of different agents for a number of different purposes. Six factors allow arguments to be extrapolated from an analysis of this discourse: the indubitably significant place that newspapers had in constituting the public; their geographical spread; their reliance on correspondents and other newspapers, even of differing political inclinations, for their material; the evidence that print culture and spoken dialogue existed in something of a continuum in this period; the sheer amount of poet laureate material in newspapers; and the fact that this material often showed at least an implicit awareness of other material that had been printed on the laureates. On the basis of these factors, it can be stated that the newspaper discourse would have furnished at least part of the framework within which the reading public viewed the poets laureate. More optimistically, that discourse may be considered as a partial representation of public opinion on the laureateship.

Public opinions

From Whitehead's accession to Southey's, it is not hard to find comment on the laureateship in the newspaper press. Some of the most significant trends will be discussed in due course; but first, a simple question needs to be asked: does this varied body of commentary suggest a positive or a negative estimation of the office? On balance, it is probably about even, or – if the routine, prominent printing of the biannual odes is considered as an acknowledgement of the laureate's importance – tending more towards a positive estimation. The odes would even be printed in radical and opposition newspapers at times of political crisis, without any adverse commentary.[13] Admittedly, when the office of laureate was specifically addressed as a subject in its own right, the attitude was more often negative, and would not uncommonly entail a call for some alteration or abolition of the office; but this is only to be expected of any institution, except those which are under threat. While the continuing existence of the office was being taken for granted, there would have been no real point in great vindications and endorsements of it appearing in print.

These negative judgements on the office took several main forms. One was the argument that the office was outdated and absurd, and akin to the old court office of fool or jester. The manifestation of this antiquated foolery was usually identified as the biannual odes.[14] Thus in 1785 the *Morning Herald* mocked the odes as repetitive nonsense, and stated that they would remain the same 'to the end of time – if the office like that of the Fool is not exiled from Court'.[15] Criticisms of the laureateship would usually at least imply that the most disgraceful thing about the office was the requirement of writing odes, but there was nonetheless a significant, continuous body of opinion that held that the office ought to be abolished irrespective of that requirement. The *Morning Chronicle* asked, upon Whitehead's death, 'Why appoint any successor …? Why not finish at nothing, and leave the place unsupplied, and its functions abolished. Or if the functions are continued, let the odes be written by the *Deans and Chapters* of the different dioceses.'[16] But this notion of the odes continuing without the office was rare. Normally, critics of the office either wished for the odes to be dispensed with so as to (at least partially) redeem it, or for the entire thing to be done away with, the odes and the office being inseparable or the office having no purpose without the odes.

[13] Eg *Middlesex Journal or Chronicle of Liberty*, 29 Dec.–1 Jan. 1770.

[14] *Gazetteer and New Daily Advertiser*, 6 Aug. 1790; *Gazetteer and New Daily Advertiser*, 19 Aug. 1790.

[15] *Morning Herald and Daily Advertiser*, 12 Sept. 1785.

[16] *Morning Chronicle and London Advertiser*, 28 April 1785.

The complicating factor in attacks on the laureateship was that it was hard to detach the office from the poet currently holding it, or from the list of poets, recent and not so recent, who had held it previously. This difficulty was particularly acute in the period 1730–1813, which saw a succession of three long-reigning laureates – Cibber, Whitehead and Pye – with Warton's five-year tenure the sole exception. From the standpoint of 1757, it must almost have seemed that there had only ever been one modern laureate, Cibber; his distant predecessor, Eusden, had been a more obscure and sheltered laureate. Half a century later, in 1813, Pye and Whitehead between them must likewise have loomed very large in understandings of the office.

On the other hand, the pseudo-history of the laureateship was widely known, and was often printed in newspapers, especially when a laureate died. Current laureates were almost invariably referred to as '(the) (poet) laureat' when mentioned in newspapers, whatever capacity they were being mentioned in, and sometimes without their actual name being given;[17] but so too were past laureates, including, most significantly, Cibber and Dryden. Especially during Whitehead's time, when the memory of celebrity laureate Cibber was still fresh, and newspapers still delighted in reporting minor anecdotes of his life or quips that he had made, it was normal to find him named simply 'the late Laureat', or some such thing.[18] Dryden was likewise so heavily identified with his office that, in one report, he was referred to as 'Erasmus Dryden, Poet Laureat to Charles II.', suggesting his official status and royal connection to have been even more identifiable than his own first name ('Erasmus' was in fact the name of Dryden's grandfather, father and one of his sons).[19]

Because of this heavy identification of office with office-holders, there were many variants and subtleties in the ways in which the office might be viewed. For example, it was a fairly common line of complaint that the office had become degraded in recent times, or even, especially after Cibber's tenure, that it was 'blasted'. Few commentators linked this idea of degradation to the idea of its being outdated; instead, the degradation was located in the quality of the office-holders. This related principally to Eusden and Cibber (whose contemporary critics had initiated the 'degradation' idea) and then, in a more complicated way, to Whitehead and Pye, whose critics did not tend to see them as culpable in their own right for the degradation,

[17] Eg Warton in connection with the Chatterton controversy, a matter unrelated to his laureate position, in *Bath Chronicle*, 11 Sept. 1788; *Public Advertiser*, 11 Sept. 1788.

[18] Eg *London Chronicle* 18–21 Feb. 1764; *Public Ledger*, 25 Sept. 1765; *Lloyd's Evening Post*, 26–9 Feb. 1768.

[19] *World and Fashionable Advertiser*, 30 April 1787.

but rather as mediocre poets who had taken on a degraded office and were happy to fulfil its disgraceful duties for money.[20] Those duties were heavily associated with Cibber, because his time in office had seen the odes printed more widely and recurrently than ever before, and because they had drawn such opprobrium from his enemies, meaning that there was some sense in which the degradation was associated with a particular practice as well as with (a) particular person(s). Equally, though, no one in the late eighteenth century was actually aware of when the laureates had begun writing the odes. Cibber's *Egotist* (1743) stated that even Dryden had written them.[21]

Hence the variation and gradation in manners of scorn for the laureateship. For some observers, its degraded state was directly attributable to the poets who held or had recently held it, or to the odes (which were themselves uncertainly but indelibly associated with Cibber), and it could therefore be redeemed, and brought back into line with the office it had supposedly been in the seventeenth century (even if no one really knew what that office had been, other than by reference to Spenser, Samuel Daniel, Jonson, Davenant and Dryden). Once a great poet took the office again, or once the odes were dispensed with – which dispensation would probably encourage or follow on from the appointment of a great poet – the laureateship would shine forth again in all its native splendour.

However, other observers felt the degradation to be fatal; the modern laureates had disgraced the office too far, and it ought to be abolished. Even to clear away the odes would not clear away the taint of Cibber (or, perhaps, of Whitehead or Pye). Lastly, there were those observers who thought the office discredited those with whom it was associated: not just Whitehead, Warton and Pye, but even the king. Because the odes were such a silly and laborious task, and because the office-holder's prominence subjected them to constant mockery and envy from other poets, no laureate could keep hold of his dignity while in office, and it was not fair or fitting to inflict a twice-yearly blast of tedious panegyric on so perspicacious a prince as George.[22]

The newspapers reveal, then, that there was certainly a significant trend of disrespect for the office running throughout the late eighteenth century. The office's reputation was tarnished; in some people's eyes it was a garish institution, standing as a disgrace to the nation, or to literature or even to

---

[20] Eg *London Evening Post*, 6–8 April 1773; *Middlesex Journal or Universal Evening Post*, 20–2 April 1773; *Gazetteer and New Daily Advertiser*, 18 Nov. 1776; *The World*, 24 March 1790.

[21] Cibber, *The Egotist: Or, Colley upon Cibber* (1743), pp. 49–50.

[22] Eg *St. James's Chronicle or the British Evening Post*, 25–7 Aug. 1778; *Morning Herald*, 9 Jan. 1786; *St. James's Chronicle or the British Evening Post*, 20–2 May 1788; *Public Advertiser*, 23 May 1788; *English Chronicle or Universal Evening Post*, 8–10 June 1790.

the laureates and king themselves. But what the newspapers also reveal is a pervasive and almost a complacent trend of exactly the opposite opinion. It has already been mentioned that the space afforded to printings of the odes, and the sheer volume of reportage on the laureates, suggest a certain respectability of standing for the office. Clearly, people were interested in it, and thought it an important aspect of literary life.

However, there is also a great deal of more explicit evidence as to the laureateship's positive reputation, and even the positive reputation of the laureate odes. The newspapers would often give such reports as the following (1762): 'Same day the Ode for the New Year, composed by William Whitehead, Esq: Poet Laureat, and set to music by Dr. Boyce, was rehearsed at the Turk's Head Tavern, in Greek-street, Soho, to a crowded audience.'[23] As early as 1765, the fare was being expanded upon: 'This day the Ode for the New Year, composed by William Whitehead, Esq; Poet Laureat … will be rehearsed at the Turk's Head Tavern in Gerrard-street, Soho, and to-morrow the same will be again rehearsed at Hickford's room in Brewer-street.'[24] The nature of these rehearsals seems to have varied a little over time; a 1766 newspaper described a 'private' performance at the Turk's Head, followed by 'a publick Rehearsal at Hickford's Great Room',[25] and in 1769 the *Middlesex Journal* (a radical paper) advertised the two rehearsals without distinguishing whether they were private or public. It then added that 'on Monday [the ode] will be publickly performed in the Great Council Chamber at St. James's'; the royal performance was thus designated as 'publick' and situated as the third performance in a sequence, rather than as something distinct from the non-court performances.[26]

Throughout the tenures of Whitehead, Warton and Pye, these rehearsals were advertised beforehand and reported on afterwards. In their evident popularity (which reached a height in the 1790s, as will be discussed below), they exemplify one of this book's major themes: the court's intimacy with the town, and its appeal to a London-centric public. Londoners were so interested in these courtly odes, which were composed specifically by the king's laureate for the king, that even the printing of the words in the newspapers was not enough; they had also to have their own public renditions of them, thus experiencing courtly culture for themselves. Some people may even have watched them both in town and in court; according to the *Middlesex Journal*, both locations were 'publick'. Evidently, not

---

[23] *Gazetteer and London Daily Advertiser*, 31 Dec. 1762.

[24] *Public Ledger*, 30 Dec. 1765.

[25] *Public Advertiser*, 30 Dec. 1766.

[26] *Middlesex Journal or Chronicle of Liberty*, 28–30 Dec. 1769.

everyone in George III's Britain thought the laureate and his odes to be either outdated or disgraceful.

Furthermore, rather than there existing a simple distinction between hostility to the odes and more positive interest in them, there was actually a powerful strand of critical interest in which each ode was read and commented upon as an individual effort within a valid literary genre, and in which many of those odes were commended as successful poems. Whitehead was the first laureate for whom this was consistently the case, and it will become most apparent in the discussion of Warton below, but it is worth briefly quoting a specifically negative (and even quite mocking) comment on Warton's first ode, so as to stress the fact that a negative critical judgement on some aspect of the laureateship could exist within a wider framework of more positive engagement. The *Morning Herald* remarked in 1785 that 'A variety of comments on *Warton's* Ode have appeared in the different prints.' Then, after jovially criticizing the ode, it advised '*Master Laureat*' that 'the best mode of defence is to write a better next year'.[27] This is not the best example of the odes being taken seriously – far better will come below – but its negativity is instructive, in that it shows how even such negative judgements could partake of a wider literary interest in the odes, in which individual responses were made in accordance with a genuine appraisal of each ode's literary merits. The odes, then, aroused a great measure of interest, both as written poems and as musical performances, and even elicited literary critical engagement in newspapers.

As explained above, there are not so many explicitly positive appraisals of the office in general as there are negative. For example, upon Whitehead's death, no one bothered to suggest that the office should be continued, because the suggestion would have been redundant. But there are more obliquely positive comments, such as this one following Warton's death: 'Many persons have been spoken of as being intended to fill the vacant place of Laureate, among whom it is surprising that Mr. Warton's brother has not been mentioned. This gentleman's talents are well known, and his genius for poetical composition is equal to that of the late Laureate.'[28] Not only does this report indicate widespread discussion about the office, but its suggestion was clearly founded on the assumption that the laureate should have a strong talent for poetry. The phrase 'poetical composition' even called to mind the compositional requirements of the office, which were thus assumed to require, and presumably not to disgrace or corrupt, a distinguished poetic 'genius'.

---

[27] *Morning Herald and Daily Advertiser*, 4 July 1785.

[28] *Diary or Woodfall's Register*, 7 June 1790.

Obviously, since the office was so heavily identified with whoever happened to be holding it at the time, and, to a diminishing extent, with its previous holders stretching back through the centuries, any attempt at establishing how contemporaries judged and understood the office must also consider the reputations of the individual laureates themselves. This has partly been done in the previous chapter, but only for the laureates' reputations prior to their appointment. Now, their reputations while in office will be described. The supposed pre-eighteenth-century laureates were essentially thought of as great poets – Chaucer, Spenser, Jonson and Dryden – or at least eminently talented ones – Skelton, Daniel and Davenant – and their association with the laureateship factored strongly in its favour. But the early eighteenth-century laureates served the opposite function. Presumably due to his short tenure, it was sometimes forgotten that Rowe had even been a laureate;[29] the eighteenth-century laureateship was therefore defined, from the standpoint of 1757 or 1760, by Tate and Eusden, two poets who had been mostly forgotten about, and Cibber, who was considered a good dramatist, and was thought of fondly as a celebrity laureate, but who had never been much respected for his laureate compositions.

The rest of this chapter will consist of more in-depth explorations of how Whitehead, Warton and Pye were perceived and responded to as individual laureates, with each poet revealing a different set of circumstances. It therefore makes sense, before continuing with the exploration of individual laureates, to pause and offer some intermediate conclusions on what has been seen so far. Clearly, the standing of the laureateship in the late eighteenth century was neither resoundingly negative, nor resoundingly positive. There was a strong, and probably well-known, trend of mockery and disapproval towards the office, which in some ways had begun during the Exclusion Crisis as part of Dryden's public battles with his literary and political enemies, but which had reached maturity during Cibber's time in office, and had then progressively hardened over the late eighteenth century. It centred on the old idea that laureates (and indeed poets in general) were paid flatterers;[30] on the related idea of the laureateship as an outdated office, no longer suited to a commercial society, a new conceptualization of literature and a proud and free British nation; and on the idea that the office had been made contemptible by the low quality of its recent occupants.

---

[29] Eg lists of laureates in *Morning Herald and Daily Advertiser*, 3 May 1785; *Whitehall Evening Post*, 3–5 May 1785; *Public Advertiser*, 5 May 1785.

[30] Prior to becoming laureate, Shadwell himself had given portrayals of poets as mercenary figures whose words were superficially attractive but void of truth and meaning: 'Ninny' in *The Sullen Lovers* (1668) and 'Poet' in *The History of Timon of Athens* (1678).

On the other hand, there was an entirely opposite point of view which was equally viable and widespread, and perhaps more so: that the laureateship and its odes were respectable and interesting, and formed an important part of the literary landscape and the interface between court and public. Certainly the office might have been held by some subpar versifiers, and the requirement for biannual panegyric odes would sometimes lead to risible results. But the office itself was still one of value and honour, its previous holders including many of the great names of English literature; and the odes, like any form of poetry, could be good as well as bad. Between these two poles of opinion, there was a spectrum of vagaries and variations, partly because of the difficulty of detaching office from office-holder, but more so for the simple reason that the office was a prominent institution, and thus gave rise to a variety of responses and interpretations. In any case, it was clearly a much bigger feature of print culture, and of public consciousness, than scholars of the late eighteenth century, or even of the laureateship itself, have realized. Newspaper and poetry readers knew about it, cared about it and subscribed to the biannual ritual of reading the odes that it produced (perhaps also going to see them performed). It is not clear whether George III himself would have viewed the laureateship as the cornerstone of court culture, but that is how it appeared to the reading public; in a sense, it was the cornerstone of a *public* court culture. It demonstrates that the court was not conceived as a separate cultural space from the nation, and that it was an appropriate cultural space for the public to inhabit. The public was too large and too abstract an audience to fit inside the physical space of the court; but in terms of the conceptual court, there were many ways that the public could enter it and enjoy the cultural products that it housed.

Whitehead's reception

Having sketched out this general picture, it is time to look at the public lives of Whitehead, Warton and Pye. The attempt will be made to establish their individual reputations as laureate, to investigate their experiences at the hands of the newspaper press and to assess where newspapers conceptually situated them.

Whitehead's reputation as a lyric poet was generally far better than Cibber's. Following his appointment, he did not publish a great deal of new work (other than the odes), and even some of these few publications were anonymous; but he was known and respected on account of that which he had published before. His most prominent and lasting works were his three full-length plays, and especially *The Roman Father*, which was revived periodically throughout his tenure as laureate, sometimes with certain alterations provided either by the company or by Whitehead himself, and with renewed notices, reviews and approbation each time. It was considered his magnum opus, and remained a repertory work beyond his death.[31] He was also well regarded as a laureate, especially at the start and end of his tenure. Richard Berenger wrote to Robert Dodsley on Whitehead's appointment, 'The Laurel has at last been properly bestow'd, and Parnassus should make bonefires and rejoicings.'[32] Likewise, Malone wrote after Whitehead's death, 'Whitehead redeem'd the fame of the place, and the crown may now be worn with honour.'[33] In 1764, one correspondent to a newspaper voiced the fairly standard distinction between Cibber and Whitehead, saying that Whitehead's odes 'are as much above Criticism, as those of his immediate Predecessor were below it'.[34] A few years earlier, another correspondent dubbed Whitehead 'the respectable Laureat'.[35] Another discussed 'one of the finest Odes that ever appeared in any language, written by the present ingenious Poet Laureat'.[36]

However, the most extended example of praise for Whitehead's laureate work came in a letter of 1758 from 'Zeno' to *Owen's Weekly Chronicle*.[37] 'I have frequently perceived a judicious selection of some pieces of poetry inserted in your paper,' Zeno began, 'which makes me expect to find Mr. Whitehead's Birth-day Ode in your next, with the following remarks.' Less than a year after Cibber's death, Zeno was thus taking it for granted that Whitehead's laureate ode would naturally be placed among 'a judicious selection' of poetry in the newspaper. Zeno then went on to contrast Whitehead and Cibber, much to the former's advantage, and opined that Whitehead's ode 'is founded upon a pretty historical event, which is delicately heightened by the graces of poetical fiction, and the whole is truly classical'. However, he had noticed that a couple of Whitehead's phrases were not ideally suited to a musical setting, and he therefore gave Whitehead a couple of pointers as to how best to write for music. This last point suggests, again, the sense

---

[31] Bod, Eng misc d. 3844, fo. 123b; Bod, Eng misc d. 3845, fos. 7b–8, 9–10b, 61; Bod, Eng misc d. 3846, fos. 26, 28–b, fo. 84b. *Public Advertiser*, 3 March 1764; *Public Advertiser*, 8 Oct. 1777; *Morning Post and Daily Advertiser*, 29 Oct. 1777; *Whitehall Evening Post*, 21–3 April 1785; 'Whitehead Memoirs', p. 55.

[32] 'Richard Berenger to Robert Dodsley, Sunday, 1 January 1758', *Electronic Enlightenment Scholarly Edition of Correspondence*.

[33] *Warton Correspondence*, lt. 482, at p. 529.

[34] *Public Advertiser*, 13 July 1764.

[35] *St. James's Chronicle or the British Evening Post*, 8–10 Sept. 1761.

[36] *Lloyd's Evening Post and British Chronicle*, 19–21 Nov. 1760.

[37] *Owen's Weekly Chronicle or Universal Journal*, 11–18 Nov. 1758.

that the laureate ode form was a valid artistic genre with its own special formal requirements, and that a certain bent of poetic talent and artifice was necessary to succeed most highly in it.

However, 'if [Whitehead's mistakes] are blemishes, they are immaterial, and last [i.e. lost?] among the beauties of this Ode'. Zeno, it appears, felt that true poetic talent was more important than the stricter formal requirements he had just pointed out. Going into detail on Whitehead's ode, Zeno observed that, in the fifth stanza, 'The Laureat … has happily imitated what we have always admired in Virgil, Milton, and Shakespear.' Without any sense of incongruity, Zeno was comparing Whitehead to perhaps the three greatest figures in the literary canon, and the two titans of English literature. The laureate's ode was a valid and even a commendable work of poetry within a framework of value and meaning set by Virgil, Milton and Shakespeare. Zeno continued:

> The address to the King breaths that simplicity which is one of the greatest ornaments among the ancient classics; and here again the author seems to have Virgil in his eye … The conclusive stanza bears a fine poetical compliment to the monarch, without the glare of adulation from the Laureat; without making the King more than a god; and even without noticing that his majesty is lineally descended from Julia the sister of Caius Julius Caesar, which is historical fact, and I hope will be regarded as such by Mr. Whitehead at another time.

Zeno then gave a paragraph illustrating this lineal descent, before signing off; his letter was followed by the printing of the ode in question.

Here, then, is found a sense of literary quality and national pride that, rather than being held in contradistinction to laureates and royal panegyrics, actually was felt as going hand in hand with such things. Whitehead's address to George was classical and Virgilian, and his panegyric was not venal flattery, but 'a fine poetical compliment'. Clearly, Zeno would not have wished to see anything too fulsome in its praise; he noticed approvingly that Whitehead had not succumbed to 'the glare of adulation', and had not deified George. Equally, though, Zeno was happy to see George complimented within the bounds of plausibility, and even felt that Whitehead could have gone further in this respect. Hence his long detailing of the lineal connection between Caesar and George, which comprised an oblique manifesto for panegyric in and of itself, supporting, as it did, the idea that laureate poetry would derive power from an appropriate, historically grounded rhetoric of praise. As long as the poet did not make George 'more than a god', panegyric could be great poetry, as determined by the standards of classical literature and the British literary heritage. As long as a poet like Whitehead, rather than Cibber, was laureate, the odes could amount to such great poetry, presenting a subject of great interest and even of pride to readers.

Of course, Zeno may not have been a disinterested observer. He may have been a political hireling, or a personal friend of Whitehead's. But the significant fact is that these points were being made at all: that a newspaper was publishing a long, effusive letter on a laureate ode, analysing that ode according to widely recognized metrics of literary quality. The letter would have been read by at least some of that paper's readers, and it would have aimed for at least a partial resonance with those readers' assumptions; otherwise, it could not have been plausible or intelligible. Wherever it came from, the letter thus played into the continuing discourse on the laureates that existed across the newspaper press, and which bore some (though undefinable) connection to the conceptual framework by which the reading public viewed the laureates. Moreover, Zeno's opinion was the extended articulation of an opinion that is seen in other newspapers, and also in other sources. For example, even Gray, in various private letters, was to express admiration for Whitehead's first ode, and for other, subsequent poems by him.[38]

As the years passed, though, Whitehead was to find himself less and less well received. Criticism of Cibber had received much of its motivation from his association with Walpole's regime; but although Whitehead was not personally as much associated with any regime as his predecessor had been, his time in office was to see the development of a furious new phase in oppositional writing, which was to identify Whitehead as one of its most promising targets. John Wilkes entered parliament in the same year as Whitehead's appointment (1757); the accession of George III was soon followed by the controversies over Bute, and Wilkes's *North Briton*; the disputed Middlesex election came in 1769; and the 1770s and 1780s witnessed a perpetual frenzy of Wilkesite agitation, the American crisis and the Association movement, with a variegated clamour of invective against the government and the king. In tandem with these events, the newspaper press was continuing to proliferate, and was perhaps becoming increasingly polarized in its views.[39] Whitehead, as a poet paid by the court and tasked with writing two public odes a year, naturally found himself encompassed in the storm, despite his personal and political mildness. From about the late

[38] Thomas Gray to Thomas Wharton (not the later poet laureate), 2 December 1758; to William Mason, 17 March 1762; to William Mason, 21 December 1762. In *Gray Correspondence*, lt. 285, at p. 602, lt. 357, at p. 777, lt. 364, at p. 789, respectively.

[39] Barker, *Late Eighteenth-Century Newspapers*, pp. 1–94; Conway, *American Independence*, pp. 85–165.

1760s, a series of scathing attacks and passing mockeries began appearing in the opposition press, taking a variety of forms.

On the most basic level, Whitehead was criticized as a bad poet, holding a ridiculous office and producing contemptible odes. In 1772 the *Middlesex Journal* published this squib: '*On reading the* Laureat's Ode: 'For two such meals of fulsome lies,/—— [i.e. George] Pays an hundred pounds a year; /—— For an OEconomist, he buys/Wretched provisions very dear!'[40] Not only was Whitehead false and venal as a poet, writing overpriced 'lies', but his badness as a poet, and the badness of his poetic role, was here being characterized by reference to the court that sponsored it. Another, longer squib, sent into the same paper by 'Paul Pinchwell', expanded on some of these themes:

> Sweet Willy Whitehead who with medium stile,
> Can never force a tear, or win a smile:
> Most simply chaste – most delicately dull,
> Nearly o'erflowing, and yet never full.
> Sweet Willy Whitehead, first in rhiming sphere,
> Who smoothly balladizes twice a year,
> Teaching his laurell'd pension'd muse to sing
> The milkwarm praises of a milk-warm King;
> Welcomes the instant year, as custom claims,
> And hails in creeping measure royal names.[41]

In these lines, the laureate was being set directly at variance with standards of literary quality, and of the literary heritage that underlay those standards.[42] For one thing, Pinchwell was emphasizing the lack of emotive force and resonance in Whitehead's verse. For another, he was casting Whitehead on the wrong side of literary history; in the couplet 'Most simply chaste … never full', he was imitating *The Dunciad*, in which Pope had adapted a famous couplet of John Denham's for an attack on Leonard Welsted.[43] Pinchwell then ironically highlighted Whitehead's status as the 'first in rhiming sphere', with a 'laurell'd pension'd muse', to contrast his official position among writers with his substandard literary talent. With the phrase 'smoothly balladizes', he further emphasized the idea of Whitehead as someone who could happily fulfil the formal act of versifying, but whose verse was empty of meaning or effect. The references to Whitehead's

[40] *Middlesex Journal or Chronicle of Liberty*, 2–4 Jan. 1772.

[41] *Middlesex Journal or Chronicle of Liberty*, 2–4 Jan. 1772.

[42] For more on these standards, see ch. 5.

[43] A. Pope, *The Poems of Alexander Pope*, ed. J. Butt (London, 1996; first published 1963), p. 410.

regularity of output were intended to further distinguish him from the sincerity and spontaneity of literary production; and the end of the poem relocated the insipidity of Whitehead's verse to its subject matter, 'a milk-warm King' and 'royal names'. The laurel was not in fact a mark of poetic achievement; it was merely a 'pension', and, because it was granted by and focused on the king, was necessarily associated with bad poetry. The court was therefore posited as forming a separate sphere and set of standards from that which the laureate was pretending to: literature.

This rhetoric of criticism was nothing new, but it was being developed in accordance with new circumstances. A picture was created in which the laureate was seen crawling off to court, and hiding there from the patriotic public that inhabited the rest of the nation. With this rhetoric, opposition writers effected a separation between the courtly on the one hand, and the public, the literary and the patriotic on the other. They portrayed the court (here elided with the government) as a kind of self-contained echo chamber, with no awareness of the people, no literary standards and no patriotism. One of the main ways in which Whitehead was attacked was as an apologist for the government's despotic policies, its disregard of national sentiment and its hostility to reform. Because he was a pensioned writer, tasked with writing biannual odes that would be promulgated to the nation through the newspapers, he was supposed to be pedalling the court line on all national affairs, including, most critically, the American War. He took his cue from court and government figures, and was therefore a kind of propagandist hireling.[44]

One variant of this line came from a correspondent for the *Morning Chronicle*, calling himself 'An Englishman'.[45] This correspondent painted Whitehead as someone who had fallen from his former principles and had taken the government's side against the country. Addressing Whitehead directly, he told him that his most recent ode 'breaths a spirit of the most contemptible servility, and is unworthy of your name and character'; flattery was to be expected of a laureate, but it could be accomplished 'without insulting the people. In some of your former odes, the friends of their country have seemed pleased, that you, though a poet-laureat, appeared still to retain some principles not wholly unworthy of an Englishman.' But the last ode had proven otherwise. The Englishman quoted one of Whitehead's former, supposedly more patriotic odes against him, observing that it had been written under George II, and that the times had now changed. He further emphasized Whitehead's newfound antagonism towards 'the people',

---

[44] Eg *London Evening Post*, 7–9 June 1774; *Morning Post and Daily Advertiser*, 5 June 1776.

[45] *Morning Chronicle and London Advertiser*, 10 June 1774.

claiming that Whitehead's ode insinuated 'that the people now begin to repent of their opposition'. But 'you have too much sense to believe this yourself, and should not endeavour to propagate so ridiculous a sentiment against others'. Whitehead was here posited as a government propagandist, peddling arguments that he knew to be untrue.

The Englishman's letter went on in this vein, complaining about the 'shameful disregard' paid to the 'interests' and 'sentiments' of 'the people', and claiming that it was the government which was in need of 'repentance and reformation'. His observation that Whitehead's 'courtly muse would not chuse to recommend' such repentance and reformation was a further suggestion that Whitehead knew the truth of the situation, but was choosing to follow the government line due to his muse having been compromised by the court. The Englishman ended with a reminder 'that it is beneath the character of a man of genius, however he may be situated, to employ his talents in gross flattery and adulation; and … he should at least be cautious not to add insult to the distresses of his country.'

This letter is noteworthy, in that it allowed Whitehead a great deal more patriotic sentiment, freedom of choice and poetic talent – even 'genius' – than most of his critics were willing to allow him. With such comments as 'however he may be situated', it even suggested that poets laureate could write in line with patriotism, public opinion and literary genius if they only wanted to. Here, there was no necessity for the laureate to side with the government against the people. At the same time, though, the Englishman was emphatically clear on the division that currently existed, between a government on the one hand, and 'the people' on the other. The government was corrupt, tyrannous and closed off; 'the people' were patriotic, and represented all the historic qualities of Englishmen, primarily a love of liberty. 'The people' *were* the nation; even literature was to be assessed and valued by reference to the sentiments, interests and values of this English people. Whitehead, formerly an admirable poet by reference to these criteria, had now chosen wrongly. He had thrown his lot in with the government, and had therefore become a poor poet, operating in opposition to the patriotic people and to national feeling.

Most criticisms of Whitehead were less sophisticated. One favoured line of attack was to point out the laureate's reticence or wrongness in points of fact and prediction.[46] In 1776, for example, came some short '*Extempore Verses*' on the New Year's ode, sneering at Whitehead's recent change in tone from bragging and belligerent to fearful and pacific, a change that was ascribed

---

[46] Eg *Morning Herald and Daily Advertiser*, 26 Dec. 1780.

to the poor fortunes of the war.[47] Another repeated tactic was to address the odes more directly, either by interlacing them with rebarbative commentary, printing parodies of them or suggesting that the praise in the odes was actually more suited to the American colonists than it was to the king.[48] In addition to these repeated tactics, the opposition press printed various other one-off angles of criticism and mockery, using the laureateship as a prominent, adaptable subject by which to express discontent with the government.[49]

Fairly consistent throughout, however, was the idea that the laureateship was a disgraceful post, used by the executive to glorify the regime and defend its policies, and necessarily filled by some bad poet who would take on any such mean, unpoetical job for money; but that there was something futile and ridiculous about the whole business, because the laureate could only ever operate in contradistinction to the true currents of public opinion, national sentiment and literary quality. At its bluntest, the opposition argued that 'the ode is that species of poetry which has commonly been found least consonant to the taste of the English nation (and indeed the very name prostituted, as it annually is, by the soporific Laureat, carries disgust along with it)'.[50] Whitehead-the-laureate was both an example and exponent of a system that was self-evidently wrong, and antithetical to national sentiment, yet which was institutionally entrenched. It required a barrage of righteous and witty criticism to dislodge it.

Whitehead's reputation as laureate, then, was generally a reasonably good one. But it became thoroughly tarnished, according to opposition newspapers, during the middle of his tenure. The growth of the newspaper press, and the various political crises of these years, had engendered a more extremely polarized newspaper discourse than had existed at the time of his appointment, meaning that this widely acceptable and even laudable laureate became a punching bag for many newspaper writers and correspondents. He never ceased to be a 'respectable laureate', as such. Malone's comment about his having redeemed the office came at his death, and was the endorsement of a reputation that had been established over the previous thirty years. This reputation rested on the assumption that the court had a natural, important

---

[47] *London Evening Post*, 9–11 Jan. 1776.

[48] Eg *Middlesex Journal and Evening Advertiser*, 23–5 June 1774; *Gazetteer and New Daily Advertiser*, 13 June 1778; and *London Courant Westminster Chronicle and Daily Advertiser*, 3 Jan. 1782.

[49] Eg *London Evening Post*, 11–13 Jan. 1774; *London Evening Post*, 7–9 June 1774; *London Chronicle*, 11–13 Jan. 1776; *Morning Post and Daily Advertiser*, 5 June 1776; *Morning Post and Daily Advertiser*, 4 Jan. 1777; *London Evening Post*, 16–19 Aug. 1777; *Morning Post and Daily Advertiser*, 20 Aug. 1777; *General Advertiser and Morning Intelligencer*, 12 June 1778.

[50] *London Evening Post*, 29 Feb.–2 March 1776.

relationship with national identity, the public and literature; it even served to bolster that assumption. But for those who considered the laureateship and the system of which it formed a part to be unrespectable, Whitehead came to seem like one more bad laureate, promulgating government lies in bad verse in exchange for a court pension, and proving the discrepancy, or even the incompatibility, between court on the one hand, and the nation, the public and literature on the other.

Warton's reception

Although the laureateship was most often characterized by reference to the odes, there had always been another understanding of the office: that it was not so much a functional position, as a mark of honour (and disinterested remuneration) for the nation's greatest poet. This had been the understanding on which Dryden, and his immediate pseudo-laureate predecessors, had received their pensions. As Chapter Three suggested, the honorific ideal persisted even after the ode function became established, playing an important part in each laureate appointment process. By the time of George III's accession, the production of odes was dominant in the way that the office appeared in print culture, but there was still a feeling that the office could be, or should be, or in fact was, a mark and reward for the greatest living poet.

Over the years, increasing numbers of observers started to notice a discrepancy between the functional requirement and the honorific ideal, or to stress these two different aspects of the office. More extremely, they expressed the desire that the ode function be dispensed with specifically so as to render the office into a purely honorific position. Thus the *Morning Chronicle* approved of Warton's appointment as laureate in terms of it being 'a reward of genius'.[51] In 1788, a correspondent named 'Candidus' gave the most suitably candid articulation of the argument for separating the function from the honour: 'For such a King does not want a Panegyrist, and such a Poet may be better employed … surely, if it is justifiable to convert any Office at Court into a Sinecure, it is in this Instance. Let the Poet Laureat be excused from rendering his annual Service of two Odes; but let the Salary be continued, as a Mark of royal Distinction conferred on Superiority of Talents.'[52] In this formulation, the court certainly had a role to play with regard to literature, and 'Superior' merit would justifiably be brought into the sphere of royal patronage. But the connection ought

---

[51] *Morning Chronicle and London Advertiser*, 29 April 1785.

[52] *St. James's Chronicle or the British Evening Post*, 20–2 May 1788; repeated, though not as a letter, in *Public Advertiser*, 23 May 1788.

to be a more abstract, honorific one, divested of any specific functional manifestation.[53]

This consciousness of a distinction between the office as functional and as honorific, and the opinion that sometimes followed – that the odes should be stripped away so as to let the honour shine forth – was to endure down to 1813, when Robert Southey accepted the office on the understanding that he could hold it as an 'honour', without being tasked with biannual odes.[54] However, a consciousness of the distinction between function and honour did not necessarily entail the abolition of the odes. With both Whitehead and Pye, there can also be identified some sense that the function and the honour were natural partners. Zeno's commentary on Whitehead's ode, quoted above, suggested that the odes ought to be written by a great poet, and that the biannual ode format gave a great poet the opportunity to write great poems.

This sense of union between function and honour reached its highest pitch with Thomas Warton. During his tenure, the office and the odes attracted new heights of attention, interest, admiration and respect, and the diligence and talent with which he fulfilled his duties meant that (according to most newspaper writers and correspondents) he was able to unite the functional and honorific aspects of the office into a seamless whole, becoming a sort of genuine national voice. (He was also helped by the relative mildness of the political climate.) Mockery did not cease, of course; but Warton's achievement was nonetheless resounding. Between 1785 and 1790, the laureateship was one of the most important aspects of the literary landscape, and each new ode was consumed avidly by newspaper writers and readers.

It helped that Warton already had an impressive reputation, and that he continued his scholarly works throughout his tenure. Indeed, those scholarly works were followed with great interest by the newspapers, and were even associated with his position as laureate. Several newspapers reported that Warton had kept up his work on Milton directly at the king's request, or 'was honoured by a Royal injunction to complete his annotations upon this mighty Bard'.[55] But what brought Warton and his office the greatest renown was the odes themselves. After his first, poorly received offering, he managed to produce a sequence of odes that, even

---

[53] *Lloyd's Evening Post*, 8–11 May 1767; *St. James's Chronicle or the British Evening Post*, 20–2 Feb. 1777.

[54] See Conclusion.

[55] *Public Advertiser*, 2 June 1790. See also *St. James's Chronicle or the British Evening Post*, 5–7 July 1785. For Warton's work on Milton, see A. Rounce, 'Scholarship', in *The Oxford Handbook of British Poetry, 1660–1800,* ed. Lynch (Oxford, 2016), p. 690.

when they did not command universal admiration, generated widespread critical engagement and discussion. Newspaper readers seem to have looked forward to them. In December 1788, the *Morning Post* read, 'If the Laureat's New Year Ode, said to have been prepared before his Majesty's illness, is not to be performed at St. James's [because of the illness], the lovers of true poetry flatter themselves, that it will at least be given to the Public by the usual channel.'[56] Likewise the *General Advertiser*: 'The subject of the New Year Ode has excited the curiosity of the Literati; the Laureat's annual tribute to Majesty, will, we hear, at this melancholy period, be dispensed with.'[57] Warton's odes, although here described as 'tribute[s] to Majesty', their performance or non-performance determined by the king's disposition, were nonetheless being identified and valued in terms of their distribution to 'the Public' and 'the Literati'. The king's illness thus served to deprive readers of the 'true poetry' it had come to look forward to twice a year. Warton's laureate odes were important literary business, and their fixed regularity of appearance only enhanced their status as literary events.

There was a continuous welter of positive remarks on the laureate's odes and talents in these years. 'The Laureat has undoubtedly added much to his fame by his second Ode,' said the *Morning Chronicle*.[58] 'The *Laureat's Ode*, the best publication of the New Year, was reviewed in the World, and with repeated approbation on the 3d of Jan,' stated the megalomaniac, self-obsessed *World*.[59] It then reviewed the ode again the next day, this time pointing out some of its flaws, but stating, 'Wharton's Ode, which though already much praised, may here meet with further panegyric, without our justly incurring the censure of adulation, is undoubtedly the happiest Lyric, the happiest Laureate Lyrick at least, that ever flowed from his pen.'[60] More unequivocal was the praise of the *St. James's Chronicle*:

> The Odes of the late Laureate, Mr. Whitehead, are confessedly superior to any of the Odes of his Predecessors: And among these predecessors, are the conspicuous Names of Dryden and Rowe. But what official Ode of Whitehead comprehends so much Variety and Vigour of Imagery, as Mr. Warton's last Ode?

---

[56] *Morning Post and Daily Advertiser*, 3 Dec. 1788.

[57] *General Advertiser*, 12 Dec. 1788.

[58] *Morning Chronicle and London Advertiser*, 9 Jan. 1786.

[59] *World and Fashionable Advertiser*, 10 Jan. 1787.

[60] *World and Fashionable Advertiser*, 11 Jan. 1787.

It then gave an extended sequence of praise for the various beauties and ingenuities of the ode in question.[61] By the end of Warton's tenure, newspapers were able to make casual remarks about 'the sublime flights and stateliness of Birth Day Odes', or to group Warton's productions with 'the best Odes in our language', comparable to 'the Odes of Gray'.[62]

There was also a tendency for deeper literary debate. The *General Evening Post* observed, 'It is a matter of no small entertainment and curiosity, to compare the different criticisms in the newspapers on the Laureat's late Ode.' It then gave a list of all the contradictory things, positive and negative, that had been said on this single ode, before concluding that, 'as the Ode is so much the object of public attention, and as abuse is too commonly excited by excellence, we may easily perceive what is its real character'.[63] Clearly, there was vigorous discussion about Warton's laureate offerings, within and beyond the newspaper press. One of the best examples came in the *Gazetteer* of 1786, precisely because it started out on a negative note, and evinced the sort of oppositional attitude that Whitehead had suffered so much from. 'Warton's Ode – with all its imperfections on its head – claims applause; but applause only as a party poem.' It was, the paper insisted, an unwarranted 'panegyrick upon the present Administration'; its 'execution' was 'well', and certain parts were 'extremely poetical' and 'extremely spirited'; however, there was a general lack of originality throughout. Following this ambivalent scrutiny, though, the *Gazetteer* concluded by saying, 'our present Laureat … is certainly superior in poetical abilities to his predecessor; and Whitehead excelled Colley Cibber. Whatever the splenetic may assert to the contrary, literature was never more encouraged, nor ever flourished as she does at present.'[64] Thus, even when an individual ode came in for some negative criticism, it was part of a wider climate of debate and approval which can leave no doubt as to the high regard in which Warton-as-laureate was held by his contemporaries.

Warton's reception is also notable in terms of what criteria he was being judged by and for what factors he was being celebrated. One correspondent in 1785, defending Warton's ode from a charge made by a critic in another newspaper – that its opening lines were ambiguous – argued instead that the lines in question led 'naturally' to Warton's 'main argument', which argument was 'exemplified in a general display of two distinguished parts of the King's character, his patronage of the arts, and the decorum of his

[61] *St. James's Chronicle or the British Evening Post*, 12–14 Jan. 1786.

[62] *The World*, 23 June 1788 and *Morning Herald*, 26 June 1788; *Public Advertiser*, 10 June 1789.

[63] *General Evening Post*, 14–17 Jan. 1786.

[64] *Gazetteer and New Daily Advertiser*, 7 Jan. 1786.

domestic life. And surely, in this display, elegance and imagery are united with perspicuity. Through the whole composition, one subject is uniformly pursued, judiciously conducted, and happily illustrated.'[65] Warton's ode was being subjected to critical literary analysis, and was found entirely successful. Moreover, it achieved literary success *as* an illustration of the king's qualities, and particularly of his role as a patron and as a father (in which latter capacity he was both a father to the nation, and an exemplar of a middle-class domestic ideal). There was no sense here, as there had been in some of the attacks on Whitehead, that praise of the king was inherently unliterary, or that a laureate ode could only ever have been vacuous. Instead, this exemplary prince and patron of the arts formed perfect subject matter for an admirable piece of poetry.

Still more emphatic in praising Warton's ode by reference to notions of literary greatness and national character was the *St. James's Chronicle*:

> As the situation of a Poet Laureate is very similar to that of Pindar ... might not our Birth-Day Odes be rendered more interesting, by interweaving agreeable Digressions [as Pindar did], and striking Parts of English History with the usual Compliments of the Day? Most of Mr. Warton's Odes have been written on this Plan; and such a Plan alone is calculated to render those periodical Productions, not only a classical Entertainment for the present Time, but a permanent and valuable Acquisition to Posterity. We are happy to hear, that Mr. Warton has very successfully pursued this Idea in his next Ode.[66]

Here, the newspaper showed awareness of the potential transience and quotidian nature of laureate odes, and yet expressed the belief that they could transcend this fate and enter the literary canon, if they were written according to Pindar's example and if they engaged with English history. Warton, the newspaper emphasized, was doing just this. His odes were being praised not just as successful examples within a limited genre, or for their courtly nature; they were being praised by reference to those public, national and literary qualities that Whitehead's enemies had claimed to be incompatible with the laureateship.

One final, interesting variation to note came in 1788, when the same newspaper stated that Warton had been 'accused of treating the transcendent and numerous Virtues of his Royal Master with a Parsimony of Panegyrick'. For some observers, the laureate was not being sycophantic enough. But

---

[65] *Public Advertiser*, 15 June 1785.

[66] *St. James's Chronicle or the British Evening Post*, 20–3 Oct. 1787. This statement heavily paraphrased Pye, without acknowledgement. For Pye's original statement, see ch. 5. H. J. Pye, *Poems on Various Subjects* (2 vols, 1787), i. 195–6.

the *Chronicle* defended him, insisting, 'the Composition turns on a very seasonable and well-chosen Topick, the singular Happiness enjoyed by the People of England, under a King, who promotes and preserves the original and constitutional Compacts of his Kingdom', which, the *Chronicle* noted, was in contrast to the despotic behaviour of Louis XVI.[67] The patriotism of the laureate could not be doubted. Nor could the unison between 'People' and 'King', which was celebrated, and in some sense enacted, in his odes.

Alongside these particular comments on his odes, Warton's tenure also saw a pronounced step-up in the amount of petty reportage to which the laureate was subjected. 'We hear that Mr. Stanley, the Royal Composer, is impatient to begin the music for the next Birth-day Ode; and at the same time we are informed, that the Laureat has not yet written a single line!' remarked the *Public Advertiser*.[68] 'The Poet Laureat yesterday presented [the manuscript of] his Ode for the New Year to their Majesties, at the Queen's House, Buckingham-Gate.'[69] As well as becoming a figure of public interest in his own right, he also served as a symbol for a wider loyalist poetic culture, invoked and looked to by those other writers who wished to celebrate the king in verse. A 'Cottage Mouse' sent in an 'Impromptu' poem in response to Warton's first birthday ode, exulting, 'O! thou, the Friend of Milton's lay,/Well chosen to record the day,/The Monarch we esteem;/Thy claim the Muse would not debar,/Content to be the evening star,/And thou the morning beam.'[70] This anonymous mousy woman, who had published panegyrics on King George and Queen Charlotte before,[71] here celebrated Warton and George in conjunction with each other, looking to the laureate as the 'morning beam' of loyalist culture, and stressing his connection with the great national bard, Milton, as the quality which rendered him suitable to 'record' the royal birthday. Others echoed the sentiment, sending their own eulogistic responses to Warton's odes into the newspapers, using the opportunity of the royal birthday to show their admiration for both laureate and king and further elaborating a public courtly culture with the laureate odes at its centre.[72]

Warton-as-laureate, then, was one of the most important figures in the literary landscape from 1785 to 1790. He stood prominently before the reading public, and his courtly odes were regarded as highly significant events, as

---

[67] *St. James's Chronicle or the British Evening Post*, 24–7 May 1788.

[68] *Public Advertiser*, 1 April 1786.

[69] *General Evening Post*, 17–19 Dec. 1789.

[70] *Public Advertiser*, 8 June 1785.

[71] *Morning Chronicle and London Advertiser*, 4 June 1784 and *Public Advertiser*, 4 June 1784.

[72] Eg *St. James's Chronicle or the British Evening Post*, 30 June–2 July 1785.

well as highly accomplished poems, deserving of critical engagement. Mockery and negativity did not disappear; but it seems unarguable that under Warton, the laureateship occupied a position of importance and respectability that would not have been expected before the detailing of this evidence. More unexpectedly still, the odes were central to this; Warton's achievement was to render the functional and the honorific notions of the office seamlessly compatible, and thus to turn the laureateship into a sort of national voice, widely regarded as speaking equally for king and people. Whitehead's role in doing something similar, and in preparing the way for Warton, should not be neglected; but he was never quite as highly regarded, and had to deal with the more factional reception provided by a more violently factional readership. It was Warton who succeeded most emphatically in setting courtly culture in harmony with ideas of literature, patriotism and public opinion. When Bishop Richard Mant came to publish Warton's *Poetical Works* in 1802, he introduced them as 'the poems of the late Laureate', and he placed the laureate odes as the culmination of Warton's lyric poetry. In the 'Memoirs' that opened the volume, Mant waxed lyrical about these laureate lyrics, which he discussed lengthily after having first surveyed the rest of Warton's English-language poetry. 'The Laureate Odes', he claimed, 'are the most striking testimony of the strength of Warton's poetical genius.'[73] It would not have been a controversial opinion.

Pye's reception

The last of the eighteenth-century laureates was Henry James Pye, whose reputation is usually thought to have been particularly poor, but whose newspaper reception was actually a mixture of Whitehead's and Warton's. Undoubtedly, there were a large number of readers who considered him a meagre poet, including the circles of William Godwin, Southey and Byron.[74] Equally, the sorts of negative press that Whitehead came in for during the crises over Wilkes, America and reform were repeated for Pye during the crisis years of the 1790s, when the French Revolutionary Wars were raging, the Jacobin scare was at its height and Pitt's government was attempting to suppress sedition. This aspect of Pye's public reception can be found in abundant evidence and diversity in the opposition press, but its tone and trends were sufficiently similar to Whitehead's for it to warrant nothing more

---

[73] R. Mant, 'Preface', in T. Warton, *The Poetical Works of the Late Thomas Warton, B.D.*, ed. R. Mant (2 vols, Oxford, 1802), i. i–v, at p. i; R. Mant, 'Memoirs of the life and writings of Thomas Warton', in Warton, *Poetical Works*, ed. Mant, i. ix–clxii, at pp. clvi–clix.

[74] Eg Thomas Lawrence to William Godwin. Bod, MS. Abinger c. 15, fo. 40.

here than a hefty footnote.[75] The only major difference was that the king and court were no longer being much targeted as part of these attacks, their place taken by Pitt's ministry. During Pye's twenty-three years as laureate, he and his office clearly had a bad reputation in some quarters. And yet, the most striking thing about Pye's tenure is that, unlike Whitehead, he embraced the potentials of his position. Rather than sitting there meekly while opposition newspapers castigated him, he made himself into a champion of loyalism, proudly placing himself at the head of loyalist culture and being celebrated as such by the loyalist press. He became a voice of the nation, as Warton had been, but within the context of a more partisan politics.

Partly, this was because he joined his role as laureate with a range of other loyalist activities. He became a Westminster magistrate in 1792, and seems to have been a tenacious official in the battle against crime and Jacobinism; in 1808, he published a *Summary of the Duties of a Justice of the Peace out of Sessions*.[76] He also wrote two anti-Jacobin novels, *The Democrat* (1795) and *The Aristocrat* (1799); plays and epic poems on patriotic, belligerent and loyalist themes; and various pieces of conservative non-fiction, including a translation of *Xenophon's Defence of the Athenian Democracy … with Notes, and an Appendix* (1794), over half of which consisted of Pye's commentary in defence of the existing British system of government. Alongside these various conservative, loyalist and Pittite endeavours there were, of course, the biannual odes.

Pye's newspaper reception was exactly as he would have wished. Due to his institutional position and spirited publications, he was accepted by the loyalist press, especially in the 1790s, as a champion of the cause, and was held up as a national bard of paramount importance. His every non-official publication was commented upon, praised for its fine loyalist tendencies and predicted to make some practical contribution to the anti-Jacobin cause.[77]

[75] Eg *The World*, 3 Jan. 1794; *Morning Post*, 8 Jan. 1794; *Morning Post*, 22 May 1794; *Morning Post and Fashionable World*, 29 Jan. 1795; *Morning Post and Fashionable World*, 29 Sept. 1795; *Oracle and Public Advertiser*, 20 Jan. 1796; *Morning Chronicle*, 25 May 1796; *Morning Chronicle*, 15 June 1796; *Morning Chronicle*, 19 Jan. 1797; *Morning Chronicle*, 5 Nov. 1799; *Morning Post and Gazetteer*, 2 Jan. 1800.

[76] Leigh Hunt's autobiography tells an anecdote in which Pye was too engrossed in reading to bother with his work arresting criminals. L. Hunt, *The Autobiography of Leigh Hunt*, ed. J. E. Morpurgo (London, 1948), p. 196. Apart from this, though, the evidence suggests Pye to have been a diligent magistrate, and his writings evince great fervour for the anti-Jacobin cause. He appears performing his work as a magistrate in official records: TNA, C 12/683/18; C 12/683/29; C 202/181/2; HO 42/22/36, fos. 94–5; HO 42/23, fos. 30–2; HO 42/45/2, fos. 8–19; HO 42/45/10, fos. 131–59; HO 42/77, fos. 178–9; HO 47/21/1; HO 47/32/16.

[77] Eg *Oracle and Public Advertiser*, 15 April 1794; *London Chronicle*, 20–2 May 1794; *Star*, 19 Jan. 1798; *Lloyd's Evening Post*, 27–9 June 1798; *Oracle and Public Advertiser*, 23 Aug. 1798;

The laureate was fulfilling a new role through his publications: 'To excite the military and patriotic ardour of his countrymen'.[78] Apparently, one line in Pye's tragedy *The Siege of Meaux* – 'Think not your private meetings are concealed from our enquiring eye,' which was an allegorical reference to the government's crackdown on Jacobin activities – produced 'one of the most marked plaudits we ever heard in a Theatre'.[79] At least one newspaper printed Pye's verses on 'the late Glorious Victory obtained by the British Fleet' of June 1794, which (it explained) had been sent by Pye to Drury Lane theatre for a public recitation there.[80]

Meanwhile, Pye made appearances at various gatherings in London, some of a courtly character, others of a broader cultural interest, successfully enacting the role of a bard of public importance and a central figure in loyalist culture. His attendance at royal Levees was reported on,[81] and so too his appointment as a Justice for the Westminster Police in 1792;[82] he was numbered among various other 'lovers and patrons of the Arts' at the Royal Academy's annual dinner;[83] he gave a recitation at the 1799 anniversary dinner of the Literary Fund;[84] and at the same event the following year, 'A poem by Mr. Pye, the laureat, was recited by another Gentleman', before a rendition of 'God Save the King'.[85] Pye even became a sort of celebrity, with papers reporting on his movements, whereabouts and appearances in public.[86] Several newspapers even reported on a minor accident suffered by 'Mr. Pye, brother to the Poet-Laureat', who fell into a cellar and lay stuck there for two hours.[87]

The odes attracted clamorous attention in a somewhat similar way to Warton's, but with a more partisan bent. As the *Sun* put it, 'The learning, the talents, and the respectable character of Mr. Pye, the Poet Laureat, cannot

---

True Briton, 9 Oct. 1798; *True Briton*, 29 July 1800; *Oracle and Daily Advertiser*, 30 July 1800.

[78] *Whitehall Evening Post*, 29–31 Jan. 1795 and *St. James's Chronicle or the British Evening Post*, 3–5 Feb. 1795.

[79] *Times*, 20 May 1794.

[80] *Whitehall Evening Post*, 8–10 July 1794.

[81] *Public Advertiser*, 25 Feb. 1792; *Morning Chronicle*, 25 Feb. 1792; *Star*, 25 Feb. 1792.

[82] *The World*, 5 July 1792.

[83] *Oracle and Public Advertiser*, 28 April 1794.

[84] *Morning Herald*, 3 May 1799.

[85] *London Packet or New Lloyd's Evening Post*, 23–5 April 1800.

[86] Eg *Star*, 26 March 1792; *Times*, 10 Aug. 1796; *St. James's Chronicle or the British Evening Post*, 5–7 July 1798; *Morning Herald*, 12 Jan. 1799; *Morning Post and Gazetteer*, 17 Jan. 1799.

[87] *Lloyd's Evening Post*, 30 April–2 May 1800; *Whitehall Evening Post*, 1–3 May 1800; *Morning Post and Gazetteer*, 3 May 1800.

exempt him from the abuse of the Seditious Prints, because his Muse is devoted to Loyalty, and because his heart feels upon that subject all that is suggested by his imagination. But the abuse is as dull as it is malignant.'[88] The products of this loyalist muse seem to have been received eagerly by many readers. In January 1792, when there was no New Year's ode, at least two newspapers filled the gap by presenting one of Pye's earlier, non-official odes, '*Written at* Eaglehurst, *which commands a View of Spithead, October 10, 1790*', in which Pye celebrated the British fleet; the *Oracle* proclaimed in preface to the ode, 'The People shall not be disappointed of an Ode from the Laureate – We present them with the following; much of which is very Poetical, in the Whitehead way, and very pleasing.'[89]

The partisan bent to Pye's public reception was not much to his cost. If anything, the necessities of partisan debate seem to have elevated the standing of the laureateship to greater heights than ever before. For example, the public rehearsals of the odes became increasingly popular and prominent events. 'The annual poetic tribute of the Laureat … yesterday was rehearsed at the Music Rooms, in Tottenham-street, to a polite and numerous audience,' reported the *Morning Herald* in 1793.[90] By 1795, the rehearsals were being witnessed by 'a crouded attendance of Musical Cognoscenti and Ladies', and being 'received with great applause, and though a gratuitous performance, some parts were unanimously *encored*'.[91] Apparently, the conductor had transitioned this ode's conclusion into 'the popular air of *Rule Britannia* with peculiar felicity and effect', further establishing the odes' position among a booming loyalist culture.[92] In 1799, 'fifteen hundred persons' attended.[93] 'The Room was, indeed, more crouded than ever we remember on any similar occasion … The whole was received with warm applause – an applause that was the due tribute to Taste, to Science, and to Genius.'[94]

Pye's odes also started cropping up in other contexts. At the 1794 annual dinner of the Royal Academy, 'Some of the chief attendants' read out 'the first two Stanzas of the Laureate's coming Ode'.[95] In 1795, numerous adverts started appearing for public, commercial vocal concerts that included a

[88] *Sun*, 10 July 1798.

[89] *Oracle*, 6 Jan. 1792; *Public Advertiser*, 9 Jan. 1792.

[90] *Morning Herald*, 3 Jan. 1793.

[91] *True Briton*, 1 Jan. 1795; *Sun*, 1 Jan. 1795.

[92] *True Briton*, 2 Jan. 1795; *Sun*, 2 Jan. 1795.

[93] *Observer*, 20 Jan. 1799.

[94] *Sun*, 18 Jan. 1799; also in *True Briton*, 18 Jan. 1799.

[95] *The World*, 28 April 1794.

'Selection from the Ode for the New Year (by permission of the Poet Laureat and the Master of His Majesty's Band)', alongside works by such composers as Handel and (an unspecified) Bach.[96] Likewise, in 1799, Ranelagh Gardens advertised the following: 'The Manager respectfully informs the Public, that by particular desire of many Persons of Distinction', he had brought in a four-year-old 'Phoenomenon' to perform 'a Concerto of Haydn's on the Grand Piano Forte; recite Collins's Ode on the Passions; and the Birth-Day Ode by the Poet-Laureat'. George III's birthday would also be honoured (the advert continued) with a fireworks display, and a 'RURAL MASQUERADE' would be put on under the patronage of the prince of Wales.[97] The same four-year-old musical prodigy popped up again in other adverts, performing Pye's ode and the two other pieces at Covent Garden theatre, as part of a performance of *Lover's Vows* put on under 'the Patronage of Her Majesty'.[98]

Nor did Pye and his supporters allow the opposition to separate the court from the spheres of public opinion, patriotism and literature, as they wished to do. Instead, for the loyalist newspapers, notions of patriotism and literature were more closely bound up with the court than ever before; they attained their highest and most natural expression in the context of courtly culture. One birthday ode was commended, as poetry, by reference to its anti-Jacobin politics: 'The Laureat's poetical description of the turbulent and dreadful situation of affairs upon the Continent, compared with the happy and harmonious agreement of all ranks to support the Constitution of Great Britain, is described in the most beautiful and impressive language.'[99] Pye's partisan, patriotic subject matter made the perfect content for fine poetry. A few years later, another ode received an even more rapturous response:

> The Poet-Laureat's address, in converting the attack on his Majesty into a compliment, has been noticed; but a Correspondent wonders that the beautiful conclusion of the Ode, which sings the birth of the young Princess, should have gone without some publick tribute of praise. Mr. Pye has narrated this joyful event in the true style of Poetry. To repeat his verse, will be to invite our readers to a repetition of pleasure.[100]

Here, Pye's courtly verse was found to be truly poetic and emphatically pleasurable to readers, on account of its treatment of royal persons and events.

---

[96] Eg *Morning Chronicle*, 30 Jan. 1795; *Oracle and Public Advertiser*, 5 Feb. 1795.

[97] *Star*, 5 June 1799.

[98] *Morning Chronicle*, 10 June 1799.

[99] *Diary or Woodfall's Register*, 24 Dec. 1792.

[100] *St. James's Chronicle or the British Evening Post*, 28–30 Jan. 1796.

The response to Pye's special *Carmen Seculare* – an ode for the new century – was, in some quarters, even more emphatic regarding his literary accomplishments. 'The whole of the work is written with true lyric enthusiasm. Gray is the model whom the Laureat has evidently studied on the present occasion, and there are many passages in this Secular Ode which would not suffer even in comparison with some of that admirable Poet's happiest flights.'[101] This courtly, patriotic ode could stand proudly alongside the great works of Gray. Meanwhile, when opposition newspapers tried to distinguish between courtly interests and literary quality, loyalist newspapers reacted with sovereign complacency: '*A Party Scribbler* says, that the Laureat's Ode smells of *the oil of influence* – This can only mean *the soft influence of the Muses*, a compliment of which the Laureat has some reason to be proud.'[102] It was the opposition, not Pye, whose literary discernment was corrupted by factional feeling; they served a '*Party*', he served '*the Muses*'.

This sort of evidence has not been much noticed by scholars. Even where Pye has been enlisted as an exemplar of loyalist sentiment, his role and reputation have been dealt with dismissively. Simon Bainbridge ended a brief discussion of him by deeming him a 'failure' in his attempts to inspire the national war effort.[103] Kevin Gilmartin, in his monograph on literary conservatism during this period, barely mentioned Pye. Where he did, he called Pye 'the much-maligned Poet Laureate and occasional *Anti-Jacobin* reviewer', and only discussed him as a representative writer of anti-Jacobin novels.[104] M. O. Grenby's treatment of Pye was more considerate. Surveying the reception of anti-Jacobin novels in the major review periodicals, he gave a nuanced, sensitive discussion of how political principles factored into matters of aesthetic criticism. However, after noting the positive reviews that Pye's anti-Jacobin novels garnered, he expressed surprise. 'Could it really be the so much maligned and notoriously dreary Henry James Pye ... whose *Aristocrat* (1799) was called "agreeable", "remarkably well-written", "pleasing", "the elegant amusements of a well-informed and accomplished writer"[?]'.[105] But the answer to Grenby's question is straightforward: yes.

---

[101] *Sun*, 18 Jan. 1800.

[102] *True Briton*, 27 Jan. 1797.

[103] S. Bainbridge, *British Poetry and the Revolutionary and Napoleonic Wars: Visions of Conflict* (Oxford, 2003), pp. 48–50 (p. 50 for quotation).

[104] K. Gilmartin, *Writing Against Revolution: Literary Conservatism in Britain, 1790–1832* (Cambridge, 2007), p. 158.

[105] M. O. Grenby, *The Anti-Jacobin Novel: British Conservatism and the French Revolution* (Cambridge, 2001), p. 198.

There was no widespread negative opinion of Pye's quality as a writer, except among those of opposition political tendencies. Even at the start of the 1790s, Hayley and Cowper had had a high opinion of Pye;[106] Isaac Disraeli had published a poetical address to him in which he had extolled him above the majority of his poetic contemporaries and identified him as a tutelary figure;[107] and the *Public Advertiser* had said upon his appointment, 'No man in Great-Britain, perhaps, could have accepted the post of Poet Laureat with so much propriety as Mr. Pye. His merits, as a Bard, are universally allowed to be striking ... The Monthly Critics ... have always spoken highly of his works.'[108] As the 1790s progressed, the tendencies of Pye's work and his position as laureate then caused him to become a champion of loyalist culture. Any positive reviews that his work might have attracted in these years should not be seen through the lens of Romantic scorn; they should be taken as evidence of Pye's complicated but prominent standing.

During the French Revolutionary and Napoleonic Wars, then, the previous trends of newspaper discussion of the laureateship reached their head. For many people, the laureateship was execrable; as a courtly office that only hireling poetasters would accept, it could only ever be so. But for many others, the laureate Pye was a loyalist champion, and his odes formed the centrepiece of loyalist culture. They were not at odds with ideas of national identity or literature, but in fact were entirely compatible with such ideas, because the court, and a spirit of loyalty to the court, were central to public opinion and national identity, and even, perhaps, to the arts. When Pye recovered from an illness in 1798, one newspaper was able to report, without a hint of irony, that 'Many of the *Literati* were wishing for his distinguished office.'[109] Thus the laureateship became, during Pye's tenure, subject to a polarization of public opinion, its reputation divided and extreme. But there can be no doubt that the office was a highly significant feature of the cultural landscape and of public consciousness. It played a key part in focusing and articulating loyalist sentiment, and it cemented the role of the court with regard to the public, national identity and literature. The reception of Pye and his odes demonstrates that eighteenth-century Britain had not in fact transitioned from a courtly culture to a post-courtly,

---

[106] Pye, *Poems on Various Subjects*, i. 49; W. Cowper, *The Letters and Prose Writings of William Cowper*, ed. J. King and C. Ryskamp (5 vols, Oxford, 1979–86), iv. 123–4.

[107] I. Disraeli, *Specimens of a New Version of Telemachus. To Which is Prefixed, A Defence of Poetry. Addressed to Henry James Pye, Esq. Poet-Laureat*, 2nd edn (1791). Looking back from 1826, John O'Keeffe stated in passing, 'Mr. Pye deservedly succeeded Warton.' J. O'Keeffe, *Recollections of the Life of John O'Keeffe* (2 vols, 1826), ii. 133.

[108] *Public Advertiser*, 26 July 1790.

[109] *Oracle and Public Advertiser*, 17 Jan. 1798.

commercial or public culture. Instead, the court remained a key location in the conceptual geography of culture, including as a forum for literary production, commercial practices, public performances and patriotism. The logistical and ideological challenges of the French Revolutionary Wars caused the court's role to become clearer and all the more important, energizing a loyalist sentiment that looked to the court, and to its poet laureate, for its voice in matters of national identity and literature.

The reviews

However, it may be objected that evidence from newspapers is insufficient to support the claims being made in this chapter, due to the problematic nature of newspapers as sources (detailed above). Therefore, this chapter will finish with a brief survey of another kind of source, which scholars generally hold to be a more representative, authoritative and accurate body of material when seeking to understand the opinions held by eighteenth-century writers and readers: the *Monthly* and *Critical* reviews. The concurrence between this evidence and the foregoing evidence will therefore not only bolster this chapter's arguments, but also emphasize just how extensive the laureateship's presence was within print culture.

The *Monthly* and *Critical*, having generally praised Whitehead's pre-laureate works, continued in this vein after his appointment.[110] The *Monthly* approved of his quasi-official *Verses to the People of England. 1758* in sentiment and, for the most part, in versification;[111] and it described Dodsley's popular *A Collection of Poems, by Several Hands* volumes as 'perhaps' the most 'excellent Miscellany … in any language', while rightly numbering Whitehead among the chief contributors to them.[112] When Whitehead was attacked in satirical works, the reviews defended him, stating that his poetic abilities and personality 'exempt[ed]' him from satire, or proved the satirist misguided.[113] When reviewing his 1774 collected works, both reviews praised him highly, and explicitly referenced his popularity with the public and his position as laureate:

> the public will receive pleasure at being furnished with a complete edition of the performances of this ingenious author, the greatest part of which, at different times, has already met with their approbation … posterity will consider the author as not undeservedly advanced to the honourable

[110] For pre-laureate reviews, see eg *MR* 10, May 1754, pp. 374–84; 16, March 1757, pp. 232–5; *CR* 1.3, April 1756, p. 267; 3, Feb. 1757, pp. 136–9.

[111] *MR* 18, April 1758, pp. 334–5.

[112] *MR* 18, June 1758, p. 533.

[113] *CR* 19, March 1765, p. 235.

distinction which he holds; and be of opinion that he has a claim to the palm of poetical genius, independent of the rank of Laureat.[114]

However, over the course of his tenure, the opinions of both reviews crystallized on a certain estimation of him: that Whitehead was a skilled, intelligent and admirable poet, among the best in the country, but that he did not evince a profuse genius. This opinion owed much to the fact that, other than in his odes, his characteristics were those of Pope, rather than of Gray and Warton. Thus his 1762 play, *The School for Lovers*, was deemed a fine '*Genteel Comedy*', but lacking in the busyness and variety demanded by English audiences.[115] The quasi-official *A Charge to the Poets* (1762) was praised for 'good sense, refined taste' and 'agreeable verses';[116] *Variety* (1776) was 'pleasing, elegant';[117] *The Goat's Beard* (1777) had 'a considerable degree of merit. It is easy and spirited.'[118] By the time of his posthumous biography and collection (1788), written and edited by Mason, both reviews reiterated that Whitehead's reputation was

> already decided upon … In poetic fire, he was not deficient; and, if he had not corrected with much coolness he might have been admired for the occasional splendour, as well as the more steady illumination. His Odes, these tedious repetitions of courtly compliment, were often spirited and poetical; and, if his successor [Warton] shines with a brighter fire, or more varied imagery, he does not excel Mr. Whitehead in precision, or the gloss, which is the effect of the limae labor et mora.[119]

This particular reviewer indicated the wider principles at stake, and one of the reasons why Whitehead slid into neglect following his death, by drawing attention to Whitehead's indebtedness to Pope and stating: 'The bolder energy, and the more varied structure of the verses of our elder poets were, for a time, forgotten in the admiration of more polished versification, of more luxuriant description, and a more elegant selection of imagery.'[120]

As this last point suggests, Warton was generally viewed differently to Whitehead. The reviews' praise of Warton was more fulsome, and

[114] *MR* 51, Oct. 1774, p. 318; *CR* 37, March 1774, pp. 199–201 (for quotation).

[115] *MR* 26, Feb. 1762, pp. 157–8 (for quotation); *CR* 13, Feb. 1762, pp. 136–8.

[116] *MR* 26, March 1762, pp. 222–3 (first quotation); *CR* 13, March 1762, p. 268 (second quotation).

[117] *MR* 54, March 1776, p. 241.

[118] *MR* 56, March 1777, pp. 188–92 (p. 192 for quotation).

[119] *MR* 78, March 1788, pp. 177–82; *CR* 65, March 1788, pp. 177–82 (p. 177 for quotation). This is not a misprint; both reviews happened to have the same page numbers.

[120] *CR* 65, March 1788, pp. 177–8.

often focused on his Gothic inclinations: 'If we had many such poets as Mr. Warton, mankind would return to their caves and their rocks; and honest Orpheus must do all his work over again.'[121] Prior to his appointment, his *History* received particularly extended and numerous reviews; after he was appointed, so too did his work on Milton.[122] When rebutting satirical attacks on Warton, the reviews placed more emphasis on the quality of his laureate odes than they had done with Whitehead: the *Critical* mentioned 'the strength, the spirit, and the true poetical ardour in Mr. Warton's last production', the 1786 New Year ode, and (correctly) pointed out in response to Peter Pindar's *Ode upon Ode* (1787) that 'Mr. Warton's late excellent Ode is only the vehicle for Peter's invective, and not the subject of his attack'.[123]

Thus the reviews bear out the impression given by the newspaper press: Warton as a poet and as a laureate was celebrated yet more highly than Whitehead, and this praise centred on his laureate odes. The best example comes in a 1793 review, which struck a similar note to Mant's:

> We have had frequent occasion to celebrate the genius and abilities of our late worthy, learned, and ingenious Laureat, as a poet, a critic, and an historian; and the chief part of the present publication has already passed our ordeal with safety and honour … We have formerly observed … that our bard was 'particularly happy in descriptive poetry;' and he has since, in his official odes, as Poet Laureat, rendered it just and necessary to extend this praise to his felicity in Gothic painting … The odes for 1787 and 1788, while the bard had no splendid foreign nor domestic events to celebrate, nor any calamities to deplore, abound with Gothic pictures and embellishments, which give that kind of mellowness to these poems, that time confers on medals and productions of the pencil.[124]

Not just in the quotidian medium of the newspapers, but in the reviews' more ruminative pages, Warton's laureate odes crowned his achievements as a poet.

For Pye, the reviews displayed less frequent interest in his role as a champion of loyalist culture than newspapers did, but were similar to them in tracing his energies across a varied range of outputs. Moreover, they

---

[121] *CR* 44, Aug. 1777, pp. 109–15 (p. 109 for quotation). However, see *MR* 56, May 1777, pp. 331–2, for praise emphasizing his 'classic taste and judgment', and his avoidance of Gothic excess.

[122] Eg *CR* 37, April 1774, pp. 275–83; 37, June 1774, pp. 435–48; 45, June 1778, pp. 417–25; 45, May 1778, pp. 321–30; 51, May 1781, pp. 321–30 (again, another coincidentally identical page range); 52, July 1781, pp. 15–23; 52, Aug. 1781, pp. 108–14; 59, May 1785, pp. 321–8; 59, June 1785, pp. 421–30.

[123] *CR* 61, Jan. 1786, pp. 71–2; *CR* 63, p. 310.

[124] *MR* 10, March 1793, pp. 271–8 (pp. 271, 277 for quotations).

reinforce the argument that it was entirely viable, and reasonably common, to view Pye-as-laureate as a major writer, but that his skill as a poet was generally ranked nearer to Whitehead's than to Warton's. Three years prior to his appointment, the *Critical* expressed 'approbation' for Pye's *Poems on Various Subjects*, and stated its judgement 'that he possesses an eminent share of classical taste, that his diction is correct and elegant, and his numbers harmonious. His invention is not equal to his judgment; whatever he adopts he embellishes, and almost makes his own, by the propriety of its application, and felicity of his expression.'[125] The *Monthly* gave a similar review.[126] In the years immediately before and after his appointment, though, his work translating, commenting on and applying the principles of Aristotle's *Poetics* gained him extended attention and praise in both reviews, and permitted him an enduring and rarefied form of positive reputation in their pages.[127] Thereafter, most if not all of his publications were reviewed in both the *Monthly* and *Critical*; even when they were criticized, his Aristotelian work was not forgotten. Moreover, as with Warton, there was at least a superficial recognition of the connection between his position as laureate and his work as a literary historian.[128]

While he was laureate, Pye's plays, novels and non-dramatic poems were sometimes criticized, and sometimes given the sort of firm but not extravagant praise bestowed on his *Poems on Various Subjects*.[129] Sometimes the reviews would indicate sentiments akin to those found in positive newspaper discussion of his odes, blending praise of his poetic talents with praise of his principles, and thus portraying him as a suitable national bard. For example, the *Monthly* referred to his long 1798 poem, *Naucratica*, as 'a performance of such superior merit', and celebrated it as a work of both British poetry and British pride:[130]

> The subject of this poem, of which the design and the execution are both highly creditable to the acknowledged abilities of Mr. Pye, is equally the

[125] *CR* 63, March 1787, pp. 185–6.

[126] *MR* 76, June 1787, pp. 504–5.

[127] *MR* 80, Feb. 1789, p. 148; 81, Nov. 1789, pp. 420–6; 81, Dec. 1789, pp. 515–22; 18 [of the *MR*'s resetting of volume numbers], Oct. 1795, pp. 121–33; *CR* 68, Nov. 1789, pp. 358–66; 68, Dec. 1789, pp. 501–16; 7 [of the *CR*'s resetting of volume numbers], Jan. 1793, pp. 1–12; 10, Feb. 1794, pp. 140–9; 12, Sept. 1794, pp. 54–66

[128] *CR* 10, Feb. 1794, p. 140; *CR* 12, Sept. 1794, p. 65.

[129] For criticism, see eg *MR* 27, Nov. 1798, p. 347; *CR* 17, July 1796, pp. 304–6; 23, July 1798, pp. 294–7; 34, April 1802, pp. 361–70. For praise, see *MR* 2, June 1790, p. 196; 29, Aug. 1799, pp. 468–9; *CR* 69, May 1790, pp. 496–9.

[130] *MR* 26, May 1798, pp. 63–8 (p. 64 for quotation).

rise and progress of the art of navigation, and of naval dominion ... We cannot conclude without expressing our hearty approbation of the author's sentiments on the importance to this country of a powerful navy: they have great merit not only as poetry, but as sound patriotism.[131]

This strain reached its highest pitch in the *Monthly*'s review of the long, semi-official *Carmen Seculare*: 'It is flattering to think that, varied as the picture [of the century] has been, the eighteenth century has afforded so much real matter for eulogy; and that the *Carmen Seculare* of the year 1800 by the Poet Laureat surpasses that of 1700 by Prior, as much in the grandeur of events recorded, as in the beauty and majesty of its versification.'[132] It is again clear that, no matter what criticism Pye may have received in some quarters, it was not unusual among contemporaries to respect him as a poet and laureate. 'The performance before us is truly poetical: while it displays both judgment and taste, it abounds with grand and suitable imagery; and the verse flows with graceful dignity. The picture of the century is pourtrayed with the skill of a master. The figures are well grouped, and, to produce effect, they are aided by a richness of colouring.'[133] Here, in the pages of the *Monthly*, laureate Pye was 'a master': as a poet, as a patriot and as an indistinguishable blend of the two.

Conclusion

The laureateship, it is evident, was of much greater prominence, much greater respectability and much greater diversity of reception than scholars have previously realized. There was certainly a powerful strain of mockery against the office, included in which were genuine appeals for its abolition; yet most of the criticism was against the manner in which the office was currently being occupied and the way in which the biannual odes were being written, or constituted that sort of gentle mockery that continues to gather about the British royal family without involving any serious opposition to it. The office attracted comments of all sorts, positive and negative, because it was an important institution in British public life.

In terms of this book's wider themes, the evidence is resounding. The periodical reception of the laureates shows that the court remained key to understandings of cultural production and consumption. Conceptually, it was nestled not just at the centre of the town, but at the centre of the nation. It was a space to which the public would gather, in order to stand

[131] *MR* 26, May 1798, pp. 63 and 68.
[132] *MR* 31, March 1800, p. 304.
[133] *MR* 31, March 1800, p. 304.

as the audience to such cultural products as the odes; it was a space which writers and artists would enter to receive the patronage that their merit had warranted. There certainly were people who saw the court as existing separately from the currents of national identity, public opinion and literature that were continually gaining ground in terms of their cultural valence and economic agency, and there certainly were people whose oppositional political position made them as keen to stress that separation as possible. But for much of the reading public, the court was a public, national space of critical importance in the production and consumption of culture. The office of poet laureate was perhaps the prime operative of this cultural space.

5. 'But odes of S—— almost choakt the way': Laureate writings of the long eighteenth century

The most prominent aspect of the eighteenth-century laureateship was the biannual odes. This had not been the case during Dryden's tenure; he had not written any, and only in a loose sense had he written any *ex cathedra* poetry at all. His immediate successors, Shadwell and Tate, had written some of these odes, without yet being considered solely or even usually responsible for them. But from the start of Rowe's tenure to the end of Pye's, the odes constituted the laureate's exclusive and comprehensive duty. Year after year, the laureate provided texts that, set to music by the master of the king's music, would be performed at court as part of the festivities of New Year's Day and the royal birthday. As a matter of course (increasingly so as the century wore on), they would also be printed for public consumption in their textual form. The odes only came to an end with George III's final incapacity and the heel-dragging of Robert Southey, who disliked the idea of writing odes to order.

In this chapter, the odes themselves will be examined. There are a great number of them: two a year for almost a century, preceded by the initial, patchy spate produced between 1689 and 1715. On a few occasions across the eighteenth century, a New Year or a birthday ode was not produced, due to some inobservance of the customary festivities; and the odes were not always published prior to 1730, meaning that there are gaps in, particularly, the surviving outputs of Tate and Eusden. But the body of surviving pre-1730 material is nonetheless large, while the post-1730 material provides an essentially unbroken run of between seventy and eighty odes.

In studying this mass of material, certain decisions of focus must therefore be made. The first is a simple one: all odes written by non-laureates have been left out. This means not only those courtly odes written before the laureates were given exclusive responsibility for the task, but also the more anomalous, voluntary odes that are found published in periodicals for New Year's Day and the royal birthdays throughout the long eighteenth century, sometimes published alongside the laureates' own official productions, and none of them ever set to music. These voluntary efforts make up a noteworthy body of material in their own right and testify to the popularity of the form, but any discussion of them would provide more of a distraction than a foil. The focus of this chapter will be entirely on the biannual courtly odes written by the laureates.

The next issue is what sort of focus to apply. In part, this chapter will have the simple intention of describing the form, content and developments of the odes. This is in keeping with a recent trend in eighteenth-century literary scholarship to analyse the form, genre and context of literary productions.[1] On this basis, more far-reaching arguments will be offered. The laureate odes have never attracted much attention from historians or literary scholars; they have generally been dismissed as poor, repetitive productions.[2] Historians of the court, individual monarchs, politics, national identity, war, culture, class, the public, or any other subject that the odes touch upon, have seldom investigated this body of material for what it might have to say; and literary scholars have likewise tended to pass over the laureate odes.

On the rare occasions that a laureate ode is made use of, it is generally lumped together with writings by other poets as a brief example of typical tendencies in loyalist or conservative verses. Kevin Sharpe and James A. Winn referred to works by Shadwell and Tate several times as part of their broader discussions of how poets celebrated later Stuart regimes; Simon Bainbridge glanced dismissively at Pye's work while giving an overview of patriotic rhetoric in 1790s poetry; and Marilyn Morris quoted one of Pye's odes as an example of a poetic celebration of Prince George's marriage to Caroline.[3] Griffin went further, arguing the laureate odes to 'constitute [a] form of patriotic verse', some of which 'had considerable reputations

---

[1] J. Lynch, 'Introduction', in *The Oxford Handbook of British Poetry, 1660–1800,* ed. Lynch (Oxford, 2016), pp. xix–xxi: see especially 'Part IV. Poetic form' and 'Part V. Poetic genres'.

[2] McGuinness, who has carried out the only study of the odes, has done so with a primarily musical interest, analysing their development as a genre of musical performance; her short chapter on 'The texts' is scathing and dismissive of them as poetry, and claims them to be tedious to the point of indistinguishability. R. McGuinness, *English Court Odes: 1660–1820* (Oxford, 1971), pp. 62–76. However, H. Smith has recently written a chapter on a 1692 non-laureate birthday ode and its context in the birthday and New Year's odes produced for William and Mary, focusing on the political and moral reformist content of the odes: H. Smith, 'Court culture and Godly monarchy: Henry Purcell and Sir Charles Sedley's 1692 birthday ode for Mary II', in *Politics, Religion and Ideas in Seventeenth- and Eighteenth-Century Britain: Essays in Honour of Mark Goldie,* ed. J. Champion, J. Coffey, T. Harris and J. Marshall (Woodbridge, 2019), pp. 219–37.

[3] S. Bainbridge, *British Poetry and the Revolutionary and Napoleonic Wars: Visions of Conflict* (Oxford, 2003), pp. 48–50 (p. 50 for quotation); M. Morris, *The British Monarchy and the French Revolution* (London, 1998), p. 167; K. Sharpe, *Rebranding Rule: Images of Restoration and Revolution Monarchy, 1660–1714* (New Haven, Conn., 2013), pp. 373-82; J. A. Winn, *Queen Anne: Patroness of Arts* (Oxford, 2014), pp. 278–9, 323, 369, 418–22, 462–3, 545–6.

in their own day and are worth a critical look'. But he only gave a brief discussion of Whitehead's odes, noted Mason's dislike of the laureate ode format and stated that the wider genre of 'the panegyrical ode had by 1750 become a genre to be used cautiously. Of the major poets, only Gray and Smart attempt it.'⁴ In all these works, the poets' laureate status is usually mentioned in passing, but not explored or given significance. This chapter will explore and give significance. While it will not be able to demonstrate the entire potentials of the laureate corpus in all the respects just mentioned, it will hopefully do something to suggest them. In particular, it will aim to show the potentials of taking an interdisciplinary approach, and of using material that lends itself particularly well to such an approach, in answering the questions that interest both historians and literary scholars.

Primarily, this chapter will discuss the odes in terms of their situation between court and public. It will ask how the laureates conceptualized the relationship between prince and people in their odes, and how they mediated that relationship to their readers. Its major argument is that the laureate odes underwent certain fundamental changes over the course of their existence, the overall tenor of which was guided by a reconceptualization of that relationship between prince and people. Initially, the main rationale of the odes had been their performance within the physical confines of the court, for an audience of royals and courtiers. The published texts of the odes enacted this performance; they gave readers a vicarious entrance into the court to witness the ceremony, to appreciate their superhuman prince and to endorse the laureate's praises. The context of the physical court was what determined the nature of the odes' production and consumption, and their meaning and value. By the time of Pye's death, the odes were doing something very different. They were eliding the court with the nation, and were portraying the king as a man among his subjects: human, sympathetic and patriotic. Where the earlier odes had sought to show the dominance of the court and its physical, ceremonial practices over the nation, the later odes sought to show that the court had a public face, a patriotic character and an active appreciation of British literature.

These developments are significant for the monograph's overall arguments. They prove that the laureate was sensitive to the concept of the public, to national identity and to standards of literature, and successfully stayed abreast of these phenomena. Coupled with the evidence from Chapter Four, this further proves the importance of the laureateship and the court in the conceptual geography of culture. The court's role as a forum for

---

⁴ D. Griffin, *Patriotism and Poetry in Eighteenth-Century Britain* (Cambridge, 2005), pp. 34, 48–50 (p. 50 for quotation).

culture, and thus as a determinant of cultural meaning, did not lapse, but was adapted. Conceptually, it evolved from a specific, physical location, to a metaphorical location that the public could enter by way of reading the published odes, to a still more abstract space that was coexistent with the nation as a whole.

First, this chapter will survey the relevant scholarship. Then, at greater length, it will explore the history of the odes, proving that they represent deliberate attempts to portray the prince, the people and the relationship between them. It will explain the various factors that rendered the laureate ode a format that was highly sensitive to the relationship between prince and people, and increasingly responsible for mediating that relationship to the reading public. At the same time, it will show that the odes were a constantly evolving format, the demands upon which became more numerous and complex over time; and it will explain what this means for a reading of the odes. Once this has been done, most of the chapter will examine the odes themselves, adopting a somewhat chronological, somewhat thematic structure. The odes will be divided into two main phases, pre-1757 and post-1757, with special attention given in sequence to Cibber, Whitehead, Warton and Pye, each of whose odes represent important developments.

The progress of poetry

As well as the scholarship discussed in the Introduction, this chapter will engage with two strands of poetry scholarship. The first is that which seeks to understand the changes in poetic taste and trends over the course of the long eighteenth century, and which plots certain changes in the sorts of poetry that were being written and valued, from panegyric and harsh satire in the late seventeenth century, through the didacticism, refined wit and polished couplets of the early eighteenth century, to the metrical experiments, lyricism and increased emphasis on passions and sentiment after the mid century, and at last to Romanticism. The mid-century fulcrum will prove especially significant here. It has been variously characterized by such terms and ideas as 'preromantic', 'Gothic', 'graveyard poetry', 'passions', 'sentimental', 'genius', 'originality', 'inspiration', 'retreat', 'introspection' and 'a reaction against Pope'. Whatever the case, it is seen as a time of new practices and ideas, justified by reference to notions of an original spirit of poetry, uncorrupted by modern refinements.[5]

[5] Eg many of the chapters in the recent *Oxford Handbook of British Poetry, 1660–1800*, ed. Lynch, reinforce this narrative, which is the same as appears in older general works. See especially M. Brown, 'The poet as genius', pp. 210–27, at pp. 216–27; L. Clymer, 'The poet as teacher', pp. 179–94, at pp. 188–93; S. Jung, 'Ode', pp. 510–27; J. Keith, 'Lyric', pp. 579–95, at

In 1984, Roger Lonsdale presented a challenge to this narrative with his anthology, *The New Oxford Book of Eighteenth-Century Verse*. He argued that scholars still know very little about the overall terrain of eighteenth-century poetry, and that the standard narrative belies the true diversity of poetic output at the time. However, he also admitted that the poetry that challenges modern notions of eighteenth-century verse tended to fall into obscurity soon after publication, and that the modern narrative is founded on the popular anthologies and compilations of the middle to late eighteenth century: the narrative was created by eighteenth-century poets, critics, publishers and readers themselves.[6] Partly for this reason, while Lonsdale's anthology has influenced subsequent attitudes to this period, the broad outlines of eighteenth-century poetics have remained mostly unchanged, and scholars' energies have been focused rather on filling out those outlines with new materials and new perspectives. David Fairer, writing one of the more recent and insightful works on eighteenth-century poetry as a whole, observed that Lonsdale ushered in exciting new approaches to the subject which circumvented the familiar stereotypes, and Fairer situated his own book in relation to such scholarship. He duly offered highly original arguments and observations for, in particular, the early eighteenth century.[7] Yet as Fairer approached the middle and later eighteenth century, he too explored the same sorts of poetic trends that formed the backbone of earlier works: experiments in form, new ideas about the essence of poetry and a reconnection with the poetry of the past.[8]

This chapter will follow Lonsdale's and Fairer's lead in using new angles and long-neglected poetry to better understand the nature of the major trends and developments in eighteenth-century poetry. The odes, it will demonstrate, were abreast of the developments that concerned eighteenth-century readers and writers, and can therefore better illuminate those developments. Whereas the nature of the mid-century developments (in particular) has generally been sought in new forms of writing, imbued with ideas of independence

---

pp. 580–2; A. Marshall, 'Satire', pp. 495–509; D. H. Radcliffe, 'Pastoral', pp. 441–56, at p. 451; D. F. Venturo, 'Poems on poetry', pp. 269–85, at pp. 281–2. See also M. Brown, *Preromanticism* (Stanford, Calif., 1991); J. Butt, *The Mid-Eighteenth Century*, ed. G. Carnall (Oxford, 1979), pp. 1–4, 57–8, 64–78, 82–6, 94; B. Hammond, *Professional Imaginative Writing in England, 1670–1740: 'Hackney for Bread'* (Oxford, 1997), p. 83; J. Sitter, 'Political, satirical, didactic and lyric poetry (II): After Pope', in *The Cambridge History of English Literature, 1660–1780*, ed. J. Richetti (Cambridge, 2005), pp. 287–315.

[6] R. Lonsdale, 'Introduction', in *The New Oxford Book of Eighteenth Century Verse*, ed. R. Lonsdale (Oxford, 1984), pp. xxxiii–xxxix.

[7] D. Fairer, *English Poetry of the Eighteenth Century 1700–1789* (London, 2003), pp. ix, 2–4, 12–16, 103–11.

[8] Fairer, *English Poetry*, pp. 144–69.

and patriotism, this chapter will reveal that newly articulated and newly popular ideals of poetry were in fact fully evidenced in the official, courtly framework of the biannual odes. An understanding of mid-century poetic developments is therefore not complete without due consideration of how it manifested there.[9] The idea that mid-century poetry (including the non-laureate ode form itself) turned away from public declamation towards personal feeling, for example, will be proven a partial truth at best.[10] The post-1757 laureate odes embody a new aesthetic of poetry that harked back to both the 'Gothic' English past and ancient Greece, and an ideology that sought to use heavily pictorial means to activate a sympathetic, emotive response in readers. The appointment of Warton as laureate, and the great acclaim that his odes received, was no accident; 1785–90 was arguably the capstone of this new aesthetic. The odes thus suggest a reconsideration of the motives behind the mid-century developments and, in particular, question the idea of these developments as being bound up with reclusiveness, introspection, disengagement from society and the unbridled spontaneity of genius.[11] If the middle to late eighteenth century was preromantic, then it was as much the Romantic apostasy of Southey, Coleridge and Wordsworth as anything else.

The second relevant strand of poetry scholarship is that on conservative and loyalist poetics. Recent years have seen scholars become increasingly interested in those tendencies of thought and action that support that status quo, and this interest has borne fruit in several significant works on eighteenth-century literature. At one end of the period is Abigail Williams's study of Whig poetics in the reigns of William and Anne; at the other is Matthew Grenby's monograph on anti-Jacobin novels and Kevin Gilmartin's on literary conservatism during the Romantic period.[12] All

---

[9] Butt's discussion of mid-century odes does include a mention of Whitehead's laureate odes, as exemplars of the tendency towards a more rigorous form of Pindaric ode, but only in passing; the emphasis is on Collins and, especially, Gray. Fairer, Sandro Jung and Marcus Walsh do not mention Whitehead in their discussion of mid-century odes. Butt, *Mid-Eighteenth Century*, pp. 70–8; D. Fairer, 'Modulation and expression in the lyric ode, 1660–1750', in *The Lyric Poem: Formations and Transformations*, ed. M. Thain (Cambridge, 2013), pp. 92–111; Jung, 'Ode', pp. 519–26; M. Walsh, 'Eighteenth-century high lyric: William Collins and Christopher Smart', in *Lyric Poem*, ed. Thain, pp. 112–34.

[10] This claim is made in eg Sitter, 'After Pope', pp. 309–15. However, for a partial refutation of it, see A. Rounce, 'Akenside's clamours for liberty', in *Cultures of Whiggism: New Essays on English Literature and Culture in the Long Eighteenth Century*, ed. D. Womersley (Newark, Del., 2005), pp. 216–33.

[11] In this respect, this chapter follows on from Griffin, *Patriotism*, pp. 3–5.

[12] K. Gilmartin, *Writing Against Revolution: Literary Conservatism in Britain, 1790–1832* (Cambridge, 2007); M. O. Grenby, *The Anti-Jacobin Novel: British Conservatism and the French Revolution* (Cambridge, 2001); A. Williams, *Poetry and the Creation of a Whig Literary*

three books reconstitute the powerful currents of conservative literature, documenting its forms and tropes and emphasizing the practical networks, motives and energies by which such literature was produced. This chapter will follow on from such work, but with a slight difference; it will seek to integrate such writing more firmly into the wider narratives of poetical change described above. Scholars of conservative literature often study it as a body of work somewhat apart from the more canonical and avant-garde work that had occupied scholarly attention before them.[13] By contrast, this chapter will argue that conservative writing should not be understood as existing separately or antagonistically from the wider currents of literary production of the time. For example, there was far more overlap between the laureate odes and the works of Thomas Gray than there was between the laureate odes and the *Anti-Jacobin Review*. In the end, perhaps even the idea of conservative literature is misleading.

The onus on the odes

There were several main factors that determined the character of the odes as negotiations of the relationship between prince and people.[14] The first is that they were a form of panegyric verse. The panegyric genre was not simply concerned with giving exorbitant praise; in fact, it centred on the idea of a public engagement between prince and people, in which the poet mediated between the two so as to effect national harmony. The best study of the panegyric tradition and its manifestation in the later Stuart period comes in James D. Garrison's monograph, *Dryden and the Tradition of Panegyric*.[15] Garrison showed that the idea of panegyric originated in the ancient world, as a public address given to a prince on a festive occasion, in which, though the prince would be praised and the loyalty of his people promised, the praise and promise would also remind him of how he was expected to rule. He would

---

Culture, 1681–1714 (Oxford, 2005).

[13] Griffin does situate the eighteenth-century *'discourse of patriotism'* firmly in the mainstream and canon of eighteenth-century poetry; however, this discourse was not conservative in the sense of supporting a social or political status quo. See Griffin, *Patriotism*, especially pp. 2–5, 7–8.

[14] The term 'prince' will be preferred in this chapter, despite the heavier use of 'king' and 'monarch' in previous chapters, because it is more appropriate in terms of the traditions of panegyric. See Garrison, cited below.

[15] J. D. Garrison, *Dryden and the Tradition of Panegyric* (Berkeley, Calif., 1975), pp. 3–15, 20–32, 38–108. Several essays in *Stuart Succession Literature: Moments and Transformations*, ed. P. Kewes and A. McRae (Oxford, 2018) cite and engage with Garrison: P. Kewes and A. McRae, 'Introduction', pp. 1–16, at pp. 11–12; R. A. McCabe, 'Panegyric and its discontents: The first Stuart succession', pp. 19–36; A. McRae, 'Welcoming the king', pp. 187–204.

be shown a princely ideal to live up to; if he failed, he would lose his people's obedience. At the same time, the panegyrist would be setting out that princely ideal to the rest of the people in attendance, reminding them of their duty to obey that ideal prince. The panegyric would thus constitute an idealized contract between prince and people. Over time, individual panegyrics became less likely to be genuinely performed on a festive occasion, and the genre, or discourse, became increasingly text-based. But it nonetheless retained the idea of being a public address, performed to the prince on behalf of his subjects.

By the late seventeenth century, the form had become heavily associated with verse (rather than with non-metrical oratory or prose), and it was becoming more diluted as a genre. It was no longer reserved for princes, or even for statesmen and military men; the sense of its being a public address was less frequently visible; and its standard tropes were falling out of fashion. The strict identity of panegyric as a form of discourse was being lost, and the idea of 'panegyric' as merely the hyperbole of 'praise' was gaining ground. Nonetheless, the traditional panegyric discourse was still visible in at least some of the late seventeenth-century poems that were called or intended as 'panegyrics'. The laureate odes, being genuine public addresses to the prince, were on this account (at least) more firmly linked to the traditional discourse than were other contemporary panegyrics. The laureate odes were thus rooted in a tradition of articulating an ideal relationship between prince and people.

Perhaps of greater importance than this tradition, though, was the nature of the laureates' position. As established in earlier chapters, the prestige and material substance of the laureates' position was based on their success both in the system of court-centred patronage and in that of commercial publication. The most obvious signal of this was the title pages to their commercially produced, non-laureate works, where their status as poet laureate would feature heavily;[16] their stature as published writers was in no small part determined by their official position as king or queen's poet. The laureates therefore had a clear incentive to make much of their prince, and of the prince's relationship with the people. Thus they could appeal to their paymasters both within and outside of the institutional court; thus they could emphasize the importance of their own position as a midpoint between prince and people.

The reception of the odes further demonstrates the onus on the laureates to try to mediate between prince and people in their official productions. Chapter Four has already shown that the reading public of the late

---

[16] Eg Eusden's *Three Poems* (1722); Whitehead's *Plays and Poems: Vol. II* (1774); Warton's posthumous *The Poems on Various Subjects* (1791).

eighteenth century did have a strong, enduring interest in the odes; but there is also evidence for something similar at the start of the century, before the publication of the odes had become routine. One newspaper printed Tate's 1715 birthday ode with the following introductory note from a correspondent: 'Since Mr. Tate, the Poet Laureat, is so modest as not to publish the Song which he compos'd on Occasion of His Majesty's Birth-Day, 'tis hop'd you will oblige the Publick, by inserting it in your Paper.'[17] Eusden's 1729 birthday ode was printed in one newspaper as part of a similar letter: 'Please to insert in your Paper the following ODE ... and you'll oblige, with many others of your Readers, Sir, *Your very humble Servant,* A. B.'[18] Such sentiments were less common under George I than under George III, but there were clearly at least some readers who felt the publication of a laureate ode to be 'oblig[ing to] the Publick'. Indeed, it was not until Whitehead's tenure that copies of the odes were specifically handed out to the newspapers; prior to that, their increasingly widespread publication in periodicals came by the agency of non-official sources and the periodical publishers themselves.[19] There were always readers in wait for the laureate odes. In the early eighteenth century, demand was greater than supply.

The reading public, then, had an interest in the odes even when they had not been specifically designed for publication. They must therefore have been interested in them *as* odes addressed to the prince and sung before him at court. Chapter Four has noted that Warton's odes were criticized in some quarters for not being sufficiently warm in their praises of George III. Moreover, especially in George III's reign, the odes were often printed in the newspapers as part of long descriptions of the courtly festivities that had taken place on the day in question. Clearly, there was a strong desire among readers to stand witness to the praises being sung to the prince. Part of the odes' appeal was that they were panegyrics to the prince. The laureates would thus have been conscious that they were writing for an audience that, at least in part, wanted the odes to articulate some particular ideal of the prince, and wanted the odes to bring the prince and people closer together, allowing the people to partake of the courtly festivities. The laureates were *selling* the idea of 'a panegyric to the prince' as much as they were effecting it.

For various reasons, then, there was an onus on the laureate odes to sing the prince's praises, pay attention to the reading public and engage with the relationship between prince and people. The laureate was rendered an interface between the two by his audiences and his genre.

[17] *The Flying Post*, 9–11 June 1715.

[18] *Universal Spectator and Weekly Journal,* 1 Nov. 1729.

[19] *Warton Correspondence*, lt. 486, at pp. 535–6.

However, the laureate was not negotiating between two static interest groups. Rather, he was dealing with a constantly evolving, expanding set of expectations, imposed upon him by an increasing diversity of interest groups. Because the odes became so prominent, they elicited a series of new demands for which the form was not originally designed, and yet which it was now the laureate's duty, in many people's eyes, to cater for. They succeeded to such an extent in their original context that they transcended that context, and their position in the conceptual geography of culture changed; hence the criteria of value by which they were judged changed also. This is partly why the odes came to be mocked and criticized in certain quarters: their original form and purpose were not immediately suited to the new criteria.

In a sense, this transformation was evident from the very start of the odes' history. The provenance of these biannual courtly entertainments is obscure, but they may have originated as part of the masques that were produced at Charles I's court for special occasions. At least one of the more popular songs from a masque by Ben Jonson is known to have become a festive courtly entertainment in its own right, being performed on one of the occasions that was later dedicated to the performance of the odes; and Jonson also wrote a series of poems on royal occasions between 1629 and 1637, two of which seem to have been performed at court.[20] Following the Restoration, the first two decades of Charles II's reign have left behind intermittent evidence of the performance of songs at court on the royal birthday and on New Year's Day (none of which had any involvement from either Davenant or Dryden), and from 1681 onwards the practice apparently became standard. Musically, these post-Restoration songs were similar to sacred music, and especially to anthems, but were generally intended as one-off performances.[21] The poets who wrote the words for them were a varying bunch, with no one poet writing many of them until Tate. There is only one, uncertain piece of evidence that any poet before Rowe was specifically commissioned.[22]

In the later Stuart period, then, the laureate odes were neither related to the laureateship, nor very often called 'odes'. They were more often entitled 'songs'. Though the term 'song' was linked to the term 'ode' in contemporary parlance, it was only in the sense that 'ode' was sometimes used to refer to any kind of lyrical, loose or non-couplet form of verse.[23] In

---

[20] McGuinness, *Court Odes*, pp. 1–11.

[21] McGuinness, *Court Odes*, pp. 9–11, 78–9.

[22] McGuinness, *Court Odes*, pp. 13–28, 49.

[23] Jung, 'Ode', p. 514.

the mid eighteenth century, Samuel Johnson's definition was to indicate this slippage. An ode was, 'A poem written to be sung to musick; a lyrick poem.'[24] Although the name 'ode' was starting to be used for the laureate odes by Shadwell's time, it was still not uncommon for them to be entitled 'songs' even as late as Eusden's tenure. Only with Cibber's appointment did the laureate productions become fixedly identified as 'odes'. However, it was also the case that, from at least Shadwell's time onwards, the texts to these productions were heavily associated with (or influenced by) the fashion for pseudo-Pindaric odes that had been brought about by Abraham Cowley's *Pindarique Odes* (1656) and by Boileau's translation of Longinus (1674). These 'Pindarics' were characterized by an exultant, effusive tone, digressive and suddenly shifting content, praise of some great figure and an irregularity of metre that went far beyond anything found in Pindar's work. The eighteenth century proper was to see increasing efforts to bring the ode form more into line with Pindar's actual practice (although there were other viable ode forms too, such as those of Anacreon and Horace); but the origins of the laureate odes were in the wild, 'sublime' pseudo-Pindaric tradition of the late seventeenth century, as well as in the older tradition of panegyric verse discussed above.[25]

Thus the later Stuart courtly 'odes' started out in a motley manner. Under Tate, the laureate odes settled down into the form that was to endure to the time of Cibber's death, and that was especially consistent in its themes, tone and language between 1692 and 1730. This was the time when the odes were most fixedly designed as one-off courtly entertainments, performed on the two major festive occasions of the year to gratify the prince and their courtiers and to emphasize the prince's glory. Sometimes they were published, sometimes not. Most of Shadwell's laureate odes appeared as independent, commercial publications. Tate, Rowe and Eusden saw their own odes intermittently put into print, either as individual publications or in periodicals, or both. Cibber's odes were almost all published in periodicals. Some of Tate's odes were published in the *Gentleman's Journal* by Peter Motteux, who had a close working relationship with Tate. This suggests that, in Tate's case at least, publication came with the laureate's own approval or instigation.[26]

[24] S. Johnson, *A Dictionary of the English Language* (2 vols, 1755–6), ii. 'Ode'.

[25] Butt, *Mid-Eighteenth Century*, pp. 64–78; Fairer, 'Lyric ode 1660–1750', pp. 94–6; Jung, 'Ode'; Sitter, 'After Pope', pp. 309–15; Walsh, 'Eighteenth-century high lyric', pp. 112–14, 121; H. D. Weinbrot, *Britannia's Issue: The Rise of British Literature from Dryden to Ossian* (Cambridge, 1994), pp. 334–58.

[26] Eg *Gentleman's Journal: Or the Monthly Miscellany*, Dec. 1692. For Motteux, the *Gentleman's Journal* and Tate's prominence in its pages, see M. J. Ezell, 'The "Gentleman's

Yet it was the fact of publication that generated new criteria of judgement for the odes. Although they were published as documents of one-off musical performance – their success or failure determined by reference to this function – their appearance as text-based poetry rendered them liable to the same sorts of reading experience and judgement to which other text-based poetry was subject. The laureates were aware of this, and sometimes seemed anxious to ensure that their odes were understood in the correct way. In a prefatory note 'To the Reader', opening a publication containing two of his odes, Tate explained:

> The Glorious Occasion upon which these Odes were written, *viz.* His Majesty's *Birth-Day*, and the *New Year*, accompanied with the Consummation of an Honourable *Peace*, requir'd the utmost Liberties of Poetry; but I was Confin'd (for the Present) to such Measures and Compass as the Musical Performance would admit; upon which Consideration the Reader's favourable allowance is requested.[27]

Tate was evidently impressed with the potential for writing royal panegyric poetry in response to designated occasions, and he imagined readers casting a critical eye over what he had produced, judging him on how well he had communicated such promising subject matter into textual, non-musical verse. But he also felt that the demands of musical performance restricted the 'Liberties of Poetry', and he made sure to establish the proper expectations among his readers. Although these odes were being published purely as texts, they had to be read as documents of performance. The title to this particular publication ended on the phrase '*Both Set to Musick, and Perform'd At Kensington*'. It was commonplace for all ode publications pre-1757 to include notes and instructions on the manner of performance, setting out such things as which voices sang which verses, or when a passage was a 'Recitativo' or an 'Air'.

Several decades after Tate's address 'To the Reader', Cibber was to write something similar. In his prose publication, *The Egotist*, he defended his odes from some of the attacks on them, making clear that he did not hold his own odes in contempt (as has sometimes been claimed by others), but that he believed that they needed to be understood in relation to their musical performance: 'without the Musick to them, they had but an

Journal" and the commercialization of restoration coterie literary practices', *Modern Philology*, lxxxix (1992), 323–40, at pp. 332, 339; Smith, 'Sedley's 1692 birthday ode', pp. 227–37.

[27] N. Tate, *The Anniversary Ode For the Fourth of December, 1697. His Majesty's Birth-Day. Another for New-Year's-Day, 1697/8* (1698), sig. A2r.

Adjective Merit'.[28] Cibber did not push this argument any further; just as he took a blasé attitude to the reception of his plays, he did not want to seem too concerned about his odes. Yet Cibber put great effort and consideration into composing those odes, working on them for months and showing them to friends for feedback, as Johnson and certain newspaper reports later attested.[29] This indicates another facet to the picture. Tate and Cibber wanted to ensure that their odes were read as the texts to courtly, musical performances, and they were keen to fend off the wrong expectations. But this emphasis on performance was also, potentially, something that *recommended* the textual poetry to readers. Fairer has emphasized the efforts of (non-laureate) ode writers in the period 1660–1750 to incorporate musical, performative elements into their odes, so as to create 'the idea of lyric eloquence without thought of any musical setting' and trigger an 'audience response'.[30] The texts of the laureate odes were doing something similar, but starting from a very different proposition: that the odes had been given their one, definitive performance already, at court in the prince's presence. To bring attention to their performative aspect was not only to defend them from judgements based on the wrong criteria; it was also to exalt them *as* texts by reference to the context of their creation and performance. The important thing was that everyone should remain aware of what the odes were, and what they were not.

Everyone did not remain aware. With print publication continuing to expand in extent and variety, and with the court's position in the cultural landscape evolving, the publication of the laureate odes became more regular. The reading public was understandably interested in the productions of that poet who held the only official claim to be the monarch of Parnassus, and in the chance to pry vicariously into the courtly festivities. When a high-profile figure such as Cibber took the baton, the demand for the odes became irresistible; from 1730 onwards, it was established as an expectation that the odes should be published. But the attendant expectation also became irresistible: these odes, being engaged with as texts, and as the poetic productions of Parnassus' king, should function not merely as texts for one-off musical performances, but as poems, and as poems worthy to have been published by Parnassian royalty. This was the decisive shift mentioned above: the point at which the odes became so successful that they found themselves attracting that expectation to be something other than what

[28] C. Cibber, *The Egotist: Or, Colley upon Cibber* (1743), p. 50.

[29] J. Boswell, *Boswell's London Journal: 1762–1763*, ed. F. A. Pottle (London, 1950), p. 282; *Public Advertiser*, 13 July 1764; *The World*, 24 March 1790.

[30] Fairer, 'Lyric ode 1660–1750', pp. 92–4.

they were, and thence the accompanying criticism. The odes transcended their context of origin, not necessarily due to the poetic ambitions of the laureate, but because they were dragged out of that context by a thousand eager pairs of hands.

Over the course of the early eighteenth century, the laureate's problems in this respect continued to intensify. Partly, this was because notions of literary quality – against which the odes were increasingly being judged – became more complicated, and developed a strain of suspicion for all forms of occasional verse. Pope led the Scriblerian effort to define good poetry both positively and negatively; Shadwell, Tate, Eusden and Cibber all fell foul of his pen.[31] After Pope's death, other writers started advancing standards of judgement that were conceived in opposition to Pope's style, seeking a greater play of fancy, imagination and passion than was permitted in the narrow compass of Pope's couplets, and finding it in various works of older English poetry. These developments were especially important for the ode form. Having been intensely discussed since the start of the century, it now became adopted by poets like Joseph Warton and William Collins as the ideal vehicle for fancy, imagination and passion.[32]

At the same time, there was developing a comparatively understudied trend in favour of a newly rigorous engagement with the forms and techniques of ancient Greek poetry, distinct from the neoclassicism of the early eighteenth century.[33] Whitehead and Mason were two of the leading figures of this trend, especially in their plays;[34] but its most famous manifestation was Gray's two odes of 1757. Gray's odes united a formal Pindaric rigour – the odes divided into metrically identical sections, each with a strophe, antistrophe and epode – with the sorts of themes and concerns shared by Joseph Warton, Collins and certain other young poets of the time.[35] The ode form was being used and scrutinized in different ways from those that had prevailed in the seventeenth century, when the laureate odes had come into being. Meanwhile, notions of the British poetic canon were becoming more precise and more sophisticated. Whitehead socialized with at least some of

---

[31] B. A. Goldgar, *Walpole and the Wits: The Relation of Politics to Literature, 1722–1742* (Lincoln, Neb., 1976), pp. 89–98; Hammond, *Hackney*, pp. 2–6, 195–202.

[32] Brown, 'Genius', pp. 216–27; Butt, *Mid-Eighteenth Century*, pp. 4–7, 57–8, 64–78; Clymer, 'Teacher', pp. 188–93; Jung, 'Ode', pp. 519–26; Rounce, 'Scholarship', pp. 685–700; Sitter, 'After Pope', pp. 309–15; Weinbrot, *Britannia's Issue*, pp. 372–401.

[33] Fairer, *English Poetry*, pp. ix, 144–65.

[34] Whitehead's *The Roman Father* (1750) and *Creusa* (1754), and Mason's *Elfrida* (1752) and *Caractacus* (1759). For Mason's discussion of these matters, see the 'Letters' prefacing *Elfrida*, pp. i–xix; 'Whitehead Memoirs', pp. 56, 72–7.

[35] Butt, *Mid-Eighteenth Century*, pp. 70–8; Jung, 'Ode', pp. 519–26.

the writers who were most prominently involved in these endeavours, and Thomas Warton was himself one of the most significant of them.[36]

The sorts of expectation against which the laureate odes were to be judged were therefore becoming more numerous, more complex and more demanding. Cibber, fifty-nine years old when appointed and having never published much lyric poetry, somewhat disregarded these new expectations, writing the same, traditional sort of laureate odes throughout his tenure. However, Whitehead brought a different attitude to the office. He wrote in sympathy with the new expectations to which the odes had become subject, sharing the sorts of principles and ambitions that underlay those expectations. Whitehead's appointment therefore marks the second main phase in the history of the odes: he, Warton and Pye would all produce odes that were intended to meet the new expectations that had been created by widespread publication, and which were, in particular, written on the understanding of the ode form as established by the poets and critics of the mid century. They were attempting to write poetry that situated itself consciously between the poetic heritage and posterity, that would impress the reading public and that would espouse an appropriately patriotic spirit.

With Pye, the case was the most complicated, as the demands of the anti-Jacobin struggle encouraged him to position his odes as patriotic, popular songs. But it was also Pye who had written the following, in a preface to his own translation of some of Pindar's odes (1787):

> As the situation of a Poet Laureat is something similar to that of our ancient Lyric Poet, might not our Birth Day Odes be rendered more interesting to the Public, by interweaving some of the popular stories which may be found in our annals, with the usual compliments of the Day? I think something of this kind was attempted by Mr. Whitehead. An idea of this nature in the hands of our present Laureat [Warton], might render those periodical productions not only a classical entertainment for the present time, but a permanent and valuable acquisition to posterity.[37]

Notwithstanding the slight unfairness here against Warton, Pye's argument demonstrated a clear sense that the odes were to be pitched as much (if not more) to 'the Public' as to the prince. He felt that if the odes were written with the classical heritage (Pindar) and British national history ('popular stories' from 'our annals') in mind, then they could become not just 'a classical entertainment' (a significant phrase in itself), but poems for 'posterity'.

---

[36] R. Terry, *Poetry and the Making of the English Literary Past: 1660–1781* (Oxford, 2001), pp. 216–51, 287–323; R. Wellek, *The Rise of English Literary History*, 2nd edn (New York, 1966), pp. 166–201.

[37] These were the lines paraphrased by the *St. James's Chronicle*, as mentioned in ch. 4. H. J. Pye, *Poems on Various Subjects* (2 vols, 1787), i. 195–6.

By the turn of the nineteenth century, there were potent new strains of radical and Romantic thought that, on the whole, did not grant much allowance to the idea of biannual laureate odes. Following Southey's appointment, these strains contributed to the death of the odes. Up to and including Southey's tenure, though, the laureates needed to remain sensitive to a host of evolving issues, or else see their work rendered ridiculous. The form had not been brought about for any purpose other than as a one-off performance at court; even its association with the laurel-crowned poet was a subsequent, accidental development. Nonetheless, over the course of the long eighteenth century, the odes became increasingly required to justify themselves without reference to their one-off performance, and to succeed by way of new criteria. Throughout it all, it remained incumbent upon the odes to negotiate the relationship between prince and people, and to mediate that relationship to the reading public. But the way in which the laureates did so underwent huge changes, which are highly instructive in terms of the position of the laureate and the role of the court in British society.

Tate's copy-text

It is now time to look at the odes themselves. This and the next two sections will survey the first phase of odes (pre-1757), showing how they presented the relationship between prince and people. It will be argued that this presentation revealed a coherent notion of the court's significance in national life, but that this notion was different from that which prevailed after 1757. Fundamentally, the earlier notion was that the court was a distinct, physical place, which directed affairs from above, and to which the eyes of the people should be turned; its ceremonial and cultural life was at the heart of the nation's culture, just as its social and political primacy was unquestioned. When published, the odes allowed the people to come to court, to witness their glorious prince and to articulate their joy in his rule. After 1757, although the odes continued to express the court's importance, they did so according to a different conceptualization.

Some of the main characteristics of the first phase of odes can be seen in the following offering from Tate, which marked New Year's Day 1693. On this occasion it was entitled an 'Ode' rather than a 'Song', and it was headed as being 'Performed Before their Majesties. *Set to* MUSICK *by Dr.* Blow. *The Words by* N. Tate, *Servant to their Majesties.*'

> The Happy, happy Year is Born,
> That wonders shall disclose;
> That Conquest with fix'd Lawrels shall adorn,
> And give our Lab'ring *HERCULES* Repose.

Ye Graces that resort
To *Virtue's Temple* blest *MARIA'S* Court,
With Incense and with Songs as Sweet,
The Long-Expected Season meet,
The Long-expected Season gently Greet.

MARIA (thus devoutly say)
MARIA - ---Oh appear! appear!
Thy Softest Charms Display,
Smile and Bless the Infant Year;
Smile on its Birth in Kindness to our Isle,
For if this Genial Day
You Cheerfully Survey,
Succeeding Years in just Return, on You and Us shall Smile.

Thus, let Departing WINTER Sing,
Approach, Advance, Thou promis'd SPRING;
And if for Action not design'd,
Together soon Together bring
Confederate Troops in *Europe's* Cause combin'd.
A Busier Prospect SUMMER yields,
Floating Navies, harrass'd Fields.
From far the *Gallick* Genius Spying
(Of Unjust War the Just Disgrace.)
Their Broken Squadrons Flying,
And *Britain's Caesar* Lightning in the Chase.

But AUTUMN does Impatient grow
To Crown the Victor's Brow;
To Wait him Home Triumphant from Alarms
To *Albion* and *MARIA'S* Arms.
Then, to conclude the Glorious Scene,
To *Europe's* Joy let *Me* Return,
When *Britain's Senate* shall Convene,
To Thank their Monarch, and no more, no more his Absence mourn.
Their kind Supplies our fainting Hopes restor'd,
Their Inspir'd Counsels shall sure means afford,
To fix the Gen'ral Peace won by our Monarch's Sword.

CHORUS.
While Tyrants their Neighbours and Subjects Oppress,
All Nations the Pious Restorer Caress.
Securely our Hero *prepares for the Field,*

His Valour his Sword, his Virtue his Shield:
He Arms in Compassion for Europe's *Release.*
He Conquers to Save, and he Warr's to give Peace.[38]

The text was typical of the pre-1757 odes in a number of ways. Firstly, the form was a Cowleyan Pindaric, exultant and eulogistic in tone, with verses and lines of varying length, and with an irregular rhyme scheme. But it was also patently designed for musical performance, with the performative elements being emphasized for the reader's benefit (although not so much here as in some other odes). The reiterations of certain words and phrases ('Happy, happy', 'The long-Expected Season', '*MARIA ... MARIA*') were intended to create an air of overflowing joy and harmonious musicality.

As for the content of the ode, the emphasis on the year and on the passing of time were likewise typical, with generic references to seasons and allusions to great contemporary events. It was rare for those allusions to be any more specific than here; in fact, especially after Tate's tenure, it was rare to find references even as specific as these, at least until 1757. Next, it was typical to have the prince celebrated as a superhuman figure ('*HERCULES*', '*our* Hero'), and to be portrayed as something between an abstraction and a real human figure (as seen in William's peculiar ability to embrace both '*Albion*' and '*MARIA*'). Classical references were particularly favoured by Tate and Eusden ('*Britain's Caesar*'), but Cibber, despite being notorious for the frequency with which he dubbed George II 'Caesar', did not much employ them.

Numerous abstract qualities were usually assigned to the prince, varying according to the writer and the prince in question.[39] Here, Tate's keen eye for '*Virtue*' was gratified by both Mary and William. The royal family would often be celebrated in terms of ideal gender and family roles (William's virtue being found on his '*Shield*', Mary's in a '*Temple*' thronged with graces, incense and sweet songs). The accession of the fertile Hanoverians allowed particularly large scope for this theme. While William, Mary and

---

[38] Tate, 1693NY.

[39] The qualities were often the sort that have been identified by recent historians as being of key and repeated importance to the way that the prince in question was celebrated and portrayed more widely, thus revealing the odes' continuities with the mainstream of courtly and loyalist rhetoric. However, due to the stated focus of this chapter, when these qualities are discussed it will be in the context of the history of the laureate odes, and of the laureate's particular aim in representing the relationship between prince and people, rather than in comparison to wider depictions of the prince in question. For those wider depictions, see especially Sharpe, *Rebranding Rule*, pp. 373–82; Morris, *British Monarchy*, passim; H. Smith, *Georgian Monarchy: Politics and Culture, 1714–1760* (Cambridge, 2006), pp. 21–58; Smith, 'Sedley's 1692 birthday ode', passim; Williams, *Whig Literary Culture*, pp. 93–134.

Anne were on the throne(s), it was typical to emphasize the great European cause that they were fighting for, and the peace, freedom and happiness that was being brought to Europe (as in this ode). But this emphasis disappeared after the Hanoverian succession, resurfacing only vaguely during times of war. Whereas William and (in a more complicated way) Anne were celebrated by reference to their actions and deeds, the Hanoverians tended to be celebrated on account of their passivity and stasis (although the word 'repose', which became one of the key words in this tendency, does appear in Tate's 1693 ode). In summary, the pre-1757 odes tended to hail their princes in exultant, musical, baroque effusions, and to paint them as glorious, semi-divine figures, sailing serenely through the skies, consorting with various allegorical figures, exemplifying various significant qualities and generally resembling the portrait of William and Mary on the ceiling of the Royal Naval College's Painted Hall.

Here Tate also demonstrated some of the more direct characteristics of the laureates' negotiation of the prince–people relationship. One was the idea that the prince was a sort of tutelary deity, guardian angel or intercessory saint on Britain's behalf, using the divine favour that was given to them personally as a way of bringing blessings upon Britain. Thus the invocation to Mary, 'Smile and Bless the Infant Year … in Kindness to our Isle', because 'Succeeding Years in just Return, on You and Us shall Smile'. Another, associated idea was that the prince's actions would effect great results for Britain. In this instance, Tate's concerns were more for the effects of William's actions on Europe ('the Gen'ral Peace won by our Monarch's Sword'), but this too was part of a wider, recurrent theme, in which it was suggested that the prince was someone for the people to take pride in as their champion, whose personal greatness reflected well on Britain and granted the nation an international pre-eminence. A related theme, not too overt in this particular ode, was that the qualities embodied by the prince were particularly British qualities, such as a love of freedom and a hatred of France ('the *Gallick* Genius').

The laureates would also give more explicit descriptions of the prince–people relationship, partly in the manner of a historian, partly in the manner of a prophet. Tate's lines, 'When *Britain's Senate* shall Convene … Their kind Supplies our fainting Hopes restor'd,/Their Inspir'd Counsels shall sure means afford,/To fix the Gen'ral Peace won by our Monarch's Sword', suggested, again in idealized form (Britain's '*Senate*'), a harmonious relationship in which both sides had their own particular roles and worked in mutual contract towards some nationally desirable end. Parliament would fund the prince, the prince would win peace and parliament would fix it in place. But the prince's interactions with the nation were cast on multiple different levels. As well as '*Britain's Senate*', William had intimate, pseudo-amorous dealings with an abstract '*Albion*', while Tate's mention of 'Us', earlier in the poem, indicated still another conception of the British people, namely, the populace of which Tate himself formed a part. This latter idea, of the poet himself as representative of the people, expressing their sentiments towards the prince and experiencing that prince's presence in some way, was also typical. In this context, it was especially common for the laureate to phrase the relationship in terms of emotion, and to express the gratitude that the people had towards their prince (the British people having 'mourn[ed]' William's 'Absence', and wanting desperately 'To Thank their Monarch').

In short, there were a range of ways that the laureates could approach the relationship between prince and people, and render it for their readers. A spirit of idealization lay behind much of this, but so too did a more personal sense of emotion. It could even be said that the rhetoric and form of the odes allowed for an affective symbiosis between (on the one hand) ideals and abstractions and (on the other) the personal and the emotive. This sense would prove highly significant in the later history of the odes, coming to occupy a more central place in them after 1757. Now, departing from this ode of Tate's, which has been used as a kind of copy-text of the quintessential early ode, the various ways in which the prince–people relationship was envisioned in the early odes will be looked at in more detail.

The early odes

The major vision of the relationship between people and prince presented in the early odes was that the two parties were joined in perfect harmony, the prince fulfilling his ideal role in terms of his qualities, actions and care for his people, the people fulfilling their ideal role in terms of their obedience and their recognition of the happiness granted to them by their prince. This unity was emphasized as right and proper, and as the source of all good things; as long as it was maintained, the nation would prosper. Yet the conditional sense was generally not explicit. Instead, the odes tended to present the relationship in a vague, idealized manner, expressing it as a sort of divine *fait accompli*, existing outside of temporality and causality. The poet expressed this relationship as a partaker of it, recorded it as a bard and witnessed its future continuation as a prophet. As will be seen below, Cibber was particularly important in developing these ideas, and in basing them around the theme of mutuality.

In this ideal form of the relationship, the prince brought good rule and the people brought due obedience. The prince cared for his people: he 'make[s] the Publick Good [his] Care'.[40] One recurrent idea was that the prince had saved Britain from recent distress, and protected it from future pain. 'Britannia, late oppress'd with dread,/Hung her declining drooping head:/A better visage now she wears … Safe beneath her mighty master,/In security she sits.'[41] Rowe's final ode included a hypnotic succession of swift, repetitive lines on this theme: 'More sweet than all, the praise/Of Caesar's golden days:/Caesar's praise is sweeter;/Britain's pleasure greater;/Still may Caesar's reign excel;/Sweet the praise of reigning well.'[42] George's praiseworthiness was bound up with his good governance of Britain, and his 'praise' corresponded vaguely but inexorably with Britain's 'pleasure'. The shortness of the lines here, and the repetition of words and noises, served to blur the two strands together, removing any hint of causation and any hint that the praise was conditional upon the pleasure, while nonetheless making clear that the two were symbiotic.

However, what the people owed to their prince in return was not onerous. Most often, the laureate stated that the people owed obedience, joy and gratitude; and, because of the nature of the laureate odes, these debts were not so much demanded, as enacted. The laureate stood in between people and prince; the tone that the ode form inclined towards was exultant, rather than argumentative; and the laureate odes were sung at court by many different voices. The laureates therefore employed the odes to express the universal, joyous gratitude of the people towards the prince. ''Tis ANNA's Day, and all around/Only Mirth and Musick sound … Shouts and Songs, and Laughing Joys.'[43]

In one ode, Tate included a chorus part reading, '*What then should Happy* Britain *do?/Blest with the Gift and Giver too.*'[44] Apparently, there was nothing for Britain to do at all; its prince had given it such perfect happiness, that Tate found himself at a loss. However, after some more praise, he rallied with this final 'Grand CHORUS': '*Happy, Happy, past Expressing,*/Britain, *if thou know'st thy Blessing;/Home-bred Discord ne'er Alarm Thee,/Other Mischief cannot Harm Thee./Happy, if you know'st thy Blessing./Happy, Happy, past Expressing.*'[45] Again, there was nothing much for Britain to do: even words could not match up to Britain's happiness, since it was '*past Expressing*'. Yet Tate was nonetheless suggesting one obligation that the people must pay,

[40] Tate, 1715BD.
[41] Rowe, 1717NY.
[42] Rowe, 1719NY.
[43] Tate, 1707BD.
[44] Tate, 1698NY.
[45] Tate, 1698NY.

and which, the word '*if*' suggested, they might fall short of. Britain was required to '*know*' its blessing. This was the people's one active requirement in the relationship: they had to acknowledge the greatness of the prince and the happiness that the prince was giving them. Again, the issue of causality was sidestepped. The happiness was ever present, yet only became true if it was acknowledged; the people were inexpressibly happy, yet would only experience their happiness if they joined Tate in his efforts to express it. It was not a hard task, Tate promised them. All they had to do was repeat after him: '*Happy, Happy … Happy, Happy …*'

The conditional clause ('*If*') was only mildly stated by Tate on this occasion, and it was never pushed hard by the laureates. In line with the odes' general inclination towards glorious assertion rather than argumentation, the norm was for joy and gratitude to be expressed, rather than demanded. A good example came in Rowe's longest and most ambitious ode (his first). 'I hear the mirth, I hear the land rejoice,/Like many waters swells the pleasing noise,/While to their monarch, thus, they raise the public voice./Father of thy country, hail! … Joy abounds in ev'ry breast,/For thee thy people all, for thee the year is blest.'[46] In this passage, Rowe initially portrayed himself as someone catching the sound of the nation's happiness from afar, and used this conceit to build up towards a crescendo of joy. He then switched role, becoming the mouthpiece of that joyous 'public voice'. It was as if the joy from 'ev'ry breast' was pouring irresistibly into the court, confirming not just the people's grateful happiness, but that the happiness originated with the prince himself: 'For thee' the people were 'blest'. This was a typical effect used by the laureates. By choosing to enact the people's emotional gratitude rather than trying to convince the people that they ought to be grateful, the laureates made that gratitude seem like something natural. They invited their readers to share in the great celebratory gratitude that had always been there, and always would be. The people's gratitude was not conditional, but was always forthcoming; it found its articulation in the people's representative, the laureate.

As well as establishing this ideal form of the prince–people relationship, the odes also illustrated the good things that resulted from its successful functioning: peace, glory and prosperity. '*Britannia* shall be shown/Still yearly with new Glories crown'd,/As *Brunswick's* Years roul on.'[47] Goodness would flow across the land. This goodness was usually presented in abstract, traditional terms, drawing upon the classical ideas of a golden age or halcyon days. 'And under Thee, our most Indulgent King,/Shall Industry and Arts

[46] Rowe, 1716NY.

[47] Eusden, 1729BD.

increase;/Quiet we shall possess, but not Inglorious Ease.//Then shall each fertile Mead, and grateful Field,/Amply reward our Care and Toil … Free from Invading force, and Intestine broil', was one typical illustration.[48] Rowe evoked the idea of halcyon days by speaking of 'the billows of the ocean' being laid to rest.[49] Tate was more explicit, hailing 'Halcyon Days of Peace'.[50] All laureates spoke of 'blessings'.[51]

The next major way in which the early odes envisioned the prince–people relationship was by relating the prince to British national identity. The sorts of qualities and frames of reference by which the prince was praised in the odes were diverse, some going back to the roots of the panegyric tradition. In terms of whether the relationship being posited was one between a prince and a people, or a prince and a British nation, it became more typical for the odes to lean towards the latter after 1757 than it had been before. Nonetheless, even from the time of Tate, and especially in Shadwell's odes, a significant trend was to praise the prince in ways that linked him to British characteristics and British history. Eusden described George I as being formed from 'the mix'd Ideas' of 'Edward, Henry, and the Lov'd Nassau' [William III]'.[52] Later, he stated that 'the rich Source of Freedom is the King'.[53] Shadwell claimed that Mary's rule eclipsed that of 'our *Eliza*'.[54] More blandly, Tate wrote on one occasion, 'Fame and Fortune ever smile/ On *Britain's* Queen, and *Britain's* Isle'.[55]

The prince thus became a sort of tutelary figure to the nation: a classical 'genius', or a patron saint. He symbolized and embodied the nation. In some sense, he interceded for it with Heaven. Eusden concluded one ode by telling Britain's previous, allegorical 'Genius' that it was now no longer needed: 'thy Guardianship may'st spare,/Britain is a Brunswick's care'.[56] The use of the word 'Brunswick' to denote George I (the Hanoverians stemming from the House of Brunswick) alliteratively emphasized the idea that the prince had become the new genius of the nation. This idea reached its height with Cibber, and with the completion of the transition from an active king like William III to a passive symbol like George II.

[48] Shadwell, 1690BD.

[49] Rowe, 1716BD.

[50] Tate, 1708NY.

[51] Eg Rowe, 1716BD.

[52] Eusden, 1720NY.

[53] Eusden, 1730NY.

[54] T. Shadwell, *Ode to the King on His Return from Ireland* (1691), p. 4.

[55] Tate, 1703NY.

[56] Eusden, 1720NY.

In many ways, then, the odes gave an explicit depiction of the prince–people relationship. Yet they also negotiated that relationship in subtler ways. The laureate was himself a prime instrument of the relationship, and the relationship was textured throughout his odes. For one thing, the laureate's praise of the prince was not simply about gratifying him personally; it was about selling him, and selling obedience, to the reading public. The laureate's odes were attempting to encourage a loyal awe and reverence for the prince (and in some ways for the prince's government of the day) and to define the manner in which that prince should be understood and responded to by his people. In so doing, he sometimes brought himself to the forefront as a prime intermediary between prince and people: leading, hearing and voicing the praise.

Some forms of praise appeared in odes from all the laureates. The prince was often portrayed as some great classical figure, with 'Caesar' and 'Augustus' being particularly favoured.[57] As mentioned above, Tate and Eusden were especially fond of classical references.[58] Other forms of praise were still more characteristic of individual laureates, with Shadwell emphasizing William and Mary's Whig qualities and Tate celebrating his princes' devotion to the cause of virtue.[59] Under the Hanoverians, the praise often focused on aspects of family, fertility and lineage.[60] One of the most noteworthy treatments of the theme came in Rowe's first ode. After hailing George I, 'Thou great Plantagenet! immortal be thy race!', the ode continued, 'See! see the sacred scyon springs,/See the glad promise of a line of kings!/Royal youth! what bard divine,/Equal to a praise like thine,/Shall in some exalted measure,/Sing thee, Britain's dearest treasure? ... Still pour the blessing forth, and give thy great increase.'[61] In the previous line, Rowe had been addressing George I directly, but here the phrase 'See! see ... see' suggested that he was turning away to address a wider audience at this point, calling their attention to the prince's flourishing line of succession as a way of telling them how grateful and invested they should be in a prince who (for the first time since Charles I) had a straightforward heir. He then pivoted once again to address the future George II; having confirmed the people's approval, and thus his own role as an intermediary between prince and people, he was able to dub the heir 'Britain's dearest treasure', while also expressing the conventional idea of the poet's unworthiness even to sing about so great a 'thee'. In these lines,

[57] Eg Tate, 1693BD; Tate, 1694BD; Rowe, 1716BD; Rowe, 1718BD.

[58] Eg Eusden, 1720NY.

[59] Eg Shadwell, 1690BD; Tate, 1705NY.

[60] Eg Tate, 1715BD; Eusden, 1720BD.

[61] Rowe, 1716NY.

the Hanoverians' fecundity was being praised not so much for their own gratification, but more so as to sell the idea of a uniquely stable monarchy to readers. The lines also showed the subtle footwork that was necessary to render such praise effective: Rowe allowed himself a brief explicit appeal to his audience, before twisting back around to face his royal patrons, and wrapped that appeal back up in the guise of an extravagant, supposedly consensual compliment. By such means, the voice of praise could come to seem like the voice of the people, even as it was being used to persuade the people as to the prince's glories (in this case, those of stability).

Moreover, the odes were rendered effective as texts by the fact of their having been performed at court. As mentioned above, the publications tended to emphasize that they had been so performed, with notations marking out things like 'CHORUS' and 'First Voice',[62] and with little explanatory paragraphs setting out things like, 'On *Monday* the 6th of this Month, the Queen was graciously pleas'd to come from *Kensington* to St. *James's*; where the foregoing Ode, set to Mr. *John* Eccles, Master of Her Majesty's Musick, was Perform'd, to the Satisfaction of the whole Court, by Her Majesty's Servants.'[63] Sometimes the publications would even name the singers.[64] Thus the meaning of the odes was partly conditioned by the ability of the reader to reconstruct the performance and imagine the prince hearing it. In the case quoted above, even 'the Satisfaction of the whole Court' was deemed worthy of note. The odes allowed readers to be present at a joyous, musical celebration of the prince's benign rule, and to participate in the enacting of an idealized prince–people relationship. Readers who were so transported were not expected to bring scepticism, criticism or dispute. They were there to bathe in the golden splendour. They were there to add their voices to the shouts of grateful joy.

The early odes thus constituted an aesthetic that was unashamedly court-centred. It was a feature of court ceremony, it emanated from the court and it transported its readers into the court so that they might partake of the court festivities and be introduced into the appropriate relationship with their prince. Having endorsed the performance, those readers would shuffle off back to their homes, duly impressed with a sense of majesty. This was a poetry that was fully in line with some of the major currents of poetry identified by scholars as pertaining to this time: it was extravagantly panegyric, pseudo-Pindaric and avowedly occasional, even seeking to recreate the occasion of its inception for its readers. In terms of the social and situational aspects of

---

[62] Eg Tate, 1711BD.

[63] Tate, 1707NY.

[64] Eg Tate, 1711BD.

poetry, it also reflected the importance of the court, and court-based coteries of literary production, with which scholars continue to characterize the later Stuart period.[65] As such, it was attuned to the contemporary poetry landscape, and it proved the court to be attuned to national life. Yet if the relationship between prince and people revealed in these odes situated the court as having a central and continuingly relevant role in society, politics and culture, then it did so with a sense that society, politics and culture looked to the court for their lead, rather than vice versa. As it had been for centuries, the court of the laureate odes was a physical space, occupied by a prince, and it dictated the nation's affairs. The court presided over the nation.

Cibber's odes

The laureate who arguably took these themes the furthest was Cibber.[66] However, his odes also signalled some of the developments to come. In his hands, the pre-1757 odes reached their culmination, but with certain changes of emphasis, tending rather to dissolve the physical presence of the court and the practical agency of the prince into a hazier, more metaphorical presence. Where the previous odes had invited their readers to court, Cibber's odes elevated that court into the clouds, and invited readers merely to look up towards it from wherever they happened to be sitting. Where the previous odes had articulated a relationship between prince and people in which the prince actively directed affairs, Cibber's prince became a more symbolic guarantee, or rubber-stamp, to affairs which were being conducted by the people themselves. His forms, tropes and techniques followed on from those of his predecessors, albeit with a narrowed range and some idiosyncratic preferences on display; but the ideas began to shift towards those which would be characteristic of his successors.

The most significant characteristic feature of Cibber's odes was that they posited a rhetoric of equilibrium, in which the court became more abstracted and the people's happiness became more heavily emphasized. This was the structuring ideology of Cibber's odes. Where the previous odes had sublimated the sense of argument, and had dampened the causal and conditional elements of the prince–people relationship, there had still been a (sometimes significant) tendency to show the prince as having

[65] Eg Ezell, 'Gentleman's Journal', pp. 323–40.

[66] Cibber's odes show some consonance with the themes and imagery of the direct political, prose writers associated with Walpole's regime, as explored in R. Browning, *Political and Constitutional Ideas of the Court Whigs* (London, 1982). Again, though, the decision made here has been to focus on each laureate's odes within the context of the history of the form; how Cibber's odes engage with partisan politics and constitutional theory has therefore not been considered here.

achieved something through action – for example, William bringing liberty to Britain – and an implication that the people's gratitude and obedience flowed from the prince's qualities of rulership. With Cibber's odes, this tendency, and its attendant implications, were further negated. Cibber's rhetoric posited a prince and people in eternal, transcendental concord, where action was not only unnecessary, but even malign. Cibber thus turned his prince into a symbolic guarantee of the nation's happiness, and suggested that, so long as his readers endorsed his recognition of that happiness, all would continue to be well.

Cibber routinely mentioned such things as 'George's gentle sway'.[67] George's rule was mild, tender and soft; there was no sense of activity to his 'sway[ing]'. Although he was 'Born to protect and bless the land!', it was only in the following manner: 'And while the laws his people form,/ His scepter glories to confirm,/Their wishes are his sole command.'[68] His people made the laws, and he followed their wishes; the diction of these lines even made it sound as if the laws in turn were 'form[ing]' the people, and that they were 'command[ing]' their prince. This rhetoric continued until Cibber's final ode: 'Our Rights, our Laws, our Liberty,/His Lenity so well maintains … So gently Caesar holds his Sway,/That Subjects with Delight Obey'. George's 'Lenity' meant that his rule was scarcely more than the confirmation of Britain's signal characteristics: rights, laws and liberty. His subjects' 'Delight' was because they had essentially nothing to obey, and were left to their own native freedoms.

Thus Cibber's George became more of a symbolic tutelary figure than his predecessors' princes had been. He guarded his people's happiness by doing nothing to tamper with it, and his people responded with a grateful but cursory obedience. In another ode, Cibber wrote, 'Now shall commerce, sailing free,/Long the boast of *Britain* be;/While our *Caesar* guards the sea,/Can our beaten foes molest us?'[69] This was not a William, guarding Britain through his martial actions. Nor was it akin to Anne's husband Prince George, who had sometimes been hailed as a guardian of the seas on account of his genuine naval rank. Instead, it was George being invoked as a sort of guardian deity, and being used to give human form and a guiding spirit to such abstract British characteristics as 'commerce' and 'the sea'. The same ode ended, 'Io *Britannia*, Io *Caesar* sound'. George II was as allegorical a figure as Britannia, to be celebrated in the same breath.

[67] Cibber, 1733NY; the phrase 'gentle Sway' also used in, eg, Cibber, 1739BD; Cibber, 1758BD.

[68] Cibber, 1732BD.

[69] Cibber, 1755BD.

Cibber depicted a king who sat happily on his throne while these verses were sung to him, smiling in vague benignity. The king thus served as Cibber's focal point for, and embodiment of, an ideal of national equilibrium. Meanwhile, the people were happy, grateful and obedient. '*Ye Grateful* Britons' and 'happy *Britons*' were typical phrases.[70] Although the people's obligation to the prince was infinite, it was never very active; Cibber continuously invoked it, but also continuously discharged it in the same breath. He positioned himself as a Levite priest, making regular offerings on behalf of the nation, while the nation nodded its head in recognition of its involvement. The nation also had to be happy; but happiness went hand in hand with gratitude, and, as in the Tate ode quoted above, also required nothing other than the people's acknowledgement. 'Awake the grateful song', Cibber called on one occasion, 'Sing, sing to George's gentle sway,/ And joy for joys receiv'd repay.'[71] The people owed their joys to their prince; but repayment was effected simply by being joyous, and Cibber's 'grateful song' was the means by which such repayment would be made. '*Augustus'* sway *demands* our song,/And *calls* for universal cheer,' Cibber insisted at the start of another ode, before continuing,

> What thanks, ye *Britons,* can repay
> So mild, so just, so tender sway?
> *Air.*
> Your annual aid when he desires,
> Less the King than land requires;
> *All the dues to him that flow*
> *Are still but Royal wants to you:*
> So the seasons lend the earth
> Their kindly rains to raise her birth;
> And well the mutual labours suit,
> *His the glory, yours the fruit.*[72]

Here, the obligation was impossible to discharge – 'What thanks ... can repay ...?' – but the debt was a light one, being composed of mildness, justice and tenderness. Moreover, the payment of the debt was not simply a payment to George, but a payment to the people themselves, from which they would reap the harvest. George's only benefit was '*glory*': again, an entirely abstract quality. The vague natural metaphors, and the refusal to be precise on the nature of an obligation which was being so insistently invoked,

---

[70] Cibber, 1731NY; for gratitude, see also eg the New Year's Day and birthday odes for 1755.

[71] Cibber, 1733NY.

[72] Cibber, 1732NY.

further created the sense that this transaction was abstract and mysterious. Thus the king became little more than a symbol of the flourishing state of the realm. The same note was struck time and time again: 'Here what you owe to Caesar's sway,/In grateful song to Caesar pay … The grateful theme demands our lays.'[73] If 'Caesar' was so immaterial a taxman as to deal only in song, and if the songs themselves were spontaneous expressions of joy, then his function was little more than a reminder of national well-being. He was an abstract quality, inspiring the proper workings of the nation: a barometer of obligation which proved to the people how happy they were based on the level of their debt.

Moreover, it was the odes themselves that enacted this immaterial transaction (or that, to continue the metaphor, took the reading of the barometer). 'Here what you owe' would be paid; the 'grateful theme' demanded 'our lyre', but it was Cibber who held that lyre, however wide was the 'our' of its ownership. Because the main substance of the transaction was joy, Cibber's odes thus became the site at which a nation's emotions would be enacted. 'The Date of Caesar's Sway … calls for universal Cheer' was the sort of sentiment with which Cibber often started his odes;[74] and he would often proceed by articulating great reams of joy, before climaxing in a thankful, joyous chorus.[75] The people were so happy that they had nothing else to do than to recognize the source of their happiness by way of Cibber's odes.

Thus Cibber continued to portray the prince–people relationship in the ways laid down by his predecessors, but with variations and new emphases that pointed the way ahead. As poetry, the odes remained somewhat responsive to the aesthetic climate in which they were being produced, but increasingly less so as the years passed, with Cibber's last efforts being very similar to his earliest. Cibber maintained a poetics of courtliness, ceremony and panegyric, and articulated the continuing importance of the court in national life both by the way in which he portrayed the relationship between prince and people and by the manner of his writing. Yet the prevailing notion of that relationship began to evolve in his odes. His predecessors had granted the court a more active, tangible leadership over society, politics and culture; they had served as a kind of a maitre d' to the court, beckoning readers inside and overseeing the relevant ceremonies; and they had at least suggested some sense of causality and practical consequence in the manner of the people's joy and obedience. Cibber turned the court into something

[73] Cibber, 1736NY.

[74] Cibber, 1758NY.

[75] Eg Cibber, 1755BD.

less tangible, trading in causality for equilibrium. He dampened the prince's agency, and argued that such dampness rendered his reign happier than any other prince's. The court's role was not diminished, but it was changing.

The later odes: Whitehead

With Whitehead's appointment, the odes reached their second major phase, and the changes took full effect. The court's role in society was no longer as a distinct, physical entity towards which the nation looked for a lead; instead, it became more equably in tune with the nation, opening itself out to the public. Courtliness became diffused and inherent throughout society; the laureate of the court was the laureate of the nation, and to celebrate either was to celebrate both. The aesthetic of the odes changed accordingly, bringing itself in line with the most recent developments in poetry and employing those developments so as to enact the celebration of court and nation.[76] Whitehead's first birthday ode for George III (1761) ran thus:

> STROPHE.
> 'Twas at the nectar'd feast of Jove,
> When fair Alcmena's son
> His destin'd course on earth had run,
> And claim'd the thrones above;
> Around their King, in deep debate,
> Conveen'd, the heav'nly synod sate,
> And meditated boons refin'd
> To grace the friend of humankind:
> When, to mark th' advancing God,
> Propitious Hermes stretch'd his rod,
> The roofs with music rung!
> 'What boon divine would heav'n bestow?
> 'Ye gods, unbend the studious brow,
> 'The fruitless search give o'er,
> 'Whilst we the just reward assign:
> 'Let Hercules with Hebe join,
> 'And Youth unite with Power!
> ANTISTROPHE.
> O sacred truth in emblem drest! –

---

[76] Kilburn notes a 'change of emphasis' between Cibber's odes and Whitehead's first ode, from 'overworked classical models … towards more "Gothic" references … in keeping with the literary tradition of the 1730s that has been associated with Prince Frederick and Bolingbrokean ideals'. M. Kilburn, 'Royalty and public in Britain: 1714–1789' (unpublished University of Oxford DPhil thesis, 1997), p. 45. However, as the 1761 birthday ode quoted here indicates, there was no wholesale rejection of classical models, and the Gothicism was more that of Gray and the Wartons than of Frederick and Bolingbroke.

Again the muses sing,
Again in Britain's blooming King
Alcides stands confest,
By temp'rance nurs'd, and early taught
To shun the smooth fallacious draught
Which sparkles high in Circe's bowl;
To tame each hydra of the soul,
Each lurking pest, which mocks its birth,
And ties the spirit down to earth
Immers'd in mortal coil;
His choice was that severer road
Which leads to Virtue's calm abode,
And well repays the toil.
In vain ye tempt, ye specious harms,
Ye flow'ry wiles, ye flatt'ring charms,
That breathe from yonder bower;
And heav'n the just reward assigns,
For Hercules with Hebe joins,
And Youth unites with Power.
EPODE.
O call'd by heav'n to fill that awful throne
Where Edward, Henry, William, George, have shone,
(Where love with rev'rence, law with pow'r agree,
And 'tis each subject's birthright to be free),
The fairest wreaths already won
Are but a prelude to the whole:
Thy arduous race is *now* begun,
And, starting from a nobler goal,
Heroes and Kings of ages past
Are Thy compeers: extended high
The trump of Fame expects the blast,
The radiant lists before Thee lie,
The field is Time, the prize Eternity!
Beyond example's bounded light
'Tis Thine to urge thy daring flight,
And heights untried explore:
O think what Thou alone canst give,
What blessings Britain may receive
When Youth unites with Power![77]

This was the style and manner of the late eighteenth-century odes. Evidently, there were still features in common with the previous odes: this particular example included a reference to music ringing out, and ended

[77] Whitehead, 1761BD.

each section on a refrain; it compared George III to various classical figures, including Hercules, and to Britain's previous great kings; it was extravagant in its praise; it celebrated the prince for mild qualities like 'temp'rance'; it emphasized the freedoms of the British subject, and the balance between 'love with rev'rence, law with pow'r'; and it even included a Tate-like passage in which the prince was shown fighting 'each hydra of the soul' as part of his zeal for 'Virtue'.

However, the entire cast of the ode was different. It was an ambitious, carefully written poem, following the structure of a genuine Pindaric ode rather than suiting itself for musical performance. 'Strophe', 'Antistrophe' and 'Epode', for example, were the three sections that Pindar had used to divide his own odes, each governed by a strict set of rules. Earlier Pindaric writers, from Cowley onwards, had ignored them in favour of wildness, but they had been rigorously reapplied by Gray and other mid-century poets. Whitehead's eagerness to use them as the governing principles of his laureate odes (rather than the old, performative divisions appropriate for music) indicated his desire to recapture the forms and methods of Greek lyricism and the supposed original spirit of poetry that certain writers were associating with it, and his attendant desire to place the emphasis on the readable text (accessible across the nation) rather than on the musical performance (a one-off event at court). Likewise, the ideas and imagery in the 1761 birthday ode were more strikingly rendered, and more elaborately figured, than previously. Whitehead's image of Hercules labouring against 'each hydra of the soul' showed more concern to draw out the evocative potentials of the metaphor than had Tate's cursory allusion. There was also a clear narrative to the poem, similar to Gray's 'Progress of poetry': it started off with the original Olympian deities, then proceeded to Hercules, thence to English kings and lastly to the future glories of George III.

After the vague musical maunderings of Cibber, Whitehead was bringing the laureate odes in line with the work of his most ambitious contemporaries. He was followed in this respect by Warton (especially) and Pye. Once in office, both Whitehead and Warton put most of their poetic efforts into the odes. Whitehead published virtually no other work throughout his long tenure; his most significant publications (other than the odes) were his *Verses to the People of England* (1758) and *Charge to the Poets* (1762), both of which had a semi-official character (as made clear in the latter's title page, reading 'Quasi ex Cathedrâ loquitur'). Warton worked diligently on his laureate odes, as shown by his correspondence and notebooks, and the only other work that he carried out during his laureate tenure was his edition of Milton's minor poems (apparently with George III's encouragement, as seen in the previous chapter).[78] The laureates channelled their poetic energies unreservedly into the odes.

The change in poetics had important ramifications for the prince–people relationship. For one thing, the laureate was now asserting himself *qua* laureate as an important, respectable poet. The court poet did not simply furnish tinkling lines to be sung on festive occasions, but produced powerful poetry to which the public should pay heed. As will become more evident in some of the following quotations, the later laureates conceived their official poetry as great national addresses; they were the poets of the nation as much as of the court. Such being the case, the odes carried with them a sense that the prince had a central patronal role in his nation, not only anointing its national poet but contributing to the way in which the nation should conceive of itself and of contemporary affairs, and doing so responsively, in harmony with national feeling.

The change in the style of the odes was also important for the way in which it portrayed the prince to the people. The previous odes, as documents of courtly performances, had suggested that readers could be vicariously present at those performances, paying their devotions and witnessing the splendour of the court. The later odes did something different. They removed the idea of courtly performance from the text itself, thus decentring the prince: the physical space of his court was replaced with a more diffuse sense of the prince's presence. Instead of transporting the reader to the court, the odes rendered the prince to his people using a variety of newly sophisticated pictorial and emotive methods, in the manner that scholars have generally linked with new poetic forms and tendencies, rather than with patronal, courtly odes. In the advertisement to his *Odes on Various Subjects* (1746), Joseph Warton, brother to the future laureate, had presented his work as a challenge to prevailing tastes, suggesting that his odes would be found 'too fanciful and descriptive'. Yet he was unrepentant: he 'looks upon Invention and Imagination to be the chief faculties of a Poet'.[79] These ideas would later be articulated more fully in *An Essay on the Genius and Writings of Pope* (1782), where Joseph Warton also made more explicit the need for a poet to cast his ideas into fully developed imagery, powerful and comprehensive enough to transport the reader to another place. 'The use, the force and the excellence of language, certainly consists in raising *clear*, *complete*, and *circumstantial* images, and in turning readers into spectators.'[80] By doing so, exponents of this rationale of poetry

---

[78] Bod, Dep d. 615; Dep d. 616; *Warton Correspondence*, lt. 523, at pp. 568–9, lt. 525, at p. 572.

[79] J. Warton, *Odes on Various Subjects* (1746), sig. A2r.

[80] J. Warton, *An Essay on the Genius and Writings of Pope* (2 vols, 1756–82), ii. 222–3. On theories concerning imagery and emotions in poetry at this time, Walsh, 'Eighteenth-century high lyric', pp. 115–22.

believed that the poet could trigger an emotional response in the reader that correlated with the poet's own ideas and emotions.[81]

The later laureate odes worked upon this rationale. They laboured to create elaborate, potent images by which their readers could envisage and understand the prince and his place in the nation. Instead of simply enacting the joyous gratitude of the prince's subjects, they used poetry's ability to communicate passions in a more deliberate way, to create a more intimate emotional relationship between prince and people. Bainbridge has noted this function of poetry to have been especially important during the French Revolutionary and Napoleonic Wars, with poets and critics conceiving poetry's chief, unique function to be its ability to mediate war to the public: it could transport readers onto the battlefield by the use of 'fancy' or 'imagination'.[82] But this function had already been present for several decades in the laureate odes, and it is therefore no wonder that, as shown in Chapter Four, laureate Pye became so central a figure to wartime loyalist culture.

Important to the later odes, then, was that the laureate was a kind of visionary, British bard, writing as much for his nation as for his prince. As seen above, the earlier odes had undoubtedly invoked British national identity and characteristics fairly regularly; but, in general, 'the people' had been figured as the prince's anonymous subjects, expressing generic praise and gratitude. The later odes contained a firmer, more sophisticated sense of 'the people' as the British nation, and of the laureate as their British poet. Whitehead's 1759 birthday ode began, 'The bard whom liberty inspires/ Wakes into willing voice th' accordant lays.'[83] He was not merely celebrating liberty, or thanking George II for his benign maintenance of it; liberty was his inspiration as a poet, and what gave him the bardic power to rouse voices into accordant music. Several years later, Whitehead described his laureate odes as proceeding from 'the *British* lyre'.[84] Sometimes, he would almost entirely forget about his prince in his fervour to sing for Britain; the 1760 New Year's ode, directly addressing Britain, gave only one passing mention to 'thy monarch', and concluded on the bombastic strain, 'The land of freedom with the land of slaves [France],/As nature's friend, *must* wage illustrious war,/ ... 'Till not on *Albion's* shores alone,/The voice of freedom shall resound,/But every realm shall equal blessings find,/And man

---

[81] J. Warton, *Pope*, ii. 222–3; Walsh, 'Eighteenth-century high lyric', pp. 115–22.

[82] Bainbridge, *Visions of Conflict*, pp. 11–31.

[83] Whitehead, 1759BD.

[84] Whitehead, 1765BD.

enjoy the birthright of his kind.'[85] Here, the old idea of freedom being spread to Europe had been resurrected; but whereas the early odes had identified this as the work of the prince, Whitehead was here attributing it to the British nation itself, its prince not even functioning as an instrument of that glorious national mission.

However, if Whitehead's emphasis was more on Britain than its prince, the prince was nonetheless central to his idea of the British nation. Especially in the birthday odes, the prince could sometimes loom overwhelmingly large. On three separate occasions, Whitehead used his birthday ode as an attempt to establish the nature of the relationship between prince and people in a more systematic, explicit manner than his predecessors had attempted.[86] Thus the 1763 birthday ode proclaimed, 'Common births, like common things,/Pass unheeded, or unknown'; but 'Born for millions monarchs rise/Heirs of Infamy or Fame ... 'Tis not our King's alone, 'tis Britain's natal morn.' The ode went on to elaborate on how 'Bright examples plac'd on high,/Shine with more distinguish'd blaze,' and 'Public is the monarch's pleasure,/Public is the monarch's care.' It ended on a description of the ideal prince, and a powerful climax which explicitly referenced Pindar with an asterisk: 'Such may *Britain* find her kings!–/Such the Muse* of rapid wings/Wafts to some sublimer sphere:/Gods and heroes mingle there./ ... O such may *Britain* ever find her kings!'[87]

In line with the sorts of theory espoused by Joseph Warton, Whitehead also brought to the odes a new sense of the emotive power of poetry. When Whitehead's predecessors had defined the prince–people relationship by reference to an emotional transaction, they had done so in a one-dimensional manner, focusing on the grateful joy of the people. Whitehead, in his more self-consciously poetic and modern odes, sought a deeper emotional response from his readers. He rendered the prince a more accessible and sympathetic figure, to whom readers could respond as a fellow man. Whitehead's George was the 'Father' and the 'Friend' of the British people.[88]

A good example came in 1765. After George III had recovered from an illness, Whitehead painted a touching scene of the emotional bonds between prince and people. George was still the object of gratitude, but also of tenderer cares. 'To HIM we pour the grateful lay/Who makes the season doubly gay;/For whom, so late, our lifted eyes/With tears besought the pitying skies,/And won the cherub health to crown/A nation's prayer, and

---

[85] Whitehead, 1760NY.

[86] Whitehead, 1763BD; Whitehead, 1773BD; Whitehead, 1784BD.

[87] Whitehead, 1763BD.

[88] Eg Whitehead, 1771BD; Whitehead, 1783BD.

ease that breast/Which feels all sorrows but its own,/And seeks by blessing to be blest.'[89] Much of this echoed Cibber, but now the prince was being characterized as someone vulnerable and sympathetic – even 'pit[iable]' – and as someone who, in turn, was racked with the sorrows being felt by his subjects. Not long after, Whitehead was hailing George as 'Friend to the poor! ... Friend to the poor', and, in celebration of a recent act of royal charity, telling of how 'His feeling heart/Inspir'd the nation's better part/With virtues like its own.'[90] Whitehead's George was a sentimental prince, not sitting airily in a court, but going about among his people, humbling himself to do them good and inspiring them with the example of charity. Thus, he gave his readers a subject to whom they could have a deeper, more sincere emotional response than had previously been the case. They were not to be bound to their prince simply by reverence, gratitude or even joy, but by the most tender and humane sentiment. He was a father and a friend to his people.

The last thing to note is the manner in which Whitehead used his position as laureate to interpret the great events through which the nation was passing, often interpreting them by reference to his prince. In an ode towards the end of the Seven Years' War, for example, he voiced his desire for peace, but also the need for all Britons to pull together against France, by reference to the marriage of George and Charlotte: 'Love commands, and beauty's queen/Rules the power who rules the sky ... /Let the war-torn legions own/Your gentler sway, and from the throne/Receive the laws of love.' But, he went on (now addressing '*ye* British dames'), 'Should *Gallia,* obstinately vain,/To her own ruin urge despair', then the British womenfolk must follow the example of '*the ladies of* Mecklenburg [Charlotte's homeland]', who, in 1395, had sold their jewels for the public good. Whitehead was confident that, inspired by their new 'fair instructress', Charlotte, Britons would 'unite [their] flame/To save the land of Liberty and Laws'.[91]

Whitehead's task became harder during the American Revolutionary War, but he persisted in interpreting events for the nation by reference to George III, and seeking to rally British hearts against France. Whitehead recurrently presented the American rebels as a prodigal son who had cast off his filial loyalty, but who could perhaps be won back again by depictions of the love, sorrow and affection of his parent. The parent in question could variably be presented as Britannia or as George.[92] When France entered

---

[89] Whitehead, 1765BD.

[90] Whitehead, 1767BD.

[91] Whitehead, 1762NY.

[92] Eg Whitehead, 1774BD; Whitehead, 1777NY.

the fray, Whitehead changed his tone, harking back to the old anti-France tropes and banging the drum for conquest.[93] Then when Spain and the Netherlands joined in against Britain, Whitehead became the poet of a distinct Britain-against-the-world sentiment, which Stephen Conway has identified as having seized the national mood at this time.[94] 'Still o'er the deep does Britain reign,/Her Monarch still the Trident bears:/Vain-glorious France, deluded Spain,/Have found their boasted efforts vain,/ … The warring world is leagu'd in vain/To conquer those who know not fear!'[95] Through the years of great international event and crisis, Whitehead-as-laureate guided his nation, telling it how to understand what was going on and voicing its valiant belligerence during its darkest moments; and he used the prince as a flexible point of reference by which to carry out his task.

Thus he continued the transformation of the prince–people relationship, from one in which the court was a distinct, physical location within which the prince was sitting and towards which the nation looked for its lead, to one in which the court was diffused and elided with Britain as a whole, the human, patriotic figure of the prince walking freely throughout the land. Whitehead and his prince were still, at this point, standing in a position of eminence over the nation, guiding its sentiments, but the overall weight and tendency of those sentiments was that of the British nation as a whole. Whitehead and his prince had power over those sentiments because they shared them too.

The later odes: Warton

Warton continued Whitehead's efforts to render the odes as both 'classical entertainment[s] for the present time' and 'permanent and valuable acquisition[s] to posterity' (as Pye had phrased it). However, whereas Whitehead had only intermittently structured his odes upon a distinct historical or pictorial conceit, and had not indulged too flamboyantly in the famous Pindaric digressions, Warton was more thoroughgoing. His odes thus resembled great poetic pageants of Britain, spreading their vision across time and space, centring on George III.[96] His first ode, which he

---

[93] Eg Whitehead, 1778BD; Whitehead, 1779NY.

[94] Eg Whitehead, 1780NY; Whitehead, 1781NY. On Britain-against-the-world sentiment, S. Conway, *The British Isles and the War of American Independence* (Oxford, 2000), pp. 197–202.

[95] Whitehead, 1780BD.

[96] Fairer touches on this aspect of Warton's laureate odes in his discussion of 'prospect' poems. He identifies both Warton and Pye as writing 'prospect' works of a conservatively patriotic hue, in which a prospect of a certain geographical area is used to survey the nation

had been rushed in writing, was the most directly focused on the prince, being an exalted description of George III's work as a patron: ''Tis his to bid neglected genius glow,/And teach the regal bounty how to flow./ His tutelary scepter's sway/The vindicated Arts obey.'[97] Thereafter, he had time to paint on a broader canvas. The 1786 New Year's ode consisted of a glorious British pageant, looking back to the past, forward to the future, and across the world; and George was situated thus within this vision: 'For our's the King, who boasts a parent's praise,/Whose hand the people's sceptre sways.'[98] The following ode presented a pictorial history of freedom, bards and 'virtuous kings', as seen in ancient Greece, climaxing on a celebration of George: 'Who, thron'd in the magnificence of peace,/Rivals [the Greek poets'] richest regal theme:/Who rules a people like their own,/In arms, in polish'd arts supreme:/Who bids his Britain vie with Greece.'[99] As in Whitehead's odes, the George being presented here was a patriot, a patron and a sympathetic human being. But Warton was more deliberate in using vast, pictorial backdrops to highlight these qualities, and to create a sense of George's importance to the nation.

The best example came in the 1787 New Year's ode, which told the history of one of Warton's favourite subjects: 'ancient Chivalry'. After surveying the 'Minstrel' and 'Bard of elder days' who had once sung to 'the Gothic Throne', Warton, becoming the bard himself, 'now ... tunes his plausive lay/To Kings, who plant the civic bay;/Who choose the patriot sovereign's part,/Diffusing commerce, peace, and art;/Who spread the virtuous pattern wide,/And triumph in a nation's pride ... To Kings, who rule a filial land,/Who claim a People's vows and pray'rs'.[100] Warton here summoned up a romantic vision of the British past, and thus created a sense that George's rule was rooted in this past, even as, by a poetic sleight of hand, he presented George's qualities as distinctly modern ones, which were best revealed against the contrast of 'the Gothic Throne'. George was a 'civic', 'patriot[ic]', parental prince, loved and cared for by his filial subjects. But he also possessed all the romance of his 'ancient' British predecessors.

A notable variant was provided by the 1789 birthday ode, which followed George III's recovery from his first major incapacity. Here, Warton gave a

---

as a whole and its past and future, and he notes that Pye succeeded Warton as laureate; but he focuses on examples of each man's pre-laureate writings, and especially Pye's *Faringdon Hill*. Fairer, *English Poetry*, pp. 205–7.

[97] Warton, 1785BD.

[98] Warton, 1786NY.

[99] Warton, 1786BD.

[100] Warton, 1787NY.

humbler, darker pageant, surveying a nation in worry and mourning, and then showing the nation's celebration at George's recovery. The image of a poor peasant lighting a candle in thanks to Heaven – 'Meek Poverty her scanty cottage grac'd,/And flung her gleam across the lonely waste' – was found especially touching by readers, according to the *Public Advertiser*.[101] Indeed, the ode created a powerful sense of a nation all going through the same emotional journey, passing from worry to exultancy, all concerned for the same subject. That subject was George: 'its Father, Friend, and Lord,/To life's career, to patriot sway, restor'd'.[102] Here was a sympathetic, sentimental prince, who animated the visionary pageant in a more emotive manner than ever before. He was a man known intimately to his subjects, and cared deeply about: not just the head, but the beating heart of the nation.

Like Whitehead, Warton had lofty ideas of the role of a poet laureate. But if Whitehead had devoted special attention to working out the relationship between prince and people, then Warton's special care was to work out where the panegyrist himself stood in this relationship. This theme was struck early on, when he insisted, 'The Muse a blameless homage pays;/To George, of Kings like these supreme,/She wishes honour'd length of days,/Nor prostitutes the tribute of her lays.'[103] But its most detailed treatment was in his 1787 birthday ode, which consisted of a survey of the laureateship itself. 'The noblest Bards of Albion's choir/Have struck of old this festal lyre,' Warton began, leaving no doubt as to the high opinion he had of his office. He then gave a stanza each to Chaucer, Spenser and Dryden, considering the ways in which they had paid tribute to their princes, and how each prince had inspired their poetry.

However, each poet presented problems. Chaucer's martial, chivalric poetry had 'moulder'd to the touch of time'. Spenser's 'visionary trappings' had been 'flung' over Elizabeth, hiding the truth with fantasy. Dryden had been worst of all: 'Does the mean incense of promiscuous praise,/Does servile fear disgrace his regal bays?/I spurn his panegyric strings,/His martial homage, turn'd to kings!/Be mine, to catch his manlier chord.' The final stanza answered all these problems by granting panegyric its most fitting subject: George III. If they had been his laureate, Chaucer would have been able to write of peace and patriotism, rather than of so archaic a subject as war; Spenser would have been able to trade 'Fiction' for 'truth'; and Dryden's flattery would have been no flattery, but 'his tribute all sincere!'[104] Thus, for all the fancy exhibited in his own laureate odes, Warton was keen to

[101] *Public Advertiser*, 10 June 1789.

[102] Warton, 1789BD.

[103] Warton, 1785BD.

[104] Warton, 1787BD.

position himself as a painter of simple truth. George III did not repudiate panegyric; instead, like Jesus with the Old Testament law, he fulfilled it. Warton's role was to mediate faithfully between prince and people, using sincere panegyric to show them how their prince really was. Thus, again, Warton was able to infuse his subject with all the romance and splendour of the past, while also characterizing George as someone distinct from the downsides of that past. He was both a monarch to be revered and a man to be loved. Warton was his faithful interpreter to the nation.

The later odes: Pye

Pye, having set out his vision for the odes in preface to his earlier Pindar translations, duly followed on from Whitehead and Warton in his approach. His first ode was a typical Wartonian pageant, celebrating British expansion, commerce and peace, employing conceits, digressions and a narrative structure.[105] But his odes also saw significant developments, spurred on by the political situation of the 1790s, with Britain facing the French threat abroad and the radical threat at home. Pye's odes thus re-embraced the musical potentials of the form, but without returning to the earlier emphasis on courtly performance; rather, Pye's odes became patriotic, popular musical pageants, with George III usually, but not invariably, figuring in some form or other. In style and language, Pye's odes were direct. In content, they mixed an earnest desire for peace with a tub-thumping jingoism. In their musical form, they were sometimes set to existing patriotic melodies, thus enabling them to occupy the important part in patriotic culture that Chapter Four showed them occupying.

As early as 1792, Pye was beginning to dispense with the labour of elaborate conceits, and to favour simpler, more direct versification than had been normal for Whitehead and Warton. The 1792 birthday ode included a few ABAB lines, but was mostly written in couplets:

> Freedom on this congenial shore
> Her holy temple rear'd of yore.
> … To welcome George's natal hour
> No vain display of empty power,
> In flattery steep'd, no soothing lay,
> Shall strains of adulation pay;
> But Commerce, rolling deep and wide
> To Albion's shores her swelling tide,
> But Themis' olive-cinctur'd head,
> And white-rob'd Peace by Vict'ry led,
> Shall fill his breast with virtuous pride,

[105] Pye, 1791NY.

Shall give him power to truth allied;
Joys, which alone a Patriot King can prove,
A nation's strength his power, his pride a people's love.[106]

Patriotic tropes came rolling along one after the other, with the prince's identity as 'a Patriot King' a commonplace by this point. It was as if Pye's predecessors had done all the hard work of establishing a set of ideas, and now Pye's job was simply to bash them out as merrily and as straightforwardly as possible.

As the 1790s wore on, Pye brought his odes more explicitly into line with the existing culture of patriotic songs. William Parsons, the master of the king's music, began setting the odes to pre-existing tunes, and the texts of the odes began making this clear to readers. The final stanza of the 1797 New Year's ode, after alluding to such things as Edward III, Agincourt and Elizabeth, climaxed with the chorus to 'Britons, Strike Home', with a footnote explaining that: 'These last lines were inserted at the desire of the King.'[107] The ode itself did not actually mention George III, because by this point there was no need; the laureate's patriotic songs were being sponsored and even directed by his patriotic prince. The 1797 New Year's ode was the first in many years to be printed in sections marked 'Air', 'Treble, Recitative' and suchlike. It ended on a section marked, 'Air and Chorus; *Tune, Rule, Britannia*', which duly closed on a quotation of that song's refrain. The 1800 birthday ode was not so explicit, but clearly ended on Pye's own version of 'God Save the King', given in three stanzas of different metre from the rest of the ode.[108]

For the most part, though, Pye's odes read as simple roll calls of loyalist rhetoric, in which patriotism and the prince had become one and the same thing. 'The notes of Triumph swell again!/Lo, Windsor boasts as high a train/Of Royal Youths, as brave as those/Who frown'd defeat on Edward's foes;/Of Royal Nymphs, as fair a race/As crown'd Philippa's chaste embrace;/Around their King, their sire, they stand,/A valiant and a beauteous band …'[109] The crown had become the most potent, but also the most natural of patriotic symbols. Its identity was seamlessly bound up with the identity of the British nation, and it was the perfect material for Pye to use in his rolling, straightforward couplets.

There is a sense with Pye's odes, then, that the relationship between

[106] Pye, 1792BD.

[107] Pye, 1797NY.

[108] Pye, 1800BD.

[109] Pye, 1805BD.

prince and people was finally settled. He was 'the royal Patriot'; 'a Patriot King'.[110] Pye's role accordingly became settled as the official British bard, and as a national cheerleader. Because he was the poet of a patriot king, who shared a mutual love with his subjects, Pye's role was to celebrate the nation, and to stir its martial spirit. There was still praise due to George III, but it was invariably a sort of national praise, channelling the nation's love and celebrating George by reference to his patriotism. 'Then let the Muse, with duteous hand,/Strike the bold lyre's responsive strings,/While ev'ry tongue through Albion's land/Joins in the hymn of praise she sings,/ … A nation's votive breath by truth consign'd/To bless a Patriot King – the friend of human kind.'[111] The prince as he appeared in this formulation also represented the sympathetic, human figure, but perfectly united with the symbolic, allegorical function that Cibber had wished upon George II. He was the genius of Britain, precisely because he was every Briton's most intimate friend. 'Faithful to him their hearts approve,/The Monarch they revere, the man they love;/Britannia's sons shall arm with patriot zeal,/Their Prince's cause their own, his rights the general weal.'[112]

As laureate, Pye held 'the British muse'.[113] Although his poetic efforts were not as much focused upon the odes as Whitehead's and Warton's had been, he conceived of all of his productions as forming a united, patriotic programme. In one ode, he referred to his long poem, *Naucratica*, with a footnote making the reference explicit, and also reminding the reader that *Naucratica* had been 'dedicated, by permission, to his Majesty'.[114] That poem had 'Sung of the wreaths that Albion's warriors bore' and of 'The naval triumphs of her George's reign'. But now, Pye observed, 'Still higher deeds the lay recording claim,/Still rise Britannia's Sons to more exalted fame.'[115] The laureate was the chronicler of British glory.

He duly commented on the great ongoing events: the first horrors of the French Revolution, the Battle of the Nile, union with Ireland, the Battle of Copenhagen and others.[116] He commonly expressed wishes for peace. Bainbridge's suggestion that there was something cursory, or insincere, about these wishes seems unfair; but it is true that Pye's pacifist imprecations

[110] For these and similar terms, see eg Pye, 1796NY; Pye, 1797BD; Pye, 1797NY; Pye, 1803BD.

[111] Pye, 1803BD.

[112] Pye, 1793NY.

[113] Pye, 1804NY.

[114] Pye, 1806NY.

[115] Pye, 1806NY.

[116] Pye, 1793BD; Pye, 1799NY; Pye, 1801NY; Pye, 1801BD.

were often mixed with such comments as 'Yet, if the stern vindictive foe,/ Insulting, arm the hostile blow,/Britain, in martial terrors dight,/Lifts high th' avenging sword, and courts the fight.'[117] However, his most passionate commentary came after the Battle of Trafalgar. 'Nelson!', Pye exclaimed; 'while a people's paeans raise/To thee the choral hymn of praise,/And while a patriot Monarch's tear/Bedews and sanctifies thy bier,/Each youth of martial hope shall feel/True Valour's animating zeal;/With emulative wish thy trophies see;/And Heroes yet unborn shall Britain owe to thee.'[118] These lines came at the end of the ode in which Pye had highlighted his own role as chronicler. As laureate, Pye led the people's 'paeans', weaving their emotions together into a 'choral hymn of praise'; as laureate, he cast Nelson's fame forward to future generations, that they might be inspired to patriotic zeal. Fittingly, at the centre of the image was the 'patriot Monarch'. He was not sitting imperiously on the throne, or exacting a debt of gratitude from his people; he was crying alongside his people, his tears falling upon Nelson's bier.

Thus under Whitehead, Warton and Pye, the odes were transformed from what they had been prior to 1757. Employing a new aesthetic of poetry, which was concerned with recapturing a supposed original spirit of poetry and stimulating the passions, these laureates continued to articulate the central role of the court in matters of national importance, but conceptualized that role in a new way. In their version of the relationship between prince and people, the prince was an intimate, human figure, caring for his people and being cared for by them on a person-to-person level, even as he occupied a position of majesty that was imbued with all the weight of British history, literary expressiveness and prophecy. The new aesthetic was particularly in tune with this conceptualization, because it reached back explicitly to the past and because it carried with it an ambitious sense of the poet's powers to paint pictures, evoke passions, create sympathy and predict the future. The poet could create pageants that spanned time and space, and would place the court at the heart of them. Thus the prince was envisioned as being at one with his people, and the court as being the symbolic, patriotic heart of national life, essential both to ideas of national identity and to literary production.

Conclusion

The laureate odes showed great changes over the course of the long eighteenth century. There was a continuing sense of the need to articulate

---

[117] Pye, 1795BD. For peace, see eg Pye, 1794NY; Pye, 1796NY. For Bainbridge, see *Visions of Conflict*, pp. 48–50.

[118] Pye, 1806NY.

the relationship between prince and people, and a continuing conviction as to the centrality of the court to national life; but conceptualizations of these matters evolved in line with wider changes in British society. The odes moved from courtly splendour and ritual, and an aesthetic appropriate for these themes, to a conscious effort to bring the prince before the people, employing a new aesthetic that was appropriate for this new emphasis. After 1757, the odes responded to modern literary demands, and were moulded into a form that elided the courtly panegyric of the prince with the patriotic panegyric of the British nation.

A study of the odes therefore reveals the increasing pressures on the laureateship, the changes to which it was required to subject itself, and the manner of its resultant adaptation. The laureate's position as cultural representative of the court and as published poet rendered him highly sensitive to the relevant developments, and ensured that the odes generally remained abreast of them. According to those odes, the court remained a vital space for cultural production and consumption, and central to public affairs and national identity; and the odes' prominence and success suggest that much of the reading public shared this interpretation. The court was viewed not as something that was marginalized by new developments, but as something that endured in the midst of them, adapting as need be.

Likewise, the developments that scholars have recognized in the fields of poetry, national identity and the public sphere cannot be completely understood without reference to the laureate odes. Those odes were regularly produced and widely read, and they entailed a continual effort to navigate these very issues, concerned particularly with understanding how they related to the court. The laureate odes show that although the middle decades of the eighteenth century were indeed of huge importance in the types of poetry being produced and the ideals of poetry being conceptualized, these developments were not exclusively associated with experimental new forms, or with notions of poetic independence and the spontaneity of inspiration. Instead, one of the most prominent ways in which these ideas were developed was through the laureate odes, produced on set occasions, twice a year, by a courtly poet. The new aesthetic of poetry was sponsored by the institutional court and it celebrated the conceptual court. It culminated in Warton's representations of a prince who somehow embodied the most admirable qualities of ancient Greece, the 'Gothic' national past and the modern world at the same time, and in Pye's depictions of a sympathetic patriot king. This was a form of conservative, loyalist poetry that was coterminous with non-courtly and non-conservative forms.

The history of the relationship between prince and people, as articulated by the odes, developed in tandem with the manner and aesthetic of articulation. At the start of the eighteenth century, the odes had been centred on the physical space of the court, forming a one-off musical performance to which the printed texts served as an imagined, carefully controlled invitation. The reading experience itself was only viable because the court's importance as a physical space was taken for granted, and because it was self-evident that a reader would wish to partake of courtly festivities and prostrate themselves before the throne. By the end of the eighteenth century, the case was otherwise; the reading experience had to stand up on its own terms, affecting the reader through the poet's imagination, imagery and emotional resonance, rather than by notes and directions pertaining to musical performance. The physical space of the court was no longer of such importance. Instead, the reader wished to be shown the glories of British history, British literature and the British people. Yet this transformation did not mean that the court or the king had been rendered irrelevant; instead, it followed wider developments in the conceptual geography of culture. Britons were increasingly favouring metaphorical spaces as the forums in which to situate cultural products and by which to determine their value. The court had evolved into one such metaphorical space. It existed throughout the nation, constituted by print culture. The court was a public court. Within it stood the king, the prime object and exemplar of patriotism; his laureate, producing panegyric odes; and the public, judging and approving.

Conclusion

> I then wrote to Croker saying that as for writing odes, like exercises, the time
> was past when I could do such things either with readiness or propriety;
> that unless I could do credit to the office, the office could do none to me;
> but that if it were understood this idle form was to be dropt & I were left
> on great public events to commemorate them in verse, or not, as the spirit
> moved, in that case I should willingly accept the situation as a mark of
> honourable distinction, which it would then become.[1]

In 1813, Robert Southey was appointed to the office of poet laureate. He
accepted on the understanding that the laureate would no longer be tasked
with writing biannual odes, but that he would instead be allowed to write
'on great public events … or not, as the spirit moved'. The king's final
descent into illness had already caused the odes to fall into partial abeyance,
yet Southey was initially disappointed. Barely had he been installed as poet
laureate when a letter reached him from the master of the king's music,
William Parsons, requesting that he send the text for 1814's New Year's
ode.[2] On this occasion, the spirit was moving anyway, and Southey wrote
a 'Carmen Triumphale' for the new year, longer than almost any previous
laureate ode, leaving Parsons to decide how much of it to set to music.
Over the next thirty years, Southey would write several more ambitiously
ex cathedra poems, but he continued to resent his paymasters' efforts to
have him write odes at stated intervals. Just as Rowe's appointment had
confirmed the identification between laureate and biannual odes that Tate
had partially effected, so too did the process reverse itself over a hundred
years later. Following Southey's resistance, Wordsworth accepted the office
in 1843 with the firmer stipulation that he would never be required to write
any official poetry. From that point on, the office was a sinecure.

   Southey's tenure therefore heralded a new era for the laureateship; the
office as it had been created between 1668 and 1715 was finished. It is fitting
that this book should end here. Yet it is not the end that might be expected
from the tenor of Southey's words, or from the manner in which he

---

[1] Southey to Charles Watkin Williams Wynn, 20 Sept. 1813, in R. Southey, *The Collected
Letters of Robert Southey*, ed. L. Pratt, T. Fulford, I. Packer et al., lt. 2305.

[2] Southey to Herbert Hill, 16 Nov. 1813, in Southey, *Collected Letters*, lt. 2330.

struggled against the eighteenth-century traditions of the office: it is neither a whimpering nor an acrimonious end. Southey disliked being required to write odes to order, and looked disdainfully on several of the eighteenth-century laureates; many of his contemporaries shared these feelings. Yet his willingness to accept the office, and his belief that it could become an 'honourable distinction' if the biannual odes were dispensed with – not all laureate writing, or even all laureate odes, but merely the biannual stipulation – indicates not the failure, but the success of the eighteenth-century laureateship. As well as being a prominent, significant feature of British cultural life, it was something that had the potential for adaptability, and something that many people believed ought to be continued in a new form. The fact that it was adapted, rather than abolished, shows that it had served its function well up to that point, and had proven itself capable of continuing to function well if only certain adjustments were made to it.

Thus the biannual odes were discontinued. The idea of the court as a distinct location in which cultural products were created and consumed, and in which cultural meaning and value were determined, had become increasingly metaphorical and abstract, and would eventually diffuse entirely. While the court as a concept became an essentially symbolic part of British society, the laureateship evolved into a primarily honorific position. Tennyson and Wordsworth, and even Ted Hughes, Carol Ann Duffy and Simon Armitage, were happy to accept the office.[3] In retrospect, it was convenient to believe that the eighteenth-century version of the office had received nothing but mockery; this belief was what lubricated the changes that the office underwent after Southey's appointment, and it gelled perfectly with the ideas that developed thereafter concerning literature, national identity, the monarchy and the character of the eighteenth century. Even Broadus, the office's foremost historian, believed 'that Warton's appointment had turned a good poet into a bad laureate', 'crystalliz[ing]' contemporary opinion against the office.[4] But whatever aesthetic judgements may be made of Warton's verse now, his tenure encouraged contemporary opinion in favour of the office, and was probably a contributory factor in Southey's and Wordsworth's acceptance of it.[5] Nor was Warton alone among eighteenth-century laureates in enjoying a widespread favourable opinion; far from it.

---

[3] For various reasons, however, some nineteenth-, twentieth- and twenty-first-century poets have turned down offers of the laureateship; eg, in recent years, Seamus Heaney and Imtiaz Dharker. *Financial Times*, 30 Aug 2013; *The Guardian*, 3 May 2019.

[4] E. K. Broadus, *The Laureateship* (Oxford, 1921), p. 154.

[5] See Southey's favourable opinion of Warton's laureate verses, cited in D. Fairer, 'Introduction: The achievement of Thomas Warton,' in *Warton Correspondence*, p. xxxvi.

As this book has argued throughout, the eighteenth-century laureateship was a highly prominent, respectable and significant office. It was perfectly in line with the sorts of practice and belief that were widespread at the time concerning culture and the court, and it served as a key instrument of those sorts of practice and belief. It was the defining element of the court's evolving place in the conceptual geography of culture: the later Stuart court nestled together with 'the town', at the centre of a metropolis to which readers throughout 'the world' looked and in which they sought to vicariously place themselves by means of print culture; the early Hanoverian court and town serving as a forum for 'the public', and as the central location for patronage, social networks and fashion; the later Hanoverian court being viewed by some as a closed-off space, alien to 'the nation', but by others, and by increasing numbers from the 1780s onwards, as an abstract space coterminous with the nation as a whole, housing royals and public in harmony.

Chapter One showed that the office was initially brought about due to the efforts of persons based both within and without the institutional court, who sought to define, and take advantage of, the conceptual court's role in culture. Such definition had become newly (and repeatedly) necessary, due to the ruptures between regimes, and due to developments in print culture, non-court institutions and the economic heft of audiences that contemporaries primarily conceptualized as the town, the world and the public. The laureateship was then fixed into a certain place within the institutional court and tasked with a specific function, again due to various persons' efforts to exploit the court's putative cultural centrality for their own gain.

These conclusions were developed in Chapter Two. By a close reading of the works of George I's poets laureate (primarily Nicholas Rowe), it was shown that literature of the time was not merely produced commercially, situated in the town, or pitched to a middle-class public, but that the court remained an important forum in terms of determining the meaning of literary works, and that writers sought to produce works that would succeed by the criteria of judgement appropriate to this courtly forum. Yet in the conceptual geography of this time, the court did not stand in opposition to the town or the public; writers like Rowe succeeded by pitching their work to court, town and public, and by appealing to each by means of the other. The laureate was a prime element of this conceptual geography, being positioned at the interface of court and town, and writing for the public while being explicitly based in court and town. The writers appointed laureate under George I – Rowe, Cibber and to some extent Eusden – were receiving their due reward for having succeeded so well according to the values connected with this conceptual geography.

Chapter Three adopted a longer timeframe, exploring all laureate appointments from Rowe to Southey. It revealed that those writers chosen for the laureateship tended to be among the few most successful and highly esteemed writers of their day, and that their appointments correlated closely to the ebbs and flows of literary taste, political power and individual royal personality. It demonstrated how the laureateship could bring various different networks into play, each attempting to access and employ it for different ends, and how, following on from this, there were different ways by which the merit that determined the bestowal of the laureateship might itself be determined. Ultimately, it offered two major conclusions: that the appointment of a laureate confirmed the court's centrality to society, in that it placed a courtly validation on those networks, cultural products and cultural practices that had the greatest valence at the time; and that the superficial randomness in the sorts of writers who were appointed laureate is a reflection of how literature was valued in the eighteenth century, when there were many different possible agents trying to make their claim for the understanding and dictation of cultural affairs.

In Chapter Four, the emphasis was on the public character of the laureate, and on the office's standing in the eyes of the reading public, during the reign of George III. Here was perhaps the most conclusive evidence as to the importance of the eighteenth-century laureateship. In exactly the period that might have been expected to see the triumph of commercial culture, the public, British identity and middle-class assertiveness, the laureateship was found to have held a massive presence in the very medium that might have been expected to reveal that triumph best: newspapers. Moreover, although mockery and hostility were certainly apportioned to the office in good supply, so too were approval, respect, consideration, esteem, enjoyment and even a sort of reverence. Although it is impossible to establish the mass of readers' genuine opinions, it would seem that much of the reading public was interested in the laureate odes, judging them by the highest standards and often finding them worthy. For Whitehead and especially Warton, it seems to have been a widespread opinion that the office had been honourably bestowed, while Pye, taking the office at the start of the French Revolutionary Wars, became a central figure in loyalist culture, his odes guiding the nation in its celebration of a patriot king. Thus the newspapers reveal the court's place in the conceptual geography of culture, and its importance in society more generally, to have endured, while also continuing to adapt; and they reveal, again, the importance of the laureateship in forming the interface between court and public.

Finally, Chapter Five surveyed the laureates' odes. Here, the laureates were found to be continually negotiating the relationship between (in the phraseology appropriate for the panegyric tradition) prince and people, and mediating that relationship to the people themselves. It was shown that, over the course of the long eighteenth century, the odes continued to affirm the centrality of the court to society and its place in the production and consumption of culture, but that the ways in which it did so communicated an understanding that the relationship between court and society was evolving. At the start of the period, the court's importance was a more traditional, hierarchical sort of importance, in which the court was a discrete location to which the rest of society actively looked for a lead; there was no greater privilege than going to court, no greater cultural product than court ceremony, and the laureate odes offered these two things to their readers. By the end of the period, however, the court had diffused across the land. Courtliness and Britishness were one and the same. A human, sympathetic, patriot king stood at one with his people, sponsoring a literature that was produced according to the highest, most ambitious and most modern understanding of literary value. The court was still perceived as being of central importance to society, and the laureateship to literature. But while the one had become an abstract part of an increasingly abstract conceptual geography of culture and its importance to society was on the way to becoming exclusively symbolic, the other was on the verge of being occupied by Southey, and thus translated into a purely honorific position.

Throughout the chapters, the main analytical framework was that of the conceptual geography of culture. However, it is now time to question what an analysis carried out within such a framework actually means, and what wider conclusions can be drawn from it. As set out in the Introduction, this conceptual geography was never a dogmatic system. Eighteenth-century Britons often used spatial concepts to frame the production and consumption of culture, and to determine the meaning and value of cultural products. There are identifiable consistencies and patterns in their manner of doing so. But such usage often tended to be casual, vague, idiosyncratic and inconsistent, even within a single document. It also coexisted with a significant trend, present throughout the long eighteenth century, of insisting upon a standard of literary quality that transcended time and space. This standard was sometimes even placed in opposition to the forms of cultural production and consumption that took place in specific spaces: the town, the court and playhouses were all sometimes described as housing corrupt taste and bad art, due to their physical and social characteristics.

Moreover, this monograph's dual intentions of using the laureateship to shed light on the subject of this conceptual geography, and of using this conceptual geography as a (putatively more authentic) framework for analysing the laureateship's meaning and function, have sometimes pulled in different directions. For example, except in Chapter Four, the conceptual geography has generally been discussed as if there was only one map of it at any given time, with all contemporaries subscribing to the same notions. In fact, there was no such accordance. Similarly, it has been argued that criteria of judgement and the value attributed to cultural products were linked to concepts of space, a rationale that has allowed arguments about contemporary understandings of spatial concepts to have been based upon quotations that sometimes do not even mention spatial concepts, simply because they mention values and criteria of judgement that other people sometimes linked to those spatial concepts. It may even be argued that by claiming to use a more authentically eighteenth-century taxonomy than Habermas's public sphere, this monograph has mixed up subject matter with methodology, and blurred the lines between the ideas of contemporaries and those of the historian.

The conclusions being made here must therefore be defined more clearly. First, the views of the laureateship and court detailed here were not universally held. It is not even possible to estimate how many people would have held them, or, insofar as an ideal model has appeared in these pages, with what differing degrees of concordance Britons would have acknowledged that model. The evidence suggests that it would be fair to call the views presented here 'mainstream', at least for the social elite resident in the town, and probably for literate English people in general. As Chapter Four indicated, there was a contrary mainstream view too; but rival mainstream views always tend to validate each other *as* mainstream views. For example, newspapers that denigrated the court and laureate did so in the acknowledgement that many literate people in Britain, and perhaps most, had a positive opinion of the court's and laureate's role in British society and culture; by opposing such views, they helped to reinforce them, and to give them greater coherence, as part of the endless dialectic of partisanship. Of course, this dialectic is not one that this monograph has engaged with much. Issues of political partisanship, social class and (other than in the emphasis on London) regional identity have been touched on somewhat incidentally, or not at all; this monograph can therefore offer no conclusions as to how these issues may have cut across the conceptual geography delineated here.

Second, spatial concepts were a widespread, useful way of understanding cultural production and consumption for eighteenth-century Britons, and they did tend towards a certain conceptual coherence, rather than being merely rhetorical. In certain ways, they would have been accepted by everyone who had any interest in culture. For example, the frequent and often casual references to the town and the court in later Stuart publications clearly assumed some common basis of understanding among readers; and no one could have been unaware that plays were performed in playhouses, and laureate odes at court. Indeed, spatial concepts would have been particularly relevant to views of the laureateship, both due to the odes and because it was certainly commonplace to use the term 'court' in discussions of the king and of the laureate.

Moreover, while it may be tempting to posit a distinction between forms of culture that were related to a certain space, such as drama and laureate odes, and forms of culture that were unrelated to particular spaces and were judged by a true standard of cultural value, this monograph's evidence has shown that no such distinction can be easily made. Print culture was intimately bound up with spatial concepts, whether that be in terms of published books being primarily intended for a town-based audience, dedicatory epistles asserting the primacy of the court, newspapers selling London and its cultural and political geography to readers throughout Britain, plays and odes transporting their readers to the space of performance or mass-produced texts constituting such abstract spatial forums as the nation. Even the transcendental standard of value was often articulated by way of spaces: the world, the country, the closet. And while some writers placed the true standard in opposition to corrupt, specific locations, others argued that the true standard was only to be found in specific locations, or reached its highest validation in them. As seen with Cibber in Chapter Two, they argued that the truest form of judgement for plays existed not in the reading experience, but in the playhouse; or, as seen with Dryden and Shadwell in Chapter One, that the best taste and judgement were to be found at court, especially in the person of the king.

Again, there were other ways of understanding culture. A thoroughgoing attempt to draw the landscape of contemporary concepts would have to depart from the landscape analogy itself, exploring (for example) the function of dedicatory epistles to aristocrats, and invocations of their powers of judgement, in determining the meaning and value of cultural products. Dedicatory epistles would sometimes make reference to the aristocrat's country seat, portraying it as a haven for writers, and as a place in which the literary work had taken shape; and, as discussed in Chapters One and Two, they would often reference the court. But they would also employ entirely non-spatial concepts and criteria of judgement. Likewise, as mentioned above, works could be judged by certain values that were sometimes explicitly linked to certain locations, but sometimes not. And, as is still the case today, though such terms as 'the nation' and 'Britain' could denote a place, they could equally or alternatively denote a body of people; that is, they could be synonymous with 'the public'.

The prevalence of different ways of making sense of culture, and the fact that they overlapped and were sometimes used interchangeably, are of significance for this monograph's main conclusions. When eighteenth-century Britons viewed the court and the laureateship in terms of a conceptual geography of culture, it was partly because it made sense to do so. There was indeed an institutional court, and several physical palaces, housing the monarch and their family members, that were resorted to by the nation's elite. St James's, Kensington, the Queen's House and Whitehall were physically intimate with the town and with Westminster, and were based in the nation's capital city. The laureate – usually one of the most successful and prominent writers in the nation – received his salary and laureate identity from the court, and wrote two odes a year that would be performed at court and widely published and read. Culture was produced and consumed in ways that were dependent upon literal geographical facts. To view culture spatially was, at least in part, to acknowledge those facts and their effects. In such an understanding, the court and laureate were clearly important; and the nature of that importance is what has been elaborated in the foregoing chapters.

However, the conceptual geography of culture was also a way – one way among many – for contemporaries to articulate broader notions about culture and their society: notions of power, authority, politics, value, identity, gender, class, nationality, the past and the future. By the same token, the casual usage of spatial concepts is highly revealing of the nature of, and developments in, eighteenth-century British society. This monograph can therefore offer conclusions about that society that could have been arrived at by means of other evidence, or another focus, but that have here been arrived at by an analysis of the poet laureateship and the conceptual geography of culture. What that analysis shows is that British society retained a hierarchical character throughout the period, focused on a traditional and metropolitan-based body of authority; the monarch and his court continued to provide the British people with the unifying ideology that allowed them to see themselves as Britons, to structure their behaviour and to evaluate the behaviour of others. Likewise, the monarch and his court served as a practical nexus of social distinction and political power. However, British society did undergo drastic changes between 1668 and 1813, due in no small part to the increasing profusion of print, which offered new bases for such a unifying ideology and partially obviated the need for physical proximity to any particular nexus. The fact that king and court retained their importance, and that print served to constitute and convey that importance in new ways, is testament to four factors: the continuing importance of physical location (including the need for print to have a base of operations, and the advantages attendant on having that base of operations in the metropole); how deeply entrenched the court was as a unifying ideology; the stability of the period; and the existence of people like the poets laureate, standing at the interface between court and reading public, responsive to developments in society as a whole (albeit such people were symptoms of the first three factors).

Indeed, the history of the eighteenth-century laureateship is of laureates (and certain other people) courting the public: both in the actual sense of the word 'courting', and in the more punning sense of bringing the public to court. By exploring this process, this monograph has made three major contributions to eighteenth-century scholarship, and particularly to eighteenth-century British cultural historiography, as set out in the Introduction. In each area, it has hopefully encouraged new agendas of research. First, it has used an interdisciplinary methodology to demonstrate the importance of the laureateship in eighteenth-century Britain. It has shown that many different agents and audiences were concerned with the office, that it was responsive to the different interest groups among which it was positioned and that it adapted as part of the eternal dialectic of old and new. Further work can be carried out in these respects not just on the laureateship, but on cultural institutions in general and on the laureate-style model of cultural producer.

Second, this monograph has placed the court and its relationship with the public in a more central place in our understanding of eighteenth-century Britain. Here, the idea of 'courting' is key. The laureates were not the only people courting the public; for example, many more odes and poems were published in affirmation of the court than came from the laureates' pens alone, and most of these came from writers who were not part of cultural institutions and do not fit the laureate-style model of cultural producer. The laureates were, so to speak, the monarchs of a public courtly culture, but they were far from absolute. Attention must now turn to the expansive, anarchic realms of that culture.

Lastly, this monograph has advanced a new paradigm for eighteenth-century cultural history: the conceptual geography of culture. This is a subject deserving of study in its own right, but is also a framework that can be used to make sense of British cultural production and consumption in the period. While there are potential risks to using this paradigm, the preceding chapters have shown that it can be highly illuminating, allowing us to ask new questions and to see eighteenth-century Britain and its cultural history in new ways. The Habermasian public sphere paradigm has been enormously, deservedly influential in the field, and also in research on other periods and countries, but its dominance necessarily involves a predetermining of the scope of our research. The conceptual geography of culture paradigm offers a new way forward, not just for scholarship on British culture of the long eighteenth century, but for earlier periods and for other European and Atlantic countries. By turning our attention to the spatial concepts that contemporaries used to map their cultural worlds and to evaluate cultural production and consumption, we will better understand what culture meant to them, why they behaved in the ways that they did and how they navigated change over time. It is by taking such a perspective that the importance of the laureateship in Britain in the long eighteenth century has been revealed, contrary to a long-standing belief that the office had been marginal and contemptible. Many more such discoveries remain to be made.

Bibliography

The biannual laureate odes

For a fairly comprehensive, very useful and highly meticulous catalogue of the surviving laureate odes and where they might be found, see Rosamond McGuinness, *English Court Odes: 1660–1820* (Clarendon Press: Oxford, 1971), 13–43. The body of published laureate odes upon which this monograph draws comprises the following (only one source given for each ode):

Thomas Shadwell

Shadwell produced a variety of odes and non-ode poems for royal occasions, but the only published odes of his which specifically addressed a royal birthday or New Year's Day were the following:

'An Ode on the Queens Birth-Day, Sang before their Majesties at Whitehal [1689]', in *Poems on Affairs of State, The Second Part* (1697), 223–4

Ode on the Anniversary of the King's Birth (1690)

Ode on the King's Birth-Day (1692)

Nahum Tate

An Ode upon the New Year (1693)

'An Ode upon Her Majesty's Birth-day, *April* the 30th [1693]', in *Gentleman's Journal, Or, The Monthly Miscellany*, April 1693, 120–1

An Ode upon His Majesty's Birth-Day (1693)

An Ode upon His Majesty's Birth-Day (1694)

The Anniversary Ode for the Fourth of December, 1697. His Majesty's Birth-Day. Another for New-Year's-Day, 1697/8 (1698)

An Ode upon the Assembling of the New Parliament. Sung before His Majesty on New-Years-Day. 1702 (1702)

The Song for the New-Years-Day, 1703 (1703)

The Triumph, Or Warriours Welcome: A Poem on the Glorious Successes of the Last Year. With the Ode for New-Year's Day. 1705 (1705)

'Song. For New-Year's Day, 1707', in *The Muses Mercury: Or, Monthly Miscellany*, January 1707, 8–9

'Song. For Her Majesty's Birth-Day, February the 6th, 1707', in *The Muses Mercury: Or, Monthly Miscellany*, February 1707, 27–8

Song for the New-Year 1708 (1708)

The Song for Her Majesty's Birth-day, February the 6th, 1710/11 (1711)
'Mr. Tate, the Poet Laureat's Song, for His Majesty's Birth-Day, May the
28th. 1715', in *The Flying Post*, 9–11 June 1715

Nicholas Rowe

Rowe's published odes are most easily accessible in Nicholas Rowe, *Poems
on Several Occasions, and Translations* (Glasgow, 1751): 'Ode for the New
Year, 1716', 105–11; 'Song For the King's Birth-Day, 28th of May, 1716', 112–
14; 'Ode for the New Year, 1717', 115–17; 'Ode to Peace for the Year, 1718',
118–20; 'Ode for the King's Birth-Day, 1718', 121–3; and 'Ode to the Thames
for the Year, 1719', 124–6.

Laurence Eusden

'Ode for the New Year, Sung before the King, Jan. 1. 1720', in *Weekly Journal
    or British Gazetteer*, 9 January 1720
'A Song Sung at Court, on His Majesty's Birth-Day', in *Weekly Journal or
    British Gazetteer*, 4 June 1720
'Ode for the Birth-Day, 1729', in *Universal Spectator and Weekly Journal*,
    1 November 1729
'The Ode for the New Year', in *Grub Street Journal*, 15 January 1730

Colley Cibber

Cibber's first two odes appeared as independent publications: *An Ode to
His Majesty, for the New-Year, 1730/31* (1731), and *An Ode for His Majesty's
Birth-Day, October 30, 1731* (1731). Thereafter, his odes are most readily and
consistently accessible in *The Gentleman's Magazine*, in its January editions
for the New Year odes and in its October or November editions (or even,
in 1748, in its December edition) for the birthday odes. Odes that do not
appear in *The Gentleman's Magazine*, and need to be found elsewhere, are:
'Ode for the King's Birth-Day, 1733', in *London Evening Post*, 27–30
    October 1733
'[Birthday ode for 1734]', in *London Evening Post*, 29–31 October 1734
'The [birthday] Ode [for 1735]', in *Daily Gazetteer*, 31 October 1735
'Ode for his Majesty's Birth-Day, 1736', in *London Evening Post*, 30 October–2
    November 1736
'Ode for the Birth-day', in *Grub Street Journal*, 3 November 1737
'The [birthday] Ode [for 1739]', in *London Evening Post*, 30 October–1
    November 1739
'The [birthday] Ode [for 1740]', in *London Evening Post*, 30 October–1
    November 1740
'An Ode for New-Year's-Day', in *London Evening Post*, 1 January 1741

'An Ode for New-Year's-Day', in *Daily Post*, 2 January 1742

'Ode for His Majesty's Birth-Day, 1746', in *London Evening Post*, 13–15 November 1746

'Ode for the New-Year, 1746–7', in *General Advertiser*, 2 January 1747

'[Birthday] Ode [for 1749]', in *Whitehall Evening Post or London Intelligencer*, 28–31 October 1749

'Ode for the New-Year', in *London Evening Post*, 30 December 1749–2 January 1750

'[New Year's ode for 1753]', in *London Evening Post*, 30 December 1752–2 January 1753

'Ode intended for the New-Year, 1758', in *Whitehall Evening Post or London Intelligencer*, 31 December 1757–3 January 1758

William Whitehead, Thomas Warton and Henry James Pye
The odes of all three laureates are most readily and consistently accessible in *The Gentleman's Magazine*, in its January editions for the New Year odes and in its June editions for the birthday odes (or in the November editions for the last two birthdays of George II). Odes that do not appear in *The Gentleman's Magazine*, and need to be found elsewhere, are:

William Whitehead, 'Ode on His Majesty's Birth-day', in *The Edinburgh Magazine*, May 1761

William Whitehead, 'Ode for His Majesty's birthday, June 4. 1769', in *The Scots Magazine*, June 1769

William Whitehead, 'Ode for the New Year, 1770', in *The Scots Magazine*, December 1769

William Whitehead, 'Ode for his Majesty's Birth-Day, 1775', in *The Weekly Magazine, or, Edinburgh amusement*, 29 June 1775

Thomas Warton, 'Ode for the New Year 1790', in *London Chronicle*, 31 December 1789–2 January 1790

Other primary sources
Modern editions of contemporary publications

[Addison, Joseph, Richard Steele et al.], *The Spectator*, ed. Donald F. Bond (5 vols, Oxford: Clarendon Press, 1965)

Dryden, John, *The Works of John Dryden*, ed. H. T. Swedenberg et al. (20 vols, Berkeley: University of California Press, 1956–2002)

Hunt, Leigh, *The Autobiography of Leigh Hunt*, ed. Jack E. Morpurgo (London: The Cresset Press, 1948)

Johnson, Samuel, *The Lives of the Poets*, ed. John H. Middendorf (3 vols, New Haven, Conn.: Yale University Press, 2010)

Pope, Alexander, *The Poems of Alexander Pope*, ed. John Butt (London: Routledge, 1996; first published 1963)

———, *The Dunciad in Four Books*, ed. Valerie Rumbold (Harlow: Longman, 1999)

Pye, Henry James, *Anti-Jacobin Novels: Volume 1, Henry James Pye, The Democrat and The Aristocrat*, ed. W. M. Verhoeven (Abingdon: Pickering and Chatto, 2005)

Shadwell, Thomas, *Complete Works*, ed. Montague Summers (5 vols, London: Fortune Press, 1927)

Southey, Robert, *Poetical Works, 1793–1810*, ed. Lynda Pratt et al. (5 vols, London: Pickering and Chatto, 2004)

———, *Later Poetical Works, 1811–1838*, ed. Lynda Pratt, Tim Fulford et al. (4 vols, London: Pickering and Chatto, 2012)

Spence, Joseph, *Observations, Anecdotes, and Characters of Books and Men: Collected from Conversation*, ed. James M. Osborn (2 vols, Oxford: Oxford University Press, 1966)

[Steele, Richard et al.], *The Tatler*, ed. Donald F. Bond (3 vols, Oxford: Clarendon Press, 1987)

Modern editions of correspondence and other private writings

Calendar of State Papers Domestic: William III, 1699–1700, ed. Edward Bateson (London: HMSO, 1937) < https://www.british-history.ac.uk/cal-state-papers/domestic/will-mary/1699-1700> [accessed 24 September 2019]

Calendar of Treasury Books: 1660–1718 (32 vols, London: PRO, 1904–58) <https://www.british-history.ac.uk/search/series/cal-treasury-books> [accessed 24 September 2019]

Berenger, Richard, 'Richard Berenger to Robert Dodsley, Sunday, 1 January 1758', *Electronic Enlightenment Scholarly Edition of Correspondence* <https://www.e-enlightenment.com/item/dodsroCU0010325a1c/?letters=decade&s=1750&r=5461> [accessed 24 September 2019]

Boswell, James, *Boswell's London Journal: 1762–1763*, ed. Frederick A. Pottle (London: Heinemann, 1950)

Byron, Lord, *Letters and Journals*, ed. Rowland E. Prothero (6 vols, London: J. Murray, 1898–1901)

Cowper, William, *The Letters and Prose Writings of William Cowper*, ed. James King and Charles Ryskamp (5 vols, Oxford: Clarendon Press, 1979–86)

Dryden, John, *The Letters of John Dryden: With Letters Addressed to Him*, ed. Charles Ward (Durham, N. C.: Duke University Press, 1942)

George III, *The Correspondence of King George the Third: From 1760 to December 1783*, ed. John Fortescue (London: Macmillan and Co., 1927)

————, *The Later Correspondence of George III*, ed. Arthur Aspinall (5 vols, Cambridge: Cambridge University Press, 1962)

Gray, Thomas, *Correspondence of Thomas Gray*, ed. Paget Toynbee and Leonard Whibley, 1st edn reprinted with corrections and additions by H. W. Starr (3 vols, Oxford: Clarendon Press, 1971)

Johnson, Samuel et al., *Johnsonian Miscellanies*, ed. George Birkbeck Hill (2 vols, London: Constable, 1966; reprint of the 1897 edn)

Nichols, John, ed. *Illustrations of the Literary History of the Eighteenth Century* (8 vols, Cambridge: Cambridge University Press, 2014; first published 1817–58)

Oldmixon, John, *The Letters, Life and Works of John Oldmixon: Politics and Professional Authorship in Early Hanoverian England*, ed. Pat Rogers (Lampeter: The Edwin Mellers Press, 2004)

Paulet, Charles, 'Charles Paulet, 2nd duke of Bolton to Joseph Addison, Monday, 4 October 1717 – [a fragment]', *Electronic Enlightenment Scholarly Edition of Correspondence* <https://www.e-enlightenment. com/item/addijoEE0060506a1c/?letters=decade&s=1710&r=2165> [accessed 29 September 2019]

————, 'Charles Paulet, 2nd duke of Bolton to Joseph Addison, Sunday, 21 November 1717', *Electronic Enlightenment Scholarly Edition of Correspondence* <https://www.e-enlightenment.com/item/ addijoEE0060501a1c/?letters=decade&s=1710&r=2268> [accessed 29 September 2019]

Pope, Alexander, *The Correspondence of Alexander Pope*, ed. George Sherburn (5 vols, Oxford: Clarendon, 1956)

Reynolds, Joshua, *The Letters of Sir Joshua Reynolds*, ed. John Ingamells and John Edgcumbe (New Haven, Conn.: Yale University Press, 2000)

Rowe, Nicholas, 'Nicholas Rowe to Alexander Pope, 1713', ed. George Sherburn, *Electronic Enlightenment Scholarly Edition of Correspondence* <https://www.e-enlightenment.com/item/popealOU0010184b1c/?le tters=decade&s=1710&r=820> [accessed 29 September 2019]

Southey, Robert, *The Collected Letters of Robert Southey*, ed. Lynda Pratt, Tim Fulford, Ian Packer et al. <https://www.rc.umd.edu/editions/ southey_letters> [accessed 19 January 2018]

Steele, Richard, *The Correspondence of Richard Steele*, ed. Rae Blanchard (Oxford: Clarendon Press, 1941)

Swift, Jonathan, *The Correspondence of Jonathan Swift*, ed. Harold Williams (5 vols, Oxford: Clarendon Press, 1963–5)

Tonson the Elder, Jacob, et al., *The Literary Correspondences of the Tonsons*, ed. Stephen Bernard (Oxford: Oxford University Press, 2016; first published 2015)

Walpole, Horace, *Memoirs of King George II*, ed. John Brooke (3 vols, London: Yale University Press, 1985)

Warton, Thomas, *The Correspondence of Thomas Warton*, ed. David Fairer (London: University of Georgia Press, 1995)

Contemporary publications

Anon., *Poems on Affairs of State, the Second Part* (1697)

Anon., *Albina, the Second Part. Or, The Coronation. A Poem on Her Present Majesty's Happy Accession to the Crown. By the Author of Albina: Or, A Poem on the Death of King William the Third* (1702)

Anon., *A Review of the Tragedy of Jane Shore* (1714)

Anon., *The Present State of the British Court* (1720)

Behn, Aphra, *The Amorous Prince* (1671)

———— *The Feign'd Curtizans, or, A Nights Intrigue* (1679)

———— *The City-Heiress* (1682)

Centlivre, Susannah, *A Bold Stroke for a Wife* (1718)

Chamberlayne, Edward, *Angliae Notitia*, 22 edns (1669–1707)

Chamberlayne, John, *Magnae Britanniae Notitia*, c.17 edns (1707–55)

Cibber, Colley, *Love's Last Shift* (1696)

———— *Woman's Wit* (1697)

———— *Xerxes* (1699)

———— *Love Makes a Man* (1701)

———— *The Non-Juror* (1718)

———— *The Non-Juror*, 5th edn (1718)

———— *Ximena* (1719)

———— *The Egotist: Or, Colley upon Cibber* (1743)

———— *Papal Tyranny in the Reign of King John* (1745)

———— *An Apology for the Life of Colley Cibber* (2 vols, 1756; first published 1740)

———— and Sir John Vanbrugh, *The Provok'd Husband* (1728)

Cibber, Theophilus [and Robert Shiels], *The Lives of the Poets* (4 vols, 1753)

Cumberland, Richard, *The Fashionable Lover* (1772)

Davies, John, *The Original, Nature, and Immortality of the Soul*, ed. Nahum Tate (1697)

Disraeli, Isaac, *Specimens of a New Version of Telemachus. To Which is Prefixed, A Defence of Poetry. Addressed to Henry James Pye, Esq. Poet-Laureat*, 2nd edn (1791)

Dryden, John, *The Critical and Miscellaneous Prose Works of John Dryden*, ed. Edmond Malone (4 vols, 1800)

Duck, Stephen, *A Poem on the Marriage of His Serene Highness the Prince of Orange, with Ann Princess-Royal of Great Britain* (1734)

D'Urfey, Thomas, *New Poems, Consisting of Satyrs, Elegies, and Odes Together with a Choice Collection of the Newest Court Songs Set to Musick by the Best Masters of the Age* (1690)

————— *A New Collection of Songs and Poems* (1683)

Eusden, Laurence, *A Letter to Mr. Addison on the King's Accession to the Throne* (1714)

————— *A Poem on the Marriage of His Grace the Duke of Newcastle to the Right Honourable The Lady Henrietta Godolphin* (1717)

————— *A Poem on the Marriage of His Grace the Duke of Newcastle to the Right Honourable The Lady Henrietta Godolphin*, 2nd edn (1717)

————— *Three Poems* (1722)

————— *An Epistle to the Noble, and Right Honourable Sir Robert Walpole, Knight of the Most Noble Order of the Garter* (1726)

Farquhar, George, *The Constant Couple* (1700)

Fielding, Henry, *The Historical Register, for the Year 1736* (1737)

Flatman, Thomas, *Poems and Songs* (1674)

Gildon, Charles, *Miscellaneous Letters and Essays on Several Subjects* (1694)

————— *Remarks on Mr. Rowe's Tragedy of the Lady Jane Gray, and Other Plays*, 2nd edn (1715)

Hayley, William, *Memoirs of the Life and Writings of William Hayley Esq.* (2 vols, 1823)

Hughes, John, *The Correspondence of John Hughes, Esq.* (2 vols, 1773)

Johnson, Samuel, *A Dictionary of the English Language* (2 vols, 1755–6)

Mant, Richard, 'Preface', in Thomas Warton, *The Poetical Works of the Late Thomas Warton, B.D.*, ed. Richard Mant (2 vols, Oxford, 1802), i. i–v

————— 'Memoirs of the life and writings of Thomas Warton', in Warton, *Poetical Works*, ed. Mant, i. ix–clxii

Mason, William, *Elfrida* (1752)

————— *Caractacus* (1759)

————— 'Memoirs of the life and writings of Mr. Gray', in Thomas Gray, *The Poems of Mr. Gray*, ed. William Mason (2 vols, 1775), spanning the entirety (1–239) of volume I and part (1–159) of II

————— 'Memoirs of the life and writings of Mr. William Whitehead', in William Whitehead, *Poems, Vol. III.*, ed. William Mason (York, 1788), 1–129

O'Keeffe, John, *Recollections of the Life of John O'Keeffe* (2 vols, 1826)

Pattison, William, *The Poetical Works of Mr. William Pattison, Late of Sidney College Cambridge* (1727)

Prior, Matthew, *An Ode, Humbly Inscrib'd to the Queen. On the Late Glorious Success of Her Majesty's Arms* (1706)

Pye, Henry James, *Poems on Various Subjects* (2 vols, 1787)

Rowe, Nicholas, *The Ambitious Step-Mother* (1701)
———— *Tamerlane* (1702)
———— *The Fair Penitent* (1703)
———— *Ulysses* (1706)
———— *The Royal Convert* (1708)
———— *The Tragedy of Jane Shore* (1714)
———— *The Tragedy of the Lady Jane Gray* (1715)
———— *The Dramatick Works of Nicholas Rowe* (1720)
Ruffhead, Owen, *The Life of Alexander Pope, Esq.* (1769)
Selden, John, *Titles of Honor*, 3rd edn (1672)
Settle, Elkanah, *The Empress of Morocco* (1673)
Shadwell, Thomas, *The Sullen Lovers* (1668)
———— *The Libertine* (1676)
———— *The History of Timon of Athens* (1678)
———— *The Medal of John Bayes* (1682)
———— *A Congratulatory Poem on His Highness the Prince of Orange* (1689)
———— *A Congratulatory Poem to the Most Illustrious Queen Mary upon Her Arrival in England* (1689)
———— *Bury-Fair* (1689)
———— *Ode on the Anniversary of the King's Birth* (1690)
———— *Poem on the Anniversary of the King's Birth* (1690)
———— *Ode to the King on His Return from Ireland* (1691)
———— *The Scowrers* (1691)
———— *Ode on the King's Birth-Day* (1692)
———— *Votum Perenne: A Poem to the King on New-Years-Day* (1692)
Sheffield, John, *The Election of a Poet Laureat* (1719), reprinted in John Sheffield, *Works* (2 vols, 1723), i. 195–200
Southerne, Thomas, *The Fatal Marriage* (1694)
Southey, Robert, 'A life of the author', in William Cowper, *The Works*, ed. Robert Southey (15 vols, London, 1835)
Steele, Richard, *Poetical Miscellanies* (1714)
Tate, Nahum, *Brutus of Alba* (1678)
———— *A Duke and No Duke* (1685)
———— *A Poem Occasioned by William III's Voyage to Holland* (1691)
———— *Characters of Vertue and Vice* (1691)
———— *A Present for the Ladies*, 2nd edn (1693)
———— *A Poem on the Late Promotion of Several Eminent Persons in Church and State* (1694)
———— *An Elegy on the Most Reverend Father in God* (1695)
———— *Elegies etc.* (1699), 71–9
———— *Panacea: A Poem upon Tea* (1700)

————— *An Elegy in Memory of the Much Esteemed and Truly Worthy Ralph Marshall, Esq* (1700)

————— *A New Version of the Psalms of David* (1700)

————— *The Kentish Worthies* (1701)

————— *The Muse's Memorial of the Happy Recovery of the Right Honourable Richard Earl of Burlington from a Dangerous Sickness in the Year 1706* (1707)

————— *A Congratulatory Poem to His Royal Highness Prince George of Denmark* (1708)

————— *The Muse's Memorial, of the Right Honourable Earl of Oxford, Lord High Treasurer of Great Britain* (1712)

————— *The Muse's Bower an Epithalamium* (1713)

————— 'To William Broughton, Esq; Marshall of the Queen's-Bench', in M. Smith, *Memoirs of the Mint and Queen's-Bench* (1713), 5–8

—————, Mr. Smith, and others, *An Entire Set of the Monitors* (1713)

————— *A Poem Sacred to the Glorious Memory of Her Late Majesty Queen Anne* (1716)

Theobald, Lewis, *Double Falshood* (1728)

————— *The Rape of Proserpine*, 3rd edn (1727)

Turner, Purbeck, *Augustus. A Poem on the Accession of His Majesty King George. Humbly Dedicated to the Right Honourable Charles, Lord Hallifax, One of the Lords Justices Appointed by His Majesty* (1714)

Otway, Thomas, *Venice Preserv'd* (1682)

Warton, Joseph, *Odes on Various Subjects* (1746)

————— *An Essay on the Genius and Writings of Pope* (2 vols, 1756–82)

Warton, Thomas, *Five Pastoral Eclogues* (1745)

————— *The Poems on Various Subjects* (1791)

Whitehead, William, *The Roman Father* (1750)

————— *Creusa* (1754)

————— *Plays and Poems: Vol. II* (1774)

Periodicals

Bath Chronicle

British Weekly Mercury

Daily Gazetteer

Daily Post

Diary or Woodfall's Register

Financial Times (2013)

Gazetteer and London Daily Advertiser

Gazetteer and New Daily Advertiser

General Advertiser

General Advertiser and Morning Intelligencer
General Evening Post
Lloyd's Evening Post
Lloyd's Evening Post and British Chronicle
London Chronicle
London Courant Westminster Chronicle and Daily Advertiser
London Evening Post
London Packet or New Lloyd's Evening Post
Middlesex Journal and Evening Advertiser
Middlesex Journal or Chronicle of Liberty
Middlesex Journal or Universal Evening Post
Morning Chronicle
Morning Chronicle and London Advertiser
Morning Herald
Morning Herald and Daily Advertiser
Morning Post
Morning Post and Daily Advertiser
Morning Post and Fashionable World
Morning Post and Gazetteer
Newcastle General Magazine
Observer
Oracle
Oracle and Public Advertiser
Owen's Weekly Chronicle or Universal Journal
Public Advertiser
Public Ledger
St. James's Chronicle or the British Evening Post
Star
Sun
The Annual Register
The Critical Review
The Edinburgh Magazine
The Flying Post
The Gentleman's Journal: Or the Monthly Miscellany
The Gentleman's Magazine
The Guardian (2019)
The Monthly Review
The Muses Mercury: Or, Monthly Miscellany
The Scots Magazine
The St. James's Evening Post
The Weekly Magazine, or, Edinburgh Amusement

The Weekly Register
The World
Times
True Briton
True Domestick Intelligence
Universal Spectator and Weekly Journal
Weekly Journal or British Gazettee
Weekly Journal with Fresh Advices Foreign and Domestick
Weekly Packet
Whitehall Evening Post
Whitehall Evening Post or London Intelligencer
World and Fashionable Advertiser

Archival sources
The Bodleian Library, Eng misc d. 3844-6
————— Dep d. 615–16
————— MS Abinger c. 15
————— MS Don. c. 75
The British Library, Add. MS. 28275
————— Add. MS. 32733
Kentish History and Library Centre, U269, A7
————— U269, A189–90
Lincolnshire Archives, ANC 5/D/15
————— MON 7/13/249
London Metropolitan Archives, Acc. 510
The National Archives, C 12/683
————— C 202/181
————— HO 42
————— HO 47
————— LC 3
————— LC 5/201–2
————— PRO 30/8/169
————— SP 44/341
North Yorkshire County Record Office, ZFW 7

Secondary sources
Archer, Stanley L., 'The epistle dedicatory in Restoration drama', *Restoration and Eighteenth-Century Theatre Research*, x (1971), 8–13
Armistead, Jack M., 'Scholarship on Shadwell since 1980: A survey and annotated chronology', *Restoration: Studies in English Literary Culture, 1660–1700*, xx (1996), 101–18

Aspinall, Arthur, *Politics and the Press c.1780–1850* (London: Home and Van Thal, 1949)

Astor, Stuart L., 'The laureate as Huckster: Nahum Tate and an early eighteenth century example of publisher's advertising', *Studies in Bibliography*, xxi (1968), 261–6

Austin, Jr, Wiltshire Stanton, and John Ralph, *The Lives of the Poets-Laureate* (London, 1853)

Bainbridge, Simon, *British Poetry and the Revolutionary and Napoleonic Wars: Visions of Conflict* (Oxford: Oxford University Press, 2003)

Barclay, Andrew, 'Mary Beatrice of Modena: The "second bless'd of woman-kind?"' in *Queenship in Britain*, ed. Orr, 74–93

Barker, Hannah, *Newspapers, Politics, and Public Opinion in Late Eighteenth-Century England* (Oxford: Clarendon, 1998)

——————— *Newspapers, Politics and English Society, 1695–1855* (Harlow: Longman, 2000)

Barry, Jonathan, 'Consumers' passions: The middle class in eighteenth-century England', *The Historical Journal*, 34 (1991), 207–16

———————, 'Bourgeois collectivism? Urban association and the middling sort', in *The Middling Sort of People*, ed. Barry and Brooks, 84–112

——————— 'Introduction', in *The Middling Sort of People*, ed. Barry and Brooks, 1–27

——————— and C. Brooks, ed., *The Middling Sort of People: Culture, Society and Politics in England, 1550–1800* (Basingstoke: Macmillan, 1994)

Beattie, John Maurice, *The English Court in the Reign of George I* (London: Cambridge University Press, 1967)

Bernard, Stephen, 'Introduction', in Tonson the Elder, Jacob, et al., *The Literary Correspondences of the Tonsons*, ed. Stephen Bernard (Oxford: Oxford University Press, 2016; first published 2015), 1–68

——————— 'General Introduction', in *The Plays and Poems of Nicholas Rowe. Volume I: The Early Plays*, ed. Stephen Bernard, Rebecca Bullard and John McTague (Abingdon: Routledge, 2016), 1–28

Beshero-Bondar, Elisa A., 'Southey's gothic science: Galvanism, automata, and heretical sorcery in *Thalaba the Destroyer*', *Genre*, xlii (2009), 1–32

Bevis, Richard D., *English Drama: Restoration and Eighteenth Century, 1660–1789* (London: Longman, 1988)

Bitter, August, *William Whitehead, Poeta Laureatus* (Halle: Niemeyer, 1933)

Black, Jeremy, *The English Press in the Eighteenth Century* (London: Croom Helm, 1987)

——————— 'Foreword to the Yale Edition', in Ragnhild Hatton, *George I*, with new foreword by Jeremy Black (New Haven, Conn.: Yale University Press, 2001), 1–8

————— *The English Press: 1621–1861* (Stroud: Sutton, 2001)

————— *George II: Puppet of the Politicians?* (Exeter: University of Exeter Press, 2007)

Blanning, T. C. W., *The Culture of Power and the Power of Culture: Old Regime Europe 1660–1789* (Oxford: Oxford University Press, 2002)

Borgman, A. S., *Thomas Shadwell* (New York: Benjamin Blom, 1969)

Borsay, Peter, *The English Urban Renaissance: Culture and Society in the Provincial Town, 1660–1770* (Oxford: Clarendon Press, 1989)

Brewer, John, *Party Ideology and Popular Politics at the Accession of George III* (Cambridge: Cambridge University Press, 1976)

————— 'Commercialization and politics', in *The Birth of a Consumer Society*, ed. McKendrick, Brewer and Plumb, 195–262

————— *The Pleasures of the Imagination: English Culture in the Eighteenth Century*, 2nd edn (London: Routledge, 2013)

Broadus, E. K., *The Laureateship* (Oxford: Clarendon Press, 1921)

Brooke, John, 'Pye, Henry (1709–66), of Faringdon, Berks', *The History of Parliament* <https://www.historyofparliamentonline.org/volume/1754-1790/member/pye-henry-1709-66> [accessed 23 March 2019]

————— 'Pye, Henry James (1745–1813), of Faringdon, Berks', *The History of Parliament* <https://www.historyofparliamentonline.org/volume/1754-1790/member/pye-henry-james-1745-1813> [accessed 23 March 2019]

Brown, Marshall, *Preromanticism* (Stanford, Calif.: Stanford University Press, 1991)

————— 'The poet as genius', in *The Oxford Handbook of British Poetry, 1660–1800*, ed. Jack Lynch (Oxford: Oxford University Press, 2016), 210–27

Brown, Wallace Cable, *Charles Churchill: Poet, Rake, and Rebel* (New York: Greenwood Press, 1968)

Browning, Reed, *Political and Constitutional Ideas of the Court Whigs* (London: Louisiana State University Press, 1982)

————— 'Thomas Pelham-Holles, duke of Newcastle upon Tyne and first duke of Newcastle under Lyme', *ODNB*

Bruce, Robert J., 'William Boyce', *ODNB*

Bucholz, R. O., *The Augustan Court: Queen Anne and the Decline of Court Culture* (Stanford, Calif.: Stanford University Press, 1993)

—————, ed., *Office-Holders in Modern Britain: Volume 11 (Revised), Court Officers, 1660–1837* (London: University of London, 2006)

Bullard, Rebecca, and John McTague, 'Introduction to *The Ambitious Step-Mother, Tamerlane*, and *The Fair Penitent*', in *The Early Plays*, ed. Bernard, Bullard and McTague, 35–55

Burke, Peter, *The Fabrication of Louis XIV* (New Haven, Conn.: Yale University Press, 1992)

Burling, William, and Timothy J. Viator, 'General Introduction', in *The Plays of Colley Cibber: Volume 1*, ed. William Burling and Timothy J. Viator (London: Associated University Presses, 2001), 11–24

Burrows, Simon, *French Exile Journalism and European Politics, 1792–1814* (Woodbridge: Boydell Press, 2000)

Butt, John, *The Mid-Eighteenth Century*, ed. Geoffrey Carnall (Oxford: Clarendon Press, 1979)

Candido, Joseph, 'Prefatory matters in the Shakespeare editions of Nicholas Rowe and Alexander Pope', *Studies in Philology*, xcvii (2000), 210–28

Chard, Chloe, and Helen Langdon, *Transports: Travel, Pleasure, and Imaginative Geography, 1600–1830* (New Haven, Conn.: Yale University Press, 1996)

Clark, J. C. D., 'On hitting the buffers: The historiography of England's Ancien Regime. A response', *Past & Present*, cxvii (1987), 195–207

————— *English Society, 1660–1832: Religion, Ideology and Politics During the Ancien Regime*, 2nd edn (Cambridge: Cambridge University Press, 2000)

Claydon, Tony, *William III and the Godly Revolution* (Cambridge: Cambridge University Press, 1996)

————— *Europe and the Making of England, 1660–1760* (Cambridge: Cambridge University Press, 2007)

————— and Ian McBride, ed., *Protestantism and National Identity: Britain and Ireland, c.1650–c.1850* (Cambridge: Cambridge University Press, 1998)

Clymer, Lora, 'The poet as teacher', in *British Poetry, 1660–1800*, ed. Lynch, 179–94

Colley, Linda, *In Defiance of Oligarchy: The Tory Party 1714–60* (Cambridge: Cambridge University Press, 1982)

————— *Britons: Forging the Nation 1707–1837*, revised edn (London: Yale University Press, 2009)

Conlin, Jonathan, ed., *The Pleasure Garden: From Vauxhall to Coney Island* (Philadelphia, Penn.: University of Pennsylvania Press, 2013)

Conway, Stephen, *The British Isles and the War of American Independence* (Oxford: Oxford University Press, 2000)

————— *War, State, and Society in Mid-Eighteenth-Century Britain and Ireland* (Oxford: Oxford University Press, 2006)

Corp, Edward, 'Catherine of Braganza and cultural politics', in *Queenship in Britain 1660–1837*, ed. Orr, 57–73

Craig, David M., *Robert Southey and Romantic Apostasy: Political Argument in Britain, 1780–1840* (Woodbridge: Boydell Press, 2007)

Davis, Rose Mary, *Stephen Duck, The Thresher-Poet* (Orono, Me: University of Maine Press, 1926)

D'Cruze, Shani, 'The middling sort in eighteenth-century Colchester: Independence, social relations and the community broker', in *The Middling Sort of People*, ed. Barry and Brooks, 181–207

DeRitter, Jones, '"Wonder not, princely Gloster, at the notice this paper brings you": Women, writing, and politics in Rowe's *Jane Shore*', *Comparative Drama*, xxxi (1997), 86–104

Dickinson, Harry Thomas, *Liberty and Property: Political Ideology in Eighteenth-Century Britain* (London: Weidenfeld and Nicolson, 1977)

Ditchfield, Grayson M., *George III: An Essay in Monarchy* (Basingstoke: Palgrave, 2002)

Dixon, Peter, 'Introduction', in Sir John Vanbrugh and Colley Cibber, *The Provoked Husband*, ed. Peter Dixon (London: Edward Arnold, 1975), xiii–xxvii

Downie, J. A., 'Foreword', in *Oldmixon*, ed. Rogers, iii–v

Draper, John W., *William Mason: A Study in Eighteenth-Century Culture* (New York: The New York University Press, 1924)

Earle, Peter, *The Making of the English Middle Class: Business, Society and Family Life in London 1660–1730* (London: Methuen, 1989)

Ennis, Daniel J., 'Honours', in *British Poetry, 1660–1800*, ed. Lynch, 732–46

Ezell, Margaret J., 'The "Gentleman's Journal" and the commercialization of Restoration coterie literary practices', *Modern Philology*, lxxxix (1992), 323–40

Fairer, David, 'Introduction: The achievement of Thomas Warton', in Thomas Warton, *The Correspondence of Thomas Warton*, ed. David Fairer (London: University of Georgia Press, 1995), xvii–xxxvi

———— *English Poetry of the Eighteenth Century 1700–1789* (London: Longman, 2003)

———— 'Modulation and expression in the lyric ode, 1660–1750', in *The Lyric Poem: Formations and Transformations*, ed. Marion Thain (Cambridge: Cambridge University Press, 2013) 92–111

Fawcett, Julia H., 'The overexpressive celebrity and the deformed king: Recasting the spectacle as subject in Colley Cibber's "Richard III"', *PMLA*, cxxvi (2011), 950–65

———— *Spectacular Disappearances: Celebrity and Privacy, 1696–1801* (Ann Arbor, Mich.: University of Michigan Press, 2016)

Field, Ophelia, '"In and out": An analysis of Kit-Cat Club membership' (Web Appendix to *The Kit-Cat Club* by Ophelia Field, 2008) <https://img1.wsimg.com/blobby/go/2d4b6719-1f56-4f40-abd6-b45a987d1775/downloads/1c3mci6ke_279827.pdf?ver=1552840569340> [accessed 23 March 2019]

———— *The Kit-Cat Club* (London: Harper Perennial, 2009; first published 2008)

Forster, Antonia, *Index to Book Reviews in England 1749–1774* (Carbondale, Ill.: Southern Illinois University Press, 1990)

———— *Index to Book Reviews in England 1775–1800* (London: British Library, 1997)

Forster, Harold, 'The rise and fall of the Cambridge Muses (1603–1763)', *Transactions of the Cambridge Bibliographical Society*, viii (1982), 141–72

Fulford, Tim, ed., *Romanticism and Millenarianism* (Basingstoke: Palgrave Macmillan, 2002)

Fuller, John, 'Cibber, *The Rehearsal at Goatham*, and the suppression of *Polly*', *The Review of English Studies*, xiii (1962), 125–34

Gaillard, Pol, 'Introduction', in Pierre Corneille, *Horace*, ed. Pol Gaillard (Paris: Bordas, 1976), 3–20

Gamer, Michael, 'Laureate policy', *Wordsworth Circle*, xlii (2011), 42–7

———— *Romanticism, Self-Canonization, and the Business of Poetry* (Cambridge: Cambridge University Press, 2017), 156–96

Garrison, James D., *Dryden and the Tradition of Panegyric* (Berkeley, Calif.: University of California Press, 1975)

Gerrard, Christine, 'Queens-in-waiting: Caroline of Anspach and Augusta of Saxe-Gotha as Princesses of Wales', in *Queenship in Britain 1660–1837*, ed. Orr, 143–61

Gibbs, A. M., 'Introduction', in William Davenant, *The Shorter Poems, and Songs from the Plays and Masques*, ed. A. M. Gibbs (Oxford: Clarendon Press, 1972), xvii–xciii

Gilmartin, Kevin, *Writing Against Revolution: Literary Conservatism in Britain, 1790–1832* (Cambridge: Cambridge University Press, 2007)

Golden, Samuel A., 'The late seventeenth century writer and the laureateship: Nahum Tate's tenure', *Hermathena*, lxxxix (1957), 30–8

Goldgar, Bertrand A., *Walpole and the Wits: The Relation of Politics to Literature, 1722–1742* (Lincoln, Neb.: University of Nebraska Press, 1976)

Gray, William Forbes, *The Poets Laureate of England: Their History and Their Odes* (London, 1914)

Greig, Hannah, *The Beau Monde: Fashionable Society in Georgian London* (Oxford: Oxford University Press, 2013)

Grenby, M. O., 'The anti-Jacobin Novel: British fiction, British conversation and the Revolution in France', *History*, lxxxiii (1998), 445–71

———— *The Anti-Jacobin Novel: British Conservatism and the French Revolution* (Cambridge: Cambridge University Press, 2001)

Griffin, Dustin, *Literary Patronage in England, 1650–1800* (Cambridge: Cambridge University Press, 1996)

———— *Patriotism and Poetry in Eighteenth-Century Britain* (Cambridge: Cambridge University Press, 2005)

Goldstein, Malcolm, 'Introduction', in Nicholas Rowe, *The Fair Penitent*, ed. Malcolm Goldstein (Lincoln, Neb.: University of Nebraska Press, 1969), xiii–xxi

Gosse, Edmund, *Gray* (London: Macmillan, 1895)

Habermas, Jürgen, *The Structural Transformation of the Public Sphere: An Enquiry into a Category of Bourgeois Society*, trans. by Thomas Burger with the assistance of Frederick Lawrence (Cambridge: Polity 1989; first published 1962 in German)

Hamilton, Walter, *The Poets Laureate of England* (London, 1879)

Hamm, Jr, Robert B., 'Rowe's Shakespear (1709) and the Tonson house style', *College Literature*, xxxi (2004), 179–205

Hammond, Brean, *Professional Imaginative Writing in England, 1670–1740: 'Hackney for Bread'* (Oxford: Clarendon Press, 1997)

Hammond, Paul, *John Dryden: A Literary Life* (Basingstoke: Macmillan, 1991)

———— *Dryden and the Traces of Classical Rome* (Oxford: Oxford University Press, 1999)

Harris, Bob, *Politics and the Rise of the Press: Britain and France, 1620–1800* (London: Routledge, 1996)

Harris, Brice, *Charles Sackville, Sixth Earl of Dorset, Patron and Poet of the Restoration* (Urbana, Ill.: The University of Illinois Press, 1940)

Harris, Tim, *Politics Under the Later Stuarts: Party Conflict in a Divided Society 1660–1715* (London: Longman, 1993)

———— 'Problematising popular culture', in *Popular Culture in England, c.1500–1800*, ed. Tim Harris (Basingstoke: Macmillan, 1995), 1–27

Harth, Phillip, *Pen for a Party: Dryden's Tory Propaganda in its Contexts* (Princeton, N. J.: Princeton University Press, 1993)

Haslett, Moyra, *Pope to Burney, 1714–1779: Scriblerians to Bluestockings* (Basingstoke: Palgrave Macmillan, 2003)

———— 'The poet as clubman', in *British Poetry, 1660–1800*, ed. Lynch, 127–43

Hatton, Ragnhild, *George I*, with new foreword by Jeremy Black (New Haven, Conn.: Yale University Press, 2001)

Heaney, Peter F., 'The laureate dunces and the death of the panegyric', *Early Modern Literary Studies*, v (1999), 4.1–4.24 [+notes] <https://extra.shu.ac.uk/emls/05-1/heandunc.html> [accessed 29 September 2019]

Hernandez, Alex Eric, *The Making of British Bourgeois Tragedy: Modernity and the Art of Ordinary Suffering* (Oxford: Oxford University Press, 2019)

Hesse, Alfred W., and Richard James Sherry, 'Two unrecorded editions of Rowe's *Lady Jane Gray*: The early editions', *The Papers of the Bibliographical Society of America*, lxxii (1978), 220–6

Holland, Peter, 'Modernizing Shakespeare: Nicholas Rowe and *The Tempest*', *Shakespeare Quarterly*, li (2000), 24–32

Holmes, Geoffrey, *British Politics in the Age of Anne*, 2nd edn (London: Hambledon, 1987)

Hoock, Holger, *The King's Artists: The Royal Academy of Arts and the Politics of British Culture 1760–1840* (Oxford: Clarendon Press, 2003)

———— *Empires of the Imagination: Politics, War, and the Arts in the British World, 1750–1850* (London: Profile Books, 2010)

Hopkins, Kenneth, *The Poets Laureate* (London: Bodley Head, 1954)

Hume, Robert D., *Henry Fielding and the London Theatre, 1728–1737* (Oxford: Clarendon Press, 1988)

———— 'Drama and theatre in the mid and later eighteenth century', in *English Literature, 1660–1780*, ed. Richetti, 316–39

Hunt, Margaret R., *The Middling Sort: Commerce, Gender, and the Family in England, 1680–1780* (Berkeley, Calif.: University of California Press, 1996)

Hunter, J. Paul, 'Political, satirical, didactic and lyric poetry (1): From the Restoration to the death of Pope', in *English Literature, 1660–1780*, ed. Richetti, 160–208

Hutton, Ronald, *Charles II: King of England, Scotland, and Ireland* (Oxford: Oxford University Press, 1991)

Jenkinson, Matthew, *Culture and Politics at the Court of Charles II, 1660–1685* (Woodbridge: Boydell Press, 2010)

Johnson, Odai, 'Empty houses: The suppression of Tate's "Richard II"', *Theatre Journal*, xlvii (1995), 503–16

Johnston, Freya, 'Richard Savage', *ODNB*

Jung, Sandro, 'Ode', in *British Poetry, 1660–1800*, ed. Lynch, 510–27

Keay, Anna, *The Magnificent Monarch: Charles II and the Ceremonies of Power* (London: Continuum, 2008)

Keegan, Bridget, 'The poet as labourer', in *British Poetry, 1660–1800*, ed. Lynch, 162–78

Keith, Jennifer, 'Lyric', in *British Poetry, 1660–1800*, ed. Lynch, 579–95

Kewes, Paulina, *Authorship and Appropriation: Writing for the Stage in England, 1660–1710* (Oxford: Clarendon, 1998)

———— '"The state is out of tune": Nicholas Rowe's *Jane Shore* and the succession crisis of 1713–14', *Huntington Library Quarterly*, lxiv (2001), 283–308

———— and Andrew McRae, 'Introduction', in *Stuart Succession Literature: Moments and Transformations*, ed. Paulina Kewes and Andrew McRae (Oxford: Oxford University Press, 2018), 1–19

Kilburn, Matthew, 'Royalty and public in Britain: 1714–1789' (unpublished University of Oxford DPhil thesis, 1997)

———— 'Charles Paulet [Powlett], second duke of Bolton', *ODNB*

Klein, Lawrence E., 'Liberty, manners, and politeness in early eighteenth-century England', *The Historical Journal*, xxxii (1989), 583–605

———— 'Coffeehouse civility, 1660–1714: An aspect of post-courtly culture in England', *Huntington Library Quarterly*, lix (1996), 30–51

Knights, Mark, *Representation and Misrepresentation in Later Stuart Britain: Partisanship and Political Culture* (Oxford: Oxford University Press, 2005)

Koon, Helene, *Colley Cibber: A Biography* (Lexington, Ky.: University Press of Kentucky, 1986)

Kramer, David Bruce, *The Imperial Dryden: The Poetics of Appropriation in Seventeenth-Century England* (Athens, Ga.: University of Georgia Press, 1994)

Kramnick, Isaac, *Bolingbroke and His Circle: The Politics of Nostalgia in the Age of Walpole* (London: Oxford University Press, 1968)

Lake, Peter, and Steven Pincus, eds, *The Politics of the Public Sphere in Early Modern England* (Manchester: Manchester University Press, 2007)

Landry, Donna, 'Poems on place', in *British Poetry, 1660–1800*, ed. Lynch, 335–55 (341–51)

Langford, Paul, *A Polite and Commercial People: England, 1727–1783* (Oxford: Oxford University Press, 1992)

Lee, Stephen M., *George Canning and Liberal Toryism, 1801–1827* (Woodbridge: Boydell Press, 2008)

Leporati, Matthew, '"Authority from heaven": Robert Southey's *Madoc* and epic Christian imperialism', *European Romantic Review*, xxv (2014), 161–80

Lipking, Lawrence, *The Ordering of the Arts in Eighteenth-Century England* (Princeton, N. J.: Princeton University Press, 1970)

Livingstone, David N. and Charles W. J. Withers, *Geography and Enlightenment* (Chicago, Ill.: University of Chicago Press, 1999)

Lonsdale, Roger, 'Introduction', in *The New Oxford Book of Eighteenth Century Verse*, ed. Roger Lonsdale (Oxford: Oxford University Press, 1984), xxxiii–xxxix

Love, Harold, 'Restoration and early eighteenth-century drama', in *English Literature, 1660–1780*, ed. Richetti, 109–31

Lynch, Jack, 'Introduction', in *British Poetry, 1660–1800*, ed. Lynch, xix–xxi

————, ed., *The Oxford Handbook of British Poetry, 1660–1800* (Oxford, 2016)

McCabe, Richard A., 'Panegyric and its discontents: The first Stuart succession', in *Stuart Succession Literature*, ed. Kewes and McRae, 19–36

McGirr, Elaine M., *Partial Histories: A Reappraisal of Colley Cibber* (London: Palgrave Macmillan, 2016)

McGuinness, Rosamond, *English Court Odes: 1660–1820* (Oxford: Clarendon Press, 1971)

McKendrick, Neil, John Brewer and J. H. Plumb, eds, *The Birth of a Consumer Society: The Commercialization of Eighteenth-Century England* (London, 1983; first published 1982).

———— 'Commercialization and the economy', in *The Birth of a Consumer Society: The Commercialization of Eighteenth-Century England*, ed. Neil McKendrick, John Brewer and John. H. Plumb (London: Hutchinson, 1983; first published 1982), 7–194

McRae, Andrew, 'Welcoming the king', in *Stuart Succession Literature*, ed. Kewes and McRae, 187–204

Mack, Robert L., *Thomas Gray: A Life* (London: Yale University Press, 2000)

Mahoney, Charles, *Romantics and Renegades: The Poetics of Political Reaction* (Basingstoke: Palgrave, 2003)

Marschner, Joanna, 'Queen Caroline of Anspach and the European princely museum tradition', in *Queenship in Britain 1660–1837*, ed. Orr, 130–42

———— *Queen Caroline: Cultural Politics at the Early Eighteenth-Century Court* (New Haven, Conn.: Yale University Press, 2014)

Marshall, Ashley, 'Satire', in *British Poetry, 1660–1800*, ed. Lynch, 495–509

Mayhew, Robert J., *Enlightenment Geography: The Political Languages of British Geography, 1650–1850* (Basingstoke: Palgrave Macmillan, 2000)

Monk, Samuel Holt, 'Commentary', in Dryden, *Works*, xvii. 327–484

Morris, Marilyn, *The British Monarchy and the French Revolution* (London: Yale University Press, 1998)

Mui, Hoh-Cheung, and Lorna H. Mui, *Shops and Shopkeeping in Eighteenth-Century England* (London: Routledge, 1989)

Munns, Jessica, 'Theatrical culture I: Politics and theatre', in *The Cambridge Companion to English Literature 1650–1740*, ed. Steven Zwicker (Cambridge: Cambridge University Press, 1998), 82–103

Nokes, David, 'John Gay', *ODNB*

Ogborn, Miles, *Spaces of Modernity: London's Geographies, 1680–1780* (London: Guildford Press, 1998)

O'Gorman, Frank, *The Emergence of the British Two-Party System, 1760–1832* (London: Edward Arnold, 1982)

O'Neill, Michael, 'Southey and Shelley reconsidered', *Romanticism*, xvii (2011), 10–24

———— and Charles W. J. Withers, *Georgian Geographies: Essays on Space, Place and Landscape in the Eighteenth Century* (Manchester: Manchester University Press, 2004)

Olsen, Thomas G., 'Apolitical Shakespeare: Or, the Restoration *Coriolanus*', *Studies in English Literature, 1500–1900*, xxxviii (1998), 411–25

Orr, Bridget, *British Enlightenment Theatre: Dramatizing Difference* (Cambridge: Cambridge University Press, 2020)

Orr, Clarissa Campbell, ed., *Queenship in Britain 1660–1837: Royal Patronage, Court Culture and Dynastic Politics* (Manchester: Manchester University Press, 2002)

———— 'Queen Charlotte, "scientific queen"', in *Queenship in Britain*, ed. Orr, 236–66

————, ed., *Queenship in Europe 1660-1815: The Role of the Consort* (Cambridge: Cambridge University Press, 2004)

Orr, Leah, 'Patronage and commercial print in conflict: Laurence Eusden's reception and afterlife', *Journal for Early Modern Cultural Studies*, xx (2020), 32–57

Oxford Dictionary of National Biography <https://www.oxforddnb.com> [accessed 23 March 2019]

Painting, Vivienne W., 'William Hayley', *ODNB*

Panecka, Ewa, *Literature and the Monarchy: The Traditional and the Modern Concept of the Office of Poet Laureate of England* (Newcastle: Cambridge Scholars Publishing, 2014)

Parry, Jonathan, *The Rise and Fall of Liberal Government in Victorian Britain* (London: Yale University Press, 1993)

Payne, Deborah C., 'Patronage and the dramatic marketplace under Charles I and II', *The Yearbook of English Studies*, xxi (1991), 137–52

Pedicord, Harry W., '*By Their Majesties' Command*': The House of Hanover at the London Theatres, 1714–1800* (London: Society for Theatre Research, 1991)

Plumb, J. H., 'Commercialization and society', in *Birth of a Consumer Society*, ed. McKendrick, Brewer and Plumb, 263–334

Pocock, J. G. A., *Virtue, Commerce, and History: Essays on Political Thought and History, Chiefly in the Eighteenth Century* (Cambridge: Cambridge University Press, 1985)

Power, Henry, *Epic Into Novel: Henry Fielding, Scriblerian Satire, and the Consumption of Classical Literature* (Oxford: Oxford University Press, 2015)

———— 'Eyes without light: University volumes and the politics of succession', in *Stuart Succession Literature*, ed. Kewes and McRae, 222–40

Pratt, Lynda, 'Revising the national epic: Coleridge, Southey and *Madoc*', *Romanticism*, ii (1996), 149–64

————, ed., *Robert Southey and the Contexts of English Romanticism* (Aldershot: Ashgate, 2006)

Radcliffe, David Hill, 'Pastoral', in *British Poetry, 1660–1800*, ed. Lynch, 441–56

Raven, James, *Publishing Business in Eighteenth-Century England* (Woodbridge: Boydell Press, 2014)

Raymond, Joad, 'The newspaper, public opinion, and the public sphere in the seventeenth century', in *News, Newspapers, and Society in Early Modern Britain*, ed. Joad Raymond (London: Frank Cass, 1999), 109–40

Richetti, John, ed., *The Cambridge History of English Literature, 1660–1780* (Cambridge: Cambridge University Press, 2005), 316–39

Rizzo, Betty, 'The patron as poet maker: The politics of benefaction', *Studies in Eighteenth-Century Culture*, xx (1991), 241–66

Rogers, Pat, 'Life', in *Oldmixon*, ed. Rogers, 13–27

———— 'Samuel Johnson', *ODNB*

Rounce, Adam, 'Akenside's clamours for liberty', in *Cultures of Whiggism*, ed. Womersley, 216–33

———— 'Scholarship', in *British Poetry, 1660–1800*, ed. Lynch, 685–700

Sambrook, James, 'Matthew Concanen', *ODNB*

———— 'Laurence Eusden', *ODNB*

———— 'John Lockman', *ODNB*

Saslow, Edward L., '"Stopp'd in other hands": The payment of Dryden's pension for 1668–1670', *Restoration: Studies in English Literary Culture, 1660–1700*, xxx (2006), 31–42

Scott, Rosemary, 'William Whitehead', *ODNB*

Seary, Peter, 'Lewis Theobald', *ODNB*

Sharpe, Kevin, *Rebranding Rule: Images of Restoration and Revolution Monarchy, 1660–1714* (New Haven, Conn.: Yale University Press, 2013)

Sherbo, Arthur, 'Nicholas Rowe', *ODNB*

Shipp, Leo, 'Appointing a poet laureate: National and poetic identities in 1813', *The English Historical Review*, cxxxvi (2021), 332–63

Sitter, John, 'Political, satirical, didactic and lyric poetry (II): After Pope', in *English Literature, 1660–1780*, ed. Richetti, 287–315

Smith, E. A., *George IV* (New Haven, Conn.: Yale University Press, 1999)

Smith, Hannah, 'The court in England, 1714–1760: A declining political institution?', *History*, xc (2005), 23–41

———— *Georgian Monarchy: Politics and Culture, 1714–1760* (Cambridge: Cambridge University Press, 2006)

———— 'Court culture and Godly monarchy: Henry Purcell and Sir Charles Sedley's 1692 birthday ode for Mary II', in *Politics, Religion and Ideas in Seventeenth- and Eighteenth-Century Britain: Essays in Honour of Mark Goldie*, ed. Justin Champion, John Coffey, Tim Harris and John Marshall (Woodbridge: Boydell Press, 2019), 219–37

Smithers, Peter, *The Life of Joseph Addison* (Oxford: Clarendon Press, 1954)

Solkin, David H., *Painting for Money: The Visual Arts and the Public Sphere in Eighteenth-Century England* (New Haven, Conn.: Yale University Press, 1992)

Speck, W. A., *Robert Southey: Entire Man of Letters* (London: Yale University Press, 2006)

Spencer, Christopher, *Nahum Tate* (New York: Twayne Publishers, 1972)

Stephens, Leslie, revised by William R. Jones, 'Stephen Duck', *ODNB*

Stobart, Jon, Andrew Hann and Victoria Morgan, *Spaces of Consumption: Leisure and Shopping in the English Town, c.1680–1830* (London: Routledge, 2007)

Sutherland, L. S. and L. G. Mitchell, eds, *The History of the University of Oxford. Volume V: The Eighteenth Century* (Oxford: Clarendon Press, 1986)

Sweet, Rosemary H., 'Topographies of politeness', *Transactions of the Royal Historical Society*, xii (2002), 355–74

———— and Penelope Lane, *Women and Urban Life in Eighteenth-Century England: 'On the Town'* (Aldershot: Ashgate, 2003)

Terry, Richard, *Poetry and the Making of the English Literary Past: 1660–1781* (Oxford: Oxford University Press, 2001)

Venturo, David F., 'Poems on poetry', in *British Poetry, 1660–1800*, ed. Lynch, 269–85

Wall, Cynthia, 'Poems on the stage', in *British Poetry, 1660–1800*, ed. Lynch, 23–39

Wallace, Beth Kowaleski, 'Reading the surfaces of Colley Cibber's "The Careless Husband"', *Studies in English Literature, 1500–1900*, xl (2000), 473–89

Walsh, Marcus, 'Eighteenth-century high lyric: William Collins and Christopher Smart', in *The Lyric Poem: Formations and Transformations*, ed. M. Thain (Cambridge, 2013), 112–34

Warner, William B., 'Novels on the market', in *English Literature, 1660–1780*, ed. Richetti, 87–105

Wauchope, Piers, 'Sir William Ellis', *ODNB*

Weatherill, Lorna, *Consumer Behaviour and Material Culture in Britain 1660–1760* (London: Routledge, 1988)

Weinbrot, Harold D., *Britannia's Issue: The Rise of British Literature from Dryden to Ossian* (Cambridge: Cambridge University Press, 1994)

Weiser, Brian, *Charles II and the Politics of Access* (Woodbridge: Boydell Press, 2003)

Welch, Anthony, 'The cultural politics of *Dido and Aeneas*', *Cambridge Opera Journal*, xxi (2009), 1–26

Wellek, René, *The Rise of English Literary History*, 2nd edn (New York: McGraw-Hill, 1966)

West, Kenyon, *The Laureates of England, from Ben Jonson to Alfred Tennyson* (London, 1895)

Wilkinson, Hazel, *Edmund Spenser and the Eighteenth-Century Book* (Cambridge: Cambridge University Press, 2017)

Williams, Abigail, *Poetry and the Creation of a Whig Literary Culture 1681–1714* (Oxford: Oxford University Press, 2005)

Wilson, Brett, 'Jane Shore and the Jacobites: Nicholas Rowe, the pretender, and the national she-tragedy', *ELH*, lxxii (2005), 823–43

Wilson, Kathleen, *The Sense of the People: Politics, Culture, and Imperialism in England, 1715–1785* (Cambridge: Cambridge University Press, 1995)

Winn, James Anderson, *John Dryden and His World* (New Haven, Conn.: Yale University Press, 1987)

———— *Queen Anne: Patroness of Arts* (Oxford: Oxford University Press, 2014)

Winstanley, D. A., *The University of Cambridge in the Eighteenth Century* (Cambridge: Cambridge University Press, 1922)

Womersley, David, ed., *'Cultures of Whiggism': New Essays on English Literature and Culture in the Long Eighteenth Century* (Newark, Del.: University of Delaware Press, 2005)

Zwicker, Steven N., *Lines of Authority: Politics and English Literary Culture, 1649–1689* (Ithaca, N. Y.: Cornell University Press, 1996), 90–199

————, ed., *The Cambridge Companion to John Dryden* (Cambridge: Cambridge University Press, 2004)

Index

CPSIA information can be obtained
at www.ICGtesting.com
Printed in the USA
JSHW050855200822
29450JS00001B/1